Charles Dudley Warner

Mummies and moslems

Charles Dudley Warner

Mummies and moslems

ISBN/EAN: 9783337281311

Printed in Europe, USA, Canada, Australia, Japan

Cover: Foto ©Lupo / pixelio.de

More available books at **www.hansebooks.com**

MUMMIES AND MOSLEMS,

BY

CHARLES DUDLEY WARNER,

Author of "My Summer in a Garden," "Back-Log Studies," etc.

TORONTO, ONT:
BELFORD BROTHERS.
MDCCCLXXVI.

O Commander of the Faithful, Egypt is a compound of black earth and green plants, between a pulverized mountain and a red sand. Along the valley descends a river, on which the blessing of the Most High reposes both in the evening and the morning, and which rises and falls with the revolutions of the sun and moon. According to the vicissitudes of the seasons, the face of the country is adorned with a silver *wave, a verdant* emerald, *and the deep yellow of a* golden *harvest.*

From Amrou, Conqueror of Egypt, to the Khalif Omar.

PREFACE.

THERE is in the Accademia at Venice a picture, painted by Paris Bordone representing what was considered at the time a miracle. A poor fisherman of the Lido, hauling his net one morning, took a fish that had in his stomach the gold ring with which the Doge had wed the Adriatic a few months before. The honest fellow carried the ring, thus miraculously rescued from the maw of the sea, to the Doge, and the council considered the event so remarkable and of such propitious augury that they ordered it to be commemorated on canvas. The picture represents the Doge upon his chair of state, surrounded by that gorgeous company of fine gentlemen with whom Paul Veronese has made us familiar, and the poor fisherman is ascending the steps of the throne and presenting the ring.

I have no doubt the event happened. For the like had occurred before. It is related that Polycrates of Samos had so much good fortune that his friend Amasis, king of Egypt, sent him a message and warned him that such prosperity was perilous : " I would rather choose," he said, " that both I and those for whom I am solicitous, should be partly successful in our undertakings and partly suffer reverses," and, accordingly, to avert divine jealousy, he advised him to cast away that which he valued most. Polycrates took his advice. The most precious thing he possessed was a seal, made of an emerald, set in gold, the cunning workmanship of a Samian named Theodorus. Having manned his fifty-oared galley, he put out a considerable distance from the island, and taking off his seal, threw it into the sea. Six days thereafter a fisherman having caught a very large and beautiful fish, presented it to Polycrates ; and his servants upon opening the fish found the ring. When he learned of this piece of good fortune, Amasis withdrew his friendship from Polycrates, satisfied that a man so prosperous could not come to a good end.

We shall look in vain for any new thing. The traveller in the Orient I suppose, always hopes to find the precious ring or the seal, a long time lost: if he should chance upon it, its story would have been already narrated.

Can one expect then to say anything new about Egypt? How many volumes, during two thousand years, have had this mysterious land for their theme! The Amasis of whom I have spoken sent a corselet to Crœsus, made of linen, with many figures of animals inwrought, and adorned with gold and cotton-wool; each thread of this corselet was worthy of admiration, for though it was fine, it contained three hundred and sixty threads, all distinct. A piece of linen found at Memphis had in each inch of warp five hundred and forty threads, or two hundred and seventy double threads. I suppose that if the lines written about Egypt were laid over the country, every part of it would be covered by as many as three hundred and sixty-five lines to the inch.

New facts about Egypt need not be expected. A *resumé* of all that has been written, in one volume, is equally out of the question. Those who find here too many details of the ancient land, must remember how many they have been spared; those who find too few, will perhaps thank me for sending them to the library.

No one can be more sensible than I am of the shortcomings of this volume. One thing, however, I have earnestly endeavoured to do :— to preserve the Oriental atmosphere. What we see in Egypt is the result of social, moral, and religious conditions, totally foreign to our experience, and not to be estimated by it. I tried to look at Egypt in its own atmosphere and not through ours, hoping thereby to be able to represent it, not photographically, but in something like its true colors and proper perspective. If I have succeeded in the slightest degree, I shall be satisfied.

C. D. W.

VENICE, October, 1875.

CONTENTS

CHAPTER I.

AT THE GATES OF THE EAST.

PAGE.

The Mediterranean—The East unlike the West—A World risked for a Woman—An unchanging World and a Fickle Sea—Still an Orient—Old Fashions—A Journey without Reasons—Off for the Orient—Leaving Naples—A Shaky Court—A deserted District—Ruins of Pæstum—Temple of Neptune—Entrance to Purgatory—Safety Valves of the World—Enterprising Natives—Sunset on the Sea—Sicily—Crete—Our Passengers—The Hottest Place on Record—An American Tourist--An Evangelical Dentist—On a Secret Mission—The Vanquished Dignitary 17

CHAPTER II.

WITHIN THE PORTALS.

Africa—Alexandria—Strange Contrasts—A New World - Nature—First View of the Orient—Hotel Europe—Mixed Nationalities—The First Backsheesh—Street Scenes in Alexandria—Familiar Pictures Idealized—Cometery Day—A Novel Turn Out—A Moslem Cemetery—New Terrors for Death—Pompey's Pillar—Our First Camel—Along the Canal—Departed Glory—A set of Fine Fellows—Our Handsome Dragomen—Bazaars—Universal Good Humor—A Continuous Holiday—Private life in Egypt—Invisible Blackness—The Land of Color and the Sun—A Casino... 28

CONTENTS.

CHAPTER III.
EGYPT OF TO-DAY.

Railways—Our Valiant Dragoman—A Hand-to-Hand Struggle—Alexandria to Cairo—Artificial Irrigation—An Arab Village—The Nile—Egyptian Festivals—Pyramids of Geezeh—Cairo—Natural Queries.. 41

CHAPTER IV.
CAIRO.

A Rhapsody—At Shepherd's—Hotel life, Egyptian plan—English Noblemen—Life in the Streets—The Valuable Donkey and his Driver—The "Swell Thing" in Cairo—A hint for Central Park—Eunuchs—"Yankee Doodles" of Cairo—A Representative Arab—Selecting Dragomen—The Great Business of Egypt—An Egyptian Market Place—A Substitute for Clothes—Dahabeëhs of the Nile—A Protracted Negotiation—Egyptian Wiles...... 45

CHAPTER V.
IN THE BAZAAR.

Sight Seeing in Cairo—An Eastern Bazaar—Courteous Merchants—The Honored Beggar—Charity to be Rewarded—A Moslem Funeral—The Gold Bazaar—Shopping for a Necklace—Conducting a Bride Home—A Partnership Matter—Early Marriages and Decay—Longings for Youth.......................... 57

CHAPTER VI.
MOSQUES AND TOMBS.

The Sirocco—The Desert—The Citadel of Cairo—Scene of the Massacre of the Memlooks—The World's Verdict—The Mosque of Mohammed Ali—Tomb of the Memlook Sultans—Life out of Death 67

CHAPTER VII.
MOSLEM WORSHIP—THE CALL TO PRAYER.

An Enjoyable City—Definition of Conscience—"Prayer is better than Sleep"—Call of the Muëzzin—Moslems at Prayer—Interior of a Mosque—Oriental Architecture—The Slipper Fitters—Devotional Washing—An Imam's Supplications........... 72

CONTENTS.

CHAPTER VIII.

THE PYRAMIDS.

Ancient Sepulchres—Grave Robbers—The Poor Old Mummy—The Oldest Monument in the World—First View of the Pyramids—The resident Bedaween—Ascending the Steps—Patent Elevators—A View from the Top—The Guide's Opinions—Origin of "Murray's Guide Book"—Speculations on the Pyramids—The Interior—Absolute Night—A Taste of Death—The Sphinx—Domestic Life in a Tomb—Souvenirs of Ancient Egypt—Backsheesh.. 79

CHAPTER IX.

PREPARATIONS FOR A VOYAGE.

A Weighty Question—The Seasons Bewitched—Poetic Dreams Realized—Egyptian Music—Public Garden—A Wonderful Rock—Its Patrons—The Playing Band—Native Love Songs—The Howling Derweeshes—An Exciting Performance—The Shakers put to Shame—Descendants of the Prophet—An Ancient Saracenic Home—The Land of the Flea and the Copt—Historical Curiosities—Preparing for our Journey—Laying in of Medicines and Rockets—A Determination to be Liberal—Official Life in Egypt—An Interview with the Bey—Paying for our Rockets—A Walking Treasury—Waiting for Wind.................... 93

CHAPTER X.

ON THE NILE.

On Board the "Rip Van Winkle"—A Farewell Dinner—The Three Months' Voyage Commenced—On the Nile—Our Pennant's Device—Our Dahabeëh—Its Officers and Crew—Types of Egyptian Races—The Kingdom of the "Stick"—The false Pyramid of Maydoon—A Night on the River—Curious Crafts—Boat Races on the Nile—Native Villages—Songs of the Sailors—Incidents of the Day—The Copts—The Patriarch—The Monks of Gebel é Tayr—Disappointment all Round—A Royal Luxury—The Banks of the Nile—Gum Arabic—Unfair Reports of Us—Speed of our Dahabeëh—Egyptian Bread—Hasheesh-Smoking—Egyptian Robbers—Sitting in Darkness—Agriculture—Gathering of Taxes—Successful Voyaging.................... 108

CONTENTS.

CHAPTER XI.

PEOPLE ON THE RIVER BANKS.

Sunday on the Nile—A Calm—A Land of Tombs—A New Divinity—Burial of a Child—A Sunday Companion on Shore—A Philosophical People—No Sunday Clothes—The Aristocratic Bedaween—The Sheykh—Rare Specimens for the Centennial—Tracts Needed—Woman's Rights—Pigeons and Cranes—Balmy Winter Nights—Tracking—Copying Nature in Dress—Resort of Crocodiles—A Hermit's Cave—Waiting for Nothing—Crocodile Mummies—The Boatmen's Song—Furling Sails—Life Again—Pictures on the Nile.................................. 131

CHAPTER XII.

SPENDING CHRISTMAS ON THE NILE.

Independence in Spelling—Asioot—Christmas Day—The American Consul—A Visit to the Pasha—Conversing by an Interpreter—The Ghawazees at Home—Ancient Sculpture—Bird's Eye View of the Nile—Our Christmas Dinner—Our Visitor—Grand Reception—The Fire Works—Christmas Eve on the Nile........ 145

CHAPTER XIII.

SIGHTS AND SCENES ON THE RIVER.

Ancient and Modern Ruins—We Pay Toll—Cold Weather—Night Sailing—Farshoot—A Visit from the Bey—The Market-Place—The Sakiyas or Water Wheels—The Nile is Egypt.......... 155

CHAPTER XIV.

MIDWINTER IN EGYPT.

Midwinter in Egypt—Slaves of Time—Where the Water Jars are Made—Coming to Anchor and how it was Done—New Years—"Smits" Copper Popularity—Great Strength of the Women—Conscripts for the Army—Conscription a Good Thing—On the Threshold of Thebes... 162

CONTENTS. xi.

CHAPTER XV.

AMONG THE RUINS OF THEBES.

Situation of the City—Ruins—Questions—Luxor—Karnak—Glorification of the Pharaohs—Sculptures in Stone—The Twin Colossi—Four Hundred Miles in Sixteen Days.................... 172

CHAPTER XVI.

HISTORY IN STONE.

A Dry City—A Strange Circumstance—A Pleasant Residence—Life on the Dahabeëh—Illustrious Visitors—Nose-Rings and Beauty—Little Fatimeh—A Mummy Hand and Thoughts upon it—Plunder of the Tombs—Exploits of the Great Sesostris—Gigantic Statues and their Object—Skill of Ancient Artists—Criticisms—Christian Churches and Pagan Temples—Society—A Peep into an Ancient Harem—Statue of Memnon—Mysteries—Pictures of Heroic Girls—Women in History................ 178

CHAPTER XVII.

KARNAK.

An Egyptian Carriage—Wonderful Ruins—The Great Hall of Sethi—The Largest Obelisk in The World—A City of Temples and Palaces.. 196

CHAPTER XVIII.

ASCENDING THE RIVER.

Ascending the River—An Exciting Boat Race—Inside a Sugar Factory—Setting Fire to a Town—Who Stole the Rockets?—Striking Contrasts—A Jail—The Kodi or Judge—What we saw at Assouan—A Gale—Ruins of Kom Ombos—Mysterious Movement—Land of Eternal Leisure.............................. 201

CHAPTER XIX.

PASSING THE CATARACT OF THE NILE.

Passing the Cataract of the Nile—Nubian Hills in Sight—Island of Elephantine—Ownership of the Cataract—Difficulties of the

Ascent—Negotiations for a Passage—Items about Assouan—
Off for the Cataracts—Our Cataract Crew—First Impressions
of the Cataract—In the Stream—Excitement—Audacious
Swimmers—Close Steering—A Comical Orchestra—The Final
Struggle—Victory—Above the Rapids—The Temple of Isis—
Ancient Kings and Modern Conquerors...................... 216

CHAPTER XX.

ON THE BORDERS OF THE DESERT.

Ethiopia—Relatives of the Ethiopians—Negro Land—Ancestry of
the Negro—Conversion Made Easy—A Land of Negative Blessings—Cool air from the Desert—Abd-el-Atti's Opinions—A
Land of Comfort—Nubian Costumes—Turning the Tables—
The Great Desert—Sin, Grease and Taxes.................. 235

CHAPTER XXI.

ETHIOPIA.

Primitive Attire—The Snake Charmer—A House full of Snakes—
A Writ of Ejectment—Natives—The Tomb of Mohammed—
Disasters—A Dandy Pilot—Nubian Beauty—Opening a Baby's
Eyes—A Nubian Pigville.................................... 244

CHAPTER XXII.

LIFE IN THE TROPICS—WADY HALFA.

Life in the Tropics—Wady Halfa—Capital of Nubia—The Centre
of Fashion—The Southern Cross—Castor Oil Plantations—Justice to a Thief—Abd-el-Atti's Court—Mourning for the Dead
—Extreme of our Journey—A Comical Celebration—The March
of Civilization.. 258

CHAPTER XXIII.

APPROACHING THE SECOND CATARACT.

Two Ways to See It—Pleasures of Canal Riding—Bird's Eye View
of the Cataracts—Signs of Wealth—Wady Halfa—A Nubian
Belle—Classic Beauty—A Greek Bride—Interviewing a Crocodile—Joking with a Widow—A Model Village............. 267

CONTENTS. xiii.

CHAPTER XXIV.

GIANTS IN STONE.

PAGE.

The Colossi of Aboo Simble, the largest in the World—Bombast—Exploits of Rameses II.—A Mysterious Temple—Fêting Ancient Deities—Guardians of the Nile—The Excavated Rock—The Temple—A Row of Sacred Monkeys—Our Last View of The Giants.. 275

CHAPTER XXV.

FLITTING THROUGH NUBIA.

Learning the Language—Models of Beauty—Cutting up a Crocodile—Egyptian Loafers—A Modern David—A Present—Our Menagerie—The Chameleon—Woman's Rights—False Prophets—Incidents—The School Master at Home—Confusion—Too Much Conversion—Charity—Wonderful Birds at Mecca...... 283

CHAPTER XXVI.

MYSTERIOUS PHILÆ.

Leave "well enough" Alone—The Myth of Osiris—The Heights of Biggeh—Cleopatra's Favorite Spot—A Legend—Mr. Fiddle—Dreamland—Waiting for a Prince—An Inland Excursion—Quarries—Adieu.. 298

CHAPTER XXVII.

RETURNING.

Downward Run—Kidnapping a Sheykh—Blessed with Relatives—Making the Chute—Artless Children—A Model of Integrity—Justice—An Accident—Leaving Nubia—A Perfect Shame.... 309

CHAPTER XXVIII.

MODERN FACTS AND ANCIENT MEMORIES.

The Mysterious Pebble—Ancient Quarries—Prodigies of Labor—Humor in Stone—A Simoon—Famous Grottoes—Naughty Attractions—Bogus Relics—Antiquity Smith.................. 320

CHAPTER XXIX.

THE FUTURE OF THE MUMMY'S SOUL.

Ancient Egyptian Literature—Mummies—A Visit to the Tombs—Disturbing the Dead—The Funeral Ritual—Unpleasant Explorations—A Mummy in Pledge—A Desolate Way—Buried Secrets—Building for Eternity—Before the Judgment Seat—Weighed in the Balance—The Habitation of the Dead—Illuminated—Accommodations for the Mummy—The Pharaoh of the Exodus—A Baby Charon—Bats.................................. 331

CHAPTER XXX.

FAREWELL TO THEBES.

Social Festivities—An Oriental Dinner—Dancing Girls—Honored by the Sultan—The Native Consul—Finger Feeding—A Dance—Ancient Style of Dancing—The Poetry of Night—Karnak by Moonlight—Amusements at Luxor—Farewell to Thebes...... 350

CHAPTER XXXI.

LOITERING BY THE WAY.

"Very Grammatick"—The Lying-in-Temple—A Holy Man—Scarecrows—Asinine Performers—Antiquity—Old Masters—Profit and Loss—Hopeless "Fellahs"—Lion's Oil—A Bad Reputation—An Egyptian Mozart....................................... 361

CHAPTER XXXII.

JOTTINGS.

Mission School—Education of Women—Contrasts—A Mirage—Tracks of Successive Ages—Bathers—Tombs of the Sacred Bulls—Religion and Grammar—Route to Darfour—Winter Residence of the Holy Family—Grottoes—Mistaken Views—Dust and Ashes—Osman Bey—A Midsummer's Night Dream—Ruins of Memphis—Departed Glory—A Second Visit to the Pyramids of Geezeh—An Artificial Mother....................... 379

CHAPTER XXXIII.

THE KHEDIVE.

At Gezereh—Aboo Yusef the Owner—Cairo Again—A Question—The Khedive—Solomon and the Viceroy—The Khedive's Family Expenses—Another Joseph—Personal Government—Docks of Cairo—Raising Mud—Popular Superstitions—Leave-Taking ... 398

CHAPTER XXXIV.

THE WOODEN MAN.

Visiting a Harem—A Reception—The Khedive at Home—Ladies of the Harem—Wife of Tufik Pasha—The Mummy—The Wooden Man—Discoveries of Mariette Bey—Egypt and Greece Compared—Learned Opinions 411

CHAPTER XXXV.

ON THE WAY HOME.

Leaving our Dahabeëh—The Baths in Cairo—Curious Mode of Execution—The Guzeereh Palace—Empress Eugenie's Sleeping Room—Medallion of Benjamin Franklin in Egypt—Heliopolis—The Bedaween Bride—Holy Places—The Resting Place of the Virgin Mary—Fashionable Drives—The Shoobra Palace—Forbidden Books—A Glimpse of a Bevy of Ladies—Uncomfortable Guardians.. 421

CHAPTER XXXVI.

BY THE RED SEA.

Following the Track of the Children of Israel—Routes to Suez—Temples—Where was the Red Sea Crossed?—In sight of the Bitter Lakes—Approaching the Red Sea—Faith—The Suez Canal—The Wells of Moses—A Sentimental Pilgrimage—Price of one of the Wells—Miriam of Marah—Water of the Wells—Returning to Suez—A Caravan of Bedaweens—Lunch Baskets searched by Custom Officers—The Commerce of the East 429

CHAPTER XXXVII.

WESTWARD HO.

Leaving Suez—Ismailia—The Lotus—A Miracle—Egyptian Steamer—Information Sought—The Great Highway—Port Saïd—Abd-el-Atti again—Great Honors Lost—Farewell to Egypt............ 440

CHAPTER I.

AT THE GATES OF THE EAST.

THE Mediterranean still divides the East from the West. Ages of traffic and intercourse across its waters have not changed this fact; neither the going of armies nor of embassies, Northmen forays nor Saracenic maraudings, Christian crusades nor Turkish invasions, neither the borrowing from Egypt of its philosophy and science, nor the stealing of its precious monuments of antiquity, down to its bones, not all the love-making, slave-trading, war-waging, not all the commerce of four thousand years, by oar and sail and steam, have sufficed to make the East like the West.

Half the world was lost at Actium, they like to say, for the sake of a woman; but it was the half that, I am convinced, we never shall gain—for though the Romans did win it, they did not keep it long, and they made no impression on it that is not, compared with its own individuality, as stucco to granite. And I suppose there is not now and never will be another woman in the East handsome enough to risk a world for.

There, across the most fascinating and fickle sea in the world —a feminine sea, inconstant as lovely, all sunshine and tears in a moment, reflecting in its quick mirror in rapid succession the skies of grey and blue, the weather of Europe and of Africa, a sea of romance and nausea—lies a world in everything unlike our own, a world perfectly known, yet never familiar and never otherwise than strange to the European and American. I had supposed it otherwise; I had been led to think that modern civilization had more or less transformed the East to its own likeness; that, for instance, the railway up the Nile had practically done for that historic stream. They say that if you run a red-hot nail through an orange, the fruit will keep its freshness and remain unchanged a long time. The thrusting of the iron into Egypt may arrest decay, but it does not appear to change the country.

There is still an Orient, and I believe there would be if it were all canaled, and railwayed, and converted; for I have great faith in habits that have withstood the influence of six or seven thousand years of changing dynasties and religions. Would you like to go a little way with me into this Orient?

The old-fashioned travellers had a formal fashion of setting before the reader the reasons that induced them to take the journey they described; and they not unfrequently made poor health an apology for their wanderings, judging that that excuse would be most readily accepted for their eccentric conduct. "Worn out in body and mind we set sail," etc.; and the reader was invited to launch in a sort of funereal bark upon the Mediterranean and accompany an invalid in search of his last resting place.

There was in fact no reason why we should go to Egypt—a remark that the reader will notice is made before he has a chance to make it—and there is no reason why any one indisposed to do so should accompany us. If information is desired, there are whole libraries of excellent books about the land of the Pharaohs, ancient and modern, historical, archæological, statistical, theoretical, geographical; if amusement is wanted, there are also excellent books, facetious and sentimental. I suppose that volumes enough have been written about Egypt to cover every foot of its arable soil if they were spread out, or to dam the Nile if they were dumped into it, and to cause a drought in either case if they were not all interesting and the reverse of dry. There is therefore no *onus* upon the traveller in the East to-day to write otherwise than suits his humour; he may describe only what he chooses. With this distinct understanding I should like the reader to go with me through a winter in the Orient. Let us say that we go to escape winter.

It is the last of November, 1874—the beginning of what proved to be the bitterest winter ever known in America and Europe, and I doubt not it was the first nip of the return of the rotary glacial period—that we go on board a little Italian steamer in the harbour of Naples, reaching it in a row-boat and in a cold rain. The deck is wet and dismal; Vesuvius is invisible, and the whole sweep of the bay is hid by a slanting mist. Italy has been in a shiver for a month; snow on the Alban hills and in the Tusculan theatre; Rome was as chilly as a stone tomb with the door left open. Naples is little better; Boston, at any season, is better than Naples—now.

We steam slowly down the harbour amid dripping ships, losing all sight of villages and the lovely coast; only Capri comes out comely in the haze, an island cut like an antique cameo. Long after dark we see the light on it and also that of the Punta della Campanella opposite, friendly beams following us down the coast. We are off Pæstum, and I can feel that its noble temple is looming there in the darkness. This ruin is in some sort a door into, an introduction to, the East.

Pæstum has been a deadly marsh for eighteen hundred years, and deserted for almost a thousand. Nettles and unsightly brambles have taken the place of the "roses of Pæstum" of which the Roman poets sang; but still, as a poetic memory, the cyclamen trails among the *débris* of the old city; and the other day I found violets waiting for a propitious season to bloom. The sea has retired away from the site of the town and broadened the marsh in front of it. There are at Pæstum three Greek temples, called, no one can tell why, the Temple of Neptune, the Basilica, and the Temple of Ceres; remains of the old town walls and some towers; a tumble-down house or two, and a wretched tavern. The whole coast is subject to tremors of the earth, and the few inhabitants hanging about there appear to have had all their bones shaken out of them by the fever and ague.

We went down one raw November morning from Naples, driving from a station on the Calabrian railway, called Battipoglia, about twelve miles over a black marshy plain, relieved only by the bold mountains, on the right and left. This plain is gradually getting reclaimed and cultivated; there is raised on it inferior cotton and some of the vile tobacco which the Government monopoly compels the free Italians to smoke, and large olive-orchards have been recently set out. The soil is rich and the country can probably be made habitable again. Now, the few houses are wretched and the few people squalid. Women were pounding stone on the road we travelled, even young girls among them wielding the heavy hammers, and all of them very thinly clad, their one sleazy skirt giving little protection against the keen air. Of course the women were hard-featured and coarse-handed; and both they and the men have the swarthy complexion that may betoken a more Eastern origin. We fancied that they had a brigandish look. Until recently this plain has been a favourite field for brigands, who spied the rich traveller from the height of St. Angelo and pounced upon him if he was unguarded. Now, soldiers are quartered along the road, patrol the country on horseback, and lounge about the ruins at Pæstum. Perhaps they retire to some height for the night, for the district is too unhealthy for an Italian even, whose health may be of no consequence. They say that if even an Englishman, who goes merely to shoot woodcock, sleeps there one night, in the right season, that night will be his last.

We saw the ruins of Pæstum under a cold grey sky, which harmonized with their isolation. We saw them best from the side of the sea, with the snow-sprinkled mountains rising behind for a background. There they stood out, impressive, majestic, time-defying. In all Europe there are no ruins better worthy the study of the admirer of noble architecture than these.

The Temple of Neptune is older than the Parthenon, its Doric sister, at Athens. It was probably built before the Persians of Xerxes occupied the Acropolis and saw from there the flight of their ruined fleet out of the Strait of Salamis. It was built when the Doric had attained the acme of its severe majesty, and it is to-day almost perfect on the exterior. Its material is a coarse travertine which time and the weather have honeycombed, showing the petrifications of plants and shells; but of its thirty-six massive exterior columns not one has fallen, though those on the north side are so worn by age that the once deep fluting is nearly obliterated. You may care to know that these columns, which are thirty feet high and seven and a half feet in diameter at the base, taper symmetrically to the capitals, which are the severest Doric.

At first we thought the temple small, and did not even realize its two hundred feet of length, but the longer we looked at it the larger it grew to the eye, until it seemed to expand into gigantic size; and from whatever point it was viewed, its harmonious proportions were an increasing delight. The beauty is not in any ornament, for even the pediment is and always was vacant, but in its admirable lines.

The two other temples are fine specimens of Greek architecture, also Doric, pure and without fault, with only a little tendency to depart from severe simplicity in the curve of the capitals, and yet they did not interest us. They are of a period only a little later than the Temple of Neptune, and that model was before their builders, yet they missed the extraordinary, many say almost spiritual, beauty of that edifice. We sought the reason, and found it in the fact that there are absolutely no straight lines in the Temple of Neptune. The side rows of columns curve a little out; the end rows curve a little in; at the ends the base line of the columns curves a trifle from the sides to the centre, and the line of the architrave does the same. This may bewilder the eye and mislead the judgment as to size and distance, but the effect is more agreeable than almost any other I know in architecture. It is not repeated in the other temples, the builders of which do not seem to have known its secret. Had the Greek colony lost the art of this perfect harmony, in the little time that probably intervened between the erection of these edifices? It was still kept at Athens, as the Temple of Theseus and the Parthenon testify.

Looking from the interior of the temple out at either end, the entrance seems to be wider at the top than at the bottom, an Egyptian effect produced by the setting of the inward and outer columns. This appeared to us like a door through which we looked into Egypt, that mother of all arts and of most of the devices of this now confused world. We were on our way to see the first columns, prototypes of the Doric order, chiselled by man.

The custodian—there is one, now that twenty centuries of war and rapine and storms have wreaked themselves upon this temple—would not permit us to take our luncheon into its guarded precincts; on a fragment of the old steps, amid the winds, we drank our red Capri wine; not the usual compound manufactured at Naples, but the last bottle of pure Capri to be found on the island, so help the soul of the landlady at the hotel there; ate one of those imperfectly nourished Italian chickens, orphan birds, owning the pitiful legs with which the *table d'hôte* frequenters in Italy are so familiar, and blessed the Government for the care, tardy as it is, of its grandest monument of antiquity.

When I looked out of the port-hole of the steamer early in the morning, we were near the volcanic Lipari islands and islets, a group of seventeen altogether; which serve as chimneys and safety-valves to this part of the world. One of the small ones is of recent creation, at least it was heaved up about two thousand years ago, and I fancy that a new one may pop up here any time. From the time of the Trojan war all sorts of races and adventurers have fought for the possession of these coveted islands, and the impartial earthquake has shaken them all off in turn. But for the mist, we should have clearly seen Stromboli, the ever active volcano, but now we can only say we saw it. We are near it, however, and catch its outline, and listen for the groan of lost souls which the credulous crusaders used to hear issuing from its depths. It was at that time the entrance of purgatory; we read in the guide books that the crusaders implored the monks of Cluny to intercede for the deliverance of those confined there, and that therefore Odilo of Cluny instituted the observance of All Souls' Day.

The climate of Europe still attends us, and our first view of Sicily is through the rain. Clouds hide the coast and obscure the base of Ætna (which is oddly celebrated in America as an assurance against loss by fire); but its wide fields of snow, banked up high above the clouds, gleam as molten silver—treasure laid up in heaven—and give us the light of the rosy morning.

Rounding the point of Faro, the *locale* of Charybdis and Scylla, we come into the harbor of Messina and take shelter behind the long, curved horn of its mole. Whoever shunned the beautiful Scylla was liable to be sucked into the strong tide Charybdis; but the rock has lost its terror for moderns, and the current is no longer dangerous. We get our last dash of rain in this strait, and there is sunny weather and blue sky at the south. The situation of Messina is picturesque; the shores both of Calabria and Sicily are mountainous, precipitous, and very rocky; there seems to be no place for vegetation except by terracing. The town is backed by lofty circling mountains, which form a dark setting for its white houses and the string of outlying villages. Mediæval forts cling to the slopes above it.

No sooner is the anchor down than a fleet of boats surrounds the steamer, and a crowd of noisy men and boys swarms on board, to sell us mussles, oranges, and all sorts of merchandise, from a hair-brush to an under-wrapper. The Sunday is hopelessly broken into fragments in a minute. These lively traders use the English language and its pronouns with great freedom. The boot-black smilingly asks: "You black my boot?"

The vendor of under-garments says: "I gif you four franc for dis one. I gif you for dese two a seven franc. No? What you gif?"

A bright orange-boy, we ask, "How much a dozen?"

"Half franc."

"Too much."

"How much you give? Tast him; he ver good; a sweet orange; you no like, you no buy. Yes, sir. Tak one. This a one, he sweet no more."

And they were sweet no more. They must have been lemons in oranges' clothing. The flattering tongue of that boy and our greed of tropical color made us owners of a lot of them, most of which went overboard before we reached Alexandria, and would make fair lemonade of the streak of water we passed through.

At noon we sail away into the warm south. We have before us the beautiful range of Aspromonte, and the village of Reggio near which in 1862 Garibaldi received one of his wounds, a sort of inconvenient love-pat of fame. The coast is rugged and steep. High up is an isolated Gothic rock, pinnacled and jagged. Close by the shore we can trace the railway track which winds round the point of Italy, and some of the passengers look at it longingly; for though there is clear sky overhead, the sea has on an ungenerous swell; and what is blue sky to a stomach that knows its own bitterness, and feels the world sinking away from under it?

We are long in sight of Italy, but Sicily still sulks in the clouds, and Mount Ætna will not show itself. The night is bright and the weather has become milder; it is the prelude to a day calm and uninteresting. Nature rallies at night, however, and gives us a sunset in a pale gold sky with cloud-islands on the horizon and palm-groves on them. The stars come out in extraordinary profusion and a soft brilliancy unknown in New England, and the sky is of a tender blue—something delicate and not to be enlarged upon. A sunset is something that no one will accept second-hand.

On the morning of December 1st we are off Crete : Greece we have left to the north, and are going at ten knots an hour towards great hulking Africa. We sail close to the island and see its long, high barren coast till late in the afternoon. There is no road visible on this side, nor any sign of human habitation, except a couple of shanties perched high up among the rocks. From this point of view, Crete is a mass of naked rock lifted out of the waves. Mount Ida crowns it, snow-capped and gigantic. Just below Crete spring up in our geography the little islands of Gozo and Antigozo, merely vast rocks, with scant patches of low vegetation on the cliffs, a sort of vegetable blush, a few stunted trees on the top of the first, and an appearance of grass which has a reddish color.

The weather is more and more delightful, a balmy atmosphere brooding on a smooth sea. The chill which we carried in our bones from New York to Naples finally melts away. Life ceases to be a mere struggle, and becomes a mild enjoyment. The blue tint of the sky is beyond all previous comparison, delicate, like the shade of a silk, fading at the horizon into an exquisite grey or nearly white. We are on deck all day and till late at night, for once enjoying, by the help of an awning, real winter weather with the thermometer at seventy-two degrees.

Our passengers are not many, but selected. There are a German baron and his sparkling wife, delightful people, who handle the English language as delicately as if it were glass, and make of it the most *naïve* and interesting form of speech. They are going to Cairo for the winter, and the young baroness has the longing and curiosity regarding the land of the sun, which is peculiar to the poetical Germans; she has never seen a black man nor a palm-tree. In charge of the captain, there is an Italian woman, whose husband lives in Alexandria, who monopolizes the whole of the ladies' cabin, by a league with the slatternly stewardess, and behaves in a manner to make a state of war and wrath between her and the rest of the passengers. There is nothing bitterer than the hatred of people for each other on shipboard. When I afterwards saw this woman in the streets of Alexandria, I had scarcely any wish to shorten her stay upon this earth. There are also two tough-fibered and strong-minded dissenting ministers from Australia, who have come round by the Sandwich Islands and the United States, and are booked for Palestine, the Suez Canal, and the Red Sea. Speaking of Aden, which has the reputation of being as hot as Constantinople is wicked, one of them tells the story of an American (the English have a habit of fastening all their dubious anecdotes upon "an American") who said that if he owned two places, one in Aden and the other in H———, he would sell the one in Aden. These ministers are distinguished lecturers at home—a solemn thought, that even the most distant land is subjected to the blessing of the popular lecture.

Our own country is well represented, as it usually is abroad, whether by appointment or self-selection. It is said that the oddest people in the world go up the Nile and make the pilgrimage of Palestine. I have even heard that one must be a little cracked who will give a whole winter to high Egypt; but this is doubtless said by those who cannot afford to go. Notwithstanding the peculiarities of so many of those one meets drifting around the East (as eccentric as the English who frequent Italian *pensions*) it must be admitted that a great many estimable and apparently sane people go up the Nile—and that such are even found among Cook's "personally conducted."

There is on board an American, or a sort of Irish-American, more or less naturalized, from Nebraska, a raw-boned, hard-featured farmer, abroad for a two-years' tour; a man who has no guide-book or literature, except the Bible which he diligently reads. He has spent twenty or thirty years in acquiring and subduing land in the new country, and without any time or taste for reading, there has come with his possessions a desire to see that old world about which he cared nothing before he breathed the vitalizing air of the West. That he knew absolutely nothing of Europe, Asia, or Africa, except the little patch called Palestine, and found a day in Rome too much for a place so run down, was actually none of our business. He was a good patriotic American, and the only wonder was that with his qualification he had not been made consul somewhere.

But a more interesting person, in his way, was a slender,

no-blooded, youngish, married man, of the vegetarian and vegetable school, also alone, and bound for the Holy Land, who was sick of the sea and otherwise. He also was without books of travel, and knew nothing of what he was going to see or how to see it. Of what Egypt was he had the dimmest notion, and why we or he or anyone else should go there. What do you go up the Nile for? we asked. The reply was that the Spirit had called him to go through Egypt to Palestine. He had been a dentist, but now he called himself an evangelist. I made the mistake of supposing that he was one of those persons who have a call to go about and convince people that religion is one part milk (skimmed) and three parts water—harmless, however, unless you see too much of them. Twice is too much. But I guaged him inadequately. He is one of those few who comprehend the future, and, guided wholly by the Spirit and not by any scripture or tradition, his mission is to prepare the world for its impending change. He is *en rapport* with the vast uneasiness, which I do not know how to name, that pervades all lands. He had felt our war in advance. He now feels a great change in the air; he is illuminated by an inner light that makes him clairvoyant. America is riper than it knows for this change. I tried to have him definitely define it, so that I could write home to my friends and the newspapers and the insurance companies; but I could only get a vague notion that there was about to be an end of armies and navies and police, of all forms of religion, of government, of property, and that universal brotherhood is to set in.

The evangelist had come abroad on an important and rather secret mission; to observe the progress of things in Europe; and to publish his observations in a book. Spiritualized as he was, he had no need of any language except the American; he felt the political and religious atmosphere of all the cities he visited without speaking to any one. When he entered a picture gallery, although he knew nothing of pictures, he saw more than any one else. I suppose he saw more than Mr. Ruskin sees. He told me, among other valuable information, that he found Europe not so well prepared for the great movement as America, but that I would be surprised at the number who were in sympathy with it, especially those in high places in society and in government. The Roman Catholic Church was going to pieces; not that he cared any more for this than for the Presbyterian—he, personally, took what was good in any church, but he had got beyond them all; he was now only working for the establishment of the truth, and it was because he had more of the truth than others that he could see further.

He expected that America would be surprised when he published his observations. "I can give you a little idea," he said, "of how things are working." This talk was late at night, and by the dim cabin lamp. "When I was in Rome, I went to see the head-man of the Pope. I talked with him over an hour, and I found that he knew all about it!"

"Good gracious! You don't say so!"

"Yes, sir. And he is in full sympathy. But he dare not say anything. He knows that his Church is on its last legs. I told him that I did not care to see the Pope, but if he wanted to meet me, and discuss the infallibility question, I was ready for him."

"What did the Pope's head-man say to that?"

"He said that he would see the Pope, and see if he could arrange an interview; and would let me know. I waited a week in Rome, but no notice came. I tell you the Pope don't dare discuss it."

"Then he didn't see you?"

"No, sir. But I wrote him a letter from Naples."

"Perhaps he won't answer it."

"Well, if he doesn't, that is a confession that he can't. He leaves the field. That will satisfy me."

I said I thought he would be satisfied.

The Mediterranean enlarges on acquaintance. On the fourth day we are still without sight of Africa, though the industrious screw brings us nearer every moment. We talk of Carthage, and think we can see the color of the Libyan sand in the yellow clouds at night. It is two o'clock on the morning of December the third, when we make the Pharos of Alexandria, and wait for a pilot.

CHAPTER II.

WITHIN THE PORTALS.

EAGERNESS to see Africa brings us on deck at dawn. The low coast is not yet visible. Africa, as we had been taught, lies in heathen darkness. It is the policy of the Egyptian government to make the harbor difficult of access to hostile men-of-war, and we, who are peacefully inclined, cannot come in till daylight, nor then without a pilot.

The day breaks beautifully, and the Pharos is set like a star in the bright streak of the East. Before we can distinguish land, we see the so-called Pompey's Pillar and the light-house, the palms, the minarets, and the outline of the domes painted on the straw-color of the sky—a dream-like picture. The curtain draws up with Eastern leisure—the sun appears to rise more deliberately in the Orient than elsewhere; the sky grows more brilliant, there are long lines of clouds, golden and crimson, and we seem to be looking miles and miles into an enchanted country. Then ships and boats, a vast number of them, become visible in the harbor, and as the light grows stronger, the city and land lose something of their beauty, but the sky grows more softly fiery till the sun breaks through. The city lies low along the flat coast, and seems at first like a brownish white streak, with fine lines of masts, palm-trees, and minarets above it.

The excitement of the arrival in Alexandria and the novelty of everything connected with the landing can never be repeated. In one moment the Orient flashes upon the bewildered traveller; and though he may travel far and see stranger sights, and penetrate the hollow shell of Eastern mystery, he never will see again at once such a complete contrast to all his previous experience. One strange, unfamiliar form takes the place of another so rapidly that there is no time to fix an impression, and everything is so *bizarre* that the new-comer has no points of comparison. He is launched into a new world, and has no time to adjust the focus of his observation. For myself, I wished the Orient would stand off a little and stand still so that I could try to comprehend it. But it would not; a revolving kaleidoscope never presented more bewildering figures and colors to a child than the port of Alexandria to us.

Our first sight of strange dress is that of the pilot and the crew who bring him off—they are Nubians, he is a swarthy Egyptian. "How black they are," says the baroness; "I don't like it." As the pilot steps on deck, in his white turban, loose robe of cotton, and red slippers, he brings the East with him; we pass into the influence of the Moslem spirit. Coming into the harbor we have pointed out to us the batteries, the palace and harem of the Pasha (more curiosity is felt about a harem than about any other building, except perhaps a lunatic asylum), and the new villas along the curve of the shore. It is difficult to see any ingress, on account of the crowd of shipping.

The anchor is not down before we are surrounded by rowboats, six or eight deep on both sides, with a mob of boatmen and guides, all standing up and shouting at us in all the broken languages of three continents. They are soon up the sides and on deck, black, brown, yellow; in turbans, in tarbooshes, in robes of white, blue, brown, in brilliant waist-shawls, slippered, and bare-legged, bare-footed, half-naked, with little on except a pair of cotton drawers and a red fez, eager, big-eyed, pushing, yelping, gesticulating, seizing hold of passengers and baggage, and fighting for the possession of the traveller's goods, which seem to him about to be shared among a lot of pirates. I saw a dazed traveller start to land, with some of his travelling-bags in one boat, his trunk in a second, and himself in yet a third, and a *commissionaire* at each arm attempting to drag him into two others. He evidently couldn't make up his mind, which to take.

We have decided upon our hotel, and ask for the *commissionaire* of it. He appears. In fact there are twenty or thirty of him. The first one is a tall, persuasive, nearly naked Ethiop, who declares that he is the only Simon Pure, and grasps our hand-bags. Instantly, a fluent, business-like Alexandrian pushes him aside—"I am the *commissionaire*"—and is about to take possession of us. But a dozen others are of like mind, and Babel begins. We rescue our property, and for ten minutes a lively and most amusing altercation goes on as to who is the representative of the hotel. They all look like pirates from the Barbary coast, instead of guardians of peaceful travellers. Quartering an orange, I stand in the centre of an interesting group, engaged in the most lively discussion, pushing, howling and fiery gesticulation. The dispute is finally between two:

"*I* Hotel Europe!"

"*I* Hotel Europe; he no hotel."

"He my brother, all same me."

"He! I never see he before," with a shrug of the utmost contempt.

As soon as we select one of them, the tumult subsides, the enemies become friends and cordially join in loading our luggage. In the first five minutes of his stay in Egypt, the traveller learns that he is to trust and be served by people who haven't the least idea that lying is not a perfectly legitimate means of attaining any desirable end. And he begins to lose any prejudice he may have in favor of a white complexion and of clothes. In a decent climate he sees how little clothing is needed for comfort, and how much artificial nations are accustomed to put on from false modesty.

We begin to thread our way through a maze of shipping, and hundreds of small boats and barges; the scene is gay and exciting beyond expression. The first sight of the colored, pictured, lounging, waiting Orient is enough to drive an impressionable person wild; so much that is novel and picturesque is crowded into a few minutes; so many colors and flying robes; such a display of bare legs and swarthy figures. We meet flat boats coming down the harbor loaded with laborers, dark, immobile groups in turbans and gowns, squatting on deck in the attitude which is the most characteristic of the East; no one stands or sits—everybody squats or reposes cross-legged. Soldiers are on the move; smart Turkish officers dart by in light boats with half a dozen rowers, the crew of an English man-of-war pull past; in all directions the swift boats fly, and with their freight of color, it is like the thrusting of quick shuttles, in the weaving of a brilliant carpet, before our eyes.

We step on shore at the Custom-House. I have heard travellers complain of the delay in getting through it. I feel that I want to go slowly, that I would like to be all day in getting through—that I am hurried along like a person who is dragged hastily through a gallery, past striking pictures of which he gets only glimpses. What a group this is on shore; importunate guides, porters, coolies. They seize hold of us, we want to stay and look at them. Did ever any civilized men dress so gayly, so little, or so much in the wrong place? If that fellow would untwist the folds of his gigantic turban, he would have cloth enough to clothe himself perfectly. Look! that's an East Indian, that's a Greek, that's a Turk, that's a Syrian Jew! No, he's Egyptian, the crook-nose is not uncommon to Egyptians; that tall round hat is Persian, that one is from Abys—there they go, we haven't half seen them! We leave our passports at the entrance, and are whisked through into the baggage-room, where our guide pays a noble official three francs for the pleasure of his chance acquaintance; some nearly naked coolie-porters, who bear long cords, carry off our luggage, and before we know it we are in a carriage, and a rascally guide and interpreter—Heaven knows how he fastened himself upon us in the past five minutes—is on the box and apparently owns us? (It took us half a day and liberal backsheesh to get rid of the evil-eyed fellow). We have gone only a little distance when half a dozen of the naked coolies rush after us, running by the carriage and laying hold of it, demanding backsheesh. It appears that either the boatman has cheated them, or they think he will, or they haven't had enough. Nobody trusts anybody else, and nobody is ever satisfied with what he gets, in Egypt. These blacks, in their dirty white gowns, swinging their porters' ropes and howling like madmen, pursue us a long way and look as if they would tear us in pieces. But nothing comes of it. We drive to the Place Mehemet Ali, the European square,—having nothing Oriental about it, a square with an equestrian statue of Mehemet Ali, some trees and a fountain—surrounded by hotels, bankers' offices and Frank shops.

There is not much in Alexandria to look at except the people, and the dirty bazaars. We never before had seen so much nakedness, filth, and dirt, so much poverty and such enjoyment of it, or at least indifference to it. We were forced to strike a new scale of estimating poverty and wretchedness. People are poor in proportion as their wants are not gratified. And here are thousands who have few of the wants that we have, and perhaps less poverty. It is difficult to estimate the poverty of those fortunate children to whom the generous sun gives a warm color for clothing, who have no occupation but to sit in the same, all day, in some noisy and picturesque thoroughfare, and stretch out the hand for the few paras sufficient to buy their food, who drink at the public fountain, wash in the tank of the mosque, sleep in street-corners, and feel sure of their salvation if they know the direction of Mecca. And the Mohammedan religion seems to be a sort of soul-compass, by which the most ignorant believer can always orient himself. The best-dressed Christian may feel certain of one thing, that he is the object of the cool contempt of the most naked, ophthalmic, flea-attended, wretched Moslem he meets. The Oriental conceit is a peg above ours—it is not self-conscious.

In a fifteen minutes' walk in the streets, the stranger finds all the pictures that he remembers in his illustrated books of Eastern life. There is turbaned Ali Baba, seated on the hindquarters of his sorry donkey, swinging his big feet in a constant effort to urge the beast forward; there is the one-eyed calender who may have arrived last night from Bagdad; there is the water-carrier, with a cloth about his loins, staggering under a full goat-skin—the skin, legs, head, and all the members of the brute distended, so that the man seems to be carrying a drowned and water-soaked animal; there is the veiled sister of Zobeide riding a grey donkey astride, with her knees drawn up (as all women ride in the East), entirely enveloped in a white garment which covers her head and puffs out about her like a balloon—all that can be seen of the woman are the toes of her pointed yellow slippers, and two black eyes; there is the seller of sherbet, a waterish, feeble, insipid drink, clinking his glasses; and the veiled woman in black, with hungry eyes, is gliding about everywhere. The veil is in two parts, a band about the forehead, and a strip of black which hangs underneath the eyes and terminates in a point at the waist; the two parts are connected by an ornamented cylinder of brass, or silver if the wearer can afford it, two and a half inches long and an inch in diameter. This ugly cylinder between the restless eyes, gives the woman an imprisoned, frightened look. Across the street from the hotel, upon the stone coping of the public square, is squatting hour after hour in the sun, a row of these forlorn creatures in black, impassive and waiting. We are told that they are washerwomen waiting for a job. I never can remove the impression that these women are half stifled behind their veils and the shawls which they draw over the head; when they move their heads, it is like the piteous dumb movement of an uncomplaining animal.

But the impatient reader is waiting for Pompey's Pillar. We drive outside the walls, through a thronged gateway, through streets and among people wretched and picturesque to the last degree. This is the road to the large Moslem cemetery, and to-day is Thursday, the day for visiting the graves. The way is lined with coffee-shops, where men are smoking and playing at draughts; with stands and booths for the sale of fried cakes and confections; and all along, under foot, so that it is difficult not to tread on them, are private markets for the sale of dates, nuts, raisins, wheat, and doora; the bare-legged owner sits on the ground and spreads his dust-covered untempting fare on a straw mat before him. It is more wretched and forlorn outside the gate than within. We are amid heaps of rubbish, small mountains of it, perhaps the ruins of old Alexandria, perhaps only the accumulated sweepings of the city for ages, piles of dust, and broken pottery. Every Egyptian town of any size is surrounded by these—the refuse of ages of weary civilization.

What a number of old men, of blind men, ragged men—though rags are no disgrace! What a lot of scrawny old women, lean old hags, some of them without their faces covered—even the veiled ones, you can see, are only bags of bones. There is a derweesh, a naked holy man, seated in the dirt by the wall, reading the Koran. He has no book, but he recites the sacred text in a loud voice, swaying his body backwards and forwards. Now and then we see a shrill-voiced, handsome boy also reading the Koran with all his might, and keeping a laughing eye upon the passing world. Here comes a novel turn-out. It is a long truck-wagon drawn by one bony horse. Upon it are a dozen women, squatting about the edges, facing each other, veiled, in black, silent, jolting along like so many bags of meal. A black imp stands in front, driving,

They carry baskets of food and flowers, and are going to the cemetery to spend the day.

We pass the cemetery, for the Pillar is on a little hillock overlooking it. Nothing can be drearier than this burying-ground—unless it may be some other Moslem cemetery. It is an uneven plain of sand, without a spear of grass or a green thing. It is covered thickly with ugly stucco, oven-like tombs, the whole inconceivably shabby and dust covered; the tombs of the men have head-stones to distinguish them from the women. Yet, shabby as all the details of this crumbling cheap place of sepulture are, nothing could be gayer or more festive than the scene before us. Although the women are in the majority, there are enough men and children present, in colored turbans, fezes, and gowns, and shawls of Persian dye, to transform the graveyard into the semblance of a parterre of flowers. About hundreds of the tombs are seated in a circle groups of women, with their food before them, and the flowers laid upon the tomb, wailing and howling in the very excess of dry-eyed grief. Here and there a group has employed a "welee" or holy man, or a boy, to read the Koran for it—and these Koran-readers turn an honest para by their vocation. The women spend nearly the entire day in this sympathetic visit to their departed friends—it is a custom as old as history, and the Egyptians used to build their tombs with a visiting ante-chamber for the accommodation of the living. I should think that the knowledge that such a group of women were to eat their luncheon, wailing and roosting about one's tomb every week, would add a new terror to death.

The Pillar, which was no doubt erected by Diocletian to his own honor, after the modest fashion of Romans as well as Egyptians, is in its present surroundings not an object of enthusiasm, though it is almost a hundred feet high, and the monolith shaft was, before age affected it, a fine piece of polished syenite. It was no doubt a few thousand years older than Diocletian, and a remnant of that oldest civilization; the base and capital he gave it are not worthy of it. Its principal use now is as a surface for the paint-brushes and chisels of distinguished travellers, who have covered it with their precious names. I cannot sufficiently admire the *naïveté* and self-depreciation of those travellers who paint and cut their names on such monuments, knowing as they must that the first sensible person who reads the same will say, "This is an ass."

We drive, still outside the walls, towards the Mahmoodeeh canal, passing amid mounds of rubbish, and getting a view of the desert-like country beyond. And now heaves in sight the unchanged quintessence of Orientalism—there is our first camel, a camel in use, in his native setting and not in a menagerie. There is a line of them, loaded with building-stones, wearily shambling along. The long bended neck apes humility, but the supercilious nose in the air expresses perfect contempt for all modern life. The contrast of this haughty "stuck-up-ativeness" (it is necessary to coin this word to express the camel's ancient conceit) with the royal ugliness of the brute, is awe-inspiring and amusing. No human royal family dare be uglier than the camel. He is a mass of bones, faded tufts, humps, lumps, splay-joints, and callosities. His tail is a ridiculous wisp, and a failure as an ornament or a fly-brush. His feet are simply big sponges. For skin covering he has patches of old Buffalo robes, faded and with the hair worn off. His voice is more disagreeable than his appearance. With a reputation for patience, he is snappish and vindictive. His endurance is overrated—that is to say he dies like a sheep on an expedition of any length, if he is not well fed. His gait moves every muscle like an ague. And yet this ungainly creature carries his head in the air, and regards the world out of his great brown eyes with disdain. The Sphinx is not more placid. He reminds me, I don't know why, of a pyramid. He has a resemblance to a palm-tree. It is impossible to make an Egyptian picture without him. What a Habsburg lip he has! Ancient, royal! The very poise of his head says plainly, "I have come out of the dim past, before history was; the deluge did not touch me; I saw Menes come and go; I helped Shoofoo build the great pyramid; I knew Egypt when it hadn't an obelisk nor a temple; I watched the slow building of the pyramid at Sakkara. Did I not transport the fathers of your race across the desert? There are three of us; the date-palm, the pyramid, and myself. Everything else is modern. Go to!"

Along the canal, where lie dahabeëhs that will by and by make their way up the Nile, are some handsome villas, palaces and gardens. This is the favorite drive and promenade. In the gardens that are open to the public, we find a profusion of tropical trees and flowering shrubs; roses are decaying, but the blossoms of the yellow acacia scent the air; there are Egyptian lilies; the plant with crimson leaves, not native here, grows as high as the arbutilon tree; the red passion-flower is in bloom, and morning-glories cover with their running vine the tall and slender cypresses. The finest tree is the sycamore, with great gnarled trunk, and down-dropping branches. Its fruit, the sycamore fig, grows directly on the branch, without stem. It is an insipid fruit, sawdusty, but the Arabs like it, and have a saying that he who eats one is sure to return to Egypt. After we had tried to eat one, we thought we should not care to return. The interior was filled with lively little flies; and a priest who was attending a school of boys taking a holiday in the grove, assured us that each fig had to be pierced when it was green, to let the flies out, in order to make it eatable. But the Egyptians eat them, flies and all.

The splendors of Alexandria must be sought in books. The traveller will see scarcely any remains of a magnificence which dazzled the world in the beginning of our era. He may like to see the mosque that marks the site of the church of St. Mark, and he may care to look into the Coptic convent whence the Venetians stole the body of the saint, about a thousand years ago. Of course we go to see that wonder of our childhood, Cleopatra's Needles, as the granite obelisks are called that were brought from Alexandria and set up before a temple of Cæsar in the time of Tiberius. Only one is standing, the other, mutilated, lies prone beneath the soil. The erect one stands near the shore and in the midst of hovels and incredible filth. The name of the earliest king it bears is that of Thothmes III., the great man of Egypt, whose era of conquest was about 1,500 years before St. Mark came on his mission to Alexandria.

The city which has had as many vicissitudes as most cities, boasting under the Cæsars a population of half a million, that had decreased to 6,000 in 1800, and has now again grown to over two hundred thousand, seems to be at a waiting point; the merchants complain that the Suez canal has killed its trade. Yet its preëminence for noise, dirt, and shabbiness will hardly be disputed; and its bazaars and streets are much more interesting, perhaps because it is the meeting-place of all races, than travellers usually admit.

We had scarcely set foot in our hotel when we were saluted and waited for by dragomans of all sorts. They knocked at our doors, they waylaid us in the passages; whenever we emerged from our rooms half a dozen rose up, bowing low; it was like being a small king, with obsequious attendants waiting every motion. They presented their cards, they begged we would step aside privately for a moment and look at the bundle of recommendations they produced; they would not press themselves, but if we desired a dragoman for the Nile they were at our service. They were of all shades of color, except white, and of all degrees of oriental splendor in their costume. There were Egyptians, Nubians, Maltese, Greeks, Syrians. They speak well all the languages of the Levant and of Europe, except the one in which you attempt to converse with them. I never made the acquaintance of so many fine fellows in the same space of time. All of them had the strongest letters of commendation from travellers whom they had served, well-known men of letters and of affairs. Travellers give these endorsements as freely as they sign applications for government appointments at home.

The name of the handsome dragoman who walked with us through the bazaars was, naturally enough, Ahmed Abdallah. He wore the red fez (tarboosh) with a gay kuffia bound about it; an embroidered shirt without collar or cravat; a long shawl of checked and bright-colored Beyrout silk girding the loins, in which was carried his watch and heavy chain; a cloth coat; and baggy silk trousers that would be a gown if they were not split enough to gather about each ankle. The costume is rather Syrian than Egyptian, and very elegant when the materials are fine; but with a suggestion of effeminacy to Western eyes.

The native bazaars, which are better at Cairo, reveal to the traveller, at a glance, the character of the Orient; its cheap tinsel, its squalor, and its occasional richness and gorgeousness. The shops on each side of the narrow street are little more than good-sized wardrobes, with room for shelves of goods in the rear and for the merchant to sit cross-legged in front. There is usually space for a customer to sit with him, and indeed two or three can rest on the edge of the platform. Upon cords stretched across the front hang specimens of the wares for sale. Wooden shutters close the front at night. These little cubbies are not only the places of sale but of manufacture of goods. Everything goes on in the view of all the world. The tailor is stitching, the goldsmith is blowing the bellows of his tiny forge, the saddler is repairing the old donkey-saddles, the shoemaker is cutting red leather, the brazier is hammering, the weaver sits at his little loom with the treadle in the ground—every trade goes on, adding its own clatter to the uproar.

What impresses us most is the good nature of the throng, under trying circumstances. The street is so narrow that three or four people abreast make a jam, and it is packed with those moving in two opposing currents. Through this mass comes a donkey with a couple of panniers of soil or of bricks, or bundles of scraggly sticks; or a camel surges in, loaded with building-joists or with lime; or a Turkish officer, with a gayly caparisoned horse impatiently stamping; a porter slams along with a heavy box on his back; the watter-carrier with his nasty skin rubs through; the vendor of sweetmeats finds room for his broad tray; the orange-man pushes his cart into the throng; the Jew auctioneer cries his antique brasses and more antique raiment. Everybody is jostled and pushed and jammed; but everybody is in an imperturbable good humor, for no one is really in a hurry, and whatever is, is as it always has been and will be. And what a cosmopolitan place it is. We meet Turks, Greeks, Copts, Egyptians, Nubians, Syrians, Armenians, Italians; tattered derweeshes, "welees" or holy Moslems, nearly naked, presenting the appearance of men who have been buried a long time and recently dug up; Greek priests, Jews, Persian Parsees, Algerines, Hindoos, negroes from Darfoor, and flat-nosed blacks from beyond Khartoom.

The traveller has come into a country of holiday which is perpetual. Under this sun and in this air there is nothing to do but to enjoy life and attend to religion five times a day. We look into a mosque; in the cool court is a fountain for washing; the mosque is sweet and quiet, and upon its clean matting a row of Arabs are prostrating themselves in prayer towards the niche that indicates the direction of Mecca. We stroll along the open streets encountering a novelty at every step. Here is a musician, a Nubian playing upon a sort of tambour on a frame; a picking, feeble noise he produces, but he is accompanied by the oddest character we have seen yet. This is a stalwart, wild-eyed son of the sand, coal-black, with a great mass of uncombed, disordered hair hanging about his shoulders. His only clothing is a breech-cloth and a round shaving-glass bound upon his forehead; but he has hung about his waist heavy strings of goats' hoofs, and those he shakes, in time to the tambour, by a tremulous motion of his big hips as he minces about. He seems so vastly pleased with himself that I covet knowledge of his language, in order to tell him that he looks like an idiot.

Near the Fort Napoleon, a hill by the harbor, we encounter another scene peculiar to the East. A yellow-skinned, cunning-eyed conjurer has attracted a ring of idlers about him, who squat in the blowing dust, under the blazing sun, and patiently watch his antics. The conjurer himself performs no wonders, but the spectators are a study of color and feature. The costumes are brilliant red, yellow, and white. The complexions exhaust the possibilities of human color. I thought I had seen black people in South Carolina; but I saw a boy just now standing in a doorway who would have been invisible but for his white shirt; and here is a fat negress in a bright yellow gown and kerchief, whose jet face has taken an incredible polish; only the most accomplished boot-black could raise such a shine on a shoe; tranquil enjoyment oozes out of her. The conjurer is assisted by two mites of children, a girl and a boy (no clothing wasted on them), and between the three a great deal of jabber and whacking with cane sticks is going on, but nothing is performed except the taking of a long snake from a bag and tying it round the little girl's neck. Paras are collected, however, and that is the main object of all performances.

A little further on, another group is gathered around a story-teller, who is reeling off one of the endless tales in which the Arab delights; love-adventures, not always the most delicate, but none the less enjoyed for that, or the story of some poor lad who has had a wonderful career and finally married the Sultan's daughter. He is accompanied in his narrative by two men thumping upon darabooka drums, in a monotonous, sleepy fashion, quite in accordance, however, with the everlasting leisure that pervades the air. Walking about are the vendors of sweets, and of greasy cakes, who carry tripods on which to rest their brass trays, and who split the air with their cries.

It is color, color, that makes all this shifting panorama so fascinating, and hides the nakedness, the squalor, the wretchedness of all this unconcealed poverty; color in flowing garments, color in the shops, color in the sky. We have come to the land of the sun.

At night when we walk around the square we stumble over bundles of rags containing men who are asleep, in all the corners, stretched on doorsteps, laid away on the edge of the sidewalk. Opposite the hotel is a *casino*, which is more Frank than Egyptian. The musicians are all women and Germans or Bohemians; the waiter-girls are mostly Italian; one of them says she comes from Bohemia, and has been in India, to which she proposes to return. The *habitués* are mostly young Egyptians in Frank dress except the tarboosh, and Italians, all effeminate fellows. All the world of loose living and wandering meets here. Italian is much spoken. There is little that is Oriental here, except it may be a complaisance toward anything enervating and languidly wicked that Europe has to offer. This cheap concert is, we are told, all the amusement at night that can be offered the traveler, by the once pleasure-loving city of Cleopatra, in the once brilliant Greek capital in which Hypatia was a star.

CHAPTER III.

EGYPT OF TO-DAY.

EGYPT has excellent railways. There is no reason why it should not have. They are made without difficulty, and easily maintained in a land of no frosts; only where they touch the desert an occasional fence is necessary against the drifting sand. The rails are laid, without wooden sleepers, on iron saucers, with connecting bands, and the track is firm and sufficiently elastic. The express train travels the 131 miles to Cairo in about four and a half hours, running with a punctuality, and with Egyptian drivers and conductors too, that is unique in Egypt. The opening scene at the station did not promise expedition or system.

We reach the station three quarters of an hour before the departure of the train, for it requires a long time—in Egypt, as everywhere in Europe—to buy tickets and get baggage weighed. The officials are slower workers than our treasury-clerks. There is a great crowd of foreigners, and the baggage-room is piled with trunks of Americans, 'boxes' of Englishmen, and chests and bundles of all sorts. Behind a high counter in a smaller room stand the scales, the weigher, and the clerks. Piles of trunks are brought in and dumped by the porters, and thrust forward by the servants and dragomans upon the counter, to gain them preference at the scales. No sooner does a dragoman get in his trunk than another is thrust ahead of it, and others are hurled on top, till the whole pile comes down with a crash. There is no system, there are neither officials nor police, and the excited travelers are free to fight it out among themselves. To venture into the *mêlée* is to risk broken bones, and it is wiser to leave the battle to luck and the dragomans. The noise is something astonishing. A score or two of men are yelling at the top of their voices, screaming, scolding, damning each other in polyglot, gesticulating, jumping up and down, quivering with excitement. This is your Oriental repose! If there were any rule by which passengers could take their turns, all the trunks could be quickly weighed and passed on; but now in the scrimmage not a trunk gets to the scales, and a half hour goes by in which no progress is made and the uproar mounts higher.

Finally, Ahmed, slight and agile, handing me his cane, kuffia and watch, leaps over the heap of trunks on the counter and comes to close quarters with the difficulty. He succeeds in getting two trunks upon the platform of the scales, but a traveller, whose clothes were made in London, tips them off and substitutes his own. The weighers stand patiently waiting the result of the struggle. Ahmed hurls off the stranger's trunk, gives its owner a turn that sends him spinning over the baggage, and at last succeeds in getting our luggage weighed. He emerges from the scrimmage an exhausted man, and we get our seats in the carriage just in time. However, it does not start for half an hour.

The reader would like to ride from Alexandria to Cairo, but he won't care to read much about the route. It is our first experience of a country living solely by irrigation—the occasional winter showers being practically of no importance. We pass along and over the vast shallows of Lake Mareotis, a lake in winter and a marsh in summer, ride between marshes and cotton-fields, and soon strike firmer ground. We are travelling, in short, through a Jersey flat, a land black, fat, and rich, without an elevation, broken only by canals and divided into fields by ditches. Every rod is cultivated, and there are no detached habitations. The prospect cannot be called lively, but it is not without interest; there are ugly buffaloes in the coarse grass, there is the elegant white heron, which travellers insist is the sacred ibis, there are some doleful-looking fellaheen, with donkeys, on the bank of the canal, there is a file of camels, and there are shadoofs. The shadoof is the primitive method of irrigation, and thousands of years have not changed it. Two posts are driven into the bank of the canal, with a cross-piece on top. On this swings a pole with a bucket of leather suspended at one end, which is outweighed by a ball of clay at the other. The fellah stands on the slope of the bank and, dipping the bucket into the water, raises it and pours the fluid into a sluiceway above. If the bank is high, two and sometimes three shadoofs are needed to raise the water to the required level. The labor is prodigiously hard and back-straining, continued as it must be constantly. All the fellaheen we saw were clad in black, though some had a cloth about their loins. The workman usually stands in a sort of a recess in the bank, and his color harmonizes with the dark soil. Any occupation more wearisome and less beneficial to the mind I cannot conceive. To the credit of the Egyptians, the men alone work the shadoof. Women here tug water, grind the corn, and carry about babies always; but I never saw one pulling at a shadoof pole.

There is an Arab village! We need to be twice assured that it is a village. Raised on a slight elevation, so as to escape high water, it is still hardly distinguishable from the land, certainly not in color. All Arab villages look like ruins; this is a compacted collection of shapeless mud-huts, flat-topped and irregularly thrown together. It is an aggregation of dog-kennels, baked in the sun and cracked. However, a clump of palm-trees near it gives it an air of repose, and if it possesses a mosque and a minaret it has a picturesque appearance, if the observer does not go too near. And such are the habitations of nearly all the Egyptians.

Sixty-five miles from Alexandria, we cross the Rosetta branch of the Nile, on a fine iron bridge—even this portion of the Nile is a broad, sprawling river; and we pass through several respectable towns which have an appearance of thrift—Tanta especially, with its handsome station and a palace of the Khedive. At Tanta is held three times a year a great religious festival and fair, not unlike the old fair of the ancient Egyptians at Bubastis in honor of Diana, with quite as many excuses, and like that, with a gramme of religion to a pound of pleasure. "Now," says Herodotus, "when they are being conveyed to the city Bubastis, they act as follows:—for men and women embark together, and great numbers of both sexes embark in every barge: some of the women have castanets on which they play, and the men play on the flute during the whole voyage; and the rest of the women and the men sing and clap their hands together at the same time." And he goes on to say that when they came to any town they moored the barge, and the women chaffed those on shore, and danced with indecent gestures ; and that at the festival more wine was consumed than all the rest of the year. The festival at Tanta is in honor of a famous Moslem saint whose tomb is there; but the tomb is scarcely so attractive as the field of the *fête*, with the story-tellers and the jugglers and booths of dancing girls.

We pass decayed Benha with its groves of Yoosef-Effendi oranges—the small fruit called Mandarin by foreigners, and preferred by those who like a slight medicinal smell and taste in the orange; and when we are yet twenty miles from Cairo, there in the south-west, visible for a moment and then hidden by the trees, and again in sight, faintly and yet clearly outlined against the blue sky, are two forms, the sight of which gives us a thrill. They stand still in that purple distance in which we have seen them all our lives. Beyond these level fields and these trees of sycamore and date-palm, beyond the Nile, on the desert's edge, with the low Libyan hills falling off behind them, as delicate in form and color as clouds, as enduring as the sky they pierce, the Pyramids of Geezeh! I try to shake off the impression of their solemn antiquity, and imagine how they would strike one if all their mystery were removed. But that is impossible. The imagination always prompts the eye. And yet I believe that standing where they do stand, and in this atmosphere, they are the most impressive of human structures. But the pyramids would be effective, as the obelisk is not, out of Egypt.

Trees increase in number; we have villas and gardens; the grey ledges of the Mokattam hills come into view, then the twin slender spires of the mosque of Mohammed Ali on the citadel promontory, and we are in the modern station of Cairo; and before we take in the situation are ignominiously driven away in a hotel-omnibus. This might happen in Europe. Yes; but then, who are these in white and blue and red, these squatters by the wayside, these smokers in the sun, these turbaned riders on braying donkeys and grumbling dromedaries; what is all this fantastic masquerade in open day? Do people live in these houses? Do women peep from these lattices? Isn't that gowned Arab conscious that he is kneeling and praying outdoors? Have we come to a land where all our standards fail, and people are not ashamed of their religion?

CHAPTER IV.

CAIRO.

CAIRO! Cairo! Masr-el-Káherah. The Victorious! City of the Caliphs, of Saláh-e'-deen, of the Memlooks! Town of mediæval romance projected into a prosaic age! More Oriental than Damascus, or Samarcand. Vast, sprawling city, with dilapidated Saracenic architecture, pretentious modern barrack-palaces, new villas and gardens, acres of compacted, squalid, unsunned dwellings. Always picturesque, lamentably dirty, and thoroughly captivating.

Shall we rhapsodize over it, or attempt to describe it? Fortunately, writers have sufficiently done both. Let us enjoy it. We are at Shepherd's. It is a caravansary through which the world flows. At its *table d' hôte* are all nations; German princes, English dukes and shopkeepers, Indian officers, American sovereigns; explorers, *savants*, travelers; they have come for the climate of Cairo, they are going up the Nile, they are going to hunt in Abyssinia, to join an advance military party on the White Nile; they have come from India, from Japan, from Australia, from Europe, from America.

We are in the Frank quarter called the Ezbekeëh, which was many years ago a pond during high water, then a garden with a canal round it, and is now built over with European houses and shops, except the square reserved for the public garden. From the old terrace in front of the hotel where the traveller used to look on trees, he will see now only raw new houses and a street usually crowded with passers and rows of sleepy donkeys and their voluble drivers. The hotel is two stories only, built round a court, damp in rainy or cloudy weather (and it is learning how to rain as high up the Nile as Cairo), and lacking the comforts which invalids require in the winter. It is kept on an ingenious combination of the American and European plans; that is, the traveller pays a fixed sum per day, and then gets a bill of particulars besides, which gives him all the pleasures of the European system. We heard that one would be more Orientally surrounded and better cared for at the Hôtel du Nil; and the Khedive, who tries his hand at everything, has set up a New Hotel on the public square; but, somehow, one enters Shepherd's as easy as he goes into a city gate.

They call the house entirely European. But there are pelicans walking about in the tropical garden; on one side is the wall of a harem, a house belonging to the Khedive's mother, a harem with closed shutters, but uninteresting, because there is no one in it, though ostriches are strutting in its paved court; in the rear of the house stretches a great grove of tall date palms standing in a dusty *débris*-strown field—a lazy wind is always singing through their tops, and a sakiya (a cow impelled water-wheel) creaks there day and night; we never lock the doors of our rooms; long-gowned attendants are always watching in the passages, and, when we want one, in default of bells, we open the door and clap the hands. All this, with a juggler performing before the house; dragomans and servants and merchants in Oriental costume; the monotonous strumming of an Arab band in a neighboring *café*; bricklayers on the unfinished house opposite us, working in white night-gowns and turbans, who might be mistaken at a distance for female sleep-walkers; and from a minaret not far away, the tenor-voiced muezzins urging us in the most musical invitation ever extended to unbelievers, to come to prayer at daylight—this cannot be called European.

An end of the dinner-table, however, is occupied by a loud party of young Englishmen, a sprinkling of dukes and earls and those attendants and attentive listeners of the nobility who laugh inordinately when my lord says a good thing, and are encouraged when my lord laughs loudly at a sally of theirs, and declares, "well, now, that's very good;" a party who seem to regard Cairo as beyond the line of civilization and its requirements. They talk loud, roar in laughing, stare at the ladies, and light their cigars before the latter have withdrawn. My comrade notices that they call for champagne before fish; we could overlook anything but that. Some travellers who are annoyed at their boisterousness speak to the landlord about them, without knowing their rank—supposing that one could always tell an earl by his superior manners. These young representatives of England have demanded that the Khedive shall send them on their hunting tour in Africa, and he is to do so at considerable cost; and it is said that he pays their hotel bills in Cairo. The desire of the Khedive to stand well with all the European powers makes him an easy prey to any nobleman who does not like to travel in Egypt at his own expense. (It ought to be added that we encountered on the Nile an Englishman of high rank who had declined the Khedive's offer of a free trip).

Cairo is a city of vast distances, especially the new part which is laid out with broad streets, and built up with isolated houses, having perhaps a garden or a green court; open squares are devoted to fountains and flower beds. Into these broad avenues the sun pours, and through them the dust swirls in clouds; everything is covered with it; it imparts its grey tint to the town, and sifts everywhere its impalpable powder. No doubt the health of Cairo is greatly improved, and epidemics are lessened, by the destruction of the pestilent old houses and by running wide streets through the old quarters of twisting lanes and sunless alleys. But the wide streets are uninteresting, and the sojourner in the city likes to escape out of their glare and dust into the cool and shady recesses of the old town. And he has not far to go to do so. A few minutes' walk from the Ezbekeëh brings one into a tangle like the crossing paths of an ants'-nest, into the very heart of the smell and colour of the Orient, among people, among shops, in the presence of manners, habits, costumes, occupations centuries old, into a life in which the western man recognizes nothing familiar.

Cairo, between the Mokattam hill of limestone and the Nile, covers a great deal of ground—about three square miles—on which dwell somewhere from a third to a half of a million of people. The traveller cannot see its stock sights in a fortnight, and though he should be three months, he will find something novel in the street-life daily, even though he does not, as Mr. Lane has so admirably done, make a study of the people. And "life" goes on in the open streets to an extent which always surprises us, however familiar we may be with Italian habits. People eat, smoke, pray, sleep, carry on all their trades in the sight of the passers-by—only into the recesses of the harem and the faces of the women one may not look. And this last mystery and reserve almost outweighs the openness of everything else. One feels as if he were in a masquerade; the part of the world which is really most important—womankind—appears to him only in shadow and flitting phantoms. What danger is he in from these wrapped and veiled figures which glide by, shooting him with a dark and perhaps wicked eye; what peril is he in as he slips through these narrow streets with their masked batteries of latticed windows! This Eastern life is all open to the sun; and yet how little of its secrets does the stranger fathom. I seem to feel, always, in an Eastern town, that there is a mask of duplicity and concealment behind which the Orientals live; that they habitually deceive the traveller in his "gropings after truth."

The best way of getting about Cairo and its environs is on the donkey. It is cheap and exhilarating. The donkey is easily mounted and easily got off from; not seldom he will weaken in his hind legs and let his rider to the ground—a sinking operation which destroys your confidence in life itself. Sometimes he stumbles and sends the rider over his head. But the *good* donkey never does either. He is the best animal, of his size and appearance, living. He has the two qualities of our greatest generals, patience and obstinacy. The *good* donkey is easy as a rocking-chair, sure-footed as a chamois; he can thread any crowd, and stand patiently dozing in any noisy thoroughfare for hours. To ride him is only a slight compromise of one's independence in walking. One is so near the ground, and so absent-mindedly can he gaze at what is around him, that he forgets that there is anything under him. When the donkey, in the excitement of company on the open street, and stimulated by the whacks and cries of his driver, breaks into the rush of a galop, there is so much flying of legs and such a general flutter, that the rider fancies he is getting over the ground at an awful rate, running a breakneck race; but it does not appear so to an observer. The rider has the feeling of the swift locomotion of the Arab steed without its danger or its expense. Besides, a long-legged man, with a cork hat and a flying linen "duster," tearing madly along on an animal as big as a sheep, is an amusing spectacle.

The donkey is abused, whacked, beaten till he is raw, saddled so that all the straps gall him, hard-ridden, left for hours to be assailed by the flies in the street, and ridiculed by all men. I wish we could know what sort of an animal centuries of good treatment would have made of him. Something no doubt quite beyond human deserts; as it is, he is simply indispensable in Eastern life. And not seldom he is a pet; he wears jingling bells and silver ornaments around his neck; his hair is shaved in spots to give him a variegated appearance, and his mane and tail are dyed with henna; he has on an embroidered cloth bridle and a handsome saddle, under which is a scarlet cloth worked with gold. The length and silkiness of his ears are signs of his gentle breeding. I could never understand why he is loaded with such an enormous saddle; the pommel of it rising up in front of the rider as big as a half-bushel measure. Perhaps it is thought well to put this mass upon his back so that he will not notice or mind any additional weight.

The donkey's saving quality, in this exacting world, is inertia. And yet he is not without ambition. He dislikes to be passed on the road by a fellow; and if one attempts it he is certain to sheer in ahead of him and shove him off the track. "Donkey jealous one anoder," say the drivers.

Each donkey has his driver or attendant, without whose presence, behind or at the side, the animal ceases to go forward. These boys, and some of them are men in stature, are the quickest-witted, most importunate, good natured vagabonds in the world. They make a study of human nature, and accurately measure every traveller the moment he appears. They are agile to do errands, some of them are better guides than the professionals, they can be entrusted with any purchases you may make, they run, carrying their slippers in their hand, all day beside the donkey, and get only a pittance of pay. They are, however, a jolly, larkish set, always skylarking with each other, and are not unlike the newspaper boys of New York; now and then one of them becomes a trader or a dragoman, and makes his fortune.

If you prefer a carriage, good vehicles have become plenty of
4

late years, since there are broad streets for driving; and some very handsome equipages are seen, especially towards evening on the Shoobra road, up and down which people ride and drive to be seen and to see, as they do in Central or Hyde park. It is *en règle* to have a saïs running before the carriage, and it is the "swell thing" to have two of them. The running saïs before a rapidly driven carriage is the prettiest sight in Cairo. He is usually a slender handsome 'black fellow, probably a Nubian, brilliantly dressed, graceful in every motion, running with perfect ease and able to keep up his pace for hours without apparent fatigue. In the days of narrow streets his services were indispensable to clear the way; and even now he is useful in the frequented ways where every one walks in the middle of the street, and the chattering, chaffing throngs are as heedless of anything coming as they are of the day of judgment. In red tarboosh with long tassel, silk and gold embroidered vest and jacket, colored girdle with ends knotted and hanging at the side, short silk trousers and bare legs, and long staff, gold-tipped, in the hand, as graceful in running as Antinous, they are most elegant appendages to a fashionable turnout. If they could not be naturalized in Central Park, it might fill some of the requirements of luxury to train a patriot from the Green Isle to run before the horses, in knee-breeches, flourishing a shillalah. Faith, I think he would clear the way.

Especially do I like to see the saïs coming down the wind before a carriage of the royal harem. The outriders are eunuchs, two in front and two behind; they are blacks, dressed in black clothes, European cut, except the tarboosh. They ride fine horses, English fashion, rising in the saddle; they have long limbs, lank bodies, cruel, weak faces, and yet cunning; they are sleek, shiny, emasculated. Having no sex, you might say they have no souls. How can these anomalies have any virtue, since virtue implies the opportunity of its opposite? These semblances of men seem proud enough of their position, however, and of the part they play to their masters, as if they did not know the repugnance they excite. The carriage they attend is covered, but the silken hangings of the glass windows are drawn aside, revealing the white-veiled occupants. They indeed have no constitutional objections to being seen; the thin veil enhances their charms, and the observer who sees their painted faces and bright languishing eyes, no doubt gives them credit for as much beauty as they possess; and as they flash by, I suppose that every one is convinced that he has seen one of the mysterious Circassian or Georgian beauties.

The minute the traveller shows himself on the hotel terrace, the donkey-boys clamor, and push forward their animals upon the sidewalk; it is no small difficulty to select one out of the tangle; there is noise enough used to fit out an expedition to the desert, and it is not till the dragoman has laid vigorously about him with his stick that the way is clear. Your nationality is known at a glance, and a donkey is instantly named to suit you—the same one being called, indifferently, "Bismarck" if you are German, "Bonaparte" if you are French, and "Yankee Doodle" if you are American, or "Ginger Bob" at a venture.

We are going to Boulak, the so-called port of Cairo, to select a dahabeëh for the Nile voyage. We are indeed only getting ready for this voyage, and seeing the city by the way. The donkey-boys speak English like natives—of Egypt. The one running beside me, a handsome boy in a long cotton shirt, is named, royally, Mahmoud Hassan.

"Are you the brother of Hassan whom I had yesterday?"

"No. He, Hassan not my brother; he better, he friend. Breakfast, lunch, supper, all together, all same, all same money. We friends."

Abd-el-Atti, our dragoman, is riding ahead on his grey donkey, and I have no difficulty in following his broad back and short legs, even though his donkey should be lost to sight in the press. He rides as Egyptians do, without stirrups, and uses his heels as spurs. Since Mohammed Abd-el-Atti Effendi first went up the Nile, it is many years ago now, with Mr. Wm. C. Prime, and got his name prominently into the Nile literature, he has grown older, stout, and rich: he is entitled by his position to the distinction of "Effendi." He boasts a good family, as good as any; most of his relatives are, and he himself has been, in government employ; but he left it because, as he says, he prefers one master to a thousand. When a boy, he went with the embassy of Mohammed Ali to England, and since that time he has travelled extensively as courier in Europe and the Levant and as mail-courier to India. Mr. Prime described him as having somewhat the complexion and features of the North American Indian; it is true, but he has a shrewd restless eye, and very mobile features, quick to image his good humor or the reverse, breaking into smiles, or clouding over upon his easily aroused suspicion. He is a good study of the Moslem and the real Oriental, a combination of the easy, procrastinating fatalism, and yet with a tindery temper and an activity of body and mind that we do not usually associate with the East. His prejudices are inveterate, and he is an unforgiving enemy and a fast, self-sacrificing friend. Not to be driven, he can always be won by kindness. Fond of money and not forgetting the last piastre due him, he is generous and lavish to a fault. A devout Moslem, he has seen too much of the world not to be liberalized. He knows the Koran and the legendary history of the Arabs, and speaks and writes Arabic above the average. An exceedingly shrewd observer and reader of character, and a mimic of other's peculiarities, he is a good *raconteur*, in his peculiar English, and capital company. It is, by the way, worth observing what sharp observers all these Eastern people become, whose business it is to study and humor the whims and eccentricities of travellers. The western man who thinks that the Eastern people are childlike or *effete*, will change his mind after a few months' acquaintance with the shrewd Egyptians. Abd-el-Atti has a good deal of influence and even authority in his sphere, and although his executive ability is without system, he brings things to pass. Wherever he goes, however, there is a ripple and a noise. He would like to go to Nubia with us this winter, he says, "for shange of air."

So much is necessary concerning the character who is to be our companion for many months. No dragoman is better known in the East; he is the sheykh of the dragomans of Cairo, and by reason of his age and experience he is hailed on the river as the sultan of the Nile. He dresses like an Englishman, except his fez.

The great worry of the voyager in Egypt, from the moment he lands, is about a dragoman; his comfort and pleasure depend very much upon a right selection. The dragoman and the dahabeëh interest him more than the sphinx and the great pyramids. Taking strangers up the Nile seems to be the great business of Egypt, and all the intricacies and tricks of it are slowly learned. Ignorant of the language and of the character of the people, the stranger may well be in a maze of doubt and perplexity. His gorgeously attired dragoman, whose recommendations would fit him to hold combined the offices of President of the American Bible Society and caterer for Delmonico, often turns out to be ignorant of his simplest duties, to have an inhabited but uninhabitable boat, to furnish a meagre table, and to be a sly knave. The traveller will certainly have no peace from the importunity of the dragomans until he makes his choice. One hint can be given; it is always best in a Moslem country to take a Moslem dragoman.

We are on our way to Boulak. The sky is full of white light. The air is full of dust; the streets are full of noise, color, vivid life, and motion. Everything is flowing, free, joyous. Naturally people fall into picturesque groups, forming, separating, shifting like scenes on the stage. Neither the rich silks and brilliant dyes, nor the tattered rags, and browns and greys are out of place; full dress and nakedness are equally *en règle*. Here is a grave, long-bearded merchant in full turban and silk gown, riding his caparisoned donkey to his shop, followed by his pipe-bearer; here is a half-naked fellah seated on the rear of his sorry-eyed beast, with a basket of greens in front of him; here are a group of women, hunched astride their donkeys, some in white silk and some in black, shapeless in their balloon mantles, peeping at the world over their veils; here a handsome saïs runs ahead of a carriage with a fat Turk lolling in it, and scatters the loiterers right and left; there are porters and beggars fast asleep by the roadside, only their heads covered from the sun; there are lines of idlers squatting in all-day leisure by the wall, smoking, or merely waiting for to-morrow.

As we get down to Old Boulak the Saturday market is encountered. All Egyptian markets occupy the street or some open place, and whatever is for sale here, is exposed to the dust and the sun; fish, candy, dates, live sheep, doora, beans, all the doubtful and greasy compounds, on brass trays, which the people eat, nuts, raisins, sugar-cane, cheap jewelry. It is difficult to force a way through the noisy crowd. The donkey-boy cries perpetually, to clear the way, "*ya*," take care, "*shimalak!*" to the left, "*yemenak!*" to the right, *ya! riglak!* look out for your left leg, look out for your right leg, make way, boy; make way old woman; but we joggle the old woman, and just escape stepping on the children and babies strewn in the street, and tread on the edge of mats spread on the ground, upon which provisions are exposed (to the dust) for sale. In the narrow, shabby streets, with dilapidated old balconies meeting overhead, we encounter loaded camels, donkeys with double panniers, hawkers of vegetables; and dodge through, bewildered by colour and stunned by noise. What is it that makes all picturesque? More dirt, shabbiness, and nakedness never were assembled. That fellow who has cut armholes in a sack for holding nuts, and slipped into it for his sole garment, would not make a good figure on Broadway, but he is in place here, and as fitly dressed as anybody. These rascals will wear a bit of old carpet as if it were a king's robe, and go about in a pair of drawers that are all rags and strings, and a coarse towel twisted about the head for turban, with a gay *insouciance* that is pleasing. In fact I suppose that a good, well-fitting black or nice brown skin is about as good as a suit of clothes.

But O! the wrinkled, flabby-breasted old women, who make a pretence of drawing the shawl over one eye; the naked, big-stomached children with spindle legs, who sit in the sand and never brush away the circle of flies around each gummy eye! The tumble-down houses, kennels in which the family sleep, the poverty of thousands of years, borne as if it were the only lot of life! in spite of all this, there is not, I venture to say, in the world beside, anything so full of color, so gay and *bizarre* as a street in Cairo. And we are in a squalid suburb.

At the shore of the swift and now falling Nile, at Boulak, are moored, four or five deep, the passenger dahabeëhs, more than a hundred of them, gay with new paint and new carpets, to catch the traveller. There are small and large, old and new (but all looking new); those that were used for freight during the summer and may be full of vermin, and those reserved exclusively for strangers. They can be hired at from sixty pounds to two hundred pounds a month; the English owner of one handsomely furnished wanted seven hundred and fifty pounds for a three-months' voyage. The Nile trip adds luxury to itself every year, and is getting so costly that only Americans will be able to afford it.

After hours of search we settle upon a boat that will suit us, a large boat that had only made a short trip, and so new that we are at liberty to christen it; and the bargaining for it begins. That is, the bargaining revolves around that boat, but glances off as we depart in a rage to this or that other, until we appear to me to be hiring half the craft on the river. We appear to come to terms; again and again Abd-el-Atti says, "Well, it is finish," but new difficulties arise.

The owners were an odd pair: a tall Arab in soiled gown and turban, named Ahmed Aboo Yoosef, a mild and wary Moslem; and Habib Bagdadli, a furtive little Jew, in Frank dress, with a cast in one of his pathetic eyes and a beseeching look, who spoke bad French fluently. Aboo Yoosef was ready to come to terms, but Bagdadli stood out; then Bagdadli acquiesced, but Aboo made conditions. Abd-el-Atti alternately coaxed and stormed; he pulled the Arab's beard; and he put his arm round his neck and whispered in his ear.

"Come, let us to go, dis Jews make me mad. I can't do anything with dis little Jews."

Our dragoman's greatest abhorrence is a Jew. "Where is this one from?" I ask.

"He from Algiers." The Algerian Jews have a bad reputation.

"*No, no, monsieur, pas Algiers*," cries the little Jew, appealing to me with a pitiful look; "I am from Bagdad." In proof of this there was his name—Habib Bagdadli.

The bargaining goes on, with fine gesticulation, despairing attitudes, tones of anger and of grief, violent protestations and fallings into apathy and dejection. It is Arab against Arab and a Jew thrown in.

"I will have this boat, but I not put you out of the way on it;" says Abd-el-Atti, and goes at it again.

My sympathies are divided. I can see that the Arab and the Jew will be ruined if they take what we offer. I know that we shall be ruined if we give what they ask. This pathetic-eyed little Jew makes me feel that I am oppressing his race; and yet I am quite certain that he is trying to overreach us. How the bargain is finally struck I know not, but made it seems to be, and clinched by Aboo reluctantly pulling his purse from his bosom and handing Abd-el-Atti a napoleon. That binds the bargain; instead of the hirer paying something, the lessor gives a pledge.

Trouble, however, is not ended. Certain alterations and additions are to be made, and it is nearly two weeks before the evasive couple complete them. The next day they offer us twenty pounds to release them. The pair are always hanging about for some mitigation or for some advance. The gentle Jew, who seems to me friendless, always excites the ire of our dragoman; "Here comes dis little Jews," he exclaims as he encounters him in the street, and forces him to go and fulfil some neglected promise.

The boat is of the largest size, and has never been above the Cataract; the owners guarantee that it can go, and there is put in the contract a forfeit of a hundred pounds if it will not. We shall see afterwards how the owners sought to circumvent us. The wiles of the Egyptians are slowly learned by the open-minded stranger.

CHAPTER V.

IN THE BAZAAR.

OUR sight-seeing in Cairo is accomplished under the superintendence of another guide and dragoman, a cheerful, willing, good-natured and careful Moslem, with one eye. He looks exactly like the one-eyed calender of the story; and his good eye has a humorous and inquiring twinkle in it. His name is Hassan, but he prefers to be called Hadji, the name he has taken since he made the pilgrimage to Mecca.

A man who has made the pilgrimage is called "the hhagg," a woman "the hhaggeh," often spelled and pronounced "hadj" and "hadgee." It seems to be a privilege of travellers to spell Arabic words as they please, and no two writers agree on a single word or name. The Arabs take a new name or discard an old one as they like, and half a dozen favourite names do duty for half the inhabitants. It is rare to meet one who hasn't somewhere about him the name of Mohammed, Ahmed, Ali, Hassan, Hosayn, or Mahmoud. People take a new name as they would a garment that strikes the fancy.

"You like go bazaar?" asks Hadji after the party is mounted on donkeys in front of the hotel.

"Yes, Hadji, go by the way of the Mooskee."

The Mooskee is the best known street in Cairo, and the only one in the old part of the town that the traveller can find unaided. It runs straight, or nearly so, a mile perhaps, into the most densely built quarters, and is broad enough for carriages. A considerable part of it is roofed lightly over with cane or palm slats, through which the sun sifts a little light, and, being watered, it is usually cool and pleasant. It cannot be called a good or even road, but carriages and donkeys pass over it without noise, the wheels making only a smothered sound: you may pass through it many times and not discover that a canal runs underneath it. The lower part of it is occupied by European shops. There are no fine shops in it like those in the Ezbekeëh, and it is not interesting like the bazaars, but it is always crowded. Probably no street in the world offers such a variety of costumes and nationalities, and in no one can be heard more languages. It is the main artery, from which branch off the lesser veins and reticulations leading into the bazaars.

If the Mooskee is crowded, the bazaars are a jam. Different trades and nationalities have separate quarters, the articles that are wanted are far apart, and one will of necessity consume a day in making two or three purchases. It is an achievement to find and bargain for a piece of tape.

In one quarter are red slippers, nothing but red slippers, hundreds of shops hung with them, shops in which they are made and sold; the yellow slippers are in another quarter, and by no chance does one merchant keep both kinds. There are the silk bazaars, the gold bazaars, the silver bazaars, the brass, the arms, the antiquity, the cotton, the spice, and the fruit bazaars. In one quarter the merchants and manufacturers are all Egyptians, in another Turks, in another Copts, or Algerines, or Persians, or Armenians, or Greeks, or Syrians, or Jews.

And what is a bazaar? Simply a lane, narrow, straight or crooked, winding, involved, interrupted by a fountain, or a mosque, intersected by other lanes, a *congeries* of lanes, roofed with matting it may be, on each side of which are the little shops, not much bigger than a dry-goods box or a Saratoga trunk. Frequently there is a story above, with hanging balconies and latticed windows. On the ledge of his shop the merchant, in fine robes of silk and linen, sits cross legged, probably smoking his chibook. He sits all day sipping coffee and gossiping with his friends, waiting for a customer. At the times of prayer he spreads his prayer-carpet and pursues his devotions in sight of all the world.

This Oriental microcosm called a bazaar is the most characteristic thing in the East, and affords most entertainment; in these cool recesses, which the sun only penetrates in glints, is all that is shabby and all that is splendid in this land of violent contrasts. The shops are rude, the passages are unpaved dirt, the matting above hangs in shreds, the unpainted balconies are about to tumble down, the lattice-work is grey with dust; fleas about; you are jostled by an unsavory throng, may be; run against by loaded donkeys; grazed by the dripping goat-skins of the water-carriers; beset by beggars; followed by Jews offering old brasses, old cashmeres, old armor; squeezed against black backs from the Soudan; and stunned by the sing-song cries of a dozen callings. But all this is nothing. Here are the perfumes of Arabia, the colours of Paradise. These narrow streets are streams of glancing colour; these shops are more brilliant than any picture—but in all is a softened harmony, the ancient art of the East.

We are sitting at a corner, pricing some pieces of old brass and arms. The merchant sends for tiny cups of coffee and offers cigarettes. He and the dragoman are wrangling about the price of something for which five times its value is asked. Not unlikely it will be sold for less than it is worth, for neither trader nor traveller has any idea of its value. Opposite is a shop where three men sit cross-legged, making cashmere shawls by piecing old bits of India scarfs. Next shop is occupied only by a boy who is reading the Koran in a loud voice, rocking forwards and backwards. A stooping seller of sherbet comes along clinking his glasses. A vendor of sweetmeats sets his tray before us. A sorry beggar, a dwarf, beseeches in figurative language.

"What does he want, Hadji?"

"He say him hungry; want piece bread; O, no matter for he."

The dragomans never interpret anything, except by short cuts. What the dwarf is really saying, according to Mr. Lane, is,

"For the sake of God! O ye charitable. I am seeking from my lord a cake of bread. I am the guest of God and the Prophet."

As we cannot content him by replying in like strain, "God enrich thee," we earn his blessing by a copper or two.

Across the street is an opening into a nest of shops, gayly hung with embroideries from Constantinople, silks from Broussa and Beyrout, stuffs of Damascus; a Persian rug is spread on the mustabah of the shop, swords and inlaid pistols with flint locks shine amid the rich stuffs. Looking down this street, one way, is a long vista of bright colour, the street passing under round arches, through which I see an old wall painted in red and white squares, upon which the sun falls in a flood of white light. The street in which we are sitting turns abruptly at a little distance, and apparently ends in a high Moorish house, with queer little latticed windows, and balconies, and dusty recesses full of mystery in this half light; and at the corner opposite that, I see part of a public fountain and hear very distinctly the "studying" of the school over it.

The public fountain is one of the best institutions of Cairo, as well as one of the most ornamental. On the street it is a rounded Saracenic structure, highly ornamented in carved marble or stucco, and gayly painted, having in front two or three faucets from which the water is drawn. Within is a tank which is replenished by water brought in skins from the Nile. Most of these fountains are charitable foundations, by pious Moslems, who leave or set apart a certain sum to ensure the yearly supply of so many skins of water. Charity to the poor is one of the good traits of the Moslems, and the giving of alms and the building of fountains are the works that will be rewarded in Paradise.

These fountains, some of which are very beautiful, are often erected near a mosque. Over them, in a room with a vaulted roof and open to the street by three or four arches with pillars, is usually a boys' school. In this room on the floor sit the master and his scholars. Each pupil has before him his lesson written on a wooden tablet, and this he is reading at the top of his voice, committing it to memory, and swaying incessantly backwards and forwards—a movement that is supposed to assist the memory. With twenty boys shouting together, the noise is heard above all the clamour of the street. If a boy looks off or stops his recitation, the stick of the schoolmaster sets him going again.

The boys learn first the alphabet, then the ninety-nine epithets of God, and then the Koran, chapter by chapter. This is the sum of human knowledge absolutely necessary; if the boy needs writing and arithmetic, he learns them from the steelyard weigher in the market; or if he is to enter any of the professions, he has a regular course of study in the Mosque el Ezher, which has thousands of students, and is the great University of the East.

Sitting in the bazaar for an hour one will see strange sights; wedding and funeral processions are not the least interesting of them. We can never get accustomed to the ungainly camel, thrusting his huge bulk into these narrow limits, and stretching his snake neck from side to side, his dark driver sitting high up in the dusk of the roof on the wooden saddle, and swaying to and fro with the long stride of the beast. The camel ought to be used in funeral processions, but I believe he is not.

We hear now a chanting down the dusky street. Somebody is being carried to his tomb in the desert outside the city. The procession has to squeeze through the crowd. First come a half dozen old men, ragged and half blind, harbingers of death, who move slowly, crying in a whining tone, " There is no deity but God; Mohammed is God's apostle; God bless and save him." Then come two or three schoolboys singing in a more lively air verses of a funeral hymn. The bier is borne by friends of the deceased, who are relieved occasionally by casual passengers. On the bier, swathed in grave clothes, lies the body, with a Cashmere shawl thrown over it. It is followed by female hired women, who beat their breasts and howl with shrill and prolonged ululations. The rear is brought up by the female mourners, relations—a group of a dozen in this case—whose hair is dishevelled, and who are crying and shrieking with a perfect abandonment to the luxury of grief. Passengers in the street stop and say, " God is most great," and the women point to the bier and say, " I testify that there is no deity but God."

When the funeral has passed and its incongruous mingling of chanting and shrieking dies away, we turn towards the gold bazaar. All the goldsmiths and silversmiths are Copts; throughout Egypt the working of the precious metals is in their hands. Descended from the ancient Egyptians, or at least having more of the blood of the original race in them than others, they have inherited the traditional skill of the ancient workers in these metals. They reproduce the old jewelry, the barbarous ornaments, and work by the same rude methods, producing sometimes the finest work with the most clumsy tools.

The gold-bazaar is the narrowest passage we have seen. We

step down into its twilight from a broader street. It is in fact about three feet wide, a lane with an uneven floor of earth, often slippery. On each side are the little shops, just large enough for the dealer and his iron safe, or for a tiny forge, bellows and anvil. Two people have to make way for each other in squeezing along this alley, and if a donkey comes through he monopolizes the way, and the passengers have to climb upon the mustubahs either side. The mustubah is a raised seat of stone or brick, built against the front of the shop and level with its floor, say two feet and a half high and two feet broad. The lower shutter of the shop turns down upon the mustubah and forms a seat upon which a rug is spread. The shopkeeper may sit upon this, or withdraw into his shop to make room for customers, who remove their shoes before drawing up their feet upon the carpet. Sometimes three or four persons will crowd into this box called a shop. The bazaar is a noisy as well as a crowded place, for to the buzz of talk and the cries of the itinerant vendors is added the clang of the goldsmiths' hammers; it winds down into the recesses of decaying houses and emerges in another direction.

We are to have manufactured a bracelet of gold of a pattern as old as the Pharaohs, and made with the same instruments that the cunning goldsmiths used three thousand years ago. While we are seated and bargaining for the work, the goldsmith unlocks his safe and shows us necklaces, bracelets, anklets, and earrings in the very forms, *bizarre* but graceful, of the jewelry of which the Israelites spoiled the Egyptian women. We see just such in the Museum at Boulak; though these are not so fine as the magnificent jewellery which Queen Aah-hotep, the mother of Amosis, attempted to carry with her into the underworld, and which the scientific violators of her tomb rescued at Thebes.

In the shop opposite to us are squeezed in three Egyptian women and a baby, who have come to spend the day in cheapening some bit of jewelry. There is apparently nothing that the Cairo women like so much as shopping—at least those who are permitted to go out at all—and they eke out its delights by consuming a day or two in buying one article. These women are taking the trade leisurely, examining slowly and carefully the whole stock of the goldsmith and deliberating on **each bead** and drop of a necklace, glancing slily at us and the passers-by out of their dark eyes meantime. They have brought cakes of bread for lunch, and the baby is publicly fed as often as he desires. These women have the power of sitting still in one spot for hours, squatting with perfect patience in a posture that would give a western woman the cramp for her lifetime. We are an hour in bargaining with the goldsmith, and are to return late in the afternoon and see the bracelet made before our eyes, for no one is expected to trust his fellow here.

Thus far the gold has only been melted into an ingot, and that with many precautions against fraud. I first count out the napoleons of which the bracelet is to be made. These are weighed. A fire is then kindled in the little forge, the crucible heated, and I drop the napoleons into it, one by one. We all carefully watch the melting, to be sure that no gold is spilled in the charcoal and no base metal added. The melted mass is then run into an ingot, and the ingot is weighed against the same number of napoleons that compose it. And I carry away the ingot.

When we return the women are still squatting in the shop in the attitude of the morning. They show neither impatience nor weariness; nor does the shopkeeper. The baby is sprawled out in his brown loveliness, and the purchase of a barbarous necklace of beads is about concluded. Our goldsmith now removes his outer garment, revealing his fine gown of striped silk, pushes up his sleeves and prepares for work. His only tools are a small anvil, a hammer and a pair of pincers. The ingot is heated and hammered and heated and hammered, until it is drawn out into an even, thick wire. This is then folded in three to the required length, and twisted, till the gold looks like molasses candy; the ends are then hammered together, and the bracelet is bent to its form. Finally it is weighed again and cleaned. If the owner wishes he can have put on it the government stamp. Gold ornaments that are stamped the goldsmith will take back at any time and give for them their weight in coin, less two per cent.

On our way home we encounter a wedding procession; this is the procession conducting the bride to the house of the bridegroom, that to the bath having taken place two days before. The night of the day before going to the bridegroom is called the "Night of Henna." The bride has an entertainment at her own house, receives presents of money, and has her hands and her feet dyed with henna. The going to the bridegroom is on the eve of either Monday or Friday. These processions we often meet in the streets of Cairo; they wander about circuitously through the town, making all the noise and display possible. The procession is a rambling affair, and generally attended by a rabble of boys and men.

This one is preceded by half a dozen shabbily dressed musicians beating different sorts of drums and blowing hautboys, each instrument on its own hook; the tune, if there was one, has become discouraged, and the melody has dropped out; thump, pound, squak, the music is more disorganized than the procession, and draggles on in noisy dissonance like a drunken militia band at the end of a day's "general training."

Next come some veiled women in black; and following them are several small virgins in white. The bride walks next, with a woman each side of her to direct her steps. This is necessary, for she is covered from head to feet with a red cashmere shawl, hanging from a sort of crown on the top of her head. She is in appearance simply a red cone. Over her and on three sides of her, but open in front, is a canopy of pink silk, borne on poles by four men. Behind straggle more musicians, piping and thumping in an independent nonchalance, followed by gleeful boys. One attendant sprinkles rose-water on the spectators, and two or three others seem to have a general direction of the course of the train, and ask backsheesh for it whenever a stranger is met.

The procession gets tired occasionally, and sits down in the dust of the road to rest. Sometimes it is accompanied by dancers and other performers to amuse the crowd. I saw one yesterday which had halted by the roadside, all the women except the bride squatting down in patient resignation. In a hollow square of spectators, in front, a male dancer was exhibiting his steps. Holding a wand perpendicularly before him with both hands, he moved backwards and forwards, with a mincing gait, exhibiting neither grace nor agility, but looking around with the most conceited expression I ever saw on a human face. Occasionally he would look down at his legs with the most approving glance, as much as to say, "I trust, God being great, that you are taking particular notice of those legs; it seems to me that they couldn't be improved." The fellow enjoyed his dancing if no one else did, and it was impossible to get him to desist and let the procession move on. At last the cortège made a *détour* round the man, who seemed to be so popular with himself, and left him to enjoy his own performance.

Sometimes the expense of this *zeffeh*, or bridal procession, is shared by two parties, and I have seen two brides walking under the same canopy, but going to different husbands. The public is not excluded from an interest in these weddings. The house of a bridegroom, near the Mooskee, was illuminated a night or two before the wedding, colored lanterns were hung across the street, and story-tellers were engaged to recite in front of the house. On the night of the marriage there was a crowd which greatly enjoyed the indelicate songs and stories of the hired performers. Late in the evening an old woman appeared at a window and proclaimed that the husband was contented with his wife.

An accompaniment of a bridal procession which we sometimes saw we could not understand. Before the procession proper, walked another, preceded by a man carrying on his head a high wooden cabinet, with four legs, the front covered with pieces of looking-glass and bits of brass; behind him were musicians and attendants, followed by a boy on horseback, dressed richly in clothes too large for him and like a girl's. It turned out to be a parade before circumcision, the friends of the lad having taken advantage of the bridal ceremony of a neighbor to make a display. The wooden case was merely the sign of the barber who walked in the procession, and was to perform the operation.

"I suppose you are married?" I ask Hadji, when the procession has gone by.

"Yes, sir, long time."

"And you have never had but one wife?"

"Have one. He quite nuff for me."

"How old was she when you married her?"

"Oh, I marry he, when he much girl! I tink he eleven, maybe twelve, not more I tink."

Girls in Egypt are marriageable at ten or eleven, and it is said that if not married before they are fourteen they have an excellent chance of being old maids. Precocious to mature, they are quick to fall away and lose their beauty; the laboring classes especially are ugly and flabby before eighteen. The low mental, not to say physical, condition of Egyptian women is no doubt largely due to these early marriages. The girl is married and is a mother before she has an opportunity to educate herself or to learn the duties of wife or mother, ignorant of how to make a home pleasant and even of housekeeping, and when she is utterly unfit to have the care and training of a child. Ignorant and foolish, and, as Mr. Lane says, passionate, women and mothers can never produce a great race. And the only reform for Egypt that will give it new vitality and a place in the world must begin with the women.

The Khedive, who either has foresight or listens to good advice, issued a firman some years ago forbidding the marriage of girls under fifteen. It does not seem to be respected either in city or country; though I believe that it has some influence in the city, and generally girls are not married so young in Cairo as in the country. Yet I heard recently in this city of a man of sixty who took a wife of twelve. As this was not his first wife, it could not be said of him, as it is said of some great geniuses, that he struck twelve the first time.

CHAPTER VI.

MOSQUES AND TOMBS.

WHAT we in Cairo like most to do, is to do nothing in the charming winter weather—to postpone the regular and necessary sight-seeing to that limbo to which the Arabs relegate everything—*bookra*, that is, to-morrow. Why not as well go to the Pyramids or to Heliopolis or to the tombs of the Memlooks to-morrow! It is to be the same fair weather; we never plan an excursion, with the proviso, "If it does not rain." This calm certainty of a clear sky adds twenty-five per cent. to the value of life.

And yet, there is the Sirocco; that enervating, depressing south wind, when all the sands of the hot desert rise up into the air and envelope everything in grit and gloom. I have been on the Citadel terrace when the city was only dimly outlined in the thick air, and all the horizon and the sky were veiled in dust as if by a black Scotch mist. We once waited three days after we had set a time to visit the Pyramids, for the air to clear. The Sirocco is bad enough in the town, the fine dust penetrates the closed recesses of all apartments; but outside the city it is unbearable. Indeed any wind raises the sand disagreeably; and dust is the great plague of Egypt. The streets of Cairo, except those that are sprinkled, are seldom free from clouds of it. And it is an ancient dust. I suppose the powdered dead of thousands of years are blowing about in the air.

The desert makes itself apparent even in Cairo. Not only is it in the air, but it lies in wait close to the walls and houses, ready to enter at the gates, sifting in through every crevice. Only by constant irrigation can it be driven back. As soon as we pass beyond the compact city eastward, we enter the desert, unless we follow the course of some refreshing canal. The drive upon it is a favorite one on summer nights. I have spoken of the desert as hot; but it is always cool at night; and it is the habit of foreigners who are detained in Cairo in the summer to go every night to the desert to cool off.

The most conspicuous object in Cairo, from all points, is the Citadel, built on a bold spur of the Mokattam range, and the adjoining Mosque of Mohammed Ali in which that savage old reformer is buried. The mosque is rather Turkish than Saracenic, and its two slender minarets are much criticised. You who have been in Constantinople are familiar with the like slight and graceful forms in that city; they certainly are not so rich or elegant as many of the elaborately carved and more robust minarets of Cairo which the genius of the old architects reared in the sun-burst of Saracenic architecture; but they are very picturesque and effective in their position, and especially against a poetic evening sky.

When Saláh-e'-deen robbed the pyramids to build the Citadel, he doubtless thought he was erecting a fortification that would for ever protect his city and be an enduring home for the Sultans of Egypt. But Mohammed Ali made it untenable as a fort by placing a commanding battery on the Mokattam ledge; and now the Citadel (by which I mean all the group of buildings) useless as a fort (except to overawe the city) and abandoned as a palace, is little more than a ghost-walk of former splendors. There are barracks in it; recruits are drilling in its squares; the minister-of-war occupies some of its stately apartments; the American General Stone, the chief officer of the Khedive's army, uses others; in some we find the primitive presses and the bureaus of the engineers and the typographical corps; but vast halls and chambers of audience, and suites of apartments of the harem, richly carved and gilded, are now vacant and echo the footsteps of sentries and servitors. And they have the shabby look of most Eastern architecture when its first freshness is gone.

We sat in the room and on the platform where Mohammed Ali sat when the slaughter of the Memlooks was going on; he sat motionless, so it is reported, and gave no other sign of nervousness than the twisting of a piece of paper in his hands. And yet he must have heard the cries under his window, and, of course, the shots of the soldiers on the walls who were executing his orders. We looked down from the balcony into the narrow, walled lane, with its closed gates, in which the five hundred Memlooks were hemmed in and massacred. Think of the nerve of the old Turk, sitting still without changing countenance while five hundred, or more, gallant swash-bucklers were being shot in cool blood under his window! Probably he would not have been so impassive if he had seen one of the devoted band escape by spurring his horse through a break in the wall and take a fearful flying leap upon the rubbish below.

The world agrees to condemn this treacherous and ferocious act of Mohammed Ali and, generally, I believe, to feel grateful to him for it. Never was there a clan of men that needed exterminating so much as the Memlooks. Nothing less would have suited their peculiarities. They were merely a band of robbers, black-mailers, and freebooters, a terror to Egypt. Dislodged from actual power, they were still greatly to be dreaded, and no ruler was safe who did not obey them. The term Memlook means "a white male slave," and is still so used. The Memlooks, who originally were mostly Circassian white slaves, climbed from the position of favorites to that of tyrants. They established a long dynasty of sultans, and their tombs yonder at the edge of the desert are among the most beautiful specimens of the Saracenic architecture. Their sovereignty was overthrown by Sultan Selim in 1517, but they remained a powerful and aristocratic band which controlled governors, corrupted even Oriental society by the introduction of monstrous vices, and oppressed the people. I suppose that in the time of the French invasion they may have been joined by bold adventurers of many nations. Egypt could have no security so long as any of them remained. It was doubtless in bad taste for Mohammed Ali to extend a friendly invitation to the Memlooks to visit him, and then murder them when they were caught in his trap; he finally died insane, and perhaps the lunacy was providentially on him at that time.

In the Citadel precincts is a hall occupied by the "parliament" of the Khedive, when it is in session; a parliament whose members are selected by the Viceroy from all over Egypt, in order that he may have information of the state of the country, but a body that has no power and certainly not so much influence in the state as the harem has. But its very assemblage is an innovation in the Orient, and it may lead in time to infinite gab, to election briberies and multitudinous legislation, the accompaniments of the highest civilization. We may yet live to see a member of it rise to enquire into the expenses of the Khedive's numerous family.

The great Mosque of Mohammed Ali is in the best repair and is the least frequented of any in Cairo. Its vast, domed interior, rich in materials and ambitious in design, is impressive, but this, like all other great mosques, strikes the Western man as empty. On the floor are beautiful rugs ; a tawdry chandelier hangs in the centre, and the great spaces are strung with lanterns. No one was performing ablution at the handsome fountain in the marble-paved court ; only a single worshipper was kneeling at prayer in all the edifice. But I heard a bird singing sweetly in the airy height of the dome.

The view from the terrace of the mosque is the finest in Egypt, not perhaps in extent, but certainly in variety and objects of interest ; and if the atmosphere and the light are both favorable, it is the most poetic. From it you command not only the city and a long sweep of the Nile, with fields of living green and dark lines of palms, but the ruins and pyramids of slumberous old Memphis, and, amid the yellow sands and backed by the desolate Libyan hills, the dreamy pyramids of Geezeh. We are advised to get this view at sunset, because then the light is soft and all the vast landscape has color. This is good advice so far as the city at our feet is concerned, with its hundreds of minarets and its wide expanse of flat roofs, palm-tops and open squares ; there is the best light then also on the purple Mokattam hills ; and the tombs of the Memlooks, north of the cemetery, with their fairy domes and exquisite minarets and the encompassing grey desert, the whole bathed in violet light, have a beauty that will linger with one who has once seen them forever. But looking beyond the Nile, you have the sun in your face. I should earnestly entreat the stranger to take this view at sunrise. I never saw it myself at that hour, being always otherwise engaged, but I am certain that the pyramids and the Libyan desert would wake at early morning in a glow of transcendant beauty.

We drive out the gate or Bab e' Nasr beyond the desolate Moslem cemetery, to go to the tombs of the Circassian Memlook Sultans. We pass round and amid hills of rubbish, dirt, and broken pottery, the dumpings of the city for centuries, and travel a road so sandy that the horses can scarcely drag the heavy carriage through it. The public horses of Cairo are sorry beasts and only need a slight excuse for stopping at any time. There is nothing agreeable about the great Moslem cemetery ; it is a field of sand-heaps, thickly dotted with little oven-shaped stucco tombs. They may be pleasanter below ground ; for the vault into which the body is put, without a coffin, is high enough to permit its occupant to sit up, which he is obliged to do, whether he is able to sit up or not, the first night of his stay there, in order to answer the questions of two angels who come to examine him on his religious practices and views.

The Tombs of the Sultans, which are in the desert, are in fact vast structures,—tombs and mosques united—and are built of parti-colored stone. They are remarkable for the beautiful and varied forms of their minarets and for their aërial domes ; the latter are covered with the most wonderful arabesque carving and tracing. They stand deserted, with the sand drifting about them, and falling to rapid decay. In the interiors are still traces of exquisite carving and color, but much of the ornamentation, being of stucco on rude wooden frames, only adds to the appearance of decay. The decay of finery is never respectable.

It is not correct, however, to speak of these mosque-tombs as deserted. Into all of them have crept families of the poor or of the vicious. And the business of the occupants, who call themselves guardians, is to extract backsheesh from the visitor. Spinning, knitting, baking, and all the simple household occupations go on in the courts and in the gaunt rooms ; one tomb is used as a grist-mill. The women and girls dwelling there go unveiled ; they were tattooed slightly upon the chin and the forehead, as most Egyptian women are ; some of the younger were pretty, with regular features and handsome dark eyes. Near the mosques are lanes of wretched homes, occupied by as wretched people. The whole mortal neighborhood swarms (life out of death) with children ; they are as thick as jars at a pottery factory ; they are as numerous as the flies that live on the rims of their eyes and noses ; they are as naked, most of them, as when they were born. The distended condition of their stomachs testifies that they have plenty to eat, and they tumble about in the dirt, in the full enjoyment of this delicious climate. People can afford to be poor when nature is their friend,

CHAPTER VII.

MOSLEM WORSHIP.—THE CALL TO PRAYER.

I SHOULD like to go once to an interesting city where there are no sights. That city could be enjoyed; and conscience—which never leaves any human being in peace until it has nagged him into a perfect condition morally, and keeps punching him about frivolous little details of duty, especially at the waking morning hour—would not come to insert her thumb among the rosy fingers of the dawn.

Perhaps I do not make myself clear about conscience. Conscience is a kind of gastric juice that gnaws upon the very coatings of a person's moral nature, if it has no indigestible sin to feed on. Of course I know that neither conscience nor gastric juice has a thumb. And, to get out of these figures, all I wish to say is, that in Cairo, when the traveller is aware of the glow of the morning stealing into his room, as if the day were really opened gently (not ripped and torn open as it is in our own cold north) by a rosy-fingered maiden, and an atmosphere of sweet leisure prevails, then Conscience suggests remorselessly: "To-day you must go to the pyramids," or, "You must take your pleasure in a drive in the Shoobra road," or "You must explore dirty Old Cairo and its Coptic churches," or "You must visit the mosques, and see the Howling Derweeshes."

But for this Conscience, I think nothing would be so sweet as the coming of an eastern morning. I fancy that the cool wind stirring in the palms is from the pure desert. It may be that these birds, so melodiously singing in the garden, are the small green birds who eat the fruits and drink the waters of Paradise, and in whose crops the souls of martyrs abide until Judgment. As I lie quite still, I hear the call of a muëzzin from a minaret not far off, the voice now full and clear and now faint, as he walks around the tower to send his entreaty over the dark roofs of the city. I am not disturbed by this early call to the unconverted, for this is not my religion. With the clamor of morning church bells in Italy it is different; for to one born in New England, Conscience is in the bells.

Sometimes at midnight I am dimly conscious of the first call to prayer, which begins solemnly.

"Prayer is better than sleep."

But the night calls are not obligatory, and I do not fully wake. The calls during the night are long chants, that of the daytime is much shorter. Mr. Lane renders it thus:

"God is most great" (four times repeated). "I testify that there is no deity but God" (twice). "I testify that Mohammed is God's Apostle" (twice). "Come to prayer" (twice). "Come to security" (twice). "God is most great" (twice). "There is no deity but God."

The muëzzin whom I hear when the first faint light appears in the east, has a most sonorous and sweet tenor voice, and his chant is exceedingly melodious. In the perfect hush of that hour his voice fills all the air, and might well be mistaken for a sweet entreaty out of heaven. This call is a long one, and is in fact a confession and proclamation as well as a call to prayer. It begins as follows:

"[I extol] the perfection of God, the Existing forever and ever" (three times): "the perfection of God, the Desired, the Existing, the Single, the Supreme: the perfection of God, the One, the Sole: the perfection of Him who taketh to Himself, in his great dominion, neither female companion nor male partner, nor any like unto Him, nor any that is disobedient, nor any deputy, nor any equal, nor any offspring. His perfection [be extolled]: and exalted be His name. He is a Deity who knew what hath been before it was, and called into existence what hath been: and he is now existing, as He was [at the first]. His perfection [be extolled]: and exalted be His name."

And it ends: "O God, bless and save and still beätify the beätified Prophet, our lord Mohammed. And may God, whose name be blessed and exalted, be well pleased with thee, O our lord El-Hassan, and with thee, O our lord El-Hoseyn, and with thee, O Aboo-Farrág, O Sheykh of the Arabs, and with all the favorites ['the welees'] of God. Amen."

The mosques of Cairo are more numerous than the churches in Rome; there are about four hundred, many of them in ruins, but nearly all in daily use. The old ones are the more interesting architecturally, but all have a certain attraction. They are always open, they are cool quiet retreats out of the glare of the sun and the noise of the street; they are democratic and as hospitable to the beggar in rags as to the pasha in silk; they offer water for the dusty feet of the pilgrim and a clean mat on which to kneel; and in their hushed walks, with no image to distract the mind and no ritual to rely on, the devout worshipper may feel the presence of the Unseen. At all hours you will see men praying there or reading the Koran, unconscious of any observers. Women I have seen in there occasionally, but rarely, at prayer; still it is not uncommon to see a group of poor women resting in a quiet corner, perhaps sewing or talking in low voices. The outward steps and open courts are refuges for the poor, the friendless, the lazy, and the tired. Especially the old and decaying mosques, do the poor frequent. There, about the fountains, the children play, and under the stately colonnades the men sleep and the women knit and sew. These houses of God are for the weary as well as for the pious or the repentant.

The mosques are all much alike. We enter by a few or by a flight of steps from the street into a large paved court, open to the sky, and surrounded by colonnades. There is a fountain in the centre, a round or octagonal structure of carved stone, usually with a fanciful wooden roof; from faucets in the exterior, water runs into a surrounding stone basin about which the worshippers crouch to perform the ablutions before prayer. At one side of the court is the entrance to the mosque, covered by a curtain. Pushing this aside you are in a spacious room lighted from above, perhaps with a dome, the roof supported by columns rising to elegant arches. You will notice also the peculiar Arabic bracketing-work, called by architects "pendentive," fitting the angles and the transitions from the corners below to the dome. In decaying mosques, where the plaster has fallen, revealing the round stick frame-work of this bracketing, the perishable character of Saracenic ornament is apparent.

The walls are plain, with the exception of gilded texts from the Koran. Above, on strings extending across the room, are little lamps, and very often hundreds of ostrich eggs are suspended. These eggs are almost always seen in Coptic and often in Greek churches. What they signify I do not know, unless the ostrich, which can digest old iron, is a symbol of the credulity that can swallow any tradition. Perhaps her eggs represent the great "cosmic egg" which modern philosophers are trying to teach (if we may be allowed the expression) their grandmothers to suck.

The stone pavement is covered with matting and perhaps with costly rugs from Persia, Smyrna, and Tunis. The end towards Mecca is raised a foot or so; in it is the prayer niche, towards which all worshippers turn, and near that is the high pulpit with its narrow steps in front; a pulpit of marble carved, or of wood cut in bewildering arabesque, and inlaid with pearl.

The oldest mosque in Cairo is Ahmed ebn e' Tooloon, built in 879 A.D., and on the spot where, according to a tradition (of how high authority I do not know), Abraham was prevented from offering up his son by the appearance of a ram. The modern name of this hill is, indeed, Kalat-el-Kebsh, the Citadel of the Ram. I suppose the tradition is as well based as is the belief of Moslems that it was Ishmael and not Isaac whose life was spared. The centre of this mosque is an open court, surrounded by rows of fine columns, five deep on the east side; and what gives it great interest is the fact that the columns all support *pointed arches*, and exceedingly graceful ones, with a slight curve of the horse-shoe at the base. These arches were constructed about three centuries before the introduction of the pointed arch into Europe; their adoption in Europe was probably one of the results of the crusades.

In this same court I raw an old nebk tree, which grows on the spot where the ark of Noah is said to have rested after its voyage. This goes to show, if it goes to show anything, that the Flood was "general" enough to reach Egypt.

The mosque of Sultan Hassan, notwithstanding its ruined and shabby condition, is the finest specimen of pure Arabic architecture in the city; and its lofty and ornamented porch is, I think, as fine as anything of its kind in the world. One may probably spend hours in the study of its exquisite details. I often found myself in front of it, wondering at the poetic invention and sensitiveness to the beautiful in form, which enabled the builders to reach the same effects that their Gothic successors only produced by the aid of images and suggestions drawn from every department of nature.

We ascend the high steps, pass through some dilapidated parts of the building, which are inhabited, and come to the threshold. Here the Moslem removes his shoes, or street-slippers, and carries them in his hand. Over this sill we may not step, shod as we are. An attendant is ready, however, with big slippers which go on over our shoes. Eager, bright little boys and girls put them on for us, and then attend us in the mosque, keeping a close watch that the slippers are not shuffled off. When one does get off, leaving the unholy shoe to touch the ground, they affect a sort of horror and readjust it with a laugh. Even the children are beginning to feel the general relaxation of bigotry. To-day the heels of my shoes actually touch the floor at every step, a transgression which the little girl who is leading me by the hand points out with a sly shake of the head. The attention of this pretty little girl looks like affection, but I know by sad experience that it means "back-sheesh." It is depressing to think that her natural, sweet, coquettish ways mean only that. She is fierce if any other girl seeks to do me the least favor, and will not permit my own devotion to her to wander.

The mosque of Sultan Hassan was built in the fourteenth century, and differs from most others. Its great, open court has a square recess on each side, over which is a noble arch; the east one is very spacious, and is the place of prayer. Behind this in an attached building, is the tomb of Hassan; lights are always burning over it, and on it lies a large copy of the Koran.

When we enter, there are only a few at their devotions, though there are several groups enjoying the serenity of the court; picturesque groups, all color and rags! In a far corner an old man is saying his prayers and near him a negro, perhaps a slave, also prostrates himself. At the fountain are three or four men preparing for devotion; and indeed the prayers begin with the washing. The ablution is not a mere form with these soiled laborers—though it does seem a hopeless task for men of the color of these to scrub themselves. They bathe the head, neck, breast, hands and arms, legs and feet; in fact, they take what might be called a fair bath in any other country. In our sight this is simply a wholesome "wash;" to them it is both cleanliness and religion, as we know, for Mr. Lane has taught us what that brown man in the blue gown is saying. It may help us to understand his acts if we transcribe a few of his ejaculations.

When he washes his face, he says:—" O God whiten my face with thy light, on the day when thou shalt whiten the faces of thy favorites; and do not blacken my face on the day when thou shalt blacken the faces of thine enemies." Washing his right arm, he entreats:—" O God, give me my book in my right hand; and reckon with me with an easy reckoning." Passing his wetted hand over his head under his raised turban, he says: " O God, cover me with thy mercy, and pour down thy blessing upon me; and shade me under the shadow of thy canopy, on the day when there shall be no shade but its shade."

One of the most striking entreaties is the prayer upon washing the right foot:—" O God make firm my feet upon the Sirát, on the day when feet shall slip upon it." " Es Sirát " is the bridge, which extends over the midst of Hell, finer than a hair and sharper than the edge of a sword, over which all must pass, and from which the wicked shall fall into Hell.

In these mosques order and stillness always reign, and the devotions are conducted with the utmost propriety, whether there are single worshippers, or whether the mosque is filled with lines of gowned and turbaned figures prostrating themselves and bowing with one consent. But, much stress as the Moslems lay upon prayer, they say that they do not expect to reach Paradise by that, or by any merit of their own, but only by faith and forgiveness. This is expressed frequently both in prayers and in the sermons on Friday. A sermon by an Imam of a Cairo mosque contains these implorings:—"O God! unloose the captivity of the captives, and annul the debts of the debtors; and make this town to be safe and secure, and blessed with wealth and plenty, and all the towns of the Moslems, O Lord of the beings of the whole earth. And decree safety and health to us and to all travellers, and pilgrims, and warriors, and wanderers, upon thy earth, and upon thy sea, such as are

Moslems, O Lord of the beings of the whole world. O Lord, we have acted unjustly towards our own souls, and if thou do not forgive us and be merciful unto us, we shall surely be of those who perish. I beg of God, the Great, that he may forgive me and you, and all the people of Mohammed, the servants of God."

CHAPTER VIII.

THE PYRAMIDS.

THE ancient Egyptians of the Upper Country excavated sepulchres for their great dead in the solid rocks of the mountain; the dwellers in the lower country built a mountain of stone in which to hide the royal mummy. In the necropolis at Thebes there are the vast rock-tombs of the kings; at Sakkara and Geezeh stand the pyramids. On the upper Nile isolated rocks and mountains cut the sky in pyramidal forms; on the lower Nile the mountain ranges run level along the horizon, and the constructed pyramids relieve the horizontal lines which are otherwise unbroken except by the palms.

The rock-tombs were walled up and their entrances concealed as much as possible, by a natural arrangement of masses of rock; the pyramids were completely encased and the openings perfectly masked. False passages leading through gorgeously carved and decorated halls and chambers to an empty pit or a blind wall, were hewn in the rock-tombs, simply to mislead the violator of the repose of the dead as to the position of the mummy. The entrance to the pyramids is placed away from the centre, and misleading passages run from it, conducting the explorer away from the royal sarcophagus. Rock-tomb and pyramid were for the same purpose, the eternal security of the mummy.

That purpose has failed; the burial place was on too grand a scale, its contents were too tempting. There is no security for any one after death but obscurity; to preserve one's body is to lose it. The bones must be consumed if they would be safe, or else the owner of them must be a patriot and gain a forgotten grave. There is nothing that men so enjoy as digging up the bones of their ancestors. It is doubtful if even the Egyptian plunderers left long undisturbed the great tombs which contained so much treasure; and certainly the Persians, the Greeks, the Romans, the Saracens, left comparatively little for the scientific grave-robbers of our excellent age. They did, however, leave the tombs, the sarcophagi, most of the sculptures, and a fair share of the preserved dead.

But time made a pretty clean sweep of the mummy and nearly all his personal and real property. The best sculptures of his tomb might legally be considered in the nature of improvements attaching themselves to the realty, but our scientists have hacked them off and carried them away as if they were personal estate. We call the Arabs thieves and ghouls who prowl in the tombs in search of valuables. But motive is everything; digging up the dead and taking his property, tomb and all, in the name of learning and investigation, is respectable and commendable. It comes to the same thing for the mummy, however, this being turned out of house and home in his old age. The deed has its comic aspect, and it seems to me that if a mummy has any humor left in his dried body, he must smile to see what a ludicrous failure were his costly efforts at concealment and repose. For there is a point where frustration of plans may be so sweeping as to be amusing; just as the mummy himself is so ghastly that his aspect is almost funny.

Nothing more impresses the mind with the antiquity of Egypt than its vast cemeteries, into which the harvests of the dead have been gathered for so many thousands of years. Of old Memphis, indeed, nothing remains except its necropolis, whose monuments have outlasted the palaces and temples that were the wonder of the world. The magnificence of the city can be estimated by the extent of its burial-ground.

On the west side of the Nile, opposite Cairo, and extending south along the edge of the desert, is a nearly continuous necropolis for fifteen miles. It is marked at intervals by pyramids. At Geezeh are three large and several small ones; at Abooseer are four; at Sakkara are eleven; at Dashoor are four. These all belonged to the necropolis of Memphis. At Geezeh is the largest, that of Cheops or Shoofoo, the third king of the fourth dynasty, reigning at Memphis about 4235 B. C., according to the chronology of Mariette Bey, which every new discovery helps to establish as the most probably correct. This pyramid was about four hundred and eighty feet high, and the length of a side of its base was about seven hundred and sixty-four feet; it is now four hundred and fifty feet high and its base line is seven hundred and forty-six feet. It is big enough yet for any practical purpose. The old pyramid at Sakkara is believed to have been built by Ouenephes, the fourth king of the first dynasty, and to be the *oldest monument in the world*. Like the mounds of the Chaldeans, it is built in degrees or stages, of which there are five. Degraded now and buried at the base in its own rubbish, it rises only about one hundred and ninety feet above the ground.

It is a drive of two hours from Cairo to the Pyramids of Geezeh, over a very good road; and we are advised to go by carriage. Hadji is on the seat with the driver, keeping his single twinkling eye active in the service of the hawadji. The driver is a polished Nubian, with a white turban and a white gown; feet and legs go bare. You wouldn't call it a stylish turnout for the Bois, but it would be all right if we had a gorgeous saïs to attract attention from ourselves.

We drive through the wide and dusty streets of the new quarter. The barrack-like palace, on the left of a broad place, is the one in which the Khedive is staying just now, though he may be in another one to-night. The streets are the same animated theatre-like scenes of vivid color and picturesque costume and indolent waiting on Providence to which we thought we should never become accustomed, but which are already beginning to lose their novelty. The fellaheen are coming in to market, trudging along behind donkeys and camels loaded with vegetables or freshly cut grass and beans for fodder. Squads of soldiers in white uniform pass; bugle notes are heard from Kasr e' Neel, a barrack of troops on the river. Here, as in Europe, the great business most seriously pursued is the drilling of men to stand straight, handle arms, roll their eyes, march with a thousand legs moving as one, and shoot on sight other human beings who have learned the same tricks. God help us, it is a pitiful thing for civilized people.

The banks of the Nile here above Boolak are high and steep. We cross the river on a fine bridge of iron, and drive over the level plain, opposite, on a raised and winding embankment.

This is planted on each side with lebbekh and sycamore trees. Part of the way the trees are large and the shade ample; the roots going down into moist ground. Much of the way the trees are small and kept alive by constant watering. On the right, by an noble avenue, are approached the gardens and the palace of Gezeereh. We pass by the new summer palace of Geezeh. Other large ones are in process of construction. If the viceroy is measured for a new suit of clothes as often as he orders a new palace, his tailors must be kept busy. Through the trees we see green fields, intersected with ditches, wheat, barley, and beans, the latter broad-sown and growing two to three feet high; here and there are lines of palms, clumps of acacias; peasants are at work or asleep in the shade; there are trains of camels, and men ploughing with cows or buffaloes. Leaving the squalid huts that are the remains of once beautiful Geezeh, the embankment strides straight across the level country.

And there before us, on a rocky platform a hundred feet higher that the meadows, are the pyramids, cutting the stainless blue of the sky with their sharp lines. They master the eye when we are an hour away, and as we approach they seem to recede, neither growing larger nor smaller, but simply withdrawing with a grand reserve.

I suppose there are more "emotions" afloat about the pyramids than concerning any other artificial objects. There are enough. It becomes constantly more and more difficult for the ordinary traveller to rise to the height of these accumulated emotions, and it is entirely impossible to say how much the excitement one experiences on drawing near them results from reading and association, and how much is due to these simple forms in such desolate surroundings. But there they stand, enduring standards, and every visitor seems inclined to measure his own height by their vastness, in telling what impression they produce upon *him*. They have been treated sentimentally, off-handedly, mathematically, solemnly, historically, humorously. They yield to no sort of treatment. They are nothing but piles of stone, and shabby piles at that, and they stand there to astonish people. Mr. Bayard Taylor is entirely right when he says that the pyramids are and will remain unchanged and unapproachably impressive, however modern life may surge about them, and though a city should creep about their bases.

Perhaps they do not appear so gigantic when the visitor is close to them as he thought they would from their mass at a distance. But if he stands at the base of the great pyramid, and casts his eye along the steps of its enormous side and up the dizzy hight where the summit seems to pierce the solid blue, he will not complain of want of size. And if he walks around one, and walks from one to another, wading in the loose sand and under a midday sun, his respect for the pyramids will increase every moment.

Long before we reach the ascent of the platform we are met by Arab boys and men, sellers of antiquities, and most persistent beggars. The antiquities are images of all sorts, of gods, beasts, and birds, in pottery or in bronze, articles from tombs, bits of mummy-cloth, beads and scarabæi, and Roman copper coins; all of them at least five thousand years old in appearance.

Our carriage is stuck in the sand, and we walk a quarter of a mile up the platform, attended by a rabble of coaxing, imploring, importunate, half-clad Bedaween. "Look a here, you take dis; dis ver much old, he from mummy; see here, I get him in tomb; one shillin; in Cairo you get him one pound; ver sheap. You no like? No anteeka, no money. How much?"

"One penny."

"Ah," ironically, "ket'-ther kháyrak (much obliged). You take him sixpence. Howadji, say, me guide, you want go top pyramid, go inside, go Sphinkee, allee tomba?"

Surrounded by an increasing swarm of guides and antiquity-hawkers, and beset with offers, entreaties, and opportunities, we come face to face with the great pyramid. The ground in front of it is piled high with its *débris*. Upon these rocks, in picturesque attitudes, some in the shade and some in the sun, others of the tribe are waiting the arrival of pyramid climbers; in the intense light their cotton garments and turbans are like white paint, brilliant in the sun, ashy in the shadow. All the shadows are sharp and deep. A dark man leaning on his spear at the corner of the pyramid makes a picture. At a kiosk near by carriages are standing and visitors are taking their lunch. But men, carriages, kiosk, are dwarfed in this great presence. It is, as I said, a shabby pile of stone, and its beauty is only that of mathematical angles; but then it is so big, it casts such a shadow; we all beside it are like the animated lines and dots which represent human beings in the etchings of Callot.

To be rid of importunities we send for the sheykh of the pyramid tribe. The Bedaween living here have a sort of ownership of these monuments, and very good property they are. The tribe supports itself mainly by tolls levied upon visitors. The sheykh assigns guides and climbers, and receives the pay for their services. This money is divided among the families; but what individuals get as backsheesh or by the sale of antiquities, they keep. They live near by, in huts scarcely distinguishable from the rocks, many of them in vacant tombs, and some have shanties on the borders of the green land. Most of them have the appearance of wretched poverty, and villainous faces abound. But handsome, intelligent faces and finely developed forms are not rare, either.

The Sheykh, venerable as Jacob, respectable as a New England deacon, suave and polite as he traditionally should be, wears a scarf of camel's hair and a bright yellow and black kuflia, put on like a hood, fastened about the head by a cord and falling over the shoulders. He apportioned his guides to take us up the pyramid and to accompany us inside. I had already sent for a guide who had been recommended to me in the city, and I found Ali Gobree the frank, manly, intelligent, quiet man I had expected, handsome also, and honesty and sincerity beaming from his countenance. How well-bred he was, and how well he spoke English. Two other men were given me; for the established order is that two shall pull and one shall push the visitor up. And it is easier to submit to the regulation than to attempt to go alone and be followed by an importunate crowd.

I am aware that every one who writes of the pyramids is expected to make a scene of the ascent, but if I were to romance I would rather do it in a fresher field. The fact is that the ascent is not difficult, unless the person is very weak in the legs or attempts to carry in front of himself a preposterous stomach. There is no difficulty in going alone; occasionally the climber encounters a step from three to four feet high, but he can always flank it. Of course it is tiresome to go up-stairs, and the great pyramid needs an "elevator"; but a person may leisurely zig-zag up the side without great fatigue. We went straight up at one corner; the guides insisting on taking me by the hand; the boosting Arab who came behind earned his money by grunting every time we reached a high step, but he didn't lift a pound.

We stopped frequently to look down and to measure with the eye the mass on the surface of which we were like flies. When we were a third of the way up, and turned from the edge to the middle, the height to be climbed seemed as great as when we started. I should think that a giddy person might have unpleasant sensations in looking back along the corner and seeing no resting-place down the sharp edges of the steps short of the bottom, if he should fall. We measure our ascent by the diminishing size of the people below, and by the widening of the prospect. The guides are perfectly civil, they do not threaten to throw us off, nor do they even mention backsheesh. Stopping to pick out shells from the nummulitic limestone blocks or to try our glasses on some distant object, we come easily to the summit in a quarter of an hour.

The top, thirty feet square, is strewn with big blocks of stone and has a flag-staff. Here ambitious people sometimes breakfast. Arabs are already here with koollehs of water and antiquities. When the whole party arrives the guides set up a perfunctory cheer; but the attempt to give an air of achievement to our climbing performance and to make it appear that we are the first who have ever accomplished the feat, is a failure. We sit down upon the blocks and look over Egypt, as if we were used to this sort of thing at home.

All that is characteristic of Egypt is in sight; to the west, the Libyan hills and the limitless stretch of yellow desert sand; to the north, desert also and the ruined pyramid of Abooroash; to the south, that long necropolis of the desert marked by the pyramids of Abooseér, Sakkarah, and Dashoor; on the east, the Nile and its broad meadows, widening into the dim Delta northward, the white line of Cairo under the Mokattam hills, and the grey desert beyond. Egypt is a ribbon of green between two deserts. Canals and lines of trees stripe the green of the foreground; white sails flicker southward along the river, winging their way to Nubia; the citadel and its mosque shine in the sun.

An Arab offers to run down the side of this pyramid, climb the second one, the top of which is still covered with the original casing, and return in a certain incredible number of minutes. We decline, because we don't like to have a half-clad Arab thrust his antics between us and the contemplation of dead yet mighty Egypt. We regret our refusal afterwards, for there is nothing people like to read about so much as facts of this sort. Humanity is more interesting than stones. I am convinced that if Martha Rugg had fallen off the pyramid instead of the rock at Niagara Falls, people would have looked at the spot where she fell and up at the stairs she came bobbing down with more interest than at the pyramid itself. Nevertheless, this Arab and another did, while we were there, climb the second pyramid like a monkey; he looked only a black speck on its side.

That accidents sometimes happen on the pyramids, I gather from the conversation of Hadji, who is full of both information and philosophy to-day.

"Sometime man, he fool, he go up. Man say, 'go this way.' Fool, he say, 'let me lone.' Umbrella he took him, threw him off; he dead in hundred pieces."

As to the selling of scarabæi to travellers, Hadji inclines to the side of the poor:—"Good one, handsome one,—one pound. Not good for much—but what to do? Gentleman he want it; man he want the money."

For Murray's Guide-Book he has not more respect than guides usually have who have acted as interpreters in the collection of information for it. For "interpret" Hadji always says "spell."

"When the Murray come here, I spell it to the man, the man to Murray and him put it down. He don't know anything before. He told me, what is this? I told him what it is. Something," with a knowing nod, "be new after Murray. Look here, Murray very old now."

Hadji understands why the cost of living has gone up so much in Egypt. "He was very sheap; now very different, dearer—because plenty people. I build a house, another people build a house, and another people he build a house. Plenty men to work, make it dear." I have never seen Hadji's dwelling, but it is probably of the style of those that he calls—

when in the street we ask him what a specially shabby mud-wall with a ricketty door in it is—"a brivate house."

About the Great Pyramid has long waged an archæological war. Years have been spent in studying it, measuring it inside and outside, drilling holes into it, speculating why this stone is in one position and that in another, and constructing theories about the purpose for which it was built. Books have been written on it, diagrams of all its chambers and passages, with accurate measurements of every stone in them, are printed. If I had control of a restless genius who was dangerous to the peace of society, I would set him at the Great Pyramid, certain that he would have occupation for a lifetime and never come to any useful result. The interior has peculiarities, which distinguish it from all other pyramids; and many think that it was not intended for a sepulchre mainly; but that it was erected for astronomical purposes, or as a witness to the true north, east, south, and west, or to serve as a standard of measure; not only has the passage which descends obliquely three hundred and twenty feet from the opening into the bed-rock, and permits a view of the sky from that depth, some connection with the observation of Sirius and the fixing of the Sothic year; not only is the porphyry sarcophagus that is in the King's Chamber, secure from fluctuations of temperature, a fixed standard of measure; but the positions of various stones in the passages (stones which certainly are stumbling-blocks to everybody who begins to think why they are there) are full of a mystic and even religious signification. It is most restful, however, to the mind to look upon this pyramid as a tomb, and that it was a sepulchre like all the others is the opinion of most scholars.

Whatever is was, it is a most unpleasant place to go into. But we wanted one idea of Cimmerian darkness, and the sensation of being buried alive, and we didn't like to tell a lie when asked if we had been in, and therefore we went. You will not understand where we went without a diagram, and you never will have any idea of it until you go. We, with a guide for each person, light candles, and slide and stumble down the incline; we crawl up an incline; we shuffle along a level passage that seems interminable, backs and knees bent double till both are apparently broken, and the torture of the position is almost unbearable; we get up the Great Gallery, a passage over a hundred and fifty feet long, twenty-eight high, and seven broad, and about as easy to ascend as a logging-sluice, crawl under three or four portcullises, and emerge, dripping with perspiration and covered with dust, into the king's chamber; a room thirty-four feet long, seventeen broad, and nineteen high. It is built of magnificent blocks of syenite, polished and fitted together perfectly, and contains the lidless sarcophagus.

If it were anywhere else and decently lighted, it would be a stylish apartment; but with a dozen torches and candles smoking in it and heating it, a lot of perspiring Arabs shouting and kicking up a dust, and the feeling that the weight of the superincumbent mass was upon us, it seemed to me too small and confined even for a tomb. The Arabs thought they ought to cheer here as they did on top; we had difficulty in driving them all out and sending the candles with them, in order that we might enjoy the quiet and blackness of this retired situation. I suppose we had for once absolute night, a room full of the original Night, brother of Chaos, night bottled up for four or five thousand years, the very night in which old Cheops lay in a frightful isolation, with all the portcullises down and the passages sealed with massive stones.

Out of this blackness the eye even by long waiting couldn't get a ray; a cat's eye would be invisible in it. Some scholars think that Cheops never occupied this sarcophagus. I can understand his feeling if he ever came in here alive. I think he may have gone away and put up "TO LET" on the door.

We scrambled about a good deal in this mountain, visited the so-called Queen's Chamber, entered by another passage, below the King's, lost all sense of time and of direction, and came out, glad to have seen the wonderful interior, but welcoming the burst of white light and the pure air, as if we were being born again. To remain long in that gulf of mortality is to experience something of the mystery of death.

Ali Gobree had no antiquities to press upon us, but he could show us some choice things in his house, if we would go there. Besides, his house would be a cool place in which to eat our lunch. We walked thither, a quarter of a mile down the sand slope on the edge of the terrace. We had been wondering where the Sphinx was, expecting it to be as conspicuous almost as the pyramids. Suddenly, turning a sand-hill, we came upon it, the rude lion's body struggling out of the sand, the human head lifted up in that stiff majesty which we all know.

So little of the body is now visible, and the features are so much damaged, that it is somewhat difficult to imagine what impression this monstrous union of beast and man once produced, when all the huge proportions stood revealed, and color gave a startling life-likeness to that giant face. It was cut from the rock of the platform; its back was patched with pieces of sandstone to make the *contour;* it head was solid. It was approached by flights of stairs descending, and on the paved platform where it stood were two small temples; between its paws was a sort of sanctuary, with an altar. Now, only the back, head and neck are above the drifting sand. Traces of the double crown of Upper and Lower Egypt, which crowned the head, are seen on the forehead, but the crown has gone. The kingly beard that hung from the chin has been chipped away. The vast wig—the false mass of hair that encumbered the shaven heads of the Egyptians, living or dead—still stands out on either side of the head, and adds a certain dignity. In spite of the broken condition of the face, with the nose gone, it has not lost its character. There are the heavy eyebrows, the prominent cheek-bones, the full lips, the poetic chin, the blurred but on-looking eyes. I think the first feeling of the visitor is, that the face is marred beyond recognition, but the sweep of the majestic lines soon becomes apparent; it is not difficult to believe that there is a smile on the sweet mouth, and the stony stare of the eyes, once caught, will never be forgotten.

The Sphinx, grossly symbolizing the union of physical and intellectual force, and hinting at one of those recondite mysteries which we still like to believe existed in the twilight of mankind, was called Hor-em-Khoo ("the Sun in his resting-place"), and had divine honors paid to it as a deity.

This figure, whatever its purpose, is older than the Pyramid of Cheops. It has sat facing the east, on the edge of this terrace of tombs, expecting the break of day, since a period that is lost in the dimness of tradition. All the achievements of the race, of which we know anything, have been enacted since that figure was carved. It has seen, if its stony eyes could see, all the procession of history file before it. Viewed now at a little distance or with evening shadows on it, its features live again, and it has the calmness, the simple majesty, that belong to high art. Old writers say that the face was once sweet and beautiful. How long had that unknown civilization lasted before it produced this art?

Why should the Sphinx face the rising sun? Why does it stand in a necropolis like a sleepy warden of the dead who sleep? Was it indeed the guardian of those many dead, the mighty who slept in pyramids, in rock-hewn tombs, in pits, their bodies ready for any pilgrimage; and does it look to the east expecting the resurrection?

Not far from the Sphinx is a marvellous temple of syenite, which the sand almost buries; in a well in one of its chambers was found the splendid red-granite statue of Chephren, the builder of the second pyramid, a piece of art which succeeding ages did not excel. All about the rock plateau are tombs, and in some of them are beautiful sculptures, upon which the coloring is fresh. The scenes depicted are of common life, the occupations and diversions of the people, and are without any religious signification. The admirable sculptures represent no gods and no funeral mysteries; when they were cut the Egyptian theology was evidently not constructed.

The residence of our guide is a tomb, two dry chambers in the rock, the entrance closed by a wooden door. The rooms are large enough for tables and chairs; upon the benches where the mummies have lain, are piled antique fragments of all sorts, set off by a grinning skull or a thigh-bone; the floor is covered with fine yellow sand. I don't know how it may have seemed to its first occupant, but we found it an excellent luncheon place, and we could sleep there calmly and securely, when the door was shut against the jackals—though I believe it has never been objected to a tomb that one couldn't sleep in it. While we sip our coffee Ali brings forth his antique images and scarabaei. These are all genuine, for Ali has certificates from most of the well-known Egyptologists as to his honesty and knowledge of antiquities. We are looking for genuine ones; those offered us at the pyramids were suspicious. We say to Ali:—

"We should like to get a few good scarabaei; we are entirely ignorant of them; but we were sent to you as an honest man.

You select half a dozen that you consider the best, and we will pay you a fair price; if they do not pass muster in Cairo you shall take them back."

"As you are a friend of Mr. Blank," said Ali, evidently pleased with the confidence reposed in him, "you shall have the best I have, for about what they cost me."

The scarabæus is the black beetle that the traveller will constantly see tumbling about in the sand, and rolling up balls of dirt, as he does in lands where he has not so sounding a name. He was sacred to the old Egyptians as an emblem of immortality, because he was supposed to have the power of self-production. No mummy went away into the shades of the nether world without one on his breast, with spread wings attached to it. Usually many scarabæi were buried with the mummy— several hundreds have been found in one mummy-case. They were cut from all sorts of stones, both precious and common, and made of limestone, or paste, hardened, glazed and baked. Some of them are exquisitely cut, the intaglio on the under side being as clean, true, and polished as Greek work. The devices on them are various; the name of a reigning or a famous king, in the royal oval, is not uncommon, and an authentic scarabæus with a royal name is considered of most value. I saw an insignificant one in soft stone and of a grey color, held at a hundred pounds; it is the second one that has ever been found with the name of Cheops on it. The scarabæi were worn in rings, carried as charms, used as seals; there are large coarse ones of blue pottery which seem to have been invitations to a funeral, by the inscriptions on them.

The scarabæus is at once the most significant and portable *souvenir* of ancient Egypt that the traveller can carry away, and although the supply was large, it could not fill the demand. Consequently antique scarabæi are now manufactured in large quantities at Thebes, and in other places, and distributed very widely over the length of Egypt; the dealers have them with a sprinkling of the genuine; almost every peasant can produce one from his deep pocket; the women wear them in their bosoms. The traveller up the Nile is pretty sure to be attacked with the fever of buying scarabæi; he expects to happen upon one of great value, which he will get for a few piastres. It is his intention to do so. The scarabæus becomes to him the most beautiful and desirable object in the world. He sees something fascinating in its shape, in its hieroglyphics, however ugly it may be to untaught eyes.

Ali selected our scarabæi. They did not seem to us exactly the antique gems that we had expected to see, and they did not give a high idea of the old Egyptian art. But they had a mysterious history and meaning; they had shared the repose of a mummy perhaps before Abraham departed from Ur. We paid for them. We paid in gold. We paid Ali for his services as guide. We gave him backsheesh on account of his kindness and intelligence, besides. We said good-bye to his honest face with regret, and hoped to see him again.

It was not long before we earnestly desired to meet him. He was a most accomplished fellow, and honesty was his best policy. There isn't a more agreeable Bedawee at the pyramids; and yet Ali is a modern Egyptian, just like his scarabæi, all the same. The traveler who thinks the Egyptians are not nimble-witted and clever is likely to pay for his knowledge to the contrary. An accumulated experience of five thousand years, in one spot, is not for nothing.

We depart from the pyramids amid a clamor of importunity; prices have fallen to zero; antiquities old as Pharoah will be given away; "backsheesh, backsheesh, O Howadji;" "I haven't any bread to *mangere*, I have six children; what is a piastre for eight persons?" They run after us, they hang upon the carriage, they follow us a mile, begging, shrieking, howling, dropping off one by one, swept behind by the weight of a copper thrown to them.

The shadows fall to the east; there is a lovely light on the plain; we meet long lines of camels, of donkeys, of fellaheen returning from city and field. All the west is rosy; the pyramids stand in a purple light; the Sphinx casts its shade on the yellow sand; its expectant eyes look beyond the Nile into the mysterious East.

CHAPTER IX.

PREPARATIONS FOR A VOYAGE.

WE are giving our minds to a name for our dahabeëh. The owners have desired us to christen it, and the task is getting heavy. Whatever we are doing; guiding a donkey through the mazes of a bazaar; eating oranges at the noon breakfast; watching the stream of color and fantastic apparel, swaying camels and dashing harem-equipage with running saïses and outriding eunuchs, flowing by the hotel; following a wedding procession in its straggling parade, or strolling vacantly along, knocked, jostled, evaded by a dozen races in a dozen minutes, and lost in the whirl, color, excitement of this perpetual masquerade, we are suddenly struck with, "what *shall* we call that boat?"

We want a name that is characteristic of the country and expressive of our own feelings, poetic and not sentimental, sensible and not common-place. It seems impossible to suggest a good name that is not already borne by a dahabeëh on the river—names such as the Lotus, the Ibis, the Gazelle, Cleopatra, Zenobia, names with an Eastern flavor. And we must have not only a name for the boat, but a motto or device for our pennant, or "distinguisher flag," as the dragoman calls the narrow fifty feet long strip of bunting that is to stream from the forward yard. We carry at the stern the flag of our country, but we float our individuality in the upper air. If we had been a bridal party we should of course have taken some such device as that of a couple who went up the river under the simple but expressive legend of "Nestledown," written on their banner.

What would *you* name a Nile dahabeëh?

The days go all too rapidly for us to catch the shifting illusions about us. It is not so much what we see of the stated sights that can be described, but it is the atmosphere in which we live that makes the strangeness of our existence. It is as if we had been born into another world. And the climate is as strange as the people, the costumes, the habits, the morals. The calendar is bewitched. December is a mixture of September and July. Alas, yes. There are the night-fogs of September, and the mosquitoes of July. You cannot tell whether the season is going backwards or forwards. But for once you are content to let Providence manage it, at least so long as there is a north wind, and you forget that the sky has any shade other than blue.

And the prophecy of the poet is realized. The nights are filled with music, and the cares that infest the day are invariably put off till to-morrow, in this deliciously procrastinating land. Perhaps, however, Mr. Longfellow would not be satisfied with the music; for it seems to be the nasal daughter of Lassitude and Monotony, ancient gods of the East. Two or three strings stretched over a sounding skin and a parchment drum suffice to express the few notes that an Arab musician commands; harmony does not enter into his plan. Yet the people are fond of what they consider music. We hear on all sides at night the picking of strings, the throb of the darabooka and the occasional outburst of a wailing and sentimental strain. Like all barbarous music, this is always minor. When the performers are sailors or common strollers, it is doubtless exactly the same music that delighted the ancient Egyptians; even the instruments are the same, and the method of clapping the hands in accentuation of the music is unchanged.

There is a *café chantant* on our side of the open, tree-grown court of a native hotel, in the Ezbekeëh, where one may hear a mongrel music, that is not inexpressive of both the morals and the mixed condition of Cairo to-day. The instruments of the band are European; the tunes played are Egyptian. When the first strain is heard we say that it is strangely wild, a weird and plaintiff minor; but that is the whole of it. The strain is repeated over and over again for a half hour, as if it were ground out of a coffee-mill, in an iteration sufficient to drive the listener insane, the dissolute scraping and thumping and barbarous dissonance never changing nor ending. From time to time this is varied with singing, of the nasal, fine-tooth-comb order, with the most extraordinary attempts at shakes and trills, and with all the agony of a moonlit cat on a house-top. All this the grave Arabs and young Egyptian rakes, who sit smoking, accept with entire satisfaction. Later in the evening dancing begins and goes on with the strumming, monotonous music till at least the call for morning prayer.

In the handsome Ezbekeëh park or garden, where there are shady walks and some fine sycamores and banyans to be seen, a military band plays every afternoon, while the foreigners of both sexes and Egyptian men promenade. Of course, no Egyptian lady or woman of respectability is ever seen in so public a place. In another part of the garden, more retired, a native band is always playing at nightfall. In this sheltered spot, under the lee of some gigantic rock and grotto-work, are tables and chairs, and a divan for the band. This rock has water pleasantly running through it, but it must have been struck by somebody besides Moses, for beer is brought out of its cool recesses, as well. Rows of men of all colors and costumes may be seen there, with pipe and mug and coffee cup; and on settees more elevated and next the grotto, are always sitting veiled women, in outer wrappers of black silk, sometimes open enough to show an underskirt of bright color and feet in white slippers. These women call for beer or something stronger, and smoke like the men; they run no risk in being in this publicity, for they have nothing to loose here or elsewhere. Opposite them on a raised divan, not unlike a roomy bedstead, sits the band.

It is the most disreputable of bands. Nothing in the whole East so expressed to me its fagged-out dissoluteness as this band and its performances. It is a sleepy, nonchalant band, as if it had been awake all the previous night; some of its members are blear-eyed, some have one eye, some have two; they are in turbans, in tarbooshes, in gowns of soiled silk, of blue cotton, of white drilling. It is the feeblest band; and yet it is subject to spurts of bacchantic fervor. Sometimes all the instruments are striving together, and then only one or two dribble the monotonous refrain; but somehow, with all the stoppings to light cigarettes and sip coffee, the tune is kept groaning on, in a minor that is as wild as the desert, and suggestive of sin.

The instruments are as African as the sunrise. There is the *darabooka*, a drum made of an earthen or wooden cylinder with a flaring head, over which is stretched a parchment; the *tír*, a kind of tambourine; *kemenyeh*, a viol of two strings, with a cocoa-nut sounding body; the *kanoon*, an instrument of strings held on the knees, and played with the fingers; the *'ood*, a sort of guitar with seven double strings; played with a plectrum, a slip of vulture's feather held between the thumb and finger; and the *náy*, a reed-flute blown at the end.

In the midst of the thumbing and scraping, a rakish youth at the end is liable, at any moment, to throw back his head and break out in a soft womanish voice, which may go no farther than a nasal *yah, ah, m-a-r-r*, that appears to satisfy his yearnings; or it may expand into a droning song, "*Yá benat Iskendereeyeh*," like that which Mr. Lane renders :—

> "O ye damsels of Alexandria !
> Your walk over the furniture is alluring :
> Ye wear the Kashmeer shawl with embroidered work,
> And your lips are sweet as sugar."

Below the divan sit some idlers or supernumeraries, who, as inclination moves them, mark the rhythm by striking the palms of the hands together, or cry out a prolonged *ah-yah*, but always in a forgetful, uninterested manner, and then subside into silence, while the picking and throbbing of the demoralized tune goes on. It is the "devilish iteration" of it, I think, that steals away the senses; this, and some occult immorality is the debased tune, that blots virtue out of the world. Yet there is something comic in these blinking owls of the night, giving sentimental tongue to the poetic imagery of the Eastern love-song—"for a solitary gazelle has taken away my soul" :—

> "The beloved came to me with a vacillating gait ;
> And her eyelids were the cause of my intoxication.
> I extended my hand to take the cup,
> And was intoxicated by her eyes.
> O thou in the rose-coloured dress! O thou in the rose-coloured dress !
> Beloved of my heart ! remain with me."

Or he pipes to the "dark-complexioned, and with two white roses":—

"O damsel! thy silk shirt is worn out, and thine arms have become visible,
And I fear for thee, on account of the blackness of thine eyes.
I desire to intoxicate myself, and kiss thy cheeks,
And do deeds that 'Antar did not."

To all of which the irresponsible chorus, swaying its head, responds *O! y-a-a-a-h!* And the motley audience sips and smokes; the veiled daughters of sin flash invitation from their kohl-stained eyes; and the cool night comes after the flaring heat of the day; and all things are as they have been for thousands of years. It is time to take you to something religious.

The Howling Derweeshes are the most active religionists in the East; I think they spend more force in devotion than the Whirling Derweeshes, though they are probably not more meritorious. They exceed our own western "Jumpers," and by contrast make the worship of our dancing Shakers tame and worldly. Of all the physical manifestations of religious feeling there is none more warming than the *zikr* of these devotees. The derweeshes are not all wanderers, beggars, saints in patched garments and filthy skin; perhaps the most of those who belong to one of the orders pursue some regular occupation; they are fishermen, labourers in the fields, artisans, and water-carriers, and only occasionally join in the ceremonies, processions and *zikrs* of their faith. I have seen a labourer drop into the ring, take his turn at a *zikr*, and drop out again, very much as the western man happens in and takes a hand in a "free fight," and then retires.

This mosque at which the Howling Derweeshes perform is circular, and large enough to admit a considerable number of spectators, who sit or stand against the wall. Since the exercise is one of the sights of the metropolis, and strangers are expected, it has a little the air of a dress-parade, and I could not but fear that the devotion lost somewhat of its singleness of purpose. When we enter, about forty men stand in an oblong ring facing each other; the ring is open towards the *mehhrâb*, or niche which marks the direction of Mecca. In the

7

opening stands the Sheykh, to direct the performance; and at his left are seated the musicians.

The derweeshes have divested themselves of turbans, fezes, outer gowns and slippers, which lie in a heap in the middle of the circle, an indistinguishable mass of old clothes, from which, when the owners come to draw, they cannot fail to get as good as they deposited. The ceremony begins with a little uneasiness on the part of the musical instruments; the sheykh bows his head and brings the palms of his hands together; and the derweeshes, standing close together, with their hands straight at their sides, begin slowly to bow and to sway to the right in a compound motion which is each time extended. The *darabooka* is beaten softly, and the *'ood* is picked to a slow measure. As the worshippers sway, they chant *Lá iláha ill-allâh* ("There is no deity but God") in endless repetition, and imperceptibly quickening the enunciation as they bow more rapidly. The music gets faster, and now and again one of the roguish boys who is thumping the drum breaks out into vocal expression of his piety or of his hilarity. The circle is now under full swing, the bowings are lower and much more rapid, and the ejaculation has become merely *Allâh*, *Allâh*, *Allâh*, with a strong stress on the final syllable.

The peculiarities of the individual performers begin to come out. Some only bow and swing in a perfunctory manner; others throw their strength into the performance, and their excitement is evinced by the working of the face and the rolling of the eyes. Many of them have long hair, which has evidently known neither scissors nor comb for years, and is matted and twisted in a hopeless tangle. One of the most conspicuous and the least clad, a hairy man of the desert, is exactly, in apparel and feature, like the conventional John the Baptist. His enormous shock of faded brown hair is two feet long, and its ends are dyed yellow with henna. When he bends forward his hair sweeps the floor, and when he throws his head back the mass whips over with a *swish* through the air. The most devout person, however, is a negro, who puts all the fervor of the tropics into his exercise. His ejaculations are rolled out with extraordinary volume, and his black skin shines with moisture; there is, too, in his swaying and bowing, an *abandon*, a laxity of muscles, and a sort of jerk that belong only to his sympathetic race.

PREPARATIONS FOR A VOYAGE.

The exercise is every moment growing more rapid, but in regular increments, as the music hastens—five minutes, ten minutes, fifteen minutes—until there is a very high pressure on, the revolutions of the cylinder are almost one in two seconds, and the piston moves quicker and quicker. The music, however, is not louder, only more intense, and now and then the reed-flute executes a little obligato, a plaintive strain, that steals into the frenzy like the note of a lost bird, sweet as love and sad as death. The performers are now going so rapidly that they can only ejaculate one syllable, 'lah, 'lah, 'lah, which is aspirated in a hoarse voice every time the head is flung forward to the floor. The hands are now at liberty, and swing with the body, or are held palm to palm before the face. The negro cannot longer contain himself, but breaks occasionally into a shrill "hoo!" He and two or three others have "the power," and are not far from an epileptic fit.

There is a limit, however, to the endurance of the body; the swaying has become so rapid that it is difficult to distinguish faces, and it is impossible for the performers to repeat even a syllable of the name of *Allah*; all they can do is to push out from the depths of the lungs a vast hoarse aspiration of *la-a-ah*, which becomes finally a gush exactly like the cut-off of a steam engine, short and quick.

The end has nearly come; in vain the cymbals clang, in vain the drum is beaten harder, and the horn calls to quicker work. The limit is reached, and while the reed expresses its plaintive fear, the speed slackens, the steam puffs are slower, and with an irregular *hoo!* from the colored brother, the circle stands still.

You expect to see them sink down exhausted. Not a bit of it. One or two having had enough of it, take their clothes and withdraw, and their places are filled by others and by some very sensible-looking men, trades-people evidently. After a short rest they go through the same or a similar performance, and so on for an hour and a half, the variations being mainly in the chanting. At the end, each derweesh affectionately embraces the Sheykh, kisses his hand without servility, resumes his garments and quietly withdraws. They seem to have enjoyed the exercise, and certainly they had plenty of it. I should like to know what they think of us, the infidel spectators, who go to look at their religious devotions as if they were a play.

That derweesh beggar in a green turban is by that token a shereef, or descendant of the prophet. No one but a shereef is allowed to wear the green turban. The shereefs are in all ranks of society, many of them wretched paupers and in the most menial occupations; the title is inherited from either parent and the representatives of the race have become common. Some who are entitled to the green turban wear the white instead, and prefer to be called Seyd (master or lord) instead of Shereef. Such a man is Seyd Sadat, the most conspicuous representative of the family of the Prophet in Cairo. His ancestors for a long period were the trustees of the funds of all the great mosques of Cairo, and consequently handled an enormous revenue and enjoyed great power. These millions of income from the property of the mosques the Khedive has diverted to his own purposes by the simple process of making himself their trustee. Thus the secular power interferes every few centuries, in all countries, with the accumulation of property in religious houses. The strict Moslems think with the devout Catholics, that it is an impious interference.

Seyd Sadat lives in the house that his family have occupied for over eight centuries! It is perhaps the best and richest specimen of Saracenic domestic architecture now standing in the East. This house, or collection of houses and disconnected rooms opening upon courts and gardens, is in some portions of it in utter decay; a part, whose elegant arches and marvelous carvings in stone, with elaborate hanging balconies and painted recesses, are still studies of beauty, is used as a stable. The inhabited rooms of the house are tiled two-thirds of the way to the lofty ceilings; the floors are of variegated marbles, and the ceilings are a mass of wood in the most intricate arabesque carving, and painted in colors as softly blended as the hues of an ancient camels' hair shawl. In one of these gorgeous apartments, the furniture of which is not at all in keeping with the decorations (an incongruity which one sees constantly in the East—shabbiness and splendor are indissolubly married), we are received by the Descendant with all the ceremony of Eastern hospitality. Seated upon the divan raised above the fountain at one end of the apartment, we begin one of those encounters of compliments through an interpreter, out of which the traveler always comes beaten out of sight. The Seyd is a handsome intelligent man of thirty-five, sleek with good living and repose, and a master of Oriental courtesy. His attire is all of silk, the blue color predominating; his only ornament is a heavy gold chain about the neck. We frame long speeches to the Seyd, and he appears to reply with equal verboseness, but what he says or what is said to him we never know. The Eastern dragoman is not averse to talking, but he always interprets in a sort of short-hand that is fatal to conversation. I think the dragomans at such interviews usually translate you into what they think you ought to say, and give you such a reply as they think will be good for you.

"Say to his lordship that we thank him for the honor of being permitted to pay our respects to a person so distinguished."

"His excellency (who has been talking two minutes) says you do him too much honor."

"We were unwilling to leave Cairo without seeing the residence of so celebrated a family."

"His excellency (who has now got fairly going) feels in deep the visit of strangers so distinguish."

"It is a great pleasure also to us to see an Arab house so old and magnificent."

"His excellency (who might have been reciting two chapters of the Koran in the interval) say not to mention it; him sorry it is not more worth you to see."

The attendants bring sherbet in large and costly cups, and chibooks elegantly mounted, and the conversation flounders along. The ladies visit the harem above, and we look about the garden and are shown into room after room, decorated in endless variety and with a festivity of invention and harmony of color which the moderns have lost. The harem turns out to be, like all ordinary harems, I think, only mysterious on the outside. We withdraw with profuse thanks, frittered away through our dragoman, and "His excellency say he hope you have pleasant voyage and come safe to your family and your country." About the outer court, and the door where we mount our donkeys, are many idlers in the sun, half beggars, half attendants, all of whom want backsheesh, besides the regular servants who expect a fee in proportion to the " distinguish " of the visitor. They are probably not unlike the clients of an ancient Roman house, or the retainers of a baronial lord of the middle ages.

If the visitor, however, really desires to see the antiquities of the Christian era, he will ride out to Old Cairo, and mouse about among the immense rubbish heaps that have been piled there since Fostat (as the ancient city was called) was reduced to ashes, more than seven hundred years ago, by a fire which raged nearly two months. There is the ruined mosque of Amer, and there are the quaint old Coptic convents and churches, built about with mud walls, and hidden away amid mounds of rubbish. To these dust-filled lanes and into these mouldering edifices the antiquarian will gladly go. These churches are the land of the flea and the home of the Copt. Anything dingier, darker, dirtier, doesn't exist. To one of them, the Sitt Miriam, Church of Our Lady, we had the greatest difficulty in getting admission. It is up-stairs in one of the towers of the old Roman gateway of Babylon. It is a small church, but it has five aisles and some very rich wood-carving and stone-mosaics. It was cleaner than the others because it was torn to pieces in the process of renovation. In these churches are hung ostrich eggs, as in the mosques, and in many of them are colored marbles, and exquisite mosaics of marble, mother-of-pearl, and glass. Aboo Sirgeh, the one most visited, has a subterranean chapel which is the seat of an historical transaction that may interest some minds. There are two niches in the wall, and in one of them, at the time of the Flight into Egypt, the Virgin Mary rested with the Child, and in the other St. Joseph reposed. That is all.

A little further on, by the river bank, opposite the southern end of the island of Rhoda, the Moslems show you the spot where little Moses lay in his little basket, when the daughter of Pharaoh came down to bathe (for Pharaoh hadn't a bath-tub in his house) and espied him. The women of the Nile do to-day exactly what Pharaoh's daughter and her maidens did, but there are no bulrushes at this place now, and no lad of the promise of Moses is afloat.

One can never have done with an exploration of Cairo, with digging down into the strata of overlying civilizations, or studying the shifting surface of its Oriental life. Here, in this Old Cairo, was an ancient Egyptian town, no doubt; the Romans constructed here massive walls and towers; the followers of St. Mark erected churches; the friends of Mohammed built mosques; and here the mongrel subjects of the Khedive, a mixture of ancient Egyptian, conquering Arabian, subject Nubian, enslaved Soudan, inheritors of all civilizations and appropriators of none, kennel amid these historic ash-heaps, caring neither for their past nor their future.

But it is drawing towards the middle of December; there are signs that warn us to be off to the south. It may rain. There are symptoms of chill in the air, especially at night, and the hotel, unwarmed, is cheerless as a barn, when the sun does not shine. Indeed, give Cairo the climate of London in November and everybody would perish in a week. Our preparations drift along. It is always "to-morrow." It requires a week to get the new name of the boat printed on a tin. The first day the bargain for it is made; the work is to be finished *bookra*, to-morrow. Next day the letters are studied. The next the tin is prepared. The next day is Friday or Wednesday or some other day in which repose is required. And the next the workman comes to know what letters the howadji desires to have upon the tin, and how big a sign is required.

Two other necessary articles remain to be procured; rockets and other fire-works to illuminate benighted Egypt, and medicines. As we were not taking along a physician and should find none of those experimenting people on the Nile, I did not see the use of carrying drugs. Besides we were going into the one really salubrious region of the globe. But everybody takes medicines; you must carry medicines. The guide-book gives you a list of absolutely essential, nasty drugs and compounds, more than you would need if you were staying at home in an artificial society, with nothing to do but take them, and a physician in every street.

I bought chunks of drugs, bottles of poisons, bundles of foul smells and bitter tastes. And then they told me that I needed balances to weigh them in. This was too much. I was willing to take along an apothecary's shop on this pleasure excursion; I was not willing to become an apothecary. No, I said, if I am to feed out these nauseous things on the Nile, I will do it generously, according to taste, and like a physician, never stinting the quantity. I would never be mean about giving medicine to other people. And it is not difficult to get up a reputation for generosity on epsom salts, rhubarb and castor oil.

We carried all these drugs on the entreaty of friends and the druggist, who said it would be very unsafe to venture so far without them. But I am glad we had them with us. The knowledge that we had them was a great comfort. To be sure we never experienced a day's illness, and brought them all back, except some doses that I was able to work off upon the crew. There was a gentle black boy, who had been stolen young out of Soudan, to whom it was a pleasure to give the most disagreeable mixtures; he absorbed enormous doses as a lily drinks dew, and they never seemed to harm him. The aboriginal man, whose constitution is not weakened by civilization, can stand a great amount of doctor's stuff. The Nile voyager is earnestly advised to carry a load of drugs with him; but I think we rather over-did the business in castor-oil; for the fact is that the people in Nubia fairly swim in it, and you can cut the cane and suck it whenever you feel like it.

By all means, go drugged on your pleasure voyage. It is such a cheerful prelude to it, to read that you will need blue-pills, calomel, rhubarb, Dover's powder, James's powder, carbolic acid, laudanum, quinine, sulphuric acid, sulphate of zinc, nitrate of silver, ipecacuanha, and blistering plaster. A few simple directions go with these. If you feel a little unwell, take a few blue pills, only about as many as you can hold in your hand; follow these with a little Dover's powder, and then repeat, if you feel worse, as you probably will; when you rally, take a few swallows of castor-oil, and drop into your throat some laudanum; and then, if you are alive, drink a dram of sulphuric acid. The consulting friends then generally add a little rice-water and a teaspoonful of brandy.

In the opinion of our dragoman it is scarcely reputable to go up the Nile without a store of rockets and other pyrotechnics. Abd-el-Atti should have been born in America. He would enjoy a life that was a continual Fourth of July. He would like his pathway to be illuminated with lights, blue, red and green, and to blaze with rockets. The supreme moment of his life is when he feels the rocket-stick tearing out of his hand. The common fire-works in the Mooskee he despised; nothing would do but the government-made, which are very good. The passion of some of the Egyptians for fire-arms and gunpowder is partly due to the prohibition. The government strictly forbids the use of guns and pistols and interdicts the importation or selling of powder. On the river a little powder and shot are more valuable than money.

We had obtained permission to order some rockets manufactured at the government works, and in due time we went with Abd-el-Atti to the bureau at the citadel to pay for them. The process was attended with all that deliberation which renders life so long and valuable in the East.

We climbed some littered and dusty steps, to a roof terrace upon which opened several apartments, brick and stucco chambers with cement floors, the walls whitewashed, but yellow with time and streaked with dirt. These were government offices, but office furniture was scarce. Men and boys in dilapidated gowns were sitting about on their heels smoking. One of them got up and led the way, and pulling aside a soiled curtain showed us into the presence of a bey, a handsomely dressed Turk, with two gold chains about his neck, squatting on a ragged old divan at one end of the little room; and this divan was absolutely all the furniture that this cheerless closet, which had one window obscured with dust, contained. Two or three officers were waiting to get the bey's signature to papers, and a heap of documents lay beside him, with an inkhorn on the cushions. Half-clad attendants or petitioners shuffled in and out of the presence of this head of the bureau. Abd-el-Atti produced his papers, but they were not satisfactory, and we were sent elsewhere.

Passing through one shabby room after another, we came into one dimmer, more stained and littered than the others. About the sides of the room upon low divans sat, cross-legged, the clerks. · Before each was a shabby wooden desk which served no purpose, however, but to hold piles of equally shabby account books. The windows were thick with dust, the floor was dirty, the desks, books and clerks were dirty. But the clerks were evidently good fellows, just like those in all government offices—nothing to do and not pay enough to make them uneasy to be rich. They rolled cigarettes and smoked continually; one or two of them were casting up columns of figures, holding the sheet of paper in the left hand and calling each figure in a loud voice (as if a little doubtful whether the figure would respond to that name); and some of them wrote a little, by way of variety. When they wrote the thin sheet of paper was held in the left hand and the writing done upon the palm (as the Arabs always write); the pen used was a blunt reed and the ink about as thick as tar. The writing resulting from these unfavorable conditions is generally handsome.

Our entry and papers were an event in that office, and the documents became the subject of a general conversation. Other public business (except the cigarettes) was suspended, and nearly every clerk gave his opinion on the question, whatever it was. I was given a seat on a rickety divan, coffee was brought in, the clerks rolled cigarettes for me and the business began to open; not that anybody showed any special interest in it, however. On the floor sat two or three boys, eating their dinner of green bean leaves and some harmless mixture of grease and flour; and a cloud of flies settled on them undisturbed. What service the ragged boys rendered to the government I could not determine. Abd-el-Atti was bandying jocularities with the clerks, and directing the conversation now and then upon the rockets.

In course of time a clerk found a scrap of paper, daubed one side of it with Arabic characters, and armed with this we went to another office and got a signature to it. This, with the other documents, we carried to another room much like the first, where the business appeared to take a fresh start; that is, we sat down and talked; and gradually induced one official after another to add a suggestion or a figure or two. Considering that we were merely trying to pay for some rockets that were ready to be delivered to us, it did seem to me that almost a whole day was too much to devote to the affair. But I was mistaken. The afternoon was waning when we went again to the bey. He was still in his little "cubby," and made room for me on the divan. A servant brought coffee. We lighted cigarettes, and, without haste, the bey inked the seal that hung to his gold chain, wet the paper and impressed his name in the proper corner. We were now in a condition to go to the treasury office and pay.

I expected to see a guarded room and heavily bolted safes. Instead of this there was no treasury apartment, nor any strong box. But we found the "treasury" walking about in one of the passages, in the shape of an old Arab in a white turban and faded yellow gown. This personage fished out of his deep breast-pocket a rag of a purse, counted out some change, and put what we paid him into the same receptacle. The Oriental simplicity of the transaction was pleasing. And the money ought to be safe, for one would as soon think of robbing a derweesh as this yellow old man.

The medicine is shipped, the rockets are on board, the crew have been fitted out with cotton drawers, at our expense (this garment is an addition to the gown they wear), the name of the boat is almost painted, the flags are ready to hoist, and the dahabeëh has been taken from Boulak and is moored above the drawbridge. We only want a north wind.

CHAPTER X.

ON THE NILE.

WE have taken possession of our dahabeëh, which lies moored under the bank, out of the current, on the west side of the river above the bridge. On the top of the bank are some structures that seem to be only mounds and walls of mud, but they are really "private houses," and each one has a wooden door, with a wooden lock and key. Here, as at every other rod of the river, where the shore will permit, the inhabitants come to fill their water-jars, to wash clothes, to bathe, or to squat on their heels and wait for the Nile to run dry.

And the Nile is running rapidly away. It sweeps under the arches of the bridge like a freshet, with a current of about three miles an hour. Our *sandal* (the broad clumsy row-boat which we take in tow) is obliged to aim far above its intended landing place when we cross, and four vigorous rowers cannot prevent its drifting rapidly down stream. The Nile is always in a hurry on its whole length; even when it spreads over flats for miles, it keeps a channel for swift passage. It is the only thing that is in a hurry in Egypt; and the more one sees it the stronger becomes the contrast of this haste with the flat valley through which it flows and the apathetic inhabitants of its banks.

We not only have taken possession of our boat, but we have begun housekeeping in it. We have had a farewell dinner-party on board. Our guests, who are foreigners, declare that they did not suppose such a dinner possible in the East; a better could not be expected in Paris. We admit that such dinners are not common in this hungry world out of New York.

Even in New York the soup would not have been made of lentils.

We have passed a night under a mosquito net, more comfortably than on shore, to be sure, but we are anxious to get into motion and change the mosquitoes, the flies, the fleas of Cairo for some less rapacious. It is the seventeenth of December. We are in the bazaars, buying the last things, when at noon we perceive that the wind has shifted. We hasten on board. Where is the dragoman! "Mohammed Effendi Abd-el-Atti goin' bazaar come directly," says the waiter. At half-past two the stout dragoman slides off his donkey and hastens on board with all the speed compatible with short legs, out of breath, but issuing a storm of orders like a belated captain of a seventy-two. He is accompanied by a black boy bearing the name of our dahabeëh, rudely painted on a piece of tin, the paint not yet dry. The dragoman regards it with some pride, and well he may, for it has cost time and trouble. No Arab on the river can pronounce the name, but they all understand its signification when the legend attached to it is related, and having a similar tale in the Koran, they have no objection to sail in a dahabeëh called the

RIP VAN WINKLE.

The name has a sort of appropriateness in the present awakening of Egypt to modern life, but exactly what it is we cannot explain.

We seat ourselves on deck to watch the start. There is as much noise and confusion as if the boat were on fire. The moment has come to cast off, when it is discovered that two of the crew are absent, no doubt dallying in some coffee-house. We cannot wait, they must catch us as they can. The stake is pulled up; the plank is drawn in; the boat is shoved off from its sand bed with grunting and yah-hoo-ing, some of the crew in the water, and some pushing with poles; the great sail drops down from the yard and the corner is hauled in to a wild chorus, and we take the stream. For a moment it seems as if we should be carried against the bridge; but the sail is large, the wind seizes us, and the three-months' voyage has begun.

We are going slowly but steadily, perhaps at the rate of

three or four miles an hour, past the receding city, drawing away from the fleet of boats and barges on the shore and the multitudinous life on its banks. It is a scene of color, motion, variety. The river is alive with crafts of all sorts, the shores are vocal with song, laughter, and the unending "chaff" of a river population. Beyond, the spires and domes of the city are lovely in the afternoon light. The citadel and the minarets gleam like silver against the purple of the Mokattam hills. We pass the long white palace of the Queen-mother; we are abreast the Isle of Rhoda, its yellow palace and its ancient Nilometer. In the cove at Geezeh are passenger-dahabeëhs, two flying the American flag, with which we exchange salutes as we go. The people on their decks are trying with a telescope to make out the device on our pennant at the yard-arm. It affords occupation for a great many people at different times during the voyage. Upon a white ground is a full sun, in red; following it in red letters is the legend *Post Nubila Phœbus*; it is the motto on the coat of arms of the City of Hartford. Here it signifies that we four Hartford people, beginning this voyage, exchange the clouds of New England for the sun of Egypt. The flag extends beyond the motto in a bifurcated blue streamer.

Flag, streamer and sail take the freshening north wind. A smaller sail is set aft. The reïs crouches on the bow, watching the channel; the steersman, a grave figure, pushes slowly back and forth the long iron handle of the tiller at the stern; the crew, waiting for their supper, which is cooking near the mast, begin to sing, one taking the solo and the others striking in with a minor response; it is not a song but a one-line ejaculation, followed by a sympathetic and barbaric assent in chorus.

The shores glide past like that land of the poet's dream where "it is always afternoon"; reposeful and yet brilliant. The rows of palms, the green fields, the lessening minarets, the groups of idlers in flowing raiment, picturesque in any attitudes they assume, the depth of blue above and the transparent soft air—can this be a permanent condition, or is it only the scene of a play?

In fact, we are sailing not only away from Europe, away from Cairo, into Egypt and the confines of mysterious Africa; we are sailing into the past. Do you think our voyage is merely a thousand miles on the Nile? We have committed ourselves to a stream that will lead us thousands of years backwards in the ages, into the depths of history. When we loosed from Cairo we let go our hold upon the modern. As we recede, perhaps we shall get a truer perspective, and see more correctly the width of the strip of time which we call " our era." There are the pyramids of Geezeh watching our departure, lifting themselves aloft in the evening sky ; there are the pyramids of Sakkara, sentinels of that long past into which we go.

It is a splendid start, for the wind blows steadily and we seem to be flying before it. It is probable that we are making five miles an hour, which is very well against such a current. Our dahabeëh proves to be an excellent sailor, and we have the selfish pleasure of passing boat after boat, with a little ripple of excitement not enough to destroy our placid enjoyments. It is much pleasanter to lift your hat to the travelers on a boat that you are drawing ahead of than it is to those of one that is dropping your boat astern.

The Nile voyage is so peculiar, and is, in fact, such a luxurious method of passing a winter, that it may be well to say a little more concerning our boat. It is about one hundred and twenty feet long, and eighteen broad in the centre, with a flat bottom and no keel; consequently it cannot tack or sail contrary to the wind. In the bow is the cook's " cubby " with the range, open to the weather forward. Behind it stands the mast, some forty feet high, and on the top of it is lashed the slender yard, which is a hundred feet long, and hangs obliquely. The enormous triangular sail stretches the length of the yard, and its point is hauled down to the deck. When it is shifted, the rope is let go, leaving the sail flapping, the end of the yard is carried round the mast, and the sail is hauled round in the opposite direction, with an amount of pulling, roaring, jabbering, and chorusing, more than would be necessary to change the course of an American fleet of war. The flat, open forward deck is capable of accommodating six rowers on a side. It is floored over now, for the sweeps are only used in descending.

Then comes the cabin, which occupies the greater part of the boat, and makes it rather top-heavy and difficult of management in an adverse wind. First in the cabin are the pantry and dragoman's room ; next a large saloon, used for dining, furnished with divans, mirrors, tables, and chairs, and lighted by large windows close together. Next are rows of bedrooms, bath-room etc; a passage between leads to the after or lounging cabin, made comfortable with divans and Eastern rugs. Over the whole cabin runs the deck, which has sofas and chairs and an awning, and is good promenading space. The rear portion of it is devoted to the steersman, who needs plenty of room for the sweep of the long tiller. The steering apparatus is of the rudest. The tiller goes into a stern-post which plays in a hole big enough for four of it, and creakingly turns a rude rudder.

If you are familiar with the Egyptian temple you will see that our dahabeëh is built on this plan. If there is no pylon, there is the mast which was always lashed to it. Then comes the *dromos* of sphinxes, the forward deck, with the crew sitting along the low bulwarks; the first cabin is the hall of columns, or *vestibulum*; behind it on each side of the passage are various chambers; and then comes the *adytum* or sanctuary—the inner cabin. The deck is the flat roof upon which wound the solemn processions; and there is a private stairway to the deck just as there was always an inner passage to the roof from one of the small chambers of the temple.

The boat is manned by a numerous company whose appearance in procession would excite enthusiasm in any American town. Abd-el-Atti has for companion and clerk his nephew, a young Egyptian (employed in the telegraph office), but in Frank dress, as all government officials are required to be.

The reïs, or captain, is Hassan. Aboo Seyda, a rather stately Arab of sixty years, with a full turban, a long gown of blue cotton, and bare-footed. He walks the deck with an ease and grace that an actor might envy; there is neither stiffness nor strut in it: it is a gait of simple majesty which may be inherited from generations of upright ancestors, but could never be acquired. Hassan is an admirable figure-head to the expedition, but he has no more pluck or authority than an old hen, and was of not much more use on board than a hen would be in a chicken-hatching establishment.

Abdel Hady Hassed, the steersman, is a Nubian from the First Cataract, shiny black in color, but with regular and delicate features. I can see him now, with his turban set well back on his head, in a loose, long-sleeved, brown garment, and without stockings or slippers, leaning against his tiller and looking straight ahead with unchanging countenance. His face had the peculiarity, which is sometimes seen, of appearing always to have a smile on it. He was born with that smile; he will die with it. An admirable person, who never showed the least excitement. That man would run us fast on a sand-bank, put us on a rock in plain sight, or let his sail jibe, without changing a muscle of his face, and in the most agreeable and good-natured manner in the world. And he never exhibited the least petulance at his accidents. I hope he will be rewarded for the number of hours he patiently stood at that tiller. The reïs would take the helm when Abdel wanted to say his prayers or to eat his simple meals; but, otherwise, I always found him at his post, late at night or in the early morning, gazing around on Egypt with that same stereotyped expression of pleasure.

The cook, Hasaneyn Mahrowan (the last name has an Irish sound, but the first is that of the sacred mosque where is buried the head of the martyr El Hoseyn) is first among his craft, and contrives to produce on his little range in the bow a dinner that would have made Rameses II. a better man. He is always at his post, like the steersman, and no matter what excitement or peril we may be in, Hasaneyn stirs his soup or bastes his chicken with perfect *sang froid*. The fact is that these Orientals have got a thousand or two thousand years beyond worry, and never feel any responsibility for what others are doing.

The waiter, a handsome Cairene, is the perfection of a trained servant, who understands signs better than English. Hoseyn Ali also rejoices in a noble name. Hasan and Hoseyn are, it is well known, the "two lords of the youths of the people of Paradise, in Paradise"; they were grandsons of the Prophet. Hoseyn was slain at the battle of the Plain of Karbalà. Hoseyn is the most smartly dressed fellow on board. His jacket and trousers are of silk; he wears a gay kuffia about his fez and his waist is girded with a fine Cashmere shawl. The fatal defect in his dress is that the full trowsers do not quite meet the stockings. There is always some point of shabbiness or lack of finish in every Oriental object.

The waiter's lieutenant is an Abyssinian boy who rejoices in the name of Ahman Abdallah (or, "Slave of God"); and the cook's boy is Gohah ebn Abdallah ("His father slave of God").

This is the poetical way of putting their condition; they were both slaves of Abd-el-Atti, but now, he says, he has freed them. For Gohah he gave two napoleons when the lad was new. Greater contrast could not be between two colored boys. Ahman is black enough, but his features are regular and well made, he has a bright merry eye, and is quick in all his intuitions, and intellectually faithful to the least particular. He divines the wants of his masters by his quick wit, and never neglects or forgets anything. Gohah is from the Soudan, and a perfect Congo negro in features and texture of skin—lips protruding and nose absolutely level with his cheeks; as faithful and affectionate as a Newfoundland dog, a mild, gentle boy. What another servant would know through his sharpened interest, Gohah comprehends by his affections.

I have described these persons, because they are types of the almost infinite variety of races and tribes in Egypt. Besides these there are fourteen sailors, and no two of the same shade or with similar features. Most of them are of Upper Egypt, and two or three of them are Nubians, but I should say that all are hopelessly mixed in blood. Ahmed, for instance, is a Nubian, and the negro blood comes out in him in his voice and laugh and a certain rolling antic movement of the body. Another sailor has that flush of red under dark in the face which marks the quadroon. The dress of the crew is usually a gown, a pair of drawers, and a turban. Ahmed wears a piece of Turkish towelling round his head. The crew is an incongruous lot altogether; a third of them smoke hasheesh whenever they can get it; they never obey an order without talking about it and suggesting something different; they are all captains in fact; they are rarely quiet, jabbering, or quarreling, or singing, when they are not hauling the sail, hoisting us from a sandbar, or stretched on deck in deep but not noiseless slumber. You cannot but like the good-natured rascals.

An irresponsible, hard-working, jolly, sullen, contradictory lot of big children, who, it is popularly reported, need a *koorbág* (a whip of hippopotamus hide) to keep them in the way of industry and obedience. It seems to me that a little kindness would do better than a good deal of whip. But the kindness ought to have begun some generations back. The koorbág is the legitimate successor of the stick, and the Egyptians have been ruled by the stick for a period of which history reports not to the contrary. In the sculptures on the earliest tombs laborers are driven to their tasks with the stick. Sailors on the old Nile boats are menaced with the stick. The overseer in the field swings the stick. Prisoners and slaves are marshalled in line with the stick. The stick is to-day also the one visible and prevalent characteristic of the government of Egypt. And I think that it is a notion among the subject classes, that a beating is now and then good for them. They might feel neglected without it. I cannot find that Egypt was ever governed in any other way than on the old plan of force and fear.

If there is anything that these officers and sailors do not understand, it is the management of a Nile boat. But this is anticipating. Just now all goes as merrily as a colored ball. The night is soft, the moon is half full; the river spreads out in shining shallows; the shores are dim and show lines of feathery palms against the sky; we meet or pass white sails which flash out of the dimness and then vanish; the long line of pyramids of Sakkara is outlined beyond the palms; now there is a light on shore, and a voice or the howling of a dog is heard; along the bank by the ruins of old Memphis a jackal runs barking in the moonlight. By half-past nine we are abreast the pyramids of Dashoor. A couple of dahabeëhs are laid up below for the night, and the lights from their rows of cabin windows gleam cheerfully on the water.

We go right on, holding our way deeper and deeper into this enchanted country. The night is simply superb, such a wide horizon, such brilliancy above! Under the night, the boat glides like a phantom ship; it is perfectly steady, and we should not know we were in motion but for the running ripple at the sides. By this lulling sound we sleep, having come, for once in the world, into a country of tranquillity, where nothing need ever be done till to-morrow, for to-morrow is certain to be like to-day.

When we came on deck at eight o'clock in the morning after "flying" all night as on birds' wings, we found that we had made thirty-five miles, and were almost abreast of the False Pyramid of Maydoon, so called because it is supposed to be built about a rock; a crumbled pyramid but curiously constructed, and perhaps older than that of Cheops. From a tomb in the necropolis here came the two life-size and striking figures that are in the Boulak Museum in Cairo. The statues, carved in calcareous limestone, represent two exceedingly respectable and intelligent looking persons, who resemble each other enough to be brother and sister; they were probably alive in the third dynasty. They sit up now, with hands on knees, having a bright look on their faces as if they hadn't winked in five thousand years, and were expecting company.

I said we were "flying" all night. This needs qualification. We went aground three times and spent a good part of the night in getting off. It is the most natural thing in navigation. We are conscious of a slight grating, then a gentle lurch, not enough to disturb a dream, followed, however, by a step on deck, and a jabber of voices forward. The sail is loosed; the poles are taken from the rack and an effort is made to shove off by the use of some muscle and a good deal of chorus; when this fails the crew jump overboard and we hear them splashing along the side. They put their backs to the boat and lift, with a grunting "*Euh-hè, euh-hè*," which changes into a rapid "halee, halee, halee," as the boat slides off; and the crew scramble on board to haul tight the sail with an emphatic "Yah! Moham*med*, Yah! Moham*med*."

We were delayed some hours altogether, we learn. But it was not delay. There can be no delay on this voyage; for there is no one on board who is in any haste. Are we not the temporary owners of this boat, and entirely irresponsible for any accident, so that if it goes down with all on board, and never comes to port, no one can hold us for damages?

The day is before us, and not only the day, but, Providence permitting, a winter of days like it. There is nothing to be done, and yet we are too busy to read even the guide-book. There is everything to be seen; it is drifting past us, we are gliding away from it. It is all old and absolutely novel. If this is laziness that is stealing over us, it is of an alert sort. In the East, laziness has the more graceful title of resignation; but we have not come to that condition even; curiosity is constantly excited, and it is a sort of employment to breathe this inspiring air.

We are spectators of a pageant that never repeats itself; for although there is a certain monotony in the character of the river and one would think that its narrow strips of arable land would soon be devoid of interest, the scenes are never twice alike. The combinations vary, the desert comes near and recedes, the mountains advance in bold precipices or fall away; the groups of people, villages, trees, are always shifting.

And yet, in fact, the scenery changes little during the day. There are great reaches of river, rapidly flowing, and wide bends across which we see vessels sailing as if in the meadows. The river is crowded all day with boats, pleasure dahabeëhs, and trading vessels uncouth and picturesque. The passenger dahabëeh is long, handsomely painted, carries an enormous sail on its long yard, has a national flag and a long streamer; and groups of white people sit on deck, under the awning; some of them are reading, some sketching, and now and then a man rises and discharges his shot-gun at a flock of birds a half a mile beyond its range.

The boats of African traders are short, high-pooped, and have the rudder stepped out behind. They usually carry no flag, and are dirty and lack paint, but they carry a load that would interest the most *blasé* European. Those bound up stream, under full sail, like ourselves, are piled with European boxes and bales, from stem to stern, and on top of the freight, in the midst of the freight, sitting on it, stretched out on it, peeping from it, is another cargo of human beings, men, women and children, black, yellow, clothed in all the hues of heaven and the rags of earth. It is an impassive load that stares at us with incurious, unwinking eyes.

The trading boats coming down with the current are even more strange and barbarous. They are piled with merchandise, but of a different sort. The sails and yards are down, and the long sweeps are in motion, balanced on outriggers, for the forward deck is filled, and the rowers walk on top of the goods as they move the oars to and fro. How black the rowers are! How black everybody on board is! They come suddenly upon us, like those nations we have read of, who sit in great darkness. The rowers are stalwart fellows whose basalt backs shine in the sun as they bend to the oar; in rowing they walk towards the cabin and pull the heavy oars as they step backwards, and every sweep is accompanied by the burst of a refrain in chorus, a wild response to a line that has been chanted by the leader as they stepped forwards. The passengers sit immoveable in the sun and regard us with a calmness and gravity which are only attainable near the equatorial regions, where things approach an equilibrium.

Sometimes we count nearly one hundred dahabeëhs in sight, each dipping or veering or turning in the sun its bird-wing sail—the most graceful in the world. A person with fancies, who is watching them, declares that the triangular sails resemble quills cut at the top for pens, and that the sails, seen over the tongue of land of a long bend ahead, look like a procession of goose quills.

The day is warm enough to call out all the birds; flocks of wild geese clang overhead, and companies of them, ranks on ranks, stand on the low sand-dunes; there are pelicans also, motionless in the shallow water near the shore, meditating like a derweesh on one leg, and not caring that the thermometer does mark 74°. Little incidents entertain us. We like to pass the dongola, flying "Ohio" from its yard, which took advantage of our stopping for milk early in the morning to go by us. We overhaul an English boat and have a mildly exciting race with her till dark, with varying fortune, the boats being nearly a match, and the victory depending upon some trick or skill on the part of the crew. All the party look at us, in a most unsympathetic manner, through goggles, which the English always put on whenever they leave the twilight of England. I do not know that we have any right to complain of this habit of wearing wire eye-screens and goggles; persons who have it mean no harm by it, and their appearance is a source of gratification to others. But I must say that goggles have a different effect in different lights. When we were sailing slowly past the Englishman, the goggles regarded us with a feeble and hopeless look. But when the Englishman was, in turn, drawing ahead of us, the goggles had a glare of "Who the devil are you?" Of course it was only in the goggles. For I have seen many of these races on the Nile, and passengers always affect an extreme indifference, leaving all demonstrations of interest to the crews of the boats.

The two banks of the river keep all day about the same relative character—the one sterile, the other rich. On the east, the brown sand licks down almost to the water; there is only a strip of green; there are few trees, and habitations only at long intervals. Only a little distance back are the Mokattam hills, which keep a rarely broken and level sky-line for two hundred and fifty miles south of Cairo.

The west side is a broad valley. The bank is high and continually caving in, like the alluvial bottoms of the Missouri; it is so high that from our deck we can see little of the land. There are always, however, palm-trees in sight, massed in groves, standing in lines, or waving their single tufts in the blue. These are the date-palms, which have no branches on their long poles; each year the old stalks are cut off for fuel, and the trunk, a mass of twisted fibres, comes to have a rough bark, as if the tree had been shingled the wrong way. Stiff in form and with only the single crown of green, I cannot account for its effect of grace and beauty. It is the life of the Nile, as the Nile is life to it. It bears its annual crop of fruit to those who want it, and a crop of taxes for the Khedive. Every palm pays in fact a poll-tax, whether it brings forth dates or not.

Where the bank slopes we can see the springing wheat and barley darkly green; it is sown under the palms even, for no foot of ground is left vacant. All along the banks are shadoofs, at which men in black stand all day raising water, that flows back in regulated streams; for the ground falls slightly away from the height of the bank. At intervals appears a little collection of mud hovels, dumped together without so much plan as you would find in a beaver settlement, but called a village, and having a mud minaret and perhaps a dome. An occasional figure is that of a man ploughing with a single ox; it has just the stiff square look of the sculptures in the tombs.

Now and then, where a zig-zag path is cut, or the bank slopes, women are washing clothes in the river, or groups of them are filling their water jars. They come in files from the villages and we hear their shrill voices in incessant chatter. These countrywomen are invariably in black or dark brown; they are not veiled, but draw their head shawl over the face as our boat passes. Their long gowns are drawn up, exposing bare feet and legs as they step into the stream. The jars are large and heavy when unfilled, and we marvel how they can raise them to their heads when they are full of water. The woman drags her jar out upon the sand, squats before it, lifts it to her head with her hands, and then rises steadily and walks up the steep bank and over the sand, holding her robe with one hand and steadying the jar with the other, with perfect grace and ease of motion. The strength of limbs required to raise that jar to the head and then rise with it, ought to be calculated by those in our own land who are striving to improve the condition of woman.

We are still flying along with the unfailing wind, and the merry progress communicates its spirit to the crew. Before sunset they get out their musical instruments, and squatting in a circle on the forward deck, prepare to enjoy themselves. One thumps and shakes the tambourine, one softly beats with his fingers the darabooka drum, and another rattles castanets. All who are not so employed beat time by a jerking motion of the raised hands, the palms occasionally coming together when the rhythm is properly accented. The leader, who has a very good tenor voice, chants a minor and monotonous love song to which the others respond either in applause of the sentiment or in a burst of musical enthusiasm which they cannot contain. Ahmed, the Nubian, whose body is full of Congoism, enters into it with a delightful *abandon*, swaying from side to side and indulging in an occasional shout, as if he were at a camp meeting. His ugly and good-natured face beams with satisfaction, an expression that is only slightly impaired by the vacant place where two front teeth ought to shine. The song is rude and barbarous but not without a certain plaintiveness; the song and scene belong together. In this manner the sailors of the ancient Egyptians amused themselves without doubt; their instruments were the same; thus they sat upon the ground, thus they clapped hands, thus they improvised ejaculations to the absent beloved:—

"The night! The night! O thou with sweet hands!
Holding the dewy peach."

The sun goes down, leaving a rosy color in the sky, that changes into an ashes-of-roses color, that gradually fades into the indefinable softness of night punctured with stars.

We are booming along all night, under the waxing moon. This is not so much a voyage as a flight, chased by the north wind. The sail is always set, the ripples are running always along the sides, the shores slide by as in a dream; the reïs is at the bow, the smiling steersman is at the helm; if we were enchanted we could not go on more noiselessly. There is something ghostly about this night-voyage through a land so imperfectly defined to the senses, but so crowded with history. If only the dead who are buried on these midnight shores were to rise, we should sail through a vast and ghastly concourse packing the valley and stretching away into the desert.

About midnight I step out of the cabin to look at the night. I stumble over a sleeping Arab. Two sailors, set to hold the sail-rope and let it go in case of a squall of wind, are nodding over it. The night is not at all gloomy or mysterious, but in all the broad sweep of it lovely and full of invitation. We are just passing the English dahabeëh, whose great sail is dark as we approach, and then takes the moon full upon it as we file abreast. She is hugging the bank and as we go by there is a snap. In the morning Abd-el-Atti says that she broke the tip of her yard against the bank. At any rate she lags behind like a crippled bird.

In the morning we are in sight of four dahabeëhs, but we overhaul and pass them all. We have contracted a habit of doing it. One of them gets her stern-sprit knocked off as she sheers before us, whereupon the sailors exchange compliments, and our steersman smiles just as he would have done if he had sent the Prussian boat to the bottom. The morning is delicious, not a cloud in the sky, and the thermometer indicating a temperature of 56°; this moderates speedily under the sun, but if you expected an enervating climate in the winter on the Nile you will be disappointed; it is on the contrary inspiring.

We pass the considerable town of Golósaneh, not caring very much about it; we have been passing towns and mounds and vestiges of ancient and many times dug-up civilizations, day and night. We cannot bother with every ash-heap described in the guide-book. Benisooef, which has been for thousands of years an enterprising city, we should like to have seen, but we went by in the night. And at night most of these towns are as black as the moon will let them be, lights being very rare. We usually receive from them only the salute of a barking dog. Inland from Golósaneh rises the tall and beautiful minaret of Semaloot, a very pretty sight above the palm-groves; so a church spire might rise out of a Connecticut meadow. At 10 o'clock we draw near the cliffs of Gebel e' Tayr, upon the long flat summit of which stands the famous Coptic convent of Sitteh Miriam el Adra, "Our Lady Mary the Virgin,"—called also Dayr el Adra.

We are very much interested in the Copts, and are glad of the opportunity to see something of the practice of their religion. For the religion is as peculiar as the race. In fact, the more one considers the Copt, the more difficult it is to define him. He is a descendant of the ancient Egyptians, it is admitted, and he retains the cunning of the ancients in working gold and silver; but his blood is crossed with Abyssinian, Nubian, Greek and Arab, until the original is lost, and to-day the representatives of the pure old Egyptian type of the sculptures are found among the Abyssinians and the Noobeh (genuine Nubians) more frequently than among the Copts. The Copt usually wears a black or brown turban or cap; but if he wore a white one it would be difficult to tell him from a Moslem. The Copts universally use Arabic; their ancient language is practically dead, although their liturgy and some of their religious books are written in it. The old language is supposed to be the spoken tongue of the old Egyptians.'

The number of Christian Copts in Egypt is small—but still large enough; they have been persecuted out of existence, or have voluntarily accepted Mohammedanism and married among the faithful. The Copts in religion are seceders from the orthodox Church, and their doctrine of the Trinity was condemned by the council of Chalcedon; they consequently hate the Greeks much more than they hate the Moslems. They reckon St. Mark their first patriarch.

Their religious practice is an odd jumble of many others. Most of them practice circumcision. The baptism of infants is held to be necessary; for a child dying unbaptized will be blind in the next life. Their fasts are long and strict; in their prayers they copy both Jews and Moslems, praying often and with endless repetitions. They confess before taking the sacrament; they abstain from swine's flesh, and make pilgrimages to Jerusalem. Like the Moslems they put off their shoes on entering the place of worship, but they do not behave there with the decorum of the Moslem; they stand always in the church, and as the service is three or four hours long, beginning often at daybreak, the long staff or crutch upon which they lean is not a useless appendage. The patriarch, who dwells in Cairo, is not, I think, a person to be envied. He must be a monk originally and remain unmarried, and this is a country where marriage is so prevalent. Besides this, he is obliged to wear always a woollen garment next the skin, an irritation in this climate more constant than matrimony. And report says that he lives under rules so rigid that he is obliged to be waked up, if he sleeps, every fifteen minutes. I am inclined to think, however, that this is a polite way of saying that the old man has a habit of dropping off to sleep every quarter of an hour.

The cliffs of Gebel e' Tayr are of soft limestone, and seem to be two hundred feet high. In one place a road is cut down to the water, partly by a zig-zag covered gallery in the face of the rock, and this is the usual landing-place for the convent. The convent, which is described as a church under ground, is in the midst of a mud settlement of lay brothers and sisters, and the whole is surrounded by a mud wall. From below it has the appearance of an earthwork fortification. The height commands the river for a long distance up and down, and from it the monks are on the lookout for the dahabeëhs of travellers. It is their habit to plunge into the water, clothed only with their professions of holiness, swim to the boats, climb on board and demand "backsheesh" on account of their religion.

It is very rough as we approach the cliffs, the waves are high, and the current is running strong. We fear we are to be disappointed, but the monks are superior to wind and waves. While we are yet half a mile off, I see two of them in the water, with their black heads under white turbans, bobbing about in the tossing and muddy waves. They make heroic efforts to reach us; we can hear their voices faintly shouting: *Ana Christian, O Howadji,* "I am a Christian, O! Howadji."

"We have no doubt you are exceptional Christians," we shout to them in reply, "Why don't you come aboard—back-shee-e-s-h ?"

They are much better swimmers than the average Christian with us. But it is in vain. They are swept by us and away from us like corks on the angry waves, and even their hail of

Christian fellowship is lost in the whistling wind. When we are opposite the convent another head is seen bobbing about in the water; he is also swept below us, but three-quarters of a mile down stream he effects a landing on another dahabeëh. As he climbs into the jolly-boat, which is towed behind, and stands erect, he resembles a statue in basalt.

It is a great feat to swim in a current so swift as this, and lashed by such a wind. I should like to have given these monks something, if only to encourage so robust a religion. But none of them succeeded in getting on board. Nothing happens to us as to other travellers, and we have no opportunity to make the usual remarks upon the degraded appearance of these Coptic monks at Dayr el Adra. So far as I saw them they were very estimable people.

At noon we are driving past Minich with a strong wind. It appears to be—but if you were to land you would find that it is not—a handsome town, for it has two or three graceful minarets, and the long white buildings of the sugar factory, with its tall chimneys, and the palace of the Khedive, stretching along the bank, give it an enterprising and cheerful aspect. This new palace of his Highness cost about half a million of dollars, and it is said that he has never passed a night in it. I confess I rather like this; it must be a royal sensation to be able to order houses made like suits of clothes without ever even trying them on. And it is a relief to see a decent building and a garden now and then, on the river.

We go on, however, as if we were running away from the sheriff, for we cannot afford to lose the advantage of such a wind. Along the banks the clover is growing sweet and green as in any New England meadow in May, and donkeys are browsing in it, tended by children; a very pleasant sight to see this ill-used animal for once in clover and trying to bury his long ears in luxury. Patches of water-melon plants are fenced about by low stockades of dried rushes stuck in the sand—for the soil looks like sand.

This vegetation is not kept alive, however, without constant labor; weeds never grow, it is true, but all green things would speedily wither if the shadoofs were not kept in motion, pouring the Nile into the baked and thirsty soil.

These simple contrivances for irrigation, unchanged since the time of the Pharaohs, have already been described. Here two tiers are required to lift the water to the level of the fields; the first dipping takes it into a canal parallel with the bank, and thence it is raised to the top. Two men are dipping the leathern buckets at each machine, and the constant bending down and lifting up of their dark bodies are fatiguing even to the spectator. Usually in barbarous countries one pities the woman; but I suppose this is a civilized region, for here I pity the men. The women have the easier tasks of washing clothes in the cool stream, or lying in the sand. The women all over the East have an unlimited capacity for sitting motionless all day by a running stream or a pool of water.

In the high wind the palm-trees are in constant motion, tossing their feather tufts in the air; some of them are blown like an umbrella turned wrong side out, and a grove presents the appearance of a crowd of people overtaken by a sudden squall. The acacia tree, which the Arabs call the *sont*, the acanthus of Strabo *(Mimosa Nilotica)* begins to be seen with the palm. It is a thorny tree, with small yellow blossoms, and bears a pod. But what interests us most is the gum that exudes from its bark; for this is the real Gum Arabic! That Heaven has been kind enough to let us see that mysterious gum manufacturing itself! The Gum Arabic of our childhood. How often have I tried to imagine the feelings of a distant and unconverted boy to whom Gum Arabic was as common as spruce gum to a New England lad.

As I said, we go on as if we were evading the law; our dahabeëh seems to have taken the bit in its teeth and is running away with us. We pass everything that sails, and begin to feel no pride in doing so; it is a matter of course. The other dahabeëhs are left behind, some with broken yards. I heard reports afterwards that we broke their yards, and that we even drowned a man. It is not true. We never drowned a man, and never wished to. We were attending to our own affairs. The crew were busy the first day or two of the voyage in cutting up their bread and spreading it on the upper deck to dry—heaps of it, bushels of it. It is a black bread, made of inferior unbolted wheat, about as heavy as lead, and sour to the uneducated taste. The Egyptians like it, however, and it is said to be very healthful. The men gnaw chunks of it with relish, but it is usually prepared for eating by first soaking it in Nile-water and warming it over a fire, in a big copper dish. Into the "stodge" thus made are sometimes thrown some "greens" snatched from the shore. The crew seat themselves about this dish when it is ready, and each one dips his right hand into the mass and claws out a mouthful. The dish is always scraped clean. Meat is very rarely had by them, only a few times during the whole voyage; but they vary their diet by eating green beans, lettuce, onions, lentils, and any sort of "greens" they can lay hands on. The meal is cooked on a little fire built on a pile of stones near the mast. When it is finished they usually gather about the fire for a pull at the "hubble-bubble." This is a sort of pipe with a cocoa-nut shell filled with water, through which the smoke passes. Usually a lump of hasheesh is put into the bowl with the tobacco. A puff or two of this mixture is enough; it sets the smoker coughing and conveys a pleasant stupor to his brain. Some of the crew never smoke it, but content themselves with cigarettes. And the cigarettes they are always rolling up and smoking while they are awake.

The hasheesh-smokers are alternately elated and depressed, and sometimes violent and noisy. A man addicted to the habit is not good for much; the hasheesh destroys his nerves and brain, and finally induces idiocy. Hasheesh intoxication is the most fearful and prevalent vice in Egypt. The government has made many attempts to stop it, but it is too firmly fixed; the use of hasheesh is a temporary refuge from poverty, hunger, and all the ills of life, and appears to have a stronger fascination than any other indulgence. In all the towns one may see the dark little shops where the drug is administered, and generally rows of victims in a stupid doze stretched on the mud benches. Sailors are so addicted to hasheesh that it is almost impossible to make up a decent crew for a dahabeëh.

Late in the afternoon we are passing the famous rock-tombs of Beni Hassan, square holes cut in the face of the cliff, high up. With our glasses we can see paths leading to them over the *débris* and along the ledges. There are two or three rows of these tombs, on different ledges; they seem to be high, dry, and airy, and I should rather live in them, dead or alive, than in the mud hovels of the fellaheen below. These places of sepulchre are older than those at Thebes, and from the pictures and sculptures in them, more than from any others, the antiquarians have reconstructed the domestic life of the ancient Egyptians. This is a desolate spot now; there is a decayed old mud village below, and a little south of it is the new town; both can barely be distinguished from the brown sand and rock in which and in front of which they stand. This is a good place for thieves, or was before Ibraheem Pasha destroyed these two villages. We are warned that this whole country produces very skilful robbers, who will swim off and glean the valuables from a dahabeëh in a twinkling.

Notwithstanding the stiff breeze the thermometer marks 74°; but both wind and temperature sink with the sun. Before the sun sets, however, we are close under the east bank, and are watching the play of light on a magnificent palm-grove, beneath which stand the huts of the modern village of Sheykh Abádeh. It adds romance to the loveliness of the scene to know that this is the site of ancient Antinoë, built by the Emperor Adrian. To be sure we didn't know it till this moment, but the traveller warms up to a fact of this kind immediately, and never betrays even to his intimate friends that he is not drawing upon his inexhaustible memory.

"That is the ancient Antinoë, built by Adrian."

Oh, the hypocrisy and deceit of the enthusiastic.

"*Is* it?"

"Yes, and handsome Antinoüs was drowned here in the Nile."

"Did they recover his body?"

Upon the bank there are more camels, dogs, and donkeys than we have seen all day; buffaloes are wallowing in the muddy margin. They are all in repose; the dogs do not bark, and the camels stretch their necks in a sort of undulatory expression of discontent, but do not bleat, or roar, or squawk, or make whatever the unearthly noise which they make is called. The men and the women are crouching in the shelter of their mud walls, with the light of the setting sun upon their dark faces. They draw their wraps closer about them to protect themselves from the north wind, and regard us stolidly and without interest as we go by. And when the light fades, what is there for them? No cheerful lamp, no book, no newspaper. They simply crawl into their kennels and sleep the sleep of "inwardness" and peace.

Just here the arable land on the east bank is broader than usual, and there was evidently a fine city built on the edge of the desert behind it. The Egyptians always took waste and desert land for dwellings and for burial-places, leaving every foot of soil available for cultivation free. There is evidence all along here of a once much larger population, though I doubt if the east bank of the river was ever much inhabited. The river banks would support many more people than we find here if the land were cultivated with any care. Its fertility, with the annual deposit, is simply inexhaustible, and it is good for two and sometimes three crops a year. But we pass fields now and then that are abandoned, and others that do not yield half what they might. The people are oppressed with taxes and have no inducement to raise more than is absolutely necessary to keep them alive. But I suppose this has always been the case in Egypt. The masters have squeezed the last drop from the people, and anything like an accumulation of capital by the laborers is unknown. The Romans used a long rake, with fine and sharp teeth, and I have no doubt that they scraped the country as clean as the present government does.

The government has a very simple method of adjusting its taxes on land and crops. They are based upon the extent of the inundation. So many feet rise, overflowing such an area, will give such a return in crops; and tax on this product can be laid in advance as accurately as when the crops are harvested. Nature is certain to do her share of the work; there will be no frost, nor any rain to spoil the harvest, nor any freakishness whatever on the part of the weather. If the harvest is not up to the estimate, it is entirely the fault of the laborer, who has inadequately planted or insufficiently watered. In the same manner a tax is laid upon each palm-tree, and if it does not bear fruit that is not the fault of the government.

There must be some satisfaction in farming on the Nile. You

are always certain of the result of your labor.* Whereas, in our country farming is the merest lottery. The season will open too wet or too dry, the seed may rot in the ground, the young plant may be nipped with frost or grow pale for want of rain, the crop runs the alternate hazards of drought or floods, it is wasted by rust or devoured by worms; and, to cap the climax, if the harvest is abundant and of good quality, the price goes down to an unremunerative figure. In Egypt you may scratch the ground, put in the seed, and then go to sleep for three months, in perfect certainty of a good harvest, if only the shadoof and the sakiya are kept in motion.

By eight o'clock in the evening, on a falling wind, we are passing Roda, whose tall chimneys have been long in sight. Here is one of the largest of the Khedive's sugar-factories, and a new palace which has never been occupied. We are one hundred and eighty-eight miles from Cairo, and have made this distance in two days, a speed for which I suppose history has no parallel; at least our dragoman says that such a run has never been made before at this time of the year, and we are quite willing to believe a statement which reflects so much honor upon ourselves, for choosing such a boat and such a dragoman.

This Nile voyage is nothing, after all; its length has been greatly overestimated. We shall skip up the river and back

---

*It should be said, however, that the ancient Egyptians found the agricultural conditions beset with some vexations. A papyrus in the British Museum contains a correspondence between Ameneman, the librarian of Rameses II, and his pupil Pentaour, who wrote the celebrated epic upon the exploits of that king on the river Orontes. One of the letters describes the life of the agricultural people :—" Have you ever conceived what sort of life the peasant leads who cultivates the soil? Even before it is ripe, insects destroy part of his harvest. . . Multitudes of rats are in the field; next come invasions of locusts, cattle ravage his harvest, sparrows alight in flocks on his sheaves. If he delays to get in his harvest, robbers come to carry it off with them; his horse dies of fatigue in drawing the plough; the tax-collector arrives in the district, and has with him men armed with sticks, negroes with palm-branches. All say, 'Give us of your corn,' and he has no means of escaping their exactions. Next the unfortunate wretch is seized, bound, and carried off by force to work on the canals; his wife is bound, his children are stripped. And at the same time his neighbors have each of them his own trouble."

again before the season is half spent, and have to go somewhere else for the winter. A man feels all-powerful, so long as the wind blows; but let his sails collapse, and there is not a more crest-fallen creature. Night and day our sail has been full, and we are puffed up with pride.

At this rate we shall hang out our colored lanterns at Thebes on Christmas night.

CHAPTER XI.

PEOPLE ON THE RIVER BANKS.

THE morning puts a new face on our affairs. It is Sunday, and the most devout could not desire a quieter day. There is a thick fog on the river, and not breeze enough stirring to show the stripes on our flag; the boat holds its own against the current by a sort of accumulated impulse. During the night we may have made five miles altogether, and now we barely crawl. We have run our race; if we have not come into a haven, we are at a stand-still, and it does not seem now as if we ever should wake up and go on again. However, it is just as well. Why should we be tearing through this sleepy land at the rate of four miles an hour?

The steersman half dozes at the helm; the reïs squats near him watching the flapping sails; the crew are nearly all asleep on the forward deck, with their burnouses drawn over their head and the feet bare, for it is chilly as late as nine o'clock, and the thermometer has dropped to 54°. Abd-el-Atti slips his beads uneasily along between his fingers, and remembers that when he said that we would reach Asioot in another day, he forgot to ejaculate: "God willing." Yet he rises and greets our coming from the cabin with a willing smile, and a—

"Morning, sir; morning, marm. I hope you enjoyin' your sleep, marm."

"Where are we now, Abd-el-Atti?"

"Not much, marm; this is a place call him Hadji Kandeel. But we do very well; I not to complain."

"Do you think we shall have any wind to-day?"

"I d' know, be sure. The wind come from Lord. Not so?"

Hadji Kandeel is in truth only a scattered line of huts, but one lands here to visit the grottoes or rock-tombs of Tel el

Amárna. All this country is gaping with tombs apparently; all the cliffs are cut into receptacles for the dead, all along the margin of the desert on each side are old necropolises and moslem cemeteries, in which generation after generation, for almost fabulous periods of time, has been deposited. Here behind Hadji Kandeel are remains of a once vast city built let us say sixteen hundred years before our era, by Amunoph IV., a wayward king of the eighteenth dynasty, and made the capital of Egypt. In the grottoes of Tel el Amárna were deposited this king and his court and favorites, and his immediate successors—all the splendor of them sealed up there and forgotten. This king forsook the worship of the gods of Thebes, and set up that of a Semitic deity, Aten, a radiating disk, a sun with rays terminating in human hands. It was his mother who led him into this, and she was not an Egyptian; neither are the features of the persons sculptured in the grottoes Egyptian.

Thus all along the stream of Egyptian history cross currents are coming in, alien sovereigns and foreign task-masters; and great breaks appear, as if one full civilization had run its course of centuries, and decay had come, and then ruin, and then a new start and a fresh career.

Early this morning, when we were close in to the west bank, I heard measured chanting, and saw a procession of men and women coming across the field. The men bore on a rude bier the body of a child. They came straight on to the bank, and then turned by the flank with military precision and marched up-stream to the place where a clumsy country ferry-boat had just landed. The chant of the men, as they walked, was deep-voiced and solemn, and I could hear in it frequently repeated the name of Mohammed. The women in straggling file followed, like a sort of ill-omened birds in black, and the noise they made, a kind of wail, was exactly like the cackle of wild geese. Indeed before I saw the procession I thought that some geese were flying overhead.

The body was laid on the ground and four men kneeled upon the bank as if in prayer. The boat meantime was unloading, men, women and children scrambling over the sides into the shallow water, and the donkeys, urged with blows, jumping after them. When they were all out the funeral took possession of the boat, and was slowly wafted across, as dismal a going to a funeral as if this were the real river of death. When the mourners had landed we saw them walking under the palm trees, to the distant burial-place in the desert, with a certain solemn dignity, and the chanting and wailing were borne to us very distinctly.

It is nearly a dead calm all day, and our progress might be imperceptible to an eye naked, and certainly it must be so to the eyes of these natives which are full of flies. It grows warm, however, and is a summer temperature when we go ashore in the afternoon on a tour of exploration. We have for attendant, Ahmed, who carries a big stick as a defence against dogs. Ahmed does not differ much in appearance from a wild barbarian, his lack of a complete set of front teeth alone preventing him from looking fierce. A towel is twisted about his head, feet and legs are bare, and he wears a blue cotton robe with full sleeves longer than his arms, gathered at the waist by a piece of rope, and falling only to the knees. A nice person to go walking with on the Holy Sabbath.

The whole land is green with young wheat, but the soil is baked and cracked three or four inches deep, even close to the shore where the water has only receded two or or three days ago. The land stretches for several miles, perfectly level and every foot green and smiling, back to the desert hills. Sprinkled over this expanse, which is only interrupted by ditches and slight dykes upon which the people walk from village to village, are frequent small groves of palms. Each grove is the nucleus of a little settlement, a half dozen sun-baked habitations, where people, donkeys, pigeons, and smaller sorts of animated nature live together in dirty amity. The general plan of building is to erect a circular wall of clay six or seven feet high, which dries, hardens, and cracks in the sun. This is the Oriental court. Inside this and built against the wall is a low mud-hut with a wooden door, and perhaps here and there are two similar huts, or half a dozen, according to the size of the family. In these hovels the floor is of smooth earth, there is a low bedstead or some matting laid in one corner, but scarcely any other furniture, except some earthen jars holding doora or dried fruit, and a few cooking utensils. A people who never sit, except on their heels, do not need chairs, and those who wear at once all the clothes they possess need no closets or wardrobes. I looked at first for a place where they could keep their "Sunday clothes" and "nice things," but this philosophical people do not have anything that is too good for daily use. It is nevertheless true that there is no hope of a people who do not have "Sunday clothes."

The inhabitants did not, however, appear conscious of any such want. They were lounging about or squatting in the dust in picturesque idleness; the children under twelve years often without clothes and not ashamed, and the women wearing no veils. The women are coming and going with the heavy water-jars, or sitting on the ground, sorting doora and preparing it for cooking; not prepossessing certainly, in their black or dingy brown gowns and shawls of cotton. Children abound. In all the fields men are at work, picking up the ground with a rude hoe shaped like an adze. Tobacco plants have just been set out, and water-melons carefully shaded from the sun by little tents of rushes. These men are all fellaheen, coarsely and scantily clad in brown cotton gowns, open at the breast. They are not bad figures, better than the women, but there is a hopeless acceptance of the portion of slaves in their bearing.

We encountered a very different race further from the river, where we came upon an encampment of Bedaween, or desert Arabs, who hold themselves as much above the fellaheen as the poor white trash used to consider itself above the negroes in our Southern States. They pretend to keep their blood pure by intermarrying only in desert tribes, and perhaps it is pure; so, I suppose, the Gipsies are pure blood enough, but one would not like them for neighbors. These Bedaween, according to their wandering and predatory habit, have dropped down here from the desert to feed their little flock of black sheep and give their lean donkeys a bite of grass. Their tents are merely strips of coarse brown cloth, probably camel's hair, like sacking, stretched horizontally over sticks driven into the sand, so as to form a cover from the sun and a protection from the north wind. Underneath them are heaps of rags, matting, old clothes, blankets, mingled with cooking utensils and the nameless and broken assortment that beggars usually lug about with them. Hens and lambs are at home there, and dogs, a small, tawny, wolfish breed, abound. The Arabs are worthy of their dwellings, a dirty, thievish lot to look at, but, as I said, no doubt of pure blood, and having all the virtues for which these nomads have been celebrated since the time when Jacob judiciously increased his flock at the expense of Laban.

A half-naked boy of twelve years escorts us to the bank of the canal near which the tents are pitched, and we are met by the sheykh of the tribe, a more venerable and courtly person than the rest of these pure-blood masqueraders in rags, but not a whit less dirty. The fellaheen had paid no attention to us; this sheykh looked upon himself as one of the proprietors of this world, and bound to extend the hospitalities of this portion of it to strangers. He received us with a certain formality. When two Moslems meet there is no end to their formal salutation and complimentary speeches, which may continue as long as their stock of religious expressions holds out. The usual first greeting is *Es-salaam 'aleykoom* "peace be on you;" to which the reply is *'Aleykoom es-salaam*, "on you be peace." It is said that persons of another religion, however, should never make use of this salutation to a Moslem, and that the latter should not and will not return it. But we were overflowing with charity and had no bigotry, and went through Egypt salaaming right and left, sometimes getting no reply and sometimes a return, to our "peace be on you," of *Wa-'aleykoom*, "and on you."

The salutations by gesture are as varied as those by speech. When Abd-el-Atti walked in Cairo with us, he constantly varied his gestures according to the rank of the people we met. To an inferior he tossed a free salaam; an equal he saluted by touching with his right hand in one rapid motion his breast, lips and head; to a superior he made the same motion except that his hand first made a dip down to his knees; and when he met a person of high rank the hand scooped down to the ground before it passed up to the head.

I flung a cheerful *salaam* at the sheykh and gave him the Oriental salute, which he returned. We then shook hands, and the sheykh kissed his after touching mine, a token of friendship which I didn't know enough to imitate, not having been brought up to kiss my own hand.

"Anglais or Francaise?" asked the sheykh.

"No," I said, "Americans."

"Ah," he ejaculated, throwing back his head with an aspiration of relief, "Melicans; *tyeb* (good)."

A ring of inquisitive Arabs gathered about us and were specially interested in studying the features and costume of one of our party ; the women, standing further off and remaining closely veiled, kept their eyes fixed on her. The sheykh invited us to sit and have coffee, but the surroundings were not tempting to the appetite and we parted with profuse salutations. I had it in mind to invite him to our American centennial; I should like to set him off against some of our dirty red brethren of the prairies. I thought that if I could transport these Bedaween, tents, children, lank, veiled women, donkeys, and all to the centennial grounds they would add a most interesting (if unpleasant) feature. But, then, I reflected, what is a centennial to this Bedawee whose ancestors were as highly civilized as he is when ours were wading about the fens with the Angles or burrowing in German forests. Besides, the Bedawee would be at a disadvantage when away from the desert, or the bank of this Nile whose unceasing flow symbolizes his tribal longevity.

As we walk along through the lush-fields which the despised fellaheen are irritating into a fair yield of food, we are perplexed with the query, what is the use of the Bedaween in this world? They produce nothing. To be sure they occupy a portion of the earth that no one else would inhabit; they dwell on the desert. But there is no need of any one dwelling on the desert, especially as they have to come from it to levy contributions on industrious folks in order to live. At this stage of the inquiry, the philosopher asks, what is the use of any one living?

As no one could answer this, we waded the water where it was shallow and crossed to a long island, such as the Nile frequently leaves in its sprawling course. This island was green from end to end, and inhabited more thickly than the mainland. We attracted a good deal of attention from the mud-villages, and much anxiety was shown lest we should walk across the wheat-fields. We expected that the dahabeëh would come and take us off, but its streamer did not advance, and we were obliged to rewade the shallow channel and walk back to the starting-place. There was a Sunday calm in the scene. At the rosy sunset the broad river shone like a mirror and the air was soft as June. How strong is habit. Work was going on as usual, and there could have been no consent of sky, earth, and people, to keep Sunday, yet there seemed to be the Sunday spell upon the landscape. I suspect that people here have got into the way of keeping all the days. The most striking way in which an American can keep Sunday on the Nile is by not going gunning, not even taking a "flyer" at a hawk from the deck of the dahabeëh. There is a chance for a tract on this subject.

Let no one get the impression that we are idling away our time, because we are on Monday morning exactly where we were on Sunday morning. We have concluded to "keep" another day. There is not a breath of wind to scatter the haze, thermometer has gone down, and the sun's rays are feeble. This is not our fault, and I will not conceal the adverse circumstances in order to give you a false impression of the Nile.

We are moored against the bank. The dragoman has gone on shore to shoot pigeons and buy vegetables. Our turkeys, which live in cages on the stern-deck, have gone ashore and are strutting up and down the sand; their gobble is a home sound and recalls New England. Women, as usual, singly and in groups, come to the river to fill their heavy water-jars. There is a row of men and boys on the edge of the bank. Behind are two camels yoked wide apart drawing a plough. Our crew chaff the shore people. The cook says to a girl,

"You would make me a good wife; we will take you along." Men, squatting on the bank say, "take her along, she is of no use."

Girl retorts, "You are not of more use than animals, you sit idle all day, while I bring water and grind the corn."

One is glad to see this assertion of the rights of women in this region where nobody has any rights; and if we had a tract we would leave it with her. Some good might be done by travellers if they would distribute biscuit along the Nile, stamped in Arabic with the words, "Man ought to do half the work," or, "Sisters rise!"

In the afternoon we explore a large extent of country, my companion carrying a shot-gun for doves. These doves are in fact wild pigeons, a small and beautiful pearly-grey bird. They live on the tops of the houses in nests formed for them by the insertion of tiles or earthen pots in the mud-walls. Many houses have an upper story of this sort on purpose for the doves;

and a collection of mere mud-cabins so ornamented is a picturesque sight, under a palm-grove. Great flocks of these birds are flying about, and the shooting is permitted, away from the houses.

We make efforts to get near the wild geese and the cranes, great numbers of which are sunning themselves on the sandbanks, but these birds know exactly the range of a gun, and fly at the right moment. A row of cranes will sometimes trifle with our feelings. The one nearest will let us approach almost within range before he lifts his huge wings and sails over the river, the next one will wait for us to come a few steps further before he flies, and so on until the sand-spit is deserted of these long-legged useless birds. Hawks are flying about the shore and great greyish crows, or ravens, come over the fields and light on the margin of sand—a most gentlemanly looking bird, who is under a queer necessity of giving one hop before he can raise himself in flight. Small birds, like sand-pipers, are flitting about the bank. The most beautiful creature, however, is a brown bird, his wing marked with white, long bill, head erect and adorned with a high tuft, as elegant as the blue-jay; the natives call it the crocodile's guide.

We cross vast fields of wheat and of beans, the Arab "food," which are sown broadcast, interspersed now and then with a melon-patch. Villages, such as they are, are frequent; one of them has a mosque, the only one we have seen recently. The water for ablution is outside, in a brick tank sunk in the ground. A row of men are sitting on their heels in front of the mosque, smoking; some of them in white gowns, and fine-looking men. I hope there is some saving merit in this universal act of sitting on the heels, the soles of the feet flat on the ground; it is not an easy thing for a Christian to do, as he will find out by trying.

Towards night a steamboat flying the star and crescent of Egypt, with passengers on board, some of "Cook's personally conducted," goes thundering down stream, filling the air with smoke and frightening the geese, who fly before it in vast clouds. I didn't suppose there were so many geese in the world.

Truth requires it to be said that on Tuesday morning the dahabeëh holds about the position it reached on Sunday morning; we begin to think we are doing well not to lose anything in this rapid current. The day is warm and cloudy, the wind is from the east and then from the south-east, exactly the direction we must go. It is in fact a sirocco, and fills one with languor, which is better than being frost-bitten at home. The evening, with the cabin windows all open, is like one of those soft nights which come at the close of sultry northern days, in which there is a dewy freshness. This is the sort of winter that we ought to cultivate.

During the day we attempt tracking two or three times, but with little success; the wind is so strong that the boat is continually blown ashore. Tracking is not very hard for the passengers, and gives them an opportunity to study the bank and the people on it close at hand. A long cable fastened on the forward deck is carried ashore, and to the far end ten or twelve sailors attach themselves at intervals by short ropes which press across the breast. Leaning in a slant line away from the river, they walk at a snail's pace, a file of parti-colored raiment and glistening legs; occasionally bursting into a snatch of a song, they slowly pull the bark along. But obstructions to progress are many. A spit of sand will project itself, followed by deep water, through which the men will have to wade in order to bring the boat round; occasionally the rope must be passed round trees which overhang the caving bank; and often freight-boats, tied to the shore, must be passed. The leisure with which the line is carried outside another boat is amusing even in this land of deliberation. The groups on these boats sit impassive and look at us with a kind of curiosity that has none of our eagerness in it. The well-bred indifferent " stare " of these people, which is not exactly brazen and yet has no element of emotion in it, would make the fortune of a young fellow in a London season. The Nubian boatmen who are tracking the freight-dahabeëh appear to have left their clothes in Cairo; they flop in and out of the water, they haul the rope along the bank, without consciousness apparently that any spectators are within miles; and the shore-life goes on all the same, men sit on the banks, women come constantly to fill their jars, these crew stripped to their toil excite no more attention than the occasional fish jumping out of the Nile. The habit seems to be general of minding one's own business.

At early morning another funeral crossed the river to a

desolate burial-place in the sand, the women wailing the whole distance of the march; and the noise was more than before like the clang of wild geese. These women have inherited the Oriental art of " lifting up the voice," and it adds not a little to the weirdness of this ululation and screeching to think that for thousands of years the dead have been buried along this valley with exactly the same feminine tenderness.

These women wear black; all the countrywomen we have seen are dressed in sombre gowns and shawls of dark or deep blue-black; none of them have a speck of color in their raiment, not a bit of ribbon nor a bright kerchief, nor any relief to the dullness of their apparel. And yet they need not fear to make themselves too attractive. The men wear all the colors that are worn; though the fellaheen as a rule wear brownish garments, blue and white are not uncommon, and a white turban or a red fez, or a silk belt about the waist gives variety and agreeable relief to the costumes. In this these people imitate that nature which we affect to admire, but outrage constantly. They imitate the birds. The male birds have all the gay plumage; the feathers of the females are sober and quiet, as befits their domestic position. And it must be admitted that men need the aid of gay dress more than women.

The next morning when the sun shows over the eastern desert, the sailors are tracking, hauling the boat slowly along an ox-bow in the river, until at length the sail can catch the light west wind which sprang up with the dawn. When we feel that, the men scramble aboard, and the dahabeëh, like a duck that has been loitering in an eddy for days, becomes instinct with life and flies away to the cliffs opposite, the bluffs called Gebel Aboofayda, part of the Mokattam range that here rises precipitously from the river and overhangs it for ten or twelve miles. I think these limestone ledges are two or three hundred feet high. The face is scarred by the slow wearing of ages, and worn into holes and caves innumerable. Immense numbers of cranes are perched on the narrow ledges of the cliff, and flocks of them are circling in front of it, apparently having nests there. As numerous also as swallows in a sand-bank is a species of duck called the diver; they float in troops on the stream, or wheel about the roosting cranes.

This is a spot famed for its sudden gusts of wind which sometimes flop over the brink and overturn boats. It also is the

PEOPLE ON THE RIVER BANKS. 141

resort of the crocodile, which seldom if ever comes lower down the Nile now. But the crocodile is evidently shy of exhibiting himself, and we scan the patches of sand at the foot of the rocks with our glasses for a long time in vain. The animal dislikes the puffing, swashing steamboats, and the rifle-balls that passing travellers pester him with. At last we see a scaly log six or eight feet long close to the water under the rock. By the aid of the glass it turns out to be a crocodile. He is asleep, and too far off to notice at all the volley of shot with which we salute him. It is a great thing to *say* you saw a crocodile. It isn't much to *see* one.

And yet the scaly beast is an interesting and appropriate feature in such a landscape, and the expectation of seeing a crocodile adds to your enjoyment. On our left are these impressive cliffs; on the right is a level island. Half-naked boys and girls are tending small flocks of black sheep on it. Abd-el-Atti raises his gun as if he would shoot the children, and cries out to them, "lift up your arm," words that the crocodile hunter uses when he is near enough to fire, and wants to attract the attention of the beast so that it will raise its fore-paw to move off, and give the sportsman a chance at the vulnerable spot. The children understand the allusion, and run laughing away.

Groups of people are squatting on the ground, doing nothing, waiting for nothing, expecting nothing; buffaloes and cattle are feeding on the thin grass, and camels are kneeling near in stately indifference; women in blue-black robes come—the everlasting sight—to draw water. The whole passes in a dumb show. The hot sun bathes all.

We pass next the late residence of a hermit, a Moslem "welee" or holy man. On a broad ledge of the cliff, some thirty feet above the water, is a hut built of stone and plaster, and whitewashed, about twelve feet high, the roof rounded like an Esquimau snow-hut with a knob at the top. Here the good man lived, isolated from the world, fed by the charity of passers-by, and meditating on his own holiness. Below him, out of the rock, with apparently no better means of support than he had, grows an acacia-tree, now in yellow blossoms. Perhaps the saint chewed the gum-arabic that oozed from it. Just above, on the river, is a slight strip of soil, where he used to raise a few cucumbers and other cooling vegetables. The farm, which is no larger than two bed blankets, is deserted now. The saint died, and is buried in his house, in a hole excavated in the rock, so that his condition is little changed, his house being his tomb, and the Nile still soothing his slumber.

But if it is easy to turn a house into a tomb, it is still easier to turn a tomb into a house. Here are two square-cut tombs in the rock, of which a family has taken possession, the original occupants probably having moved out hundreds of years ago. Smoke is issuing from one of them, and a sorry-looking woman is pulling dead grass among the rocks for fuel. There seems to be no inducement for any one to live in this barren spot, but probably rent is low. A little girl seven or eight years old comes down and walks along the bank, keeping up with the boat, incited, of course, by the universal expectation of backsheesh. She has on a head-veil, covering the back of the head and neck, and a single shirt of brown rags hanging in strings. I throw her an apple, a fruit she has probably never seen, which she picks up and carries until she is joined by an elder sister, to whom she shows it. Neither seems to know what it is. The elder smells it, sticks her teeth into it, and then takes a bite. The little one tastes, and they eat it in alternate bites, growing more and more eager for fair bites as the process goes on.

Near the southern end of the cliffs of Gebel Aboofayda are the crocodile-mummy pits which Mr. Prime explored; caverns in which are stacked up mummied crocodiles and lizards by the thousands. We shall not go nearer to them. I dislike mummies; I loathe crocodiles; I have no fondness for pits. What could be more unpleasant than the three combined! To crawl on one's stomach through crevices and hewn passages in the rock, in order to carry a torch into a stifling chamber, packed with mummies and cloths soaked in bitumen, is an exploit that we willingly leave to Egyptologists. If one takes a little pains, he can find enough unpleasant things above ground.

It requires all our skill to work the boat round the bend above these cliffs; we are every minute about to go aground on a sand-bar, or jibe the sail, or turn about. Heaven only knows how we ever get on at all, with all the crew giving orders and no one obeying. But by five o'clock we are at the large market town of Manfaloot, which has half a dozen minarets, and is sheltered by a magnificent palm-grove. You seem to be approaching an earthly paradise; and one can keep up the illusion if he does not go ashore. And yet this is a spot that ought to interest the traveller, for here Lot is said to have spent a portion of the years of his exile, after the accident to his wife.

At sunset old Abo Arab comes limping along the bank with a tin pail, having succeeded at length in overtaking the boat; and in reply to the question where he has been asleep all day, pulls out from his bosom nine small fish as a peace-offering. He was put off at sunrise to get milk for breakfast. What a happy-go-lucky country it is.

After sundown, the crew, who have worked hard all day, on and off, tacking, poling, and shifting sail, get their supper round an open fire on deck, take each some whiffs from the "hubble-bubble," and, as we sail out over the broad, smooth water, sing a rude and plaintive melody to the subdued thump of the darabooka. Towards dark, as we are about to tie up, the wind, which had failed, rises, and we voyage on, the waves rippling against the sides in a delicious lullaby. The air is soft, the moon is full, and peeps out from the light clouds which obscure the sky and prevent dew.

The dragoman asleep on the cabin deck, the reïs crouched, attentive of the course, near him, part of the sailors grouped about the bow in low chat, and part asleep in the shadow of the sail, we voyage along under the wide night, still to the south and warmer skies, and seem to be sailing through an enchanted land.

Put not your trust in breezes. The morning finds us still a dozen miles from Asioot, where we desire to celebrate Christmas; we just move with sails up, and the crew poling. The head man chants a line or throws out a word, and the rest come in with a chorus, as they walk along, bending the shoulder to the pole. The leader—the "shanty man" the English sailors call their leader, from the French *chanter*, I suppose—ejaculates a phrase, sometimes prolonging it, or dwelling on it with a variation, like "O! Mohammed!" or "O! Howadji!" or some scraps from a love-song, and the men strike in in chorus: "Hā Yālēsah, hā Yālēsah," a response that the boatmen have used for hundreds of years.

We sail leisurely past a large mud village dropped in a splendid grove of palms and acacias. The scene is very poetical before details are inspected, and the groves, we think, ought to be the homes of refinement and luxury. Men are building a boat under the long arcade of trees, women are stooping with the eternal water-jars, which do not appear to retain fluid any better than the sieves of the Danaïdes, and naked children run along the bank crying "Backsheesh, O Howadji." Our shotgun brings down a pigeon-hawk close to the shore. A boy plunges in and gets it, handing it to us on deck from the bank, but not relinquishing his hold with one hand until he feels the half-piastre in the other. So early is distrust planted in the human breast.

Getting away from this idyllic scene, which has not a single resemblance to any civilized town, we work our way up to El Hamra late in the afternoon. This is the landing-place for Asioot; the city itself is a couple of miles inland, and could be reached by a canal at high water. We have come again into an active world, and there are evidences that this is a busy place. New boats are on the stocks, and there is a forge for making some sort of machinery. So much life has not been met with since we left Cairo. The furling our great sail is a fine sight as we round in to the bank, the sailors crawling out on the slender, hundred-feet-long yard, like monkeys, and drawing up the hanging slack with both feet and hands.

It is long since we have seen so many or so gaily-dressed people as are moving on shore; a procession of camels passes along; crowds of donkeys are pushed down to the boat by their noisy drivers; old women come to sell eggs, and white grease that pretends to be butter, and one of them pulls some live pigeons from a bag. We lie at the mud-bank, and classes of half-clad children, squatting in the sand, study us. Two other dahabeëhs are moored near us, their passengers sitting under the awning and indolently observing the novel scene, book in hand, after the manner of Nile voyagers.

These are the pictures constantly recurring on the river, only they are never the same in grouping or color, and they never weary one. It is wonderful, indeed, how satisfying the Nile is in itself, and how little effort travellers make for the society of each other. Boats pass or meet and exchange salutes, but with little more effusion than if they were on the Thames. Nothing afloat is so much like a private house as a dahabeëh, and I should think, by what we hear, that sociability decreases on the Nile with increase of travel and luxury.

CHAPTER XII.

SPENDING CHRISTMAS ON THE NILE.

PROBABLY this present writer has the distinction of being the only one who has written about the Nile and has not invented a new way of spelling the name of the town whose many minarets and brown roofs are visible over the meadows.

It is written Asioot, Asyoot, Asiüt, Ssout, Siôout, Osyoot, Osioot, O'Sioót, Siüt, Sioot, O'siout, Si-ôôt, Siout, Syouth, and so on, indefinitely. People take the liberty to spell names as they sound to them, and there is consequently a pleasing variety in the names of all places, persons, and things in Egypt; and when we add to the many ways of spelling an Arabic word, the French, the German, and the English translation or equivalent, you are in a hopeless jumble of nomenclature. The only course is to strike out boldly and spell everything as it seems good in your eyes, and differently in different moods. Even the name of the Prophet takes on half a dozen forms; there are not only ninety-nine names of the attributes of God, but I presume there are ninety-nine ways of spelling each of them.

This Asioot has always been a place of importance. It was of old called Lycopolis, its divinity being the wolf or the wolf-headed god; and in a rock-mountain behind the town were not only cut the tombs of the inhabitants, but there were deposited the mummies of the sacred wolves. About these no one in Asioot knows or cares much, to-day. It is a city of twenty-five thousand people, with a good many thriving Copt Christians; the terminus, to-day, of the railway, and the point of arrival and departure of the caravans to and from Darfoor—a desert march of a month. Here are made the best clay pipe-bowls in Egypt, and a great variety of ornamented dishes and vases in clay, which the traveller buys and doesn't know what to do with. The artisans also work up elephants' tusks and ostrich feathers into a variety of "notions."

Christmas day opens warm and with an air of festivity. Great palm-branches are planted along the bank and form an arbor over the gang-plank. The cabin is set with them, in gothic arches over windows and doors, with yellow oranges at the apex. The forward and saloon decks are completely embowered in palms, which also run up the masts and spars. The crew have entered with zeal into the decoration, and in the early morning transformed the boat into a floating bower of greenery; the effect is Oriental, but it is difficult to believe that this is really Christmas day. The weather is not right, for one thing. It is singularly pleasant, in fact like summer. We miss the usual snow and ice and the hurtling of savage winds that bring suffering to the poor and make charity meritorious. Besides, the Moslems are celebrating the day for us, and, I fear, regarding it simply as an occasion of backsheesh. The sailors are very quick to understand so much of our religion as is profitable to themselves.

In such weather as this it would be possible for "shepherds to watch their flocks by night."

Early in the day we have a visit from Wasef el Khyat, the American consul here for many years, a Copt and a native of Asioot, who speaks only Arabic; he is accompanied by one of his sons, who was educated at the American college in Beyrout. So far does that excellent institution send its light; scattered rays, to be sure, but it is from it and such schools that the East is getting the real impetus of civilization. I do not know what the consul at Asioot does for America, but our flag is of great service to him, protecting his property from the exactions of his own government. Wasef is consequently very polite to all Americans, and while he sipped coffee and puffed cigars in our cabin he smiled unutterable things. This is the pleasantest kind of intercourse in a warm climate, where a puff and an occasional smile will pass for profuse expressions of social enjoyment.

His Excellency Shakirr Pasha, the governor of this large and rich province, has sent word that he is about to put carriages and donkeys at our disposal, but this probably meant that the consul would do it; and the consul has done it. The carriage awaits us on the bank. It is a high, paneled, venerable ark, that moves with trembling dignity; and we choose the donkeys as less pretentious and less liable to come to pieces. This is no doubt the only carriage between Cairo and Kartoom, and its appearance is regarded as an event.

Our first visit is paid to the pasha, who has been only a few days in his province, and has not yet transferred his harem from Cairo. We are received with distinguished ceremony, to the lively satisfaction of Abd-el-Atti, whose face beams like the morning, in bringing together such "distinguish" people as his friend the pasha, and travellers in his charge. The pasha is a courtly Turk, of most elegant manners, and the simplicity of high breeding, a man of the world, and one of the ablest governors in Egypt. The room into which we are ushered, through a dirty alley and a mud wall court, is hardly in keeping with the social stilts on which we are all walking. In our own less favored land, it would answer very well for a shed or an out-house to store beans in, or for a "reception room" for sheep; a narrow oblong apartment, covered with a flat roof of palm logs, with a couple of dirty little windows high up, the once whitewashed walls stained variously, the cheap divans soiled.

The hospitality of this gorgeous *salon* was offered us with effusion, and we sat down and exchanged compliments as if we had been in a palace. I am convinced that there is nothing like the Oriental imagination. An attendant (and the servants were in keeping with the premises) brought in *fingans* of coffee. The servant presents the cup in his right hand, holding the bottom of the silver receptacle in his thumb and finger; he takes it away empty with both hands, placing the left under and the right on top of it. These formalities are universal and all-important. Before taking it you ought to make the salutation by touching breast, lips, and forehead, with the right hand —an acknowledgment not to the servant but to the master. Cigars are then handed round, for it is getting to be considered on the Nile that cigars are more "swell" than pipes; more's the pity.

The exchange of compliments meantime went on, and on the part of the pasha with a fineness, adroitness, and readiness that showed the practice of a lifetime in social fence. He surpassed our most daring invention with a smiling ease, and topped all our extravagances with an art that made our poor efforts appear clumsy. And what the effect would have been if we could have understood the flowery Arabic I can only guess; nor can we ever know how many flowers of his own the dragoman cast in.

"His excellency say that he feel the honor of your visit."

"Say to his excellency that although we are only spending one day in his beautiful capital, we could not forego the pleasure of paying our respects to his excellency." This sentence is built by the critic, and strikes us all favorably.

"His excellency himself not been here many days, and sorry he not know you coming, to make some preparations to receive you."

"Thank his excellency for the palms that decorate our boat."

"They are nothing, nothing, he say not mention it; the dahabeëh look very different now if the Nile last summer had not wash away all his flower-garden. His excellency say, how you enjoyed your voyage?"

"It has been very pleasant; only for a day or two we have wanted wind."

"Your misfortune, his excellency say, his pleasure; it give him the opportunity of your society. But he say if you want wind he sorry no wind; it cause him to suffer that you not come here sooner."

"Will his excellency dine with us to-day?"

"He say he think it too much honor."

"Assure his excellency that we feel that the honor is conferred by him."

And he consents to come. After we have taken our leave, the invitation is extended to the consul, who is riding with us.

The way to the town is along a winding, shabby embankment, raised above high water, and shaded with sycamore-trees. It is lively with people on foot and on donkeys, in more colored and richer dress than that worn by country-people; the fields are green, the clover is springing luxuriantly, and spite of the wrecks of unburned-brick houses, left gaping by the last flood and spite of the general untidiness of everything, the ride is enjoyable. I don't know why it is that an irrigated country never is pleasing on close inspection, neither is an irrigated garden. Both need to be seen from a little distance, which conceals the rawness of the alternately dry and soaked soil, the frequent thinness of vegetation, the unkempt swampy appearance of the lowest levels, and the painful whiteness of paths never wet and the dustiness of trees unwashed by rain. There is no Egyptian landscape or village that is neat, on near inspection.

Asioot has a better entrance than most towns, through an old gateway into the square (which is the court of the palace), and the town has extensive bazaars and some large dwellings; But as we ride through it, we are always hemmed in by mud-walls, twisting through narrow alleys, encountering dirt and poverty at every step. We pass through the quarter of the Ghawázees, who, since their banishment from Cairo, form little colonies in all the large Nile towns. These are the dancing-women whom travellers are so desirous of seeing; the finest-looking women and the most abandoned courtesans, says Mr. Lane, in Egypt. In showy dresses of bright yellow and red, adorned with a profusion of silver-gilt necklaces, earrings, and bracelets, they sit at the doors of their hovels in idle expectation. If these happen to be the finest-looking women in Egypt, the others are wise in keeping their veils on.

Outside the town we find a very pretty cemetery of the Egyptian style, staring white tombs, each dead person resting under his own private little stucco oven. Near it is encamped a caravan just in from Darfoor, bringing cinnamon, gum-arabic, tusks, and ostrich feathers. The camels are worn with the journey; their drivers have a fierce and free air in striking contrast with the bearing of the fellaheen. Their noses are straight, their black hair is long and shaggy, their garment is a single piece of coarse brown cloth; they have the wildness of the desert.

The soft limestone ledge back of the town is honeycombed with grottoes and tombs, rising in tiers from the bottom to the top. Some of them have merely square-cut entrances into a chamber of moderate size, in some part of which, or in a passage beyond, is a pit cut ten or twenty feet deep in the rock, like a grave, for the mummy. One of them has a magnificent entrance through a doorway over thirty feet high and fifteen deep; upon the jambs are gigantic figures cut in the rock. Some of the chambers are vast and were once pillared, and may have served for dwellings. These excavations are very old. The hieroglyphics and figures on the walls are not in relief on the stone, but cut in at the outer edge and left in a gradual swell in the centre—an *intaglio relievato*. The drawing is generally spirited, and the figures show knowledge of form and artistic skill. It is wonderful that such purely conventional figures, the head almost always in profile and the shoulders square to the front, can be so expressive. On one wall is a body of infantry marching, with the long pointed shields mentioned by Xenophon in describing Egyptian troops. Everywhere are birds, gracefully drawn and true to species, and upon some of them the blue color is fresh. A ceiling of one grotto is wrought in ornamental squares—a "Greek pattern," executed long before the time of the Greeks. Here we find two figures with the full face turned towards us, instead of the usual profile.

These tombs have served for a variety of purposes. As long as the original occupants rested here, no doubt their friends came and feasted and were mournfully merry in these sightly chambers overlooking the Nile. Long after they were turned out, Christian hermits nested in them, during that extraordinary period of superstition when men thought they could best secure their salvation by living like wild beasts in the deserts of Africa. Here one John of Lycopolis had his den, in which he stayed fifty years, without ever opening the door or seeing the face of a woman. At least, he enjoyed that reputation. Later, persecuted Christians dwelt in these tombs, and after them have come wanderers, and jackals, and houseless Arabs. I think I should rather live here than in Asioot; the tombs are cleaner and better built than the houses of the town, and there is good air here and no danger of floods.

When we are on the top of the bluff, the desert in broken ridges is behind us. The view is one of the best of the usual views from hills near the Nile, the elements of which are similar; the spectator has Egypt in all its variety at his feet. The valley here is broad, and we look a long distance up and down the river. The Nile twists and turns in its bed like one of the chimerical serpents sculptured in the chambers of the dead; canals wander from it through the plain; and groves of palms and lines of sycamores contrast their green with that of the fields. All this level expanse is now covered with wheat, barley and thick clover, and the green has a vividness that we have never seen in vegetation before. This owes somewhat to the brown contrast near at hand and something maybe to the atmosphere, but, I think the growing grain has a lustre unknown to other lands. The smiling picture is enclosed by the savage frame of the desert, gaunt ridges of rocky hills, drifts of stones, and yellow sand that sends its hot tongues in long darts into the plain. At the foot of the mountain lies Asioot, brown as the mud of the Nile, a city built of sun-dried bricks, but presenting a singular and not unpleasing appearance on account of the dozen white stone minarets, some of them worked like lace, which spring out of it.

The consul's home is one of the best in the city, but outside it shows only a mud-wall like the meanest. Within is a paved court, and offices about it; the rooms above are large, many-windowed, darkened with blinds, and not unlike those of a plain house in America. The furniture is European mainly, and ugly, and of course out of place in Africa. We see only the male members of the family. Confectionery and coffee are served and some champagne, that must have been made by the Peninsular and Oriental Steamship Company; their champagne is well known in the Levant, and there is no known decoction that is like it. In my judgment, if it is proposed to introduce Christianity and that kind of wine into Egypt, the country would better be left as it is.

During our call the consul presents us fly-whisks with ivory handles, and gives the ladies beautiful fans of ostrich feathers mounted in ivory. These presents may have been due to a broad hint from the Pasha, who said to the consul at our interview in the morning:—

"I should not like to have these distinguished strangers go away without some remembrance of Asioot. I have not been here long; what is there to get for them?"

"O, your excellency, I will attend to that," said the consul.

In the evening, with the dahabeëh beautifully decorated and hung with colored lanterns, upon the deck, which, shut in with canvas and spread with Turkish rugs, was a fine reception-room, we awaited our guests, as if we had been accustomed to this sort of thing in America from our infancy, and as if we usually celebrated Christmas outdoors, fans in hand, with fireworks. A stand for the exhibition of fireworks had been erected on shore. The pasha was received as he stepped on board, with three rockets (that being, I suppose, the number of his official "tails,"), which flew up into the sky and scattered their bursting bombs of color amid the stars, announcing to the English dahabeëhs, the two steamboats and the town of Asioot, that the governor of the richest province in Egypt was about to eat his dinner.

The dinner was one of those perfections that one likes to speak of only in confidential moments to dear friends. It wanted nothing either in number of courses or in variety, in meats, in confections, in pyramids of gorgeous construction, in fruits and flowers. There was something touching about the lamb roasted whole, reclining his head on his own shoulder. There was something tender about the turkey. There was a terrible moment when the plum-pudding was borne in on fire, as if it had been a present from the devil himself. The pasha regarded it with distrust, and declined, like a wise man, to eat flame. I fear that the English have fairly introduced this dreadful dish into the Orient, and that the natives have come to think that all foreigners are Molochs who can best be pleased by offering up to them its indigestible ball set on fire of H. It is a fearful spectacle to see this heathen people offering this incense to a foreign idol, in the subserviency which will sacrifice even religion to backsheesh.

The conversation during dinner is mostly an exchange of compliments, in the art of which the pasha is a master, displaying in it a wit, a variety of resource and a courtliness that make the game a very entertaining one. The Arabic language gives full play to this sort of social *espièglerie*, and lends a delicacy to encounters of compliment which the English language does not admit.

Coffee and pipes are served on deck, and the fireworks begin to tear and astonish the night. The Khedive certainly employs very good pyrotechnists, and the display by Abd-el-Atti and his equally excited helpers, although simple, is brilliant. The intense delight that the soaring and bursting of a rocket gives to Abd-el-Atti is expressed in unconscious and unrestrained demonstration. He might be himself in flames but he would watch the flight of the rushing stream of fire, jumping up and down in his anxiety for it to burst:—

"There! there! that's-a he, hooray!"

Every time one bursts, scattering its colored stars, the crew, led by the dragoman, cheer,

"Heep, heep, hooray! heep, heep, hooray!"

A whirligig spins upon the river, spouting balls of fire, and the crew come in with a "Heep, heep, hooray! heep, heep, hooray!"

The steamer, which has a Belgian prince on board, illuminates, and salutes with shot guns. In the midst of a fusillade of rockets and Roman candles, the crew develope a new accomplishment. Drilled by the indomitable master of ceremonies, they attempt the first line of that distinctively American melody,

"We won't go home till morning."

They really catch the air, and make a bubble, bubble of sounds, like automata, that somewhat resemble the words. Probably they think that it is our national anthem, or perhaps a Christmas hymn. No doubt, "won't-go-home-till-morning" sort of Americans have been up the river before us.

The show is not over when the pasha pleads an engagement to take a cup of tea with the Belgian prince, and asks permission to retire. He expresses his anguish at leaving us, and he will not depart if we say "no." Of course, our anguish in letting the pasha go exceeds his suffering in going, but we sacrifice ourselves to the demand of his station, and permit him to depart. At the foot of the cabin stairs he begs us to go no further, insisting that we do him too much honor to come so far.

The soft night grows more brilliant. Abd-el-Atti and his minions are still blazing away. The consul declares that Asioot in all his life has never experienced a night like this. We express ourselves as humbly thankful in being the instruments of giving Asioot (which is asleep there two miles off) such an "eye-opener." (This remark has a finer sound when translated into Arabic.)

The spectacle closes by a voyage out upon the swift river in the sandal. We take Roman candles, blue, red, and green lights and floaters which Abd-el-Atti lets off, while the crew hoarsely roar "We won't go home till morning," and mingle "Heep, heep, hooray," with "Hā Yalēsah, hā Yalēsah."

The long range of lights on the steamers, the flashing lines and pyramids of colors on our own dahabeëh, the soft June-like night, the moon coming up in fleecy clouds, the broad Nile sparkling under so many fires, kindled on earth and in the sky, made a scene unique, and as beautiful as any that the Arabian Nights suggest.

To end all, there was a hubbub on shore among the crew, caused by one of them who was crazy with hasheesh, and threatened to murder the reïs and dragoman, if he was not permitted to go on board. It could be demonstrated that he was less likely to slay them if he did not come on board, and he was therefore sent to the governor's lock-up, with a fair prospect of going into the Khedive's army. We left him behind, and about one o'clock in the morning stole away up the river with a gentle and growing breeze.

Net result of pleasure:—one man in jail, and Abd-el-Atti's wrist so seriously burned by the fireworks, that he has no use of his arm for weeks. But, "'twas a glorious victory." For a Christmas, however, it was a little too much like the Fourth of July.

CHAPTER XIII.

SIGHTS AND SCENES ON THE RIVER.

AS WE sail down into the heart of Egypt and into the remote past, living in fact by books and by eye-sight, in eras so far-reaching that centuries count only as years in them, the word "ancient" gets a new signification. We pass every day ruins, ruins of the Old Empire, of the Middle Empire, of the Ptolomies, of the Greeks, of the Romans, of the Christians, of the Saracens; but nothing seems ancient to us any longer except the remains of Old Egypt.

We have come to have a singular contempt for anything so modern as the work of the Greeks, or Romans. Ruins pointed out on shore as Roman do not interest us enough to force us to raise the field-glass. Small antiquities that are of the Roman period are not considered worth examination. The natives have a depreciatory shrug when they say of an idol or a brick-wall, "Roman!"

The Greeks and the Romans are moderns like ourselves. They are as broadly separated in the spirit of their life and culture from those ancients as we are; we can understand them; it is impossible for us to enter into the habits of thought and of life of the early Pharaonic times. When the variation of two thousand years in the assignment of a dynasty seems to us a trifle, the two thousand years that divide us and the Romans shrink into no importance.

In future ages the career of the United States and of Rome will be reckoned in the same era; and children will be taught the story of George Washington suckled by the wolf, and Romulus cutting the cherry-tree with his little hatchet. We must have distance in order to put things in their proper relations. In America, what have we that will endure a thousand years? Even George Washington's hatchet may be forgotten sooner than the *flabellum* of Pharaoh.

The day after Christmas we are going with a stiff wind, so fresh that we can carry only the forward sail. The sky is cloudy and stormy-looking. It is in fact as disagreeable and as sour a fall day as you can find anywhere. We keep the cabin, except for a time in the afternoon, when it is comfortable sitting on deck in an overcoat. We fly by Abooteeg; Raáineh, a more picturesque village, the top of every house being a pigeon-tower; Gow, with its remnants of old Antæopolis—it was in the river here that Horus defeated Typhon in a great battle, as, thank God! he is always doing in this flourishing world, with a good chance of killing him outright some day, when Typhon will no more take the shape of crocodile or other form of evil, war, or paper currency; Tahtah, conspicuous by its vast mounds of an ancient city; and Gebel Sheykh Hereédee, near the high cliffs of which we run, impressed by the grey and frowning crags.

As we are passing these rocks a small boat dashes out to our side, with a sail in tatters and the mast carrying a curiously embroidered flag, the like of which is in no signal-book. In the stern of this fantastic craft sits a young and very shabbily clad sheykh, and demands backsheesh, as if he had a right to demand toll of all who pass his dominions. This right our reïs acknowledges and tosses him some paras done up in a rag. I am sure I like this sort of custom-house better than some I have seen.

We go on in the night past Soohag, the capital of the province of Girgeh; and by other villages and spots of historic interest, where the visitor will find only some heaps of stones and rubbish to satisfy a curiosity raised by reading of their former importance; by the White Monastery and the Red Convent; and, coming round a bend, as we always are coming round a bend, and bringing the wind ahead, the crew probably asleep; we ignominiously run into the bank, and finally come to anchor in mid-stream.

As if to crowd all weathers into twenty-four hours, it clears off cold in the night; and in the morning when we are opposite the pretty town of Ekhmeem, a temperature of 51° makes it rather fresh for the men who line the banks working the shadoofs, with no covering but breech-cloths. The people here, when it is cold, bundle up about the head and shoulders with thick wraps, and leave the feet and legs bare. The natives are huddled in clusters on the bank, out of the shade of the houses, in order to get the warmth of the sun; near one group a couple of discontented camels kneel; and the naked boy, making no pretence of a superfluous wardrobe by hanging his shirt on a bush while he goes to bed, is holding it up to dry.

We skim along in almost a gale the whole day, passing in the afternoon an American dahabeëh tied up, repairing a broken yard, and giving Bellianeh the go-by as if it were of no importance. And yet this is the landing for the great Abydus, a city once second only to Thebes, the burial-place of Osiris himself, and still marked by one of the finest temples in Egypt. But our business now is navigation, and we improve the night as well as the day; much against the grain of the crew. There is always more or less noise and row in a night sail, going aground, splashing, and boosting in the water to get off, shouting and chorusing and tramping on deck, and when the thermometer is as low as 52° these night-baths are not very welcome when followed by exposure to keen wind, in a cotton shirt. And with the dragoman in bed, used up like one of his burnt-out rockets, able only to grumble at "dese fellow care for nothing but smoke hasheesh," the crew are not very subordinate. They are liable to go to sleep and let us run aground, or they are liable to run aground in order that they may go to sleep. They seem to try both ways alternately.

But moving or stranded, the night is brilliant all the same; the night-skies are the more lustrous the farther we go from the moisture of Lower Egypt, and the stars scintillate with splendor, and flash deep colors like diamonds in sunlight. Late, the moon rises over the mountains under which we are sailing, and the effect is magically lovely. We are approaching Farshoot.

Farshoot is a market-town and has a large sugar-factory, the first set-up in Egypt, built by an uncle of the Khedive. It was the seat of power of the Howara tribe of Arabs, and famous for its breed of Howara horses and dogs, the latter bigger and fiercer than the little wolfish curs with which Egypt swarms. It is much like other Egyptian towns now, except that its inhabitants, like its dogs, are a little wilder and more ragged than the fellaheen below. This whole district of Hamram is exceedingly fertile and bursting with a tropical vegetation.

The Turkish governor pays a formal visit and we enjoy one of those silent and impressive interviews over chibooks and coffee, in which nothing is said that one can regret. We finally make the governor a complimentary speech, which Hoseyn, who only knows a little table-English, pretends to translate The bey replies, talking very rapidly for two or three minutes. When we asked Hoseyn to translate, he smiled and said—" Thank you "—which was no doubt the long palaver.

The governor conducts us through the sugar-factory, which is not on so grand a scale as those we shall see later, but hot enough and sticky enough, and then gives us the inevitable coffee in his office ; seemingly, if you clap your hands anywhere in Egypt, a polite and ragged attendant will appear with a tiny cup of coffee.

The town is just such a collection of mud-hovels as the others, and we learn nothing new in it. Yes, we do. We learn how to scour brass dishes. We see at the doorway of a house where a group of women sit on the ground waiting for their hair to grow, two boys actively engaged in this scouring process. They stand in the dishes, which have sand in them, and, supporting themselves by the side of the hut, whirl half-way round and back. The soles of their feet must be like leather. This method of scouring is worth recording, as it may furnish an occupation for boys at an age when they are usually, and certainly here, useless.

The weekly market is held in the open air at the edge of the town. The wares for sale are spread upon the ground, the people sitting behind them in some sort of order, but the crowd surges everywhere and the powdered dust rises in clouds. It is the most motley assembly we have seen. The women are tattooed on the face and on the breast; they wear anklets of bone and of silver, and are loaded with silver ornaments. As at every other place where a fair, a wedding, or a funeral attracts a crowd, there are some shanties of the Ghawazees, who are physically superior to the other women, but more tattooed, their necks, bosoms and waists covered with their whole fortune of silver, their eyelids heavily stained with kohl —bold-looking jades, who come out and stare at us with a more than masculine impudence.

The market offers all sorts of green country produce, and eggs, corn, donkeys, sheep, lentils, tobacco, pipe-stems, and cheap ornaments in glass. The crowd hustles about us in a troublesome manner, showing special curiosity about the ladies, as if they had rarely seen white women. Ahmed and another sailor charge into them with their big sticks to open a passage for us, but they follow us, commenting freely upon our appearance. The sailors jabber at them and at us, and are anxious to get us back to the boat, where we learn that the natives "not like you." The feeling is mutual, though it is discouraging to our pride to be despised by such barbarous half-clad folk.

Beggars come to the boat continually for backsheesh; a tall juggler in a white, dirty tunic, with a long snake coiled about his neck, will not go away for less than half a piastre. One tariff piastre (five cents) buys four eggs here, double the price of former years, but still discouraging to a hen. However, the hens have learned to lay their eggs small. All the morning we are trading in the desultory way in which everything is done here, buying a handful of eggs at a time, and live chickens by the single one.

In the afternoon the boat is tracked along through a land that is bursting with richness, waving with vast fields of wheat, of lentils, of sugar-cane, interspersed with melons and beans. The date-palms are splendid in stature and mass of crown. We examine for the first time the Dôm palm, named from its shape, which will not flourish much lower on the river than here. Its stem grows up a little distance, and then branches in two, and these two limbs each branch in two; always in two. The leaves are shorter than those of the date-palm, and the tree is altogether more scraggy, but at a little distance it assumes the dome form. The fruit, now green, hangs in large bunches a couple of feet long; each fruit is the size of a large Flemish Beauty pear. It has a thick rind, and a stone, like vegetable ivory, so hard that it is used for drill-sockets. The fibrous rind is gnawed off by the natives when it is ripe, and is said to taste like gingerbread. These people live on gums and watery vegetables and fibrous stuff that wouldn't give a northern man strength enough to gather them.

We find also the *sont* acacia here, and dig the gum-arabic from its bark. In the midst of a great plain of wheat, intersected by ditches and raised footways, we come upon a *sakiya*, embowered in trees, which a long distance off makes itself known by the most doleful squeaking. These water-wheels, which are not unlike those used by the Persians, are not often seen lower down the river, where the water is raised by the shadoof. Here we find a well sunk to the depth of the Nile, and bricked up. Over it is a wheel, upon which is hung an endless rope of palm fibres, and on its outer rim are tied earthen jars. As the wheel revolves these jars dip into the well, and coming up discharge the water into a wooden trough, whence it flows into channels of earth. The cogs of this wheel fit into another, and the motive power of the clumsy machine is furnished by a couple of oxen or cows, hitched to a pole swinging round an upright shaft. A little girl, seated on the end of the pole, is driving the oxen, whose slow hitching gait sets the machine rattling and squeaking as if in pain. Nothing is exactly in gear, the bearings are never oiled; half the water is spilled before it gets to the trough; but the thing keeps grinding on, night and day, and I suppose has not been improved or changed in its construction for thousands of years.

During our walk we are attended by a friendly crowd of men and boys; there are always plenty of them who are as idle as we are, and are probably very much puzzled to know why we roam about in this way. I am sure a New England farmer, if he saw a troop of these Arabs strolling through his corn-field, would set his dogs on them.

Both sides of the river are luxuriant here. The opposite bank, which is high, is lined with shadoofs, generally in sets of three, in order to raise the water to the required level. The view is one long to remember:—the long curving shore, with the shadoofs and the workmen, singing as they dip; people in flowing garments moving along the high bank, and processions of donkeys and camels as well; rows of palms above them, and beyond the purple Libyan hills, in relief against a rosy sky, slightly clouded along the even mountain line. In the foreground the Nile is placid and touched with a little colour.

We feel more and more that the Nile is Egypt. Everything takes place on its banks. From our boat we study its life at our leisure. The Nile is always vocal with singing, or scolding, or calling to prayer; it is always lively with boatmen or work-

SIGHTS AND SCENES ON THE RIVER.

men, or picturesque groups, or women filling their water-jars. It is the highway; it is a spectacle a thousand miles long. It supplies everything. I only wonder at one thing. Seeing that it is so swift, and knowing that it flows down and out into a world whence so many wonders come, I marvel that its inhabitants are contented to sit on its banks year after year, generation after generation, shut in behind and before by desert hills, without any desire to sail down the stream and get into a larger world. We meet rather intelligent men who have never journeyed so far as the next large town.

Thus far we have had only a few days of absolutely cloudless skies; usually we have some clouds, generally at sunrise and sunset, and occasionally an overcast day like this. But the cloudiness is merely a sort of shade; there is no possibility of rain in it.

And, sure of good weather, why should we hasten? In fact, we do not. It is something to live a life that has in it neither worry nor responsibility. We take an interest, however, in How and Disnah and Fow, places where people have been living and dying now for a long time, which we cannot expect you to share. In the night while we are anchored a breeze springs up, and Abd-el-Atti roars at the sailors to rouse them, but unsuccessfully, until he cries,

"Come to prayer!"

The sleepers, waking, answer,

"God is great, and Mohammed is his prophet."

They then get up and set the sail. This is what it is to carry religion into daily life.

To-day we have been going northward, for variety. Keneh, which is thirty miles higher up the river than How, is nine minutes further north. The Nile itself loiters through the land. As the crew are poling slowly along, this hot summer day, we have nothing to do but to enjoy the wide and glassy Nile, its fertile banks vocal with varied life. The songs of Nubian boatmen, rowing in measured stroke down the stream, come to us. The round white wind-mills of Keneh are visible on the sand-hills above the town. Children are bathing, and cattle and donkeys wading in the shallows, and the shrill chatter of women is heard on the shore. If this is winter, I wonder what summer here is like.

CHAPTER XIV.

MIDWINTER IN EGYPT.

WHETHER we go north or south, or wait for some wandering, unemployed wind to take us round the next bend, it is all the same to us. We have ceased to care much for time, and I think we shall adopt the Assyrian system of reckoning.

The period of the precession of the equinoxes was regarded as *one day* of the life of the universe; and this day equals 43,200 of our years. This day, of 43,200 years, the Assyrians divided into twelve cosmic *hours* or "sars," each one of 3,600 years; each of these hours into six "ners," of 6000 years; and the "ner" into ten "sosses" or cosmic *minutes*, of 600 years. And thus, as we reckon sixty seconds to a minute, our ordinary year was a *second* of the great chronological period. What then is the value of a mere second of time? What if we do lie half a day at this bank, in the sun, waiting for a lazy breeze? There certainly is time enough, for we seem to have lived a cosmic hour since we landed in Egypt.

One sees here what an exaggerated importance we are accustomed to attach to the exact measurement of time. We constantly compare our watches, and are anxious that they should not gain or lose a second. A person feels his own importance somehow increased if he owns an accurate watch. There is nothing that a man resents more than the disparagement of his watch. (It occurs to me, by the way, that the superior attractiveness of women, that quality of repose and rest which the world finds in them, springs from the same amiable *laisser aller* that suffers their watches never to be correct. When the day comes that women's watches keep time, there will be no peace in this world.) When two men meet, one of the most frequent interchanges of courtesies is to compare watches; certainly, if the question of time is raised, as it is sure to be shortly among a knot of men with us, every one pulls out his watch, and comparison is made.

We are, in fact, the slaves of time and of fixed times. We think it a great loss and misfortune to be without the correct time; and if we are away from the town-clock and the noon-gun, in some country place, we importune the city stranger, who appears to have a good watch, for the time; or we lie in wait for the magnificent conductor of the railway express, who always has the air of getting the promptest time from headquarters.

Here in Egypt we see how unnatural and unnecessary this anxiety is. Why should we care to know the exact time? It is 12 o'clock, Arab time, at sunset, and that shifts every evening, in order to wean us from the rigidity of iron habits. Time is flexible, it waits on our moods and we are not slaves to its accuracy. Watches here never agree, and no one cares whether they do or not. My own, which was formerly as punctual as the stars in their courses, loses on the Nile a half hour or three quarters of an hour a day (speaking in our arbitrary, artificial manner); so that, if I were good at figures, I could cypher out the length of time which would suffice, by the *loss* of time by my watch, to set me back into the age of Thothmes III.—a very good age to be in. We are living now by great cosmic periods and have little care for minute divisions of time.

This morning we are at Ballás, no one knows how, for we anchored three times in the night. At Ballás are made the big earthen jars which the women carry on their heads, and which are sent from here the length of Egypt. Immense numbers of them are stacked upon the banks, and boat-loads of them are waiting for the wind. Rafts of these jars are made and floated down to the Delta; a frail structure, one would say, in the swift and shallow Nile, but below this place there are neither rocks in the stream nor stones on the shore.

The sunrise is magnificent, opening a cloudless day, a day of hot sun, in which the wheat on the banks and under the palm groves, now knee-high and a vivid green, sparkles as if it had dew on it. At night there are colors of salmon and rose in the sky and on the water; and the end of the mountain, where Thebes lies, takes a hue of greyish or pearly pink. Thebes! And we are really coming to Thebes! It is fit that it should lie in such a bath of color. Very near to-night seems that great limestone ledge in which the Thebans entombed their dead; but it is by the winding river thirty miles distant.

The last day of the year 1874 finds us lounging about in this pleasant Africa, very much after the leisurely manner of an ancient maritime expedition, the sailors of which spent most of their time in marauding on shore, watching for auguries, and sailing a little when the deities favored. The attempts, the failures, the mismanagements of the day add not a little to your entertainment on the Nile.

In the morning a light breeze springs up and we are slowly crawling forward, when the wind expires, and we come to anchor in mid-stream. The Nile here is wide and glassy, but it is swift, and full of eddies that make this part of the river exceedingly difficult of navigation. We are too far from the shore for tracking, and another resource is tried. The sandal is sent ahead with an anchor and a cable, the intention being to drop the anchor and then by the cable pull up to it, and repeat the process until we get beyond these eddies and treacherous sand-bars.

Of course the sailors in the sandal, who never think of two things at the same time, miscalculate the distance, and after they drop the anchor, have not rope enough to get back to the dahabeëh. They are, just above us, and just out of reach, in a most helpless condition, but quite resigned to it. After various futile experiments they make a line with their tracking-cords and float an oar to us, and we send them rope to lengthen their cable. Nearly an hour is consumed in this. When the cable is attached, the crew begin slowly to haul it in through the pullies, walking the short deck in a round and singing chorus of, "O Mohammed," to some catch-word or phrase of the leader. They like this, it is the kind of work that boys prefer, a sort of frolic:—

    Allah, Allah!"

And in response,

"O Mohammed!"
"God forgive us!"
"O Mohammed!"
"God is most great!"
"O Mohammed!"
"El Hoseyn!"
"O Mohammed!"

And so they go round as hilarious as if they played at leap-frog, with no limit of noise and shouting. They cannot haul a rope or pull an oar without this vocal expression. When the anchor is reached it is time for the crew to eat dinner.

We make not more than a mile all day, with hard work, but we reach the shore. We have been two days in this broad, beautiful bend of the river, surrounded by luxuriant fields and palm-groves, the picture framed in rosy mountains of limestone which glow in the clear sunshine. It is a becalmment in an enchanted place, out of which there seems to be no way, and if there were we are loosing the desire to go. At night, as we lie at the bank, a row of ragged fallaheen line the high shore, like buzzards, looking down on us. There is something admirable in their patience, the only virtue they seem to practise.

Later, Abd-el-Atti is thrown into a great excitement upon learning that this is the last day of the year. He had set his heart on being at Luxor, and celebrating the New Year with a grand illumination and burst of fire-works. If he had his way we should go blazing up the river in a perpetual fizz of pyrotechnic glory. At Luxor especially, where many boats are usually gathered, and which is for many the end of the voyage, the dragomans like to outshine each other in display. This is the fashionable season at Thebes, and the harvest-time of its merchants of antiquities; entertainments are given on shore, boats are illuminated, and there is a general rivalry in gaiety. Not to be in Thebes on New Year's is a misfortune. Something must be done. The sheykh of the village of Tookh is sent for, in the hope that he can help us round the bend. The sheykh comes, and sits on the deck and smokes. Orion also comes up the eastern sky, like a conqueror, blazing amid a blazing heaven. But we don't stir.

Upon the bank sits the guard of men from the village, to protect us; the sight of the ragamuffins grouped round their lanterns is very picturesque. Whenever we tie up at night we are obliged to procure from the sheykh of the nearest village a guard to keep thieves from robbing us, for the thieves are not only numerous but expert all along the Nile. No wonder. They have to steal their own crops, in order to get a fair share of the produce of the land they cultivate under the exactions of the government. The sheykh would not dare to refuse the guard asked for. The office of sheykh is still hereditary from father to eldest son, and the sheykh has authority over his own village, according to the ancient custom, but he is subject to a bey, set by the government to rule a district.

New Year's morning is bright, sparkling, cloudless. When I look from my window early, the same row of buzzards sit on the high bank, looking down upon our deck and peering into our windows. Brown, ragged heaps of humanity; I suppose they are human. One of the youngsters makes mouths and faces at me; and, no doubt, despises us, as dogs and unbelievers. Behold our critic:—he has on a single coarse brown garment, through which his tawny skin shows in spots, and he squats in the sand.

What can come out of such a people? Their ignorance exceeds their poverty; and they appear to own nothing save a single garment. They look not ill-fed, but ill-conditioned. And the country is skinned; all the cattle, the turkeys, the chickens are lean. The fatness of the land goes elsewhere.

In what contrast are these people, in situation, in habits, in every thought, to the farmers of America. This Nile valley is in effect cut off from the world; nothing of what we call news enters it, no news, or book, no information of other countries, nor of any thought, or progress, or occurrences. These people have not, in fact, the least conception of what the world is; they know no more of geography than they do of history. They think the world is flat, with an ocean of water round it. Mecca is the centre. It is a religious necessity that the world should be flat in order to have Mecca its centre. All Moslems believe that it is flat, as a matter of faith, though a few intelligent men know better.

These people, as I say, do not know anything, as we estimate knowledge. And yet these watchmen and the group on the bank talked all night long; their tongues were racing incessantly, and it appeared to be conversation and not monologue or narration. What could they have been talking about? Is talk in the inverse ratio of knowledge, and do we lose the power or love for mere talk, as we read and are informed ?

These people, however, know the news of the river. There is a sort of freemasonry of communication by which whatever occurs is flashed up and down both banks. They know all about the boats and who are on them, and the name of the dragomans, and hear of all the accidents and disasters.

There was an American this year on the river by the name of Smith—not that I class the coming of Smith as a disaster—who made the voyage on a steamboat. He did not care much about temples or hieroglyphics, and he sought to purchase no antiquities. He took his enjoyment in another indulgence. Having changed some of his pounds sterling into copper paras, he brought bags of this money with him. When the boat stopped at a town Smith did not go ashore. He stood on deck and flung his coppers with a free hand at the group of idlers he was sure to find there. But Smith combined amusement with his benevolence, by throwing his largesse into the sand and into the edge of the river, where the recipients of it would have to fight and scramble and dive for what they got. When he cast a handful there was always a tremendous scrimmage, a rolling of body over body, a rending of garments, and a tumbling into the river. This feat not only amused Smith, but it made him the most popular man on the river. Fast as the steamer went, his fame ran before him, and at every landing there was sure to be a waiting crowd, calling "Smit, Smit." There has been no one in Egypt since Cambyses who has made so much stir as Smit.

I should not like to convey the idea that the inhabitants here are stupid ; far from it ; they are only ignorant, and oppressed by long misgovernment. There is no inducement for any one to do more than make a living. The people have sharp countenances, they are lively, keen at a bargain, and, as we said, many of them expert thieves. They are full of deceit and cunning, and their affability is unfailing. Both vices and good qualities are products not of savagery, but of a civilization worn old and threadbare. The Eastern civilization generally is only one of manners, and I suspect that of the old Egyptian was no more.

These people may or may not have a drop of the ancient

Egyptian blood in them; they may be no more like the Egyptians of the time of the Pharoahs than the present European Jews are like the Jews of Judea in Herod's time; but it is evident that, in all the changes in the occupants of the Nile valley, there has been a certain continuity of habits, of modes of life, a holding to ancient traditions; the relation of men to the soil is little changed. The Biblical patriarchs, fathers of nomadic tribes, have their best representatives to-day, in mode of life and even in poetical and highly figurative speech, not in Israelite bankers in London nor in Israelite beggars in Jerusalem, but in the Bedaween of the desert. And I think the patient and sharp-witted, but never educated, Egyptians of old times are not badly represented by the present settlers in the Nile valley.

There are ages of hereditary strength in the limbs of the Egyptian women, who were here, carrying these big water-jars, before Menes turned the course of the Nile at Memphis. I saw one to-day sat down on her heels before a full jar that could not weigh less than a hundred pounds, lift it to her head with her hands, and then rise straight up with it, as if the muscles of her legs were steel. The jars may be heavier than I said, for I find a full one not easy to lift, and I never saw an Egyptian man touch one.

We go on towards Thebes slowly; though the river is not swifter here than elsewhere, we have the feeling that we are pulling up-hill. We come in the afternoon to Negádeh, and into one of the prettiest scenes on the Nile. The houses of the old town are all topped with pigeon-towers, and thousands of these birds are circling about the palm-groves or swooping in large flocks along the shore. The pigeons seem never to be slain by the inhabitants, but are kept for the sake of the fertilizer they furnish. It is the correct thing to build a second story to your house for a deposit of this kind. The inhabitants here are nearly all Copts, but we see a Roman Catholic Church with its cross; and a large wooden cross stands in the midst of the village—a singular sight in a Moslem country.

A large barge lies here waiting for a steamboat to tow it to Keneh. It is crowded, packed solidly, with young fellows who have been conscripted for the army, so that it looks like a floating hulk covered by a gigantic swarm of black bees. And they are all buzzing in a continuous hum, as if the queen bee had not arrived. On the shore are circles of women, seated in the sand, wailing and mourning as if for the dead—the mothers and wives of the men who have just been seized for the service of their country. We all respect grief, and female grief above all; but these women enter into grief as if it were a pleasure, and appear to enjoy it. If the son of one of the women in the village is conscripted, all the women join in with her in mourning.

I presume there are many hard cases of separation, and that there is real grief enough in the scene before us. The expression of it certainly is not wanting; relays of women relieve those who have wailed long enough; and I see a little clay hut into which the women go, I have no doubt for refreshments, and from which issues a burst of sorrow every time the door opens.

Yet I suppose that there is no doubt that the conscription (much as I hate the trade of the soldier) is a good thing for the boys and men drafted, and for Egypt. Shakirr Pasha told us that this is the first conscription in fifteen years, and that it does not take more than two per cent. of the men liable to military duty—one or two from a village. These lumpish and ignorant louts are put for the first time in their lives under discipline, are taught to obey; they learn to read and write, and those who show aptness and brightness have an opportunity, in the technical education organized by General Stone, to become something more than common soldiers. When these men have served their time, and return to their villages, they will bring with them some ideas of the world and some habits of discipline and subordination. It is probably the speediest way, this conscription, by which the dull clodishness of Egypt can be broken up. I suppose that in time we shall discover something better, but now the harsh discipline of the military service is often the path by which a nation emerges into a useful career.

Leaving this scene of a woe over which it is easy to be philosophical—the raw recruits, in good spirits, munching black bread on the barge while the women howl on shore—we celebrate the night of the New Year by sailing on, till presently the breeze fails us, when it is dark; the sailors get out the small anchor forward, and the steersman calmly lets the sail jibe, and there is a shock, a prospect of shipwreck, and a great tumult, everybody commanding, and no one doing anything to prevent the boat capsizing or stranding. It is exactly like boys' play, but at length we get out of the tangle, and go on, Heaven knows how, with much pushing and hauling, and calling upon "Allah" and "Mohammed."

No. We are not going on, but fast to the bottom, near the shore.

In the morning we are again tracking with an occasional puff of wind, and not more than ten miles from Luxor. We can, however, outwalk the boat; and we find the country very attractive and surprisingly rich; the great fields of wheat, growing rank, testify to the fertility of the soil, and when the fields are dotted with palm trees the picture is beautiful.

It is a scene of wide cultivation, teeming with an easy, ragged, and abundant life. The doleful sakiyas are creaking in their ceaseless labor; frequent mud-villages dot with brown the green expanse, villages abounding in yellow dogs and coffee-colored babies; men are working in the fields, directing the irrigating streams, digging holes for melons and small vegetables, and ploughing. The plough is simply the iron-pointed stick that has been used so long, and it scratches the ground five or six inches deep. The effort of the government to make the peasants use a modern plough, in the Delta, failed. Besides the wheat, we find large cotton-fields, the plant in yellow blossoms, and also ripening, and sugar-cane. With anything like systematic, intelligent agriculture, what harvests this land would yield!

"Good morning!"

The words were English, the speaker was one of two eager Arabs, who had suddenly appeared at our side.

"Good morning. O, yes. Me guide Goorna."

"What is Goorna?"

"Yes. Temp de Goorna. Come bime by."

"What is Goorna?"

"Plenty. I go you. You want buy any *antiques?* Come bime by."

"Do you live in Goorna?"

"All same. Memnonium, Goorna, I show all gentlemens. Me guide. Antiques! O plenty. Come bime by."

Come Bime By's comrade, an older man, loped along by his side, unable to join in this intelligent conversation, but it turned out that he was the real guide, and all the better in that he made no pretence of speaking any English.

"Can you get us a mummy, a real one, in the original package, that hasn't been opened?"

"You like. Come plenty mummy. Used be. Not now. You like, I get. Come bime by, *bookra*."

We are in fact on the threshold of great Thebes. These are two of the prowlers among its sepulchres, who have spied our dahabeëh approaching from the rocks above the plain, and have come to prey on us. They prey equally upon the living and the dead, but only upon the dead for the benefit of the living. They try to supply the demand which we tourists create. They might themselves be content to dwell in the minor tombs, in the plain, out of which the dead were long ago ejected; but Egyptologists have set them the example, and taught them the profit of digging. If these honest fellows cannot always find the ancient scarabæi and the vases we want, they manufacture very good imitations of them. So that their industry is not altogether so ghastly as it may appear.

We are at the north end of the vast plain upon which Thebes stood; and in the afternoon we land, and go to visit the northernmost ruin on the west bank, the Temple of Koorneh (Goorneh), a comparatively modern structure, begun by Sethi I., a great warrior and conqueror of the nineteenth dynasty, before the birth of Moses.

CHAPTER XV.

AMONG THE RUINS OF THEBES.

YOU need not fear that you are to have inflicted upon you a description of Thebes, its ruins of temples, its statues, obelisks, pylons, tombs, holes in the ground, mummy-pits and mounds, with an attempt to reconstruct the fabric of its ancient splendor, and present you, gratis, the city as it was thirty-five hundred years ago, when Egypt was at the pinnacle of her glory, the feet of her kings were on the necks of every nation, and this, her capital, gorged with the spoils of near and distant maraudings, the spectator of triumph succeeding triumph, the *depôt* of all that was precious in the ancient world, at once a treasure-house and a granary, ruled by an aristocracy of cruel and ostentatious soldiers, and crafty and tyrannical priests, inhabited by abject Egyptians and hordes of captive slaves—was abandoned to a sensuous luxury rivalling that of Rome in her days of greatest wealth and least virtue in man or woman.

I should like to do it, but you would go to sleep before you were half through it, and forget to thank the cause of your comfortable repose. We can see, however, in a moment, the unique situation of the famous town.

We shall have to give up, at the outset, the notion of Homer's "hundred-gated Thebes." It is one of his generosities of speech. There never were any walls about Thebes, and it never needed any; if it had any gates they must have been purely ornamental structures; and perhaps the pylons of the many temples were called gates. If Homer had been more careful in slinging around his epithets he would have saved us a deal of trouble.

Nature prepared a place here for a vast city. The valley of

the Nile, narrow above and below, suddenly spreads out into a great circular plain, the Arabian and Libyan ranges of mountains falling back to make room for it. In the circle of these mountains, which are bare masses of limestone, but graceful and bold in outline, lies the plain, with some undulation of surface, but no hills: the rim of the setting sun is grey, pink, purple, according to the position of the sun; the enclosure is green as the emerald. The Nile cuts this plain into two unequal parts. The east side is the broader, and the hills around it are neither so near the stream nor so high as the Libyan range.

When the Nile first burst into this plain it seems to have been undecided what course to take through it. I think it has been undecided ever since, and has wandered about, shifting from bluff to bluff, in the long ages. Where it enters, its natural course would be under the eastern hills, and there, it seems to me, it once ran. Now, however, it sweeps to the westward, leaving the larger portion of the plain on the right bank.

The situation is this: on the east side of the river are the temple of Luxor on a slight elevation, and the modern village built in and around it: a mile and a half below and further from the river, are the vast ruins of Karnak; two or three miles north-east of Karnak are some isolated columns and remains of temples. On the west side of the river is the great necropolis. The crumbling Libyan hills are pierced with tombs, The desert near them is nothing but a cemetery. In this desert are the ruins of the great temples, Medeenet Háboo, Dayr el Bahree, the Memnonium (or Rameseum, built by Rameses II., who succeeded in affixing his name to as many things in Egypt as Michael Angelo did in Italy), the temple of Koorneh, and several smaller ones. Advanced out upon the cultivated plain, a mile or so from the Memnonium, stand the two Colossi. Over beyond the first range of Libyan hills, or precipices, are the Tombs of the Kings, in a wild gorge, approached from the north by a winding sort of cañon, a defile so hot and savage that a mummy passing through it couldn't have had much doubt of the place he was going to.

The ancient city of Thebes spread from its cemetery under and in the Libyan hills, over the plain beyond Karnak. Did the Nile divide that city? Or did the Nile run under the eastern bluff and leave the plain and city one.

It is one of the most delightful questions in the world, for no one knows anything about it, nor ever can know. Why, then, discuss it? Is it not as important as most of the questions we discuss? What, then, would become of learning and scholarship, if we couldn't dispute about the site of Troy, and if we all agreed that the temple of Pandora Regina was dedicated to Neptune and not to Jupiter? I go in for united Thebes.

Let the objector consider. Let him stand upon one of the terraces of Dayr el Bahree, and casting his eye over the plain and the Nile in a straight line to Karnak, notice the conformity of directions of the lines of both temples, and that their avenues of sphinxes produced would have met; and let him say whether he does not think they did meet.

Let the objector remember that the Colossi, which now stand in an alluvial soil that buries their bases over seven feet and is annually inundated, were originally on the hard sand of the desert; and that all the arable land of the west side has been made within a period easily reckoned; that every year adds to it the soil washed from the eastern bank.

Farther, let him see how rapidly the river is eating away the bank at Luxor; wearing its way back again, is it not? to the old channel under the Arabian bluff, which is still marked. The temple at Luxor is only a few rods from the river. The English native consul, who built his house between the pillars of the temple thirty years ago, remembers that, at that time, he used to saddle his donkey whenever he wanted to go to the river. Observation of the land and stream above, at Ermont, favors the impression that the river once ran on the east side and that it is working its way back to the old channel.

The village of Ermont is about eight miles above Luxor, and on the west side of the river. An intelligent Arab at Luxor told me that one hundred and fifty years ago Ermont was on the east side. It is an ancient village, and boasts ruins; among the remaining sculptures is an authentic portrait of Cleopatra, who appears to have sat to all the stone-cutters in Upper Egypt. Here then is an instance of the Nile going round a town instead of washing it away.

One thing more: Karnak is going to tumble into a heap some day, Great Hall of Columns and all. It is slowly having its foundations sapped by inundations and leachings from the

Nile. Now, does it stand to reason that Osirtasen, who was a sensible king and a man of family; that the Thothmes people, and especially Hatasoo Thothmes, the woman who erected the biggest obelisk ever raised; and that the vain Rameses II., who spent his life in an effort to multiply his name and features in stone, so that time couldn't rub them out, would have spent so much money in structures that the Nile was likely to eat away in three or four thousand years?

The objector may say that the bed of the Nile has risen; and may ask how the river got over to the desert of the west side without destroying Karnak on its way. There is Erment, for an example.

Have you now any idea of the topography of the plain? I ought to say that along the western bank, opposite Luxor, stretches a long sand island joined to the main, in low water, and that the wide river is very shallow on the west side.

We started for Koorneh across a luxuriant wheat-field, but soon struck the desert and the *débris* of the old city. Across the river we had our first view of the pillars of Luxor and the pylons of Karnak, sights to heat the imagination and set the blood dancing. But how far off they are; on what a grand scale this Thebes is laid out—if one forgets London and Paris and New York.

The desert we pass over is full of rifled tombs, hewn horizontally in rocks that stand above the general level. Some of them are large chambers, with pillars left for support. The doors are open and the sand drifts in and over the rocks in which they are cut. A good many of them are inhabited by miserable Arabs, who dwell in them and in huts among them. I fancy that, if the dispossessed mummies should reappear, they would differ little, except perhaps in being better clad, from these bony living persons who occupy and keep warm their sepulchres.

Our guide leads us at a lively pace through these holes and heaps of the dead, over sand hot to the feet, under a sky blue and burning, for a mile and a half. He is the first Egyptian I have seen who can walk. He gets over the ground with a sort of skipping lope, barefooted, and looks not unlike a tough North American Indian. As he swings along, holding his thin cotton robe with one hand, we feel as if we were following a shade despatched to conduct us to some Unhappy Hunting-Grounds.

Near the temple are some sycamore-trees and a collection of hovels called Koorneh, inhabited by a swarm of ill-conditioned creatures, who are not too proud to beg and probably are not ashamed to steal. They beset us there and in the ruins to buy all manner of valuable antiquities, strings of beads from mummies, hands and legs of mummies, small green and blue images, and the like, and raise such a clamor of importunity that one can hold no communion, if he desires to, with the spirits of Sethi I., and his son Rameses II., who spent the people's money in erecting these big columns and putting the vast stones on top of them.

We are impressed with the massiveness and sombreness of the Egyptian work, but this temple is too squat to be effective, and is scarcely worth visiting, in comparison with others, except for its sculptures. Inside and out it is covered with them; either the face of the stone cut away, leaving the figures in relief, or the figures are cut in at the sides and left in relief in the centre. The rooms are small—from the necessary limitations of roof-stones that stretched from wall to wall, or from column to column; but all the walls, in darkness or in light, are covered with carving.

The sculptures are all a glorification of the Pharaohs. We should like to know the unpronounceable names of the artists, who, in the conventional limits set them by their religion, drew pictures of so much expression, and figures so life-like, and chiseled these stones with such faultless execution; but there are no names here but of Pharaoh and of the gods.

The king is in battle, driving his chariot into the thick of the fight; the king crosses rivers, destroys walled cities, routs armies; the king appears in a triumphal procession with chained captives, sacks of treasure, a menagerie of beasts, and a garden of exotic trees and plants borne from conquered countries; the king is making offerings to his predecessors, or to gods many, hawk-headed, cow-headed, ibis-headed, man-headed. The king's scribe is taking count of the hands, piled in a heap, of the men the king has slain in battle. The king, a gigantic figure, the height of a pylon, grasps by the hair of the head a bunch of prisoners, whom he is about to slay with a raised club—as one would cut off the tops of a handful of radishes.

There is a vein of "Big Injun" running through them all. The same swagger and boastfulness, and cruelty to captives. I was glad to see one woman in the mythic crowd, doing the generous thing: Isis, slim and pretty, offers her breast to her son, and Horus stretches up to the stone opportunely and takes his supper like a little gentleman. And there is color yet in her cheek and robe that was put on when she was thirty-five hundred years younger than she is now.

Towards the south we saw the more extensive ruins of the Memnonium, and, more impressive still, the twin Colossi, one of them the so-called vocal statue of Memnon, standing up in the air against the evening sky more than a mile distant. They rose out of a calm green plain of what seemed to be wheat, but which was a field of beans. The friendly green about them seemed to draw them nearer to us in sympathy. At this distance we could not see how battered they were. And the unspeakable calm of these giant figures, sitting with hands on knees, fronting the east, like the Sphinx, conveys the same impression of lapse of time and of endurance that the pyramids give.

The sunset, as we went back across the plain, was gorgeous in vermillion, crimson, and yellow. The Colossi dominated the great expanse, and loomed up in the fading light like shapes out of the mysterious past.

Our dahabeëh had crept up to the east side of the island, and could only be reached by passing through sand and water. A deep though not wide channel of the Nile ran between us and the island. We were taken over this in a deep tub of a ferry-boat. Laboriously wading through the sand and ploughed fields of the island, we found our boat anchored in the stream, and the shore so shallow that even the sandal could not land. The sailors took us off to the row-boat on their backs.

In the evening the dahabeëh is worked across and secured to the crumbling bank of the Luxor. And the accomplishment of a voyage of four hundred and fifty miles in sixteen days is, of course, announced by rockets.

CHAPTER XVI.

HISTORY IN STONE.

IT NEVER rains at Thebes; you begin with that fact. But everybody is anxious to have it rain, so that he can say, "It rained when I was at Thebes, for the first time in four thousand years."

It has not rained for four thousand years, and the evidence of this is that no representation of rain is found in any of the sculptures on temples or monuments; and all Egyptologists know that what is not found thus represented has had no existence.

To day, it rained for the first time in four thousand years. The circumstances were these. We were crossing at sunset from the west side to the island, in a nasty little ferry, built like a canal-barge, its depths being full of all uncleanliness and smell—donkeys, peasants, and camels using it for crossing. (The getting of a camel in and out of such a deep trough is a work of time and considerable pounding and roaring of beast and men.) The boat was propelled by two half-clad, handsome, laughing Egyptian boys, who rowed with some crooked limbs of trees, and sang "Hā! Yālesah," and "Yah! Mohammed" as they stood and pulled the unwieldy oars.

We were standing above the reek, on a loose platform of sticks at the stern, when my comrade said, "It rains, I think I felt a drop on my hand."

"It can't be," I said, "it has not rained here in four thousand years;" and I extended my hand. I felt nothing. And yet I could not swear that a drop or two did not fall into the river. It had that appearance, nearly. And we have seen no flies skipping on the Nile at this season.

In the sculpture we remember that the king is often represented extending his hand. He would not put it out for nothing, for everthing done anciently in Egypt, every scratch on a rock, has a deep and profound meaning. Pharaoh is in the attitude of fearing that it is going to rain. Perhaps it did rain last night. At any rate, there were light clouds over the sky.

The morning opens with a cool west wind, which increases and whirls the sand in great clouds over the Libyan side of the river, and envelopes Luxor in its dry storm. Luxor is for the most part a collection of miserable mud-hovels on a low ridge, with the half-buried temple for a nucleus, and a few houses of a better sort along the bank, from which float the consular flags.

The inhabitants of Luxor live upon the winter travellers. Sometimes a dozen or twenty gay dahabeëhs and several steamboats are moored here, and the town assumes the appearance of a fashionable watering-place. It is the best place on the river, on the whole, considering its attractions for scholars and sightseers, to spend the winter, and I have no doubt it would be a great resort if it had any accommodations for visitors. But it has not; the stranger must live in his boat. There is not indeed in the whole land of Egypt above Cairo such a thing as an inn; scarcely a refuge where a clean Christian, who wishes to keep clean, can pass a night, unless it be in the house of some governor or a palace of the Khedive. The perfection of the world's climate in winter is, to be sure, higher up, in Nubia; but that of Thebes is good enough for people accustomed to Europe and New England. With steamboats making regular trips and a railroad crawling up the river, there is certain to be the Rameses Hotel at Thebes before long, and its rival a Thothmes House; together with the Mummy Restaurant, and the Scarabæus Saloon.

You need two or three weeks to see properly the ruins of Thebes, though Cook's "personally conducted tourists" do it in four days, and have a *soirée* of the dancing-girls besides. The region to be travelled over is not only vast (Strabo says the city was nine miles long) but it is exceedingly difficult getting about, and fatiguing if haste is necessary. Crossing the swift Nile in a sandal takes time; you must wade or be carried over shallows to the island beach; there is a weary walk or ride over this; another stream is to be crossed, and then begins the work of the day. You set out with a cavalcade of mules, servants, water-carriers, and a retinue of hungry, begging Arabs, over the fields and through the desert to the temples and tombs. The distances are long, the sand is glaring, the incandescent sun is reflected in hot waves from the burning Libyan chain. It requires hours to master the plan of a vast temple in its ruins, and days to follow out the story of the wonderful people who built it, in its marvellous sculptures—acres of inside and outside walls of picture cut in stone.

Perhaps the easiest way of passing the time in an ancient ruin was that of two Americans, who used to spread their rugs in some shady court, and sit there, drinking brandy and champagne all day, letting the ancient civilization gradually reconstruct itself in their brains.

Life on the dahabeëh is much as usual; in fact, we are only awaiting a favorable wind to pursue our voyage, expecting to see Thebes satisfactorily on our return. Of the inhabitants and social life of Luxor we shall have more to say by and by. We have daily a *levée* of idlers on the bank, who spend twilight hours in watching the boat; we are visited by sharp-eyed dealers in antiquities, who pull out strings of scarabæi from their bosoms, or cautiously produce from under their gowns a sculptured tablet, or a stone image, or some articles from a mummy-case—*antiques* really as good as new. Abd-el-Atti sits on the forward-deck cheapening the poor chickens with old women, and surrounded by an admiring group of Arab friends, who sit all day smoking and sipping coffee, and kept in a lively enjoyment by his interminable *facetiæ* and *badinage*.

Our most illustrious visitors are the American consul, Ali Effendi Noorad, and the English consul, Mustapha Aga. Ali is a well-featured, bronze-complexioned Arab of good family (I think of the Ababdehs), whose brother is sheykh of a tribe at Karnak. He cannot speak English, but he has a pleasanter smile than any other American consul I know. Mustapha, now very old and well known to all Nile travellers, is a venerable wise man of the East, a most suave, courtly Arab, plausible, and soft of speech; under his bushy eyebrows one sees eyes that are keen and yet glazed with a film of secrecy; the sort of eye that you cannot look into, but which you have no doubt looks into you.

Mustapha, as I said, built his house between two columns of the temple of Luxor. These magnificent columns, with flaring lotus capitals, are half-buried in sand, and the whole area is so built in and over by Arab habitations that little of the once extensive and splendid structure can be seen. Indeed, the visitor will do well to be content with the well-known poetic view of the columns from the river. The elegant obelisk, whose mate is in Paris, must however be seen, as well as the statues of Rameses II. sitting behind it up to their necks in sand—as if a sitz-bath had been prescribed. I went one day into the interior of the huts, in order to look at some of the sculptures, especially that of a king's chariot which is shaded by a parasol —an article which we invented three or four thousand years after the Egyptians, who first used it, had gone to the shades where parasols are useless. I was sorry that I went. The private house I entered was a mud enclosure with a creaky wooden door. Opening this I found myself in what appeared to be a private hen-yard, where babies, chickens, old women, straw, flies, and dust, mingled with the odors of antiquity; about this were the rooms in which the family sleep—mere dog-kennels. Two of the women had nose-rings put through the right nostril, hoops of gold two or three inches across. I cannot say that a nose-ring adds to a woman's beauty, but if I had to manage a harem of these sharp-tongued creatures I should want rings in their noses—it would need only a slight pull of the cord in the ring to cause the woman to cry, in Oriental language, "where thou goest, I will go." The parasol sculpture was half-covered by the mud-wall and the oven; but there was Pharaoh visible, riding on in glory through all this squalor. The Pharaohs and priests never let one of the common people set foot inside these superb temples; and there is a sort of base satisfaction now in seeing the ignorant and oppressed living in their palaces, and letting the hens roost on Pharaoh's sun-shade. But it was difficult to make picturesque the inside of this temple-palace, even with all the flowing rags of its occupants.

We spend a day in a preliminary visit to the Memnonium and the vast ruins known as those of Medeenet Háboo. Among our attendants over the plain are half a dozen little girls, bright, smiling lasses, who salute us with a cheery "Good-morning,' and devote themselves to us the whole day. Each one carries on her head a light, thin water-*koolleh*, that would hold about a quart, balancing it perfectly as she runs along. I have seen mere infants carrying very small *koollehs*, beginning thus young to learn the art of walking with the large ones, which is to be the chief business of their lives.

One of the girls, who says her name is Fatimeh (the name of the Prophet's favorite daughter is in great request), is very pretty, and may be ten or eleven years old, not far from the marriageable age. She has black hair, large, soft, black eyes, the lids stained with kohl, dazzling white teeth and a sweet smile. She wears cheap earrings, a necklace of beads and metal, and a slight ring on one hand; her finger-nails and the palms of her little hands are stained with henna. For dress she has a sort of shawl used as a head-veil, and an ample outergarment, a mantle of dark-blue cotton, ornamented down the front seams with colored beads—a coquettish touch that connects her with her sisters of the ancient *régime* who seem to have used the cylindrical blue bead even more profusely than ladies now-a-day the jet "bugles," in dress trimming. I fear the pretty heathen is beginning to be aware of her attractions.

The girls run patiently beside us or wait for us at the temples all day, bruising their feet on the stony ways, getting nothing to eat unless we give them something, chatting cheerfully, smiling at us and using their little stock of English to gain our good will, constantly ready with their *koollehs*, and say nothing of backsheesh until they are about to leave us at night and go to their homes. But when they begin to ask, and get a copper or two, they beg with a mixture of pathos and anxiety and a use of the pronouns that is irresistible.

"You tired. Plenty backsheesh for little girl. Yes."

"Why don't you give us backsheesh? We are tired too," we reply.

"Yes. Me give you backsheesh you tired all day."

Fatimeh only uses her eyes, conscious already of her power. They are satisfied with a piastre; which the dragoman says is too much, and enough to spoil them. But, after all, five cents is not a magnificent gift, from a stranger who has come five thousand miles, to a little girl in the heart of Africa, who has lighted up the desert a whole day with her charming smiles?

The donkey-boy pulls the strings of pathos for his backsheesh, having no beauty to use; he says, "Father and mother *all* dead." Seems to have belonged to a harem.

Before we can gain space or quiet either to examine or enjoy a temple, we have to free ourselves of a crowd of adhesive men, boys, and girls, who press upon us their curiosities, relics of the dead, whose only value is their antiquity. The price of these relics is of course wholly "fancy," and I presume that Thebes, where the influence of the antique is most strong, is the best market in the world for these trifles; and that, however cheaply they may be bought here, they fetch a better price than they would elsewhere.

I suppose if I were to stand in Broadway and offer passers-by such a mummy's hand as this which is now pressed upon my notice, I could scarcely give it away. This hand has been "doctored" to sell; the present owner has re-wrapped its bitumen soaked flesh in mummy-cloth, and partially concealed three rings on the fingers. Of course the hand is old and the cheap rings are new. It is pleasant to think of these merchants in dried flesh prowling about among the dead, selecting a limb here and there that they think will decorate well, and tricking out with cheap jewelry these mortal fragments. This hand, which the rascal has chosen, is small, and may have been a source of pride to its owner long ago; somebody else may have been fond of it, though even he—the lover—would not care to hold it long now. A pretty little hand; I suppose it has in its better days given many a caress and love-pat, and many a slap in the face; belonged to one of the people, or it would not have been found in a common mummy-pit; perhaps the hand of a sweet water-bearer like Fatimeh, perhaps of some slave-girl whose fatal beauty threw her into the drag-net that the Pharaohs occasionally cast along the Upper Nile— slave-hunting raids that appear on the monuments as great military achievements. This hand, naked, supple, dimpled, henna-tipped, may have been offered for nothing once; there are wanted for it four piastres now, rings and all. A dear little hand!

Great quantities of antique beads are offered us in strings, to one end of which is usually tied a small image of Osiris, or the winged sun, or the scarabæus with wings. The inexhaustible supply of these beads and images leads many to think that they are manufactured to suit the demand. But it is not so. Their blue is of a shade that is not produced now-a-days. And, besides, there is no need to manufacture what exists in the mummy-pits in such abundance. The beads and bugles are of glass; they were much used for necklaces and are found covering the breasts of mummies, woven in a network of various patterns, like old bead purses. The vivid blue color was given by copper.

The little blue images of Osiris which are so abundant are also genuine. They are of porcelain, a sort of porcelain-glass, a sand-paste, glazed, colored blue, and baked. They are found in great quantities in all tombs; and it was the Egyptian practice to thickly strew with them the ground upon which the foundations and floors of temples were laid. These images found in tombs are more properly figures of the dead under the form of Osiris, and the hieroglyphics on them sometimes give the name and quality of the departed. They are in fact a sort of "P.P.C." visiting-card, which the mummy has left for future ages. The Egyptians succeeded in handing themselves down to posterity; but the manner in which posterity has received them is not encouraging to us to salt ourselves down for another age.

The Memnonium, or more properly Rameseum, since it was built by Rameses II., and covered with his deeds, writ in stone, gives you even in its ruins a very good idea of one of the most symmetrical of Egyptian temples; the vast columns of its great hall attest its magnificence, while the elaboration of its sculpture, wanting the classic purity of the earlier work found in the tombs of Geezeh and Sakkara, speak of a time when art was greatly stimulated by royal patronage.

It was the practice of the Pharaohs when they came to the throne to make one or more military expeditions of conquest and plunder, slay as many enemies as possible (all people being considered "enemies" who did not pay tribute), cut as wide a swath of desolation over the earth as they were able, loot the cities, drag into captivity the pleasing women, and return laden with treasure and slaves and the evidences of enlarged dominion. Then they spent the remainder of their virtuous days in erecting huge temples and chiseling their exploits on them. This is, in a word, the history of the Pharaohs.

But I think that Rameses II., who was the handsomest and most conceited swell of them all, was not so particular about doing the deeds as he was about recording them. He could not have done much else in his long reign than erect the temples, carve the hieroglyphics, and set up the statues of himself, which proclaim his fame. He literally spread himself all over Egypt, and must have kept the whole country busy, quarrying, and building, and carving for his glorification. That he did a tenth of the deeds he is represented performing, no one believes now; and I take a vindictive pleasure in abusing him. By some historic fatality he got the name of the Great Sesostris, and was by tradition credited with the exploits of Thothmes III., the greatest of the Pharaohs, a real hero and statesman, during whose reign it was no boast to say that Egypt "placed her frontier where it pleased herself," and with those of his father Sethi I., a usurper in the line, but a great soldier.

However, this Rameses did not have good luck with his gigantic statues; I do not know one that is not shattered, defaced, or thrown down. This one at the Rameseum is only a wreck of gigantic fragments. It was a monolith of syenite, and if it was the largest statue in Egypt, as it is said, it must have been over sixty feet high. The arithmeticians say that it weighed about eight hundred and eighty-seven tons, having a solid content of three times the largest obelisk in the world, that at Karnak. These figures convey no idea to my mind. When a stone man is as big as a four-story house, I cease to grasp him. I climbed upon the arm of this Rameses, and found his name cut deeply in the hard granite, the cutting polished to the very bottom like the finest intaglio. The polishing alone of this great mass must have been an incredible labor. How was it moved from its quarry in Assouan, a hundred and thirty miles distant? And how was it broken into the thousand fragments in which it lies? An earthquake would not do it. There are no marks of drilling or the use of an explosive material. But if Cambyses broke it—and Cambyses must have been remembered in Egypt as Napoleon I. is in Italy, the one for smashing, the other for stealing—he had something as destructive as nitro-glycerine.

Rameses II. impressed into his service not only art but literature. One of his achievements depicted here is his victory over the Khitas (Hittites), an Asiatic tribe; the king is in the single-handed act of driving the enemy over the river Orontes, — a blueish streak meandering down the wall. This scene is the subject of a famous poem, known as the Poem of Pantaoor, which is carved in hieroglyphics at Karnak and at Luxor. The battle is very spiritedly depicted here. On the walls are many side-scenes and acts characteristic of the age and the people. The booty from the enemy is collected in a heap; and the quantity of gold is indicated by the size of a bag of it which is breaking the back of an ass; a soldier is pulling the beard of his prisoner, and another is beating his captives, after the brutal manner of the Egyptians.

The temples at Medeenet Haboo are to me as interesting as those at Karnak. There are two; the smaller one is of various ages; but its oldest portions were built by Amun-noo-het, the sister of Thothmes, the woman who has left more monuments of her vigor than any other in history, and, woman-like, the monuments are filial offerings, and not erections to her own greatness; the larger temple is the work of Rameses III. The more you visit it, the more you will be impressed with the splendor of its courts, halls, and columns, and you may spend days in the study of its sculptures without exhausting them.

Along these high-columned halls stalk vast processions, armies going to battle, conquerors in triumphal entry, priests and soldiers bearing sacrifices, and rows of stone deities of the Egyptian pantheon receiving them in a divine indifference. Again the battle rages, the chariots drive furiously, arrows fill the air, the foot-troops press forward with their big spears and long shields, and the king is slaying the chief, who tumbles from his car. The alarm has spread to the country beyond; the terrified inhabitants are in flight; a woman, such is the detail, is seen to snatch her baby and run into the woods, leaving her pot of broth cooking on the fire.

The carving in this temple is often very deep, cut in four or five inches in the syenite, and beautifully polished to the bottom, as if done with emery. The colors that once gave each figure its character, are still fresh, red, green, blue, and black. The ceilings of some of the chambers yet represent the blue and star-sprinkled sky. How surpassingly brilliant these must have been once! We see how much the figure owed to color, when the color designated the different nationalities, the enemies or the captives, the shade of their skin, hair, beard and garments. We recognize even textures of cloth, and the spotted leopard-skins worn by the priests. How gay are the birds of varied plumage!

There is considerable variety in sculpture here, but, after all, an endless repetition on wall after wall, in chamber after chamber, of the same royal persons, gods, goddesses, and priests. There is nothing on earth so tiresome as a row of stone gods, in whom I doubt if anybody ever sincerely believed, standing to receive the offerings of a Turveydrop of a king. Occasionally the gods take turn about, and pour oil on the head of a king, at his coronation, and with this is usually the very pretty device of four birds flying to the four quarters of the globe to announce the event. But whatever the scene, warlike or religious, it is for the glorification of Pharaoh, all the same. He is commonly represented of gigantic size, and all the other human figures about him are small in comparison. It must have kept the Pharaoh in a constantly inflated condition, to walk these halls and behold, on all sides, his extraordinary apotheosis. But the Pharaoh was not only king but high priest, and the divine representative on earth of, and about to become, in a peculiar sense, Osiris himself, at his death.

The Egyptians would have saved us much trouble if they had introduced perspective into these pictures. It is difficult to feel that a pond of water, a tree, and a house, one above the other on a wall, are intended to be on the same level. We have to accustom ourselves to figures always in profile, with the eye cut in full as if seen in front, and both shoulders showing. The hands of prisoners are tied behind them, but this is shown by bringing both elbows, with no sort of respect for the man's anatomy, round to the side toward us, yet it is wonderful what character and vivacity they gave to their figures, and how by simple profile they represent nationalities and races, Ethiops, Nubians, Jews, Assyrians, Europeans.

These temples are inlaid and overlaid, and surrounded with heaps of rubbish, and the *débris* of ancient and modern mud and unbaked-brick dwellings; part of the great pillars are entirely covered. The Christians once occupied the temples, and there are remains of a church, and a large church, in one of the vast courts, built of materials at hand, but gone to ruin more complete than the structure around it. The early Christians hewed away the beautiful images of Osiris from the pillars (an Osiride pillar is one upon one side of which, and the length of it, is cut in full relief only attached at the back, a figure of Osiris), and covered the hieroglyphics and sculptures with plaster. They defaced these temples as the Reformers hacked and whitewashed the cathedrals of Germany. And sometimes the plaster which was meant to cover forever from sight the images of a mysterious religion, has defeated the intentions of the plasterers, by preserving, to an age that has no fear of stone gods, the ancient pictures, sharp in outline and fresh in colour.

It is indeed marvelous that so much has been preserved, considering what a destructive creature man is, and how it pleases his ignoble soul to destroy the works of his forerunners on the earth. The earthquake has shaken up Egypt time and again, but Cambyses was worse; he was an earthquake with malice and purpose, and left little standing that he had leisure to overturn. The ancient Christians spent a great deal of time in rubbing out the deep-cut hieroglyphics, chiseling away the heads of strange gods, covering the pictures of ancient ceremonies and sacrifices, and painting on the walls their own rude conceptions of holy persons and miraculous occurrences. And then the Moslems came, hating all images and pictorial representations alike, and scraped away or battered with bullets the work of pagans and Christians.

There is much discussion whether these so-called temples were not palaces and royal residences as well as religious edifices. Doubtless many of them served a double purpose; the great pylons and propylons having rooms in which men might have lived, who did not know what a comfortable house is. Certainly no palaces of the Pharaohs have been discovered in Egypt, if these temples are not palaces in part; and it is not to be supposed that the Pharaoh dwelt in a mud-house with a palm-roof, like a common mortal. He was the religious as well as the civil head, Pope and Cæsar in one, and it is natural that he should have dwelt in the temple precincts.

The pyramidal towers of the great temple of Medeenet Haboo are thought to be the remains of the palace of Rameses III. Here indeed the Egyptologists point out his harem and the private apartments, when the favoured of Amun-Re unbent himself from his usual occupation of seizing a bunch of captives by the hair and slashing off their heads at a blow, in the society of his women and the domestic enjoyments of a family man. Here we get an insight into the private life of the awful monarch, and are able to penetrate the mysteries of his retirement. It is from such sculptures as one finds here that scholars have been able to rehabilitate old Egyptian society and tell us not only what the Egyptians did but what they were thinking about. The scholar, to whom we are most indebted for the reconstruction of the ancient life of the Egyptians, Sir Gardner Wilkinson, is able not only to describe to us a *soirée*, from paintings in tombs at Thebes, but to tell us what the company talked about and what their emotions were. "In the meantime," he says, "the conversation became animated" (as it sometimes does at parties) "and the ladies fluently discussed the question of dress," "the maker of an earring and the shop where it was purchased was anxiously inquired after." On one occasion, when the guests were in "raptures of admiration" over something, an awkward youth overturned a pedestal, creating great confusion and frightening the women, who screamed; however, no one was hurt, and harmony being restored, "the incident afforded fresh matter for conversation, to be related in full details to their friends when they returned home."

This is very wonderful art, and proves that the Egyptians excelled all who came after them in the use of the chisel and brush; since they could not only represent in a drawing on the wall of a tomb the gaiety of an evening party and the subject of its conversation, but could make the picture convey as well the talk of the guests to their friends after they returned home!

We had read a good deal about the harem of Rameses III., and it was naturally the first object of our search at Medeenet Haboo. At the first visit we could not find it, and all our expectation of his sweet domestic life was unrealized. It was in vain that we read over the description:—"Here the king is attended by his harem, some of whom present him with flowers, or wave before him fans and flabella; and a favourite is caressed, or invited to divert his leisure hours with a game of draughts." We climbed everywhere, and looked into every room, but the king and his harem were not visible. And yet the pictures, upon which has been built all this fair fabric of the domestic life of Rameses, must exist somewhere in these two pyramidal towers. And what a gallery of delights it must be, we thought. The king attended by his harem!

Upon a subsequent visit, we insisted that the guide should take us into this harem. That was not possible, but he would show it to us. We climbed a broken wall, from the top of which we could look up, through a window, into a small apartment in the tower. The room might be ten feet by twelve in size, probably smaller. There was no way of getting to it by any interior stairway or by any exterior one, that we could see, and I have no doubt that if Pharaoh lived there he climbed up by a ladder and pulled his harem up after him.

But the pictures on the walls, which we made out by the help of an opera-glass, prove this to have been one of the private apartments, they say. There are only two pictures, only one, in fact, not defaced; but as these are the only examples of the interior decoration of an ancient royal palace in all Egypt, it is well to make the most of them. They are both drawn in spirited outlines and are very graceful, the profile faces having a Greek beauty. In one Rameses III., of colossal size, is represented seated on an elegant *fauteuil*, with his feet on a stool. He wears the royal crown, a necklace, and sandals. Before him stands a lady of his harem, clad in a high crown of lotus-stems, a slight necklace, and sandals turned up like skates. It must be remembered that the weather was usually very warm in Thebes, especially on this side the river. The lady is holding up a lotus-flower, but it is very far from the royal nose, and indeed she stands so far off that the king has to stretch out his arm to chuck her under the chin. The Pharaoh's beautiful face preserves its immortal calm, and the "favourite is caressed" in accordance with the chastest requirements of high art.

In the other picture, the Pharaoh is seated as before, but he is playing at draughts. In his left hand he holds some men, and his right is extended lifting a piece from the draught-board. His antagonist has been unfortunate. Her legs are all gone; her hand has disappeared. There remains of this "favorite" only the outline of part of the body, the right arm and the hand which lifts a piece, and a suggestion of the left arm extended at full length and pushing a lotus-bud close to the king's nose. It is an exhibition of man's selfishness. The poor woman is not only compelled to entertain the despot at the game, but she must regale his fastidious and scornful nose at the same time; it must have been very tiresome to keep the left hand thus extended through a whole game. What a passion the Egyptians had for the heavy perfume of this flower. They are smelling it in all their pictures.

We climbed afterwards, by means of a heap of rubbish, into a room similar to this one, in the other tower, where we saw remains of the same sculpture. It was like the Egyptians to repeat that picture five hundred times in the same palace.

The two Colossi stand half a mile east of the temple of Medeenes Haboo, and perhaps are the survivors of like figures which lined an avenue to another temple. One of them is better known to fame than any other ancient statue, and rests its reputation on the most shadowy basis. In a line with these statues are the remains of other colossi of nearly the same size, buried in the alluvial deposit. These figures both represent Amunoph III. (about 1500 or 1600 B. C.); they are seated; and on either side of the legs of the king, and attached to the throne, are the statues of his mother and daughter, little women, eighteen feet high. The colossi are fifty feet high without the bases, and must have stood sixty feet in the air before the Nile soil covered the desert on which they were erected. The pedestal is a solid stone thirty-three feet long.

Both were monoliths. The southern one is still one piece, but shockingly mutilated. The northern one is the famous Vocal Statue of Memnon; though why it is called of Memnon and why "vocal" is not easily explained. It was broken into fragments either by some marauder, or by an earthquake at the beginning of our era, and built up from the waist by blocks of stone, in the time of the Roman occupation, during the reign of Septimius Severus.

There was a tradition—perhaps it was only the tradition of a tradition—that it used to sing every morning at sunrise. No mention is made of this singing property, however, until after it was overthrown; and its singing ceased to be heard after the Roman Emperor put it into the state in which we now see it. It has been assumed that it used to sing, and many theories have been invented to explain its vocal method. Very likely the original report of this prodigy was a Greek or Roman fable; and the noise may have been produced by a trick for Hadrian's benefit (who is said to have heard it) in order to keep up the reputation of the statue.

Amunoph III. (or Amenōphis, or Amen-hotep—he never knew how to spell his name) was a tremendous slasher-about over the territories of other people; there is an inscription down at Samneh (above the second cataract) which says that he brought, in one expedition, out of Soudan, seven hundred and forty negro prisoners, half of whom were women and children. On the records which this modest man made, he is "Lord of both worlds, absolute master, Son of the Sun." He is Horus, the strong bull. "He marches and victory is gained, like Horus, son of Isis, like the Sun in heaven." He also built almost as extensively as Rameses II.; he covered both banks of the Nile with splendid monuments; his structures are found from Ethiopia to the Sinaitic peninsula. He set up his image in this Colossus, the statue which the Greeks and Romans called Memnon, the fame of which took such possession of the imagination of poets and historians. They heard, or said they heard, Memnon, the Ethiopian, one of the defenders of Troy, each morning saluting his mother, Aurora.

If this sound was heard, scientists think it was produced by the action of the sun's rays upon dew fallen in the crevices of the broken figure. Others think the sound was produced by a priest who sat concealed in the lap of the figure and struck a metallic stone. And the cavity and the metallic stone exist there now. Of course the stone was put in there and the cavity left, when the statue was repaired, it having been a monolith. And as the sound was never heard before the statue was broken nor after it was repaired, the noise was not produced by the metallic stone. And if I am required to believe that the statue sang with his head off, I begin to doubt altogether. I incline to think that we have here only one of those beautiful myths in which the Greeks and Romans loved to clothe the distant and the gigantic.

One of the means of accounting for a sound which may never have been heard, is that the priests produced it in order to strike with awe the people. Now, the Egyptian priests never cared anything about the people, and wouldn't have taken the trouble; indeed, in the old times "people" wouldn't have been allowed anywhere within such a sacred inclosure as this in which the Colossus stood. And, besides, the priest could not have got into the cavity mentioned. When the statue was a monolith, it would puzzle him to get in ; and there is no stairway or steps by which he could ascend now. We sent an Arab up, who scaled the broken fragments with extreme difficulty, and struck the stone. The noise produced was like that made by striking the metallic stones we find in the desert,—not a resonance to be heard far.

So that I doubt that there was any singing at sunrise by the so-called Memnon (which was Amunoph), and I doubt that it was a priestly device.

This Amunoph family, whose acquaintance we have been obliged to make, cut a wide swath in their day; they had eccentricities, and there are told a great many stories about them, which might interest you if you could believe that the Amunophs were as real as the Habsburgs and the Stuarts and the Grants.

Amunoph I. (or Amen-hotep) was the successor of Amosis (or Ahmes) who expelled the Shepherds, and even pursued them into Canaan and knocked their walled-towns about their heads. Amunoph I. subdued the Shasu or Bedaween of the desert between Egypt and Syria, as much as those hereditary robbers were ever subdued. This was in the seventeenth century B. C. This king also made a naval expedition up the Nile into Ethiopia, and it is said that he took captive there the "chief of the mountaineers." Probably then he went into Abyssinia, and did not discover the real source of the Nile.

The fourth Amunoph went conquering in Asia, as his predecessors had done, for nations did not stay conquered in those days. He was followed by his seven daughters in chariots of war. These heroic girls fought, with their father, and may be seen now, in pictures, gently driving their chariot-wheels over the crushed Asiatics. When Amunoph IV. came home and turned his attention to religion, he made lively work with the Egyptian pantheon. This had grown into vast proportions from the time of Menes, and Amunoph did not attempt to improve

13

it or reform it; he simply set it aside, and established a new religion. He it was who abandoned Thebes and built Tel-el-Amarna, and there set up the worship of a single god, Aten, represented by the sun's disc. He shut up the old temples, effaced the images of the ancient gods, and persecuted mercilessly their worshippers throughout the empire.

He was prompted to all this by his mother, for he himself was little better than an imbecile. It was from his mother that he took his foreign religion as he did his foreign blood, for there was nothing of the Egyptian type in his face. His mother, Queen Taia, wife of Amunoph III., had light hair, blue eyes and rosy cheeks, the characteristics of northern women. She was not of royal family, and not Egyptian; but the child of a foreign family then living in the Delta, and probably the king married her for her beauty and cleverness.

M. Lenormant thinks she was a Hebrew. That people were then very numerous in the Delta, where they lived unmolested, keeping their own religion, a very much corrupted and materialized monotheism. Queen Taia has the complexion and features of the Hebrews—I don't mean of the Jews who are now dispersed over the continents. Lenormant credits the Hebrews, through the Queen Taia, with the overthrow of the Pharaonic religion and the establishment of the monotheism of Amunoph IV.—a worship that had many external likenesses to the Hebrew forms. At Tel-el-Amarna we see, among the utensils of the worship of Aten, the Israelitish "Table of Shew-bread." It is also noticed that the persecution of the Hebrews coincides with the termination of the religious revolution introduced by the son of Taia.

Whenever a pretty woman of talent comes into history she makes mischief. The episode of queen Taia is however a great relief to the granite-faced monotony of the conservative Pharaohs. Women rulers and regents always make the world lively for the time being—and it took in this case two or three generations to repair the damages. Smashing things and repairing damages —that is history.

History starts up from every foot of this Theban plain, piled four or five deep with civilizations. These temples are engulfed in rubbish; what the Persians and the earthquake spared,

Copts and Arabs for centuries have overlaid with their crumbling habitations. It requires a large draft upon the imagination to reinstate the edifices that once covered this vast waste; but we are impressed with the size of the city, when we see the long distances that the remaining temples are apart, and the evidence, in broken columns, statues, and great hewn blocks of stone shouldering out of the sand, of others perhaps as large.

CHAPTER XVII.

KARNAK.

THE weather is almost unsettled. There was actually a dash of rain against the cabin window last night— over before you could prepare an affidavit to the fact —and to-day is cold, more or less cloudy with a drop, only a drop, of rain occasionally. Besides, the wind is in the southwest and the sand flies. We cannot sail, and decide to visit Karnak, in spite of the entreaty of the hand-book to leave this, as the crown of all sight-seeing, until we have climbed up to its greatness over all the lesser ruins.

Perhaps this is wise; but I think I should advise a friend to go at once to Karnak and outrageously astonish himself, while his mind is fresh, and before he becomes at all sated with ruins or familiar with other vast and exceedingly impressive edifices. They are certain to dull a little his impression of Karnak even.

"Madam—" it is Abd-el-Atti who comes in, rubbing his hands—"your carriage stops the way."

"Carriage?"

"Yes, ma'am, I just make him."

The carriage was an arm-chair slung between two pushing-poles; between each end of them was harnessed a surly, diminutive donkey who seemed to feel his degradation. Each donkey required a driver; Ahmed, with his sleeves rolled up and armed with a big club, walked beside, to steady the swaying chair, and to beat the boys when their donkeys took a fancy to lie down; and a cloud of interested Arabs hovered about it, running with it, adding to the noise, dust, and picturesqueness of our cavalcade.

On the outskirts of the mud-cabins we pass through the

KARNAK. 197

weekly market, a motley assemblage of country-folks and produce, camels, donkeys, and sheep. It is close by the Ghawazee quarter, where is a colony of a hundred or more of these dancing-girls. They are always conspicuous among Egyptian women by their greater comeliness and gay apparel. They wear red and yellow gowns, many tinkling ornaments of silver and gold, and their eyes are heavily darkened with kohl. I don't know what it is in this kohl, that gives women such a wicked and dangerous aspect. They come out to ask for backsheesh in a brazen but probably intended to be a seductive manner; they are bold, but some of them rather well-looking. They claim to be an unmixed race of ancient lineage; but I suspect their blood is no purer than their morals. There is not much in Egypt that is *not* hopelessly mixed.

Of the mile-and-a-half avenue of sphinxes that once connected Luxor with Karnak, we see no trace until we are near the latter. The country is open and beautiful with green wheat, palms, and sycamores. Great Karnak does not show itself until we are close upon it; its vast extent is hidden by the remains of the wall of circuit, by the exterior temples and pylons. It is not until we have passed beyond the great—but called small—temple of Rameses III., at the north entrance, and climbed the pyramidal tower to the west of the Great Hall, that we begin to comprehend the magnitude of these ruins, and that only days of wandering over them and of study would give us their gigantic plan.

Karnak is not a temple, but a city rather; a city of temples, palaces, obelisks, colossal statues. It is, like a city, a growth of many centuries. It is not a conception or the execution of a purpose; it is the not always harmonious accretion of time and wealth and vanity. Of the slowness of its growth some idea may be gained from the fact that the hieroglyphics on one face of one of its obelisks were cut two hundred and fifty years after those on the opposite face. So long ago were both chiseled, however, they are alike venerable to us. I shouldn't lose my temper with a man who differed with me only a thousand years about the date of any event in Egypt.

They were working at this mass of edifices, sacred or profane, all the way from Osirtasen I. down to Alexander II.; that is from about 3064 B. C. according to Mariette (Bunsen, 2781,

Wilkinson, 2080,—it doesn't matter) to only a short time before our era. There was a modest beginning in the plain but chaste temple of Osirtasen; but each king sought to outdo his predecessor until Sethi I. forever distanced rivalry in building the Great Hall. And after him it is useless for anyone else to attempt greatness by piling up stones. The length of the temples, pylons, and obelisks, *en suite* from west to east, is 1180 feet; but there are other outlying and gigantic ruins; I suppose it is fully a mile and a half round the wall of circuit.

There is nothing in the world of architecture like the Great Hall; nothing so massive, so surprising, and, for me, at least, so crushingly oppressive. What monstrous columns! And how thickly they are crowded together! Their array is always compared to a forest. The comparison is apt in some respects; but how free, uplifting is a forest, how it expands into the blue air, and lifts the soul with it. A piece of architecture is to be judged, I suppose, by the effect it produces. It is not simply that this hall is pagan in its impression; it misses the highest architectural effect by reason of its unrelieved heaviness. It is wonderful; it was a prodigious achievement to build so many big columns.

The setting of enormous columns so close together that you can only see a few of them at one point of view is the architecture of the Great Hall. Upon these, big stones are put for a roof. There is no reason why this might not have been repeated over an acre of ground. Neither from within nor from without can you see the extent of the hall.* The best view of it is down the centre aisle, formed by the largest columns; and as these have height as well as bulk, and the sky is now seen above them, the effect is of the highest majesty. This hall was dimly lighted by windows in the clere story, the frames of which exhibit a freedom of device and grace of carving worthy of a Gothic cathedral. These columns, all richly sculptured, are

---

* The Great Hall measures one hundred and seventy feet by three hundred and twenty-nine; in this space stand one hundred and thirty-four columns; twelve of these, forming the central avenue of one hundred and seventy feet, are sixty-two feet high, without plinth and abacus, and eleven feet six inches in diameter; the other one hundred and twenty-two columns are forty-two feet five inches in height and about nine feet in diameter. The great columns stand only fifteen or sixteen feet apart.

laid up in blocks of stone of half the diameter, the joints broken. If the Egyptians had dared to use the arch, the principle of which they knew, in this building, so that the columns could have stood wide apart and still upheld the roof, the sight of the interior would have been almost too much for the human mind. The spectator would have been exalted, not crushed by it.

Not far off is the obelisk which Amunoo-het erected to the memory of her father. I am not sure but it will stand long after The Hall of Sethi is a mass of ruins; for already is the water sapping the foundations of the latter, some of the columns lean like reeling drunken men, and one day, with crash after crash, these giants will totter, and the blocks of stone of which they are built will make another of those shapeless heaps to which sooner or later our solidest works come. The red granite shaft of the faithful daughter lifts itself ninety-two feet into the air, and is the most beautiful as it is the largest obelisk ever raised.

The sanctuary of red granite was once very rich and beautiful; the high polish of its walls and the remains of its exquisite carving, no less than the colors that still remain, attest that. The sanctuary is a heap of ruins, thanks to that ancient Shaker, Cambyses, but the sculptures in one of the chambers are the most beautiful we have seen; the colors, red, blue, and green are still brilliant, the ceiling is spangled with stars on a blue firmament. Considering the hardness of this beautiful syenite and the difficulty of working it, I think this is the most admirable piece of work in Thebes.

It may be said of some of the sculptures here, especially of the very spirited designs and intelligent execution of those of the Great Hall, that they are superior to those on the other side of the river. And yet there is endless theological reiteration here; there are dreary miles of the same gods in the same attitudes; and you cannot call all of them respectable gods. The longer the religion endured the more conventional and repetitious its representations became. The sculptors came to have a traditional habit of doing certain scenes and groups in a certain way; and the want of life and faith in them becomes very evident in the sculptures of the Ptolemaic period.

In this vast area you may spend days and not exhaust the objects worth examination. On one of our last visits we found near the sacred lake very striking colossal statues which we had never seen before.

When this city of temples and palaces, the favorite royal residence, was entire and connected with Luxor by the avenue of sphinxes, and the great edifices and statues on the west side of the river were standing, this broad basin of the Nile, enclosed by the circle of rose-colored limestone mountains, which were themselves perforated with vast tombs, must have been what its splendid fame reports, when it could send to war twenty thousand chariots. But, I wonder, whether the city, aside from its conspicuous temples and attached palaces, was one of mud-hovels, like those of most peoples of antiquity, and of the modern Egyptians.

CHAPTER XVIII.

ASCENDING THE RIVER.

WE resume our voyage on the sixth of January, but we leave a hostage at Luxor as we did at Asioot. This is a sailor who became drunk and turbulent last night on hasheesh, and was sent to the governor.

We found him this morning with a heavy chain round his neck and tied to a stake in one corner of the court-yard of the house where the governor has his office. I think he might have pulled up the stake and run away; but I believe it is not considered right here for a prisoner to escape. The common people are so subdued that they wilt, when authority puts its heavy hand on them. Near the sailor was a mud-kennel into which he could crawl if he liked. This is the jail of Luxor. Justice is summary here. This sailor is confined without judge or jury, and will be kept till he refunds his advance wages, since he was discharged from the boat as a dangerous man.

The sailors dread the lock-up, for they may be forced into the army as the only way out of it; they would much prefer the stick. They are used to the stick; four thousand years of Egyptians have been accustomed to the stick. A beating they do not mind much, or at least are not humiliated by it as another race would be. But neither the prospect of the jail nor the stick will wean them from hasheesh, which is the curse of Egypt.

We spread our sails to a light breeze and depart in company with two other dahabeëhs, one English (the *Philæ*) and one American (the *Dongola*). Africa and weeks of leisure and sunny skies are before us. We loiter along in company, in friendly company one may say, now passing a boat and now falling behind, like three ducks coquetting in a swift current.

We are none of us in a hurry, we are indifferent to progress, our minds are calm, and our worst passions not excited. We do not appear to be going rapidly, I sometimes doubt if we are going forward at all, but it gradually becomes apparent that we are in the midst of a race!

Everything in this world is relative. I can imagine a fearfully exciting match of mud-turtles on a straight track. Think of the agony, prolonged, that the owner of the slow turtle would suffer! We are evidently in for it; and a race like this, that lasts all day, will tire out the hardiest sportsman.

The *Rip Van Winkle* is the largest boat and happens to have the lead; but the *Philæ*, a very graceful, gay boat, is crawling up to us; the *Dongola* also seems to feel a breeze that we have not. We want a strong wind—the *Rip Van Winkle* does not wake up in a mild air. As we desire, it freshens a little, the big sail swells, and the ripples are louder at the bow. Unfortunately there is breeze enough for three, and the other vessels shake themselves out like ducks about to fly. It is a pretty sight just now: the spread of three great bird-wing sails, the long gayly-painted cabins and decks, the sweeping yards and the national colors and variegated streamers flying!

They are gaining on us; the *Philæ* gets inside, and taking our wind, for a moment, creeps ahead, and attempts to sheer across our bow to force us into the swifter current; the *Dongola* sails in at the same time, and a jam and collision appear inevitable. A storm of language bursts out of each boat; men run to stern and bow, to ward off intruders or to disengage an entangled spar; all the crew, sailors, reïses, and dragomans are in the most active vociferation. But the *Philæ* sails out of the coil, the *Dongola* draws ahead at the risk of going into the bank, and our crew seize the punt-poles and have active work to prevent going fast on a sand-bar to leeward.

But the prosperity of the wicked is short. The wind falls flat. Instantly our men are tumbling into the water and carrying the rope ashore to track. The lines are all out, and the men are attempting to haul us round a deep bend. The steersmen keep the head of the vessels off shore, and the strain on the trackers is tremendous. The cables flop along the bank and scrape over the shadoofs, raking down a stake now and then, and bring out from their holes the half-naked, protesting proprietors, who get angry and gesticulate,—as if they had anything to do with our race!

The men cannot hold the cable any longer; one by one they are forced to let go, at the risk of being drawn down the crumbling bank, and the cable splashes into the water. The sailors run ahead and come down upon a sand-spit; there are puffs of wind in our sail, and we appear to have made a point, when the men wade on board and haul in the rope. The *Dongola* is close upon us; the *Philœ* has lost by keeping too far out in the current. Oh, for a wind!

Instead of a wind, there is a bland smile in the quiet sky. Why, O children, do you hasten? Have not Nile sailors been doing this for four thousand years? The boats begin to yaw about. Poles are got out. We are all in danger of going aground; we are all striving to get the inside track at yonder point; we are in danger of collision; we are most of all in danger of being left behind. The crews are crazy with excitement; as they hurriedly walk the deck, rapidly shifting their poles in the shallow water, calling upon Yalēsah in quicker and quicker respirations, "Hā Yalēsah," "Hā Yalēsah," as they run to change the sail at the least indication of a stray breeze, as they see first one dahabeëh and then the other crawling ahead, the contest assumes a serious aspect, and their cries are stronger and more barbaric.

The *Philœ* gets inside again and takes the bank. We are all tracking, when we come to the point, beyond which is a deep bay. If we had wind we should sail straight across; the distance round the bay is much greater—but then we can track along the bank; there is deep water close under the bank and there is deep water in mid-river. The *Philœ* stands away into the river, barely holding its own in the light zephyr. The *Dongola* tries to follow the *Philœ*, but swings round, and her crew take to the poles. Our plan appears to be more brilliant. Our men take the cable out upon a sand-bank in the stream, and attempt to tow us along the centre channel. All goes well. We gain on the *Philœ* and pass it. We see the *Dongola* behind, struggling in the shallows. But the sand-bank is a failure. The men begin to go from it into deeper water; it is up to their knees, it reaches our "drawers," which we bought for the crew; it comes to the waist; their shoulders are going under. It is useless; the cable is let go, and the men rush back to the sandbar. There they are. Our cable is trailing down stream; we have lost our crew, and the wind is just coming up. While we are sending the sandal to rescue our mariners, the *Philæ* sails away, and the *Dongola* shows her stern.

The travellers on the three boats, during all this contest, are sitting on the warm, sunny decks, with a pretence of books, opera-glasses in hand, apparently regarding the scene with indifference, but no doubt, underneath this mask, longing to "lick" the other boats.

After all, we come to Erment (which is eight miles from Luxor) not far apart. The race is not to the swift. There is no swift on the Nile. But I do not know how there could be a more exciting race of eight miles a day!

At Erment is a large sugar factory belonging to the Khedive; and a governor lives here in a big house and harem. The house has an extensive garden laid out by old Mohammed Ali, and a plantation of oranges, Yusef Effendis, apples, apricots, peaches, lemons, pomegranates, and limes. The plantation shows that fruit will grow on the Upper Nile, if one will take the trouble to set out and water the trees. But we see none. The high Nile here last September so completely washed out the garden that we can get neither flowers nor vegetables. And some people like the rapidly-grown watery vegetables that grow along the Nile.

Our dragoman wanted some of the good, unrefined loaf-sugar from the factory here, and I went with him to see how business is transacted. We had difficulty in finding any office or place of sale about the establishment.

But a good-natured dwarf, who seemed to spring out of the ground on our landing, led us through courts and amid dilapidated warehouses to a gate, in which sat an Arab in mixed costume. Within the gate hung a pair of steelyards, and on one side was a bench. The gate, the man, the steelyards and the bench constituted an office. Beyond was an avenue, having low enclosures on each side, that with broken pillars and walls of brick looked very much like Pompeii; in a shallow bin was a great heap of barley, thrashed, and safe and dry in the open air.

The indifferent man in the gate sent for a slow boy, who, in his own time, came, bearing a key, a stick an inch square and a foot long, with four short iron spikes stuck in one side near the end. He led us up a dirty brick stairway outside a building, and inserting the key in a wooden lock to match (both lock and key are unchanged since the Pharaohs) let us into a long, low room, like an old sail loft, full of dust, packages of sugar-paper and old account books. When the shutters were opened we found at one end a few papers of sugar, which we bought, and our own sailor carried down to the steelyards. The indifferent man condescended to weigh the sugar, and took the pay, but he lazily handed the money to the boy, who sauntered off with it. Naturally, you wouldn't trust that boy; but there was an indescribable sense of the worthlessness of time and of money and of all trade, about this transaction, that precluded the possibility of the smartness of theft.

The next day the race is resumed, with little wind and a good deal of tracking; we pass the *Dongola* and are neck-and-neck with the *Philæ* till afternoon, when we bid her good-bye; and yet not with unmixed pleasure.

It is a pleasure to pass a boat and leave her toiling after; but the pleasure only lasts while she is in sight. If I had my way, we should constantly overhaul boats and pass them, and so go up the stream in continual triumph. It is only the cold consciousness of duty performed that sustains us, when we have no spectators of our progress.

We go on serenely. Hailing a crossing ferry-boat, loaded with squatting, turbaned tatterdemalion Arabs, the dragoman cries " *Salaam 'aleykoom.*"

The reply is, " *Salaam ;* peace be with you; may God meet you in the way; may God receive you to himself." The Old Testament style.

While we were loitering along by Mutáneh—where there is a sugar-factory, and an irrigating steam pump—trying to count the string of camels, hundreds of them moving along the bank against the sunset—camels that bring the cane to be ground—and our crew were eating supper, I am sorry to say that the *Philæ* poled ahead of us, and went on to Esneh. But something happened at Esneh.

It was dark when we arrived at that prosperous town, and, of course, Abd-el-Atti, who would like to have us go blazing through Egypt like Cambyses, sent up a rocket. Its fiery serpent tore the black night above us, exploded in a hundred colored stars, and then dropped its stick into the water. Splendid rockets! The only decent rockets to be had in Egypt are those made by the government; and Abd-el-Atti was the only dragoman who had been thoughtful enough to make interest with the authorities and procure government rockets. Hence our proud position on the river. We had no fireman, and the Khedive did not pay our expenses, but the Viceroy himself couldn't out-rocket us.

As soon as we had come to shore and tied up, an operation taking some time in the darkness, we had a visit from the governor, a friend of our dragoman; but this visit was urgent and scarcely friendly. An attempt had been made to set the town on fire! A rocket from an arriving boat had been thrown into the town, set fire to the straw on top of one of the houses and—

"Did it spread?"

"No, but it might. Allah be praised, it was put out. But the town might have been burned down. What a way is this, to go along the Nile firing the towns at night?"

"'Twasn't our rocket. Ours exploded in the air and fell into the river. Did the other boat, did the *Philæ*, send up a rocket when she arrived?"

"Yes. There was another rocket."

"Dat's it, dat's it," says Abd-el-Atti. "Why you no go on board the *Philæ* and not come here?" And then he added to us, as if struck by a new idea, "Where the *Philæ* get dat rocket? I think he have no rocket before. Not send any up Christmas in Asioot, not send any up in Luxor. I think these very strange. Not so?"

"What kind of rocket was it, that burnt the town?" we ask the governor.

"I have it." The governor ran to the cabin door and called. A servant brought in the exploded missile. It was a large-sized rocket, like our own; twice as large as the rockets that are not made by the government, and which travellers usually carry.

"Seems like our stick," cries Abd-el-Atti, getting excited. He examined the sheath with great care. We all gathered round the cabin lamp to look at the fatal barrel. It had a mark on it, something in Arabic. Abd-el-Atti turned it sideways and upside down, in an effort to get at the meaning of the writing.

"That is government; make 'em by the government; no doubt," he says, standing off and becoming solemn. "Dat rocket been stole. Looks like our rocket."

Abd-el-Atti flies out, and there is a commotion outside. "Who has been stealing rockets and sell 'em to that dragoman?" Boxes are opened. Rockets are brought in and compared. The exploded one has the same mark as ours, it is the same size.

A new anxiety dawns upon Abd-el-Atti. What if the *Philæ* has government rockets? Our distinction is then gone. No. It can't be. "I know what every dragoman do in Cairo. He can't get dese rocket. Nobody get 'em dis year 'cept us." Abd-el-Atti is for probing the affair to the bottom. Perhaps the hasheesh eating sailor we discharged at Luxor stole some of our rockets and sold them, and thus they came into possession of the dragoman of the *Philæ*.

The young governor, however, has had enough of it. He begins to see a great deal of vexation to himself, and a row with an English and an American dahabeëh and with natives besides. Let it drop, he says. The governor sits on the divan smoking a cigar. He is accompanied by a Greek friend, a merchant of the place. When the governor's cigar goes out, in his distraction, the Greek takes it, and re-lights it, puffing it till it is well enflamed, and then handing it again to the governor. This is a custom of the East. The servant often "starts" the cigarette for his master.

"Oh, let it go," says the governor, appealing to us: "It is finish now. It was no damage done it."

"But it might," cries Abd-el-Atti, "it might burn the town," taking now the *rôle* which the governor had dropped.

"But you are not to blame. It is not you have done it."

"Then why you come to me, why you come to us wid de rocket? Why you no go to the *Philæ*? Yes. You know that we, nobody else on the river got government rockets. This government rocket—look the mark," seizing the exploded one and a new one, and bringing the ends of both so near the lamp that we all fear an explosion. "There is something underhands here."

"'But it's all right now."

"How it's all right? Story go back to Cairo; *Rip Van Winkle* been gone set fire to Esneh. Whose rockets? Government rockets. Nobody have government rockets 'cept Abd-el-Atti."

A terrific confab goes on in the cabin for nearly an hour between the dragoman, the governor, and the Greek; a lively entertainment and exhibition of character which we have no desire to curtail. The governor is a young, bright, presentable fellow, in Frank dress, who for liveliness of talk and gesture would pass for an Italian.

When the governor has departed, our reïs comes in and presents us a high-toned "certificate" from the gentleman on board the *Philæ*:—he has learned from our reïs, steersman, and some sailors (who are in a panic) that they are all to be hauled before the governor and punished on a charge of stealing rockets and selling them to his dragoman. He certifies that he bought his own rockets in the Mooskee; that his dragoman was with him when he bought them; and that our men are innocent. The certificate further certifies that our conduct toward our crew is unjustifiable and an unheard of cruelty!

Here was a *casus belli!* Foreign powers had intervened. The right of search and seizure was again asserted; the war of 1812 was about to be renewed. Our cruelty unheard of? We should think so. All the rest of it was unheard of also. We hadn't the slightest intention of punishing anybody or hauling anybody before the governor. When Abd-el-Atti hears the certificate, he shakes his head:—

"Buy 'em like this in the Mooskee? Not be. Not find government rockets in any shop in the Mooskee. Something underhands by that dragoman!"

Not wishing to light the flames of war in Africa, we immediately took servants and lanterns and called on the English Man-of-War. The Man-of-War had gone to bed. It was nine o'clock.

"What for he send a certificate and go to bed?" Abd-el-Atti wants to know. "I not like the looks of it." He began to be suspicious of all the world.

In the morning the gentleman returned our call. He did not know or care whose rocket set fire to the town. Couldn't hurt these towns much to burn them ; small loss if all were burned. The governor had called on him to say that no damage was done. Our dragoman had, however, no right to accuse his of buying stolen rockets. His were bought in Cairo, etc., etc. And the matter dropped amicably and without bloodshed. But Abd-el-Atti's suspicions widened as he thought it over :—

"What for de Governor come to me ? What for he not go to dat boat what fire de rocket ? What for de Governor come been call on me wid a rocket ? The Governor never come been call on me wid a rocket before ! "

It is customary for all boats which are going above the first cataract to stop at Esneh twenty-four hours to bake bread for the crew; frequently they are detained longer, for the wheat has to be bought, ground in one of the little ox-power mills, mixed and baked; and the crew hire a mill and oven for the time being, and perform the labor. We had sent sailors ahead to bake the bread, and it was ready in the morning; but we stayed over, according to immemorial custom. The sailors are entitled to a holiday, and they like to take it where there are plenty of coffee-houses and a large colony of Ghawazee girls.

Esneh is not a bad specimen of an Egyptian town. There is a temple here, of which only the magnificent portico has been excavated; the remainder lies under the town. We descend some thirty feet to get to the floor of the portico,—to such a depth has it been covered. And it is a modern temple, after all, of the period of the Roman occupation. We find here the cartouches of the Cæsars. The columns are elegant and covered with very good sculpture ; each of the twenty-five has a different capital, and some are developed into a hint of the Corinthian and the composite. The rigid constraints of the Egyptian art are beginning to give way.

The work in the period of the Romans differs much from the ancient; it is less simple, more ornamented and debased. The hieroglyphics are not so carefully and nicely cut. The figures are not so free in drawing, and not so good as the old, except that they show more anatomical knowledge, and begin to exhibit a little thought of perspective. The later artists attempt to work out more details in the figure, to show muscles and various members in more particularity. Some of the forms and faces have much beauty, but most of them declare a decline of art, or perhaps an attempt to reconcile the old style with new knowledge, and consequent failure.

We called on the governor. He was absent at the mosque, but his servant gave us coffee. The Oriental magnificence of the gubernatorial residence would impress the most faithless traveller. The entrance was through a yard that would be a fair hen-yard (for common fowl) at home, and the small apartment into which we were shown might serve for a stable; but it had a divan, some carpets and chairs, and three small windows. Its roof was flat, made of rough split palm-trees, covered with palm-leaves. The governor's lady lives somewhere in the rear of this apartment of the ruler, in a low mud-house, of which we saw the outside only.

Passing near the government house, we stopped in to see the new levy of soldiers, which amounts to some four hundred from this province. Men are taken between the ages of eighteen and twenty-four, and although less than three per cent. of those liable are seized, the draft makes a tremendous excitement all along the river. In some places the bazaars are closed and there is a general panic as if pestilence had broken out.

Outside the government house, and by the river bank, are women, squatting in the sand, black figures of woe and dirt, bewailing their relations taken away. In one mud-hovel there is so much howling and vocal grief that we think at first a funeral is in progress. We are permitted to look into the lock-up where the recruits are detained waiting transportation down the river. A hundred or two fellaheen, of the average as to nakedness and squalor of raiment, are crowded into a long room with a dirt floor, and among them are many with heavy chains on their ankles. These latter are murderers and thieves, awaiting trial or further punishment. It is in fact the jail, and the soldiers are forced into this companionship until their departure. One would say this is a bad nursery for patriots.

The court of justice is in the anteroom of this prison; and the two ought to be near together. The kadi, or judge, sits cross-legged on the ground, and others squat around him, among them a scribe. When we enter, we are given seats on a mat near the judge, and offered coffee and pipes. This is something like a court of justice, sociable and friendly. It is impossible to tell who is prisoner, who are witnesses, and who are spectators. All are talking together, the prisoner (who is pointed out) louder than any other, the spectators all joining in with the witnesses. The prisoner is allowed to "talk back," which must be a satisfaction to him. When the hubbub subsides, the judge pronounces sentence; and probably he does as well as an ordinary jury.

The remainder of this town is not sightly. In fact I do not suppose that six thousand people could live in one dirtier, dustier, of more wretched houses; rows of unclean, shriveled women, with unclean babies, their eyes plastered with flies, sitting along the lanes called streets; plenty of men and boys in no better case as to clothing; but the men are physically superior to the women. In fact we see no comely women except the Ghawazees. Upon the provisions, the grain, the sweet-cakes exposed for sale on the ground, flies settle so that all look black.

Not more palaces and sugar-mills, O! Khedive, will save this Egypt, but some plan that will lift these women out of dirt and ignorance!

Our next run is to Assouan. Let us sketch it rapidly, and indicate by a touch the panorama it unrolled for us.

We are under way at daylight, leaving our two companions of the race asleep. We go on with a good wind, and by lovely sloping banks of green; banks that have occasionally a New England-river aspect; but palm-trees are behind them, and beyond are uneven mountain ranges, the crumbling limestone of which is so rosy in the sun. The wind freshens, and we spin along five miles an hour. The other boats have started, but they have a stern chase, and we lose them round a bend.

The atmosphere is delicious, a little under a summer heat, so that it is pleasant to sit in the sun; we seem to fly, with our great wings of sails, by the lovely shores. An idle man could desire nothing more. The crew are cutting up the bread baked yesterday and spreading it on the deck to dry. They prefer this to bread made of bolted wheat; and it would be very good, if it were not heavy and sour, and dirty to look at, and somewhat gritty to the teeth.

In the afternoon we pass the new, the Roman, and the old

town of El-Kab, back of which are the famous grottoes of Eilethyas with their pictures of domestic and agricultural life. We go on famously, leaving Edfoo behind, to the tune of five miles an hour; and, later, we can distinguish the top of the sail of the *Philæ* at least ten miles behind. Before dark we are abreast of the sandstone quarries of Silsilis, the most wonderful in the world, and the river is swift, narrower, and may be rocky. We have accomplished fifty-seven miles since morning, and wishing to make a day's run that shall astonish Egypt, we keep on in the dark. The wind increases, and in the midst of our career we go aground. We tug and push and splash, however, get off the sand, and scud along again. In a few moments something happens. There is a thump and a lurch, and bedlam breaks loose on deck.

We have gone hard on the sand. The wind is blowing almost a gale, and in the shadow of these hills the night is black. Our calm steersman lets the boat swing right about, facing downstream, the sail jibes, and we are in great peril of upsetting, or carrying away yard, mast and all. The hubbub is something indescribable. The sailors are ordered aloft to take in the sail. They fear to do it. To venture out upon that long slender yard, which is foul and threatens to snap every moment, the wind whipping the loose sail, is no easy or safe task. The yelling that ensues would astonish the regular service. Reïs and sailors are all screaming together, and above all can be held the storming of the dragoman, who is most alive to the danger, his voice broken with excitement and passion. The crew are crouching about the mast, in terror, calling upon Mohammed. The reïs is muttering to the Prophet, in the midst of his entreaty. Abd-el-Atti is rapidly telling his beads, while he raves. At last Ahmed springs up the rigging, and the others, induced by shame and the butt-end of a hand-spike, follow him, and are driven out along the shaking yard. Amid intense anxiety and with extreme difficulty, the sail is furled and we lie there, aground, with an anchor out, the wind blowing hard and the waves pounding us, as if we were making head against a gale at sea. A dark and wildish night it is, and a lonesome place, the rocky shores dimly seen; but there is starlight. We should prefer to be tied to the bank, sheltered from the wind rather than lie swinging and pounding here.

However, it shows us the Nile in a new aspect. And another good comes out of the adventure. Ahmed, who saved the boat, gets a new suit of clothes. Nobody in Egypt needed one more. A suit of clothes is a blue cotton gown.

The following morning (Sunday) is cold, but we are off early as if nothing had happened, and run rapidly against the current —or the current against us, which produces the impression of going fast. The river is narrower, the mountains come closer to the shores, and there is, on either side, only a scant strip of vegetation. Egypt, along here, is really only three or four rods wide. The desert sands drift down to the very shores, and the desert hills, broken, jagged, are savage walls of enclosure.

The Nile no doubt once rose annually and covered these now bleached wastes, and made them fruitful. But that was long ago. At Silsilis, below here, where the great quarries are, there was once a rocky barrier, probably a fall, which set the Nile back, raising its level from here to Assouan. In some convulsion this was carried away. When? There is some evidence on this point at hand. By ten o'clock we have rounded a long bend, and come to the temples of Kom Ombos, their great columns conspicuous on a hill close to the river. They are rather fine structures, for the Ptolemies. One of them stands upon foundations of an ancient edifice built by Thothmes I. (eighteenth dynasty); and these foundations rest upon alluvial deposit. Consequently the lowering of the Nile above Silsilis, probably by breaking through the rock-dam there, was before the time of Thothmes I. The Nile has never risen to the temple site since. These striking ruins are, however, destined to be swept away; opposite the bend where they stand a large sand-island is forming, and every hour the soil is washing from under them. Upon this sand-island this morning are flocks of birds, sunning themselves, and bevies of sand-grouse take wing at our approach. A crocodile also lifts his shoulders and lunges into the water, when we get near enough to see his ugly scales with the glass.

As we pass the desolate Kom Ombos, a solitary figure emerges from the ruins and comes down the slope of the sand-hill, with turban flowing, ragged cotton robe, and a long staff; he runs along the sandy shore and then turns away into the desert, like a fleeing Cain, probably with no idea that it is Sunday, and that the "first bell" is about to ring in Christian countries.

The morning air is a little too sharp for idle comfort, although we can sit in the sun on deck and read. This west wind coming from the mountains of the desert brings always cold weather, even in Nubia.

Above Kom Ombos we come to a little village in a palm-grove —a scene out of the depths of Africa,—such as you have often seen in pictures—which is the theatre of an extraordinary commotion. There is enacted before us in dumb-show something like a pantomime in a play-house; but this is even more remote and enigmatical than that, and has in it all the elements of a picture of savagery. In the interior of Africa are they not all children, and do they not spend their time in petty quarreling and fighting?

On the beach below the village is moored a trading vessel, loaded with ivory, cinnamon, and gum-arabic, and manned by Nubians, black as coals. People are climbing into this boat and jumping out of it, splashing in the water, in a state of great excitement; people are running along the shore, shouting and gesticulating wildly, flourishing long staves; parties are chasing each other, and whacking their sticks together; and a black fellow, in a black gown and white shoes, is chasing others with an uplifted drawn sword. It looks like war or revolution, picturesque war in the bright sun on the yellow sand, with all attention to disposition of raiment and colour and striking attitudes. There are hurryings to and fro, incessant clamours of noise and shoutings and blows of cudgels; some are running away, and some are climbing into palm trees, but we notice that no one is hit by cane or sword. Neither is anybody taken into custody, though there is a great show of arresting somebody. It is a very animated encounter, and I am glad that we do not understand it.

Sakiyas increase in number along the bank, taking the place of the shadoof, and we are never out of hearing of their doleful songs. Labour here is not hurried. I saw five men digging a well in the bank—into which the sakiya buckets dip; that is, there were four, stripped, coal-black slaves from Soudan, superintended by an Arab. One man was picking up the dirt with a pick-axe hoe. Three others were scraping out the dirt with a contrivance that would make a lazy man laugh;—one fellow held the long handle of a small scraper, fastened on like a shovel; to this upright scraper two ropes were attached, which the two others pulled, indolently, thus gradually scraping the dirt out of the hole a spoonful at a time. One man with a shovel would have thrown it out four times as fast. But why should it be thrown out in a hurry? Must we always intrude our haste into this land of eternal leisure?

By afternoon the wind falls, and we loiter along. The desert apparently comes close to the river on each side. On one bank are a hundred camels, attended by a few men and boys, browsing on the coarse tufts of grass and the scraggy bushes; the hard surroundings suit the ungainly animals. It is such pictures of life, differing in all respects from ours, that we come to see. A little boat with a tattered sail is towed along close to the bank by half a dozen ragged Nubians, who sing a not unmelodious refrain as they walk and pull,—better at any rate than the groan of the sakiyas.

There is everywhere a sort of Sabbath calm—a common thing here, no doubt, and of great antiquity. It must be easy here to keep not only Sunday but all the days of the week.

As we advance the scenery becomes more Nubian, the river narrower and apparently smaller, when it should seem larger. This phenomenon of a river having more and more water as we ascend is one that we cannot get accustomed to. The Nile, having no affluents, loses, of course, continually by evaporation, by canals, and the constant drain on it for irrigation. No wonder the Egyptians were moved by its mystery no less than by its beneficence to a sort of worship of it.

The rocks are changing their character; granite begins to appear amid the limestone and sandstone. Along here, seven or eight miles below Assouan, there is no vegetation in sight from the boat, except strips of thrifty palm-trees, but there must be soil beyond, for the sakiyas are always creaking. The character of the population is changed also; above Kom Ombos it is mostly Nubian—who are to the fellaheen as granite is to sandstone. The Nubian hills lift up their pyramidal forms in the south, and we seem to be getting into real Africa.

CHAPTER XIX.

PASSING THE CATARACT OF THE NILE.

AT LAST, twenty-four days from Cairo, the Nubian hills are in sight, lifting themselves up in the south, and we appear to be getting into the real Africa—Africa, which still keeps its barbarous secret, and dribbles down this commercial highway the Nile, as it has for thousands of years, its gums and spices and drugs, its tusks and skins of wild animals, its rude weapons and its cunning work in silver, its slave-boys and slave-girls. These native boats that we meet, piled with strange and fragrant merchandise, rowed by antic crews of Nubians, whose ebony bodies shine in the sun as they walk backward and forward at the long sweeps, chanting a weird, barbarous refrain,—what tropical freights are these for the imagination!

At sunset we are in a lonesome place, the swift river flowing between narrow rocky shores, the height beyond Assouan grey in the distance, and vultures watching our passing boat from the high crumbling sandstone ledges. The night falls sweet and cool, the soft new moon is remote in the almost purple depths, the thickly strewn stars blaze like jewels, and we work slowly on at the rate of a mile an hour, with the slightest wind, amid the granite rocks of the channel. In this channel we are in the shadow of the old historical seat of empire, the island of Elephantine; and, turning into the narrow passage to the left, we announce by a rocket to the dahabeëhs moored at Assouan the arrival of another inquisitive American. It is Sunday night. Our dragoman despatches a messenger to the chief reïs of the cataract, who lives at Philæ, five miles above. A second one is sent in the course of the night; and a third meets the old patriarch on his way to our boat at sunrise. It is necessary to impress the Oriental mind with the importance of the travellers who have arrived at the gate of Nubia.

The Nile voyager who moors his dahabeëh at the sand-bank with the fleet of merchant boats, above Assouan, seems to be at the end of his journey. Travellers from the days of Herodotus even to this century have followed each other in saying that the roar of the cataract deafened the people for miles around. Civilization has tamed the rapids. Now there is neither sight nor sound of them here at Assouan. To the southward, the granite walls which no doubt once dammed the river have been broken through by some pre-historic convulsion that strewed the fragments about in grotesque confusion. The island of Elephantine, originally a long heap of granite, is thrown into the middle of the Nile, dividing it into two narrow streams. The southern end rises from the water, a bold mass of granite. Its surface is covered with ruins, or rather with the *débris* of many civilizations; and into this mass and hills of brick, stone, pottery, and ashes, Nubian women and children may be seen constantly poking, digging out coins, beads and images, to sell to the howadji. The north portion of the island is green with wheat; and it supports two or three mud-villages, which offer a good field for the tailor and the missionary.

The passage through the east channel, between Assouan and Elephantine, is through walls of granite rocks; and southward at the end of it the view is bounded by a field of broken granite gradually rising, and apparently forbidding egress in that direction. If the traveller comes for scenery, as some do, nothing could be wilder and at the same time more beautiful than these fantastically piled crags; but considered as a navigable highway the river here is a failure.

Early in the morning the head sheykh of the cataract comes on board, and the long confab which is preliminary to any undertaking, begins. There are always as many difficulties in the way of a trade or an arrangement as there are quills on a porcupine; and a great part of the Egyptian bargaining is the preliminary plucking out of these quills. The cataracts are the hereditary property of the Nubian sheykhs and their tribes who live near them—belonging to them more completely than the rapids of the St. Lawrence to the Indian pilots; almost their whole livelihood comes from helping boats up and down the rapids, and their harvest season is the winter when the dahabeëhs of the howadji require their assistance. They magnify the difficulties and dangers and make a mystery of their skill and knowledge. But, with true Orientalism, they appear to seek rather to lessen than to increase their business. They oppose intolerable delays to the traveller, keep him waiting at Assouan by a thousand excuses, and do all they can to drive him discouraged down the river. During this winter boats have been kept waiting two weeks on one frivolous excuse or another—the day was unlucky, or the wind was unfavorable, or some prince had the preference. Princes have been very much in the way this winter; the fact would seem to be that European princes are getting to run up the Nile in shoals, as plenty as shad in the Connecticut, more being hatched at home than Europe has employment for.

Several thousand people, dwelling along the banks from Assouan to three or four miles above Philæ, share in the profits of the passing boats; and although the sheykhs, and head reïses (or captains) of the cataract get the elephant's share, every family receives something—it may be only a piastre or two—on each dahabeëh; and the sheykhs draw from the villages as many men as are required for each passage. It usually takes two days for a boat to go up the cataract and not seldom they are kept in it three or four days, and sometimes a week. The first day the boat gets as far as the island of Séhayl, where it ties up and waits for the cataract people to gather next morning. They may take it into their heads not to gather, in which case the traveller can sun himself all day on the rocks, or hunt up the inscriptions which the Pharaohs, on their raids into Africa for slaves and other luxuries, cut in the granite in their days of leisure three or four thousand years ago, before the world got its present impetus of hurry. Or they may come and pull the boat up a rapid or two, then declare they have not men enough for the final struggle, and leave it for another night in the roaring desolation. To put on force enough, and cables strong enough not to break, and promptly drag the boat through in one day would lessen the money-value of the achievement perhaps in the mind of the owner of the boat. Nature has done a great deal to make the First Cataract an obstacle to navigation, but the wily Nubian could teach nature a lesson; at any rate he has never relinquished the key to the gates. He owns the cataracts as the Bedawees own the pyramids of Geezeh and the routes across the desert to Sinai and Petra.

The aged reïs comes on board; and the preliminary ceremonies, exchange of compliments, religious and social, between him and our astute dragoman begin. Coffee is made, the reïs's pipe is lighted, and the conversation is directed slowly to the ascent of the cataracts. The head reïs is accompanied by two or three others of inferior dignity and by attendants who squat on the deck in attitudes of patient indifference. The world was not made in a day. The reïs looks along the deck and says:

"This boat is very large; it is too long to go up the cataract."

There is no denying it. The dahabeëh is larger than almost any other on the river; it is one hundred and twenty feet long. The dragoman says:

"But you took up General McClellan's boat, and that is large."

"Very true, effendi; but why the howadji no come when Genel Clemen come, ten days ago?"

"We chose to come now."

"Such a long boat never went up. Why you no come two months ago when the river was high?" This sort of talk goes on for half an hour. Then the other sheykh speaks:—

"What is the use of talking all this stuff to Mohammed Abd-el-Atti Effendi; he knows all about it."

"That is true. We shall go."

"Well, it is 'finish'," says Abd-el-Atti.

When the long negotiation is concluded, the reïs is introduced into the cabin to pay his respects to the howadji; he seats himself with dignity and salutes the ladies with a watchful self-respect. The reïs is a grown Nubian, with finely cut features but a good many shades darker than would be fellowshipped by the Sheltering Wings Association in America, small feet, and small hands with long tapering fingers that confess an aristocratic exemption from manual labor. He wears a black gown, and a white turban; a camel's hair scarf distinguishes him from the vulgar. This sheykh boasts I suppose as ancient blood as runs in any aristocratic veins, counting his ancestors back in unbroken succession to the days of the Prophet at least, and not improbably to Ishmael. That he wears neither stockings nor slippers does not detract from his simple dignity. Our conversation while he pays his visit is confined to the smoking of a cigar and some well-meant grins and smiles of mutual good feeling.

While the morning hours pass we have time to gather all the knowledge of Assouan that one needs for the enjoyment of life in this world. It is an ordinary Egyptian town of sunbaked brick, brown, dusty, and unclean, with shabby bazaars containing nothing, and full of importunate beggars and insatiable traders in curiosities of the upper country. Importunate vendors beset the traveller as soon as he steps ashore, offering him all manner of trinkets which he is eager to purchase and doesn't know what to do with when he gets them. There are crooked, odd-shaped knives and daggers, in ornamental sheaths of crocodile skin, and savage spears with great round hippopotamus shields from Kartoom or Abyssinia; jagged iron spears and lances and ebony clubs from Darfoor; cunning Nubian silver-work, bracelets and great rings that have been worn by desert camel-drivers; moth-eaten ostrich feathers; bows and arrows tipped with flint from the Soudan, necklaces of glass and dirty leather charms (containing words from the Koran); broad bracelets and anklets cut out of big tusks of elephants and traced in black, rude swords that it needs two hands to swing; bracelets of twisted silver cord and solid silver as well; earrings so large that they need to be hitched to a strand of the hair for support; nose-rings of brass and silver and gold, as large as the earrings; and "Nubian costumes" for women—a string with leather fringe depending to tie about the loins—suggestions of a tropical life under the old dispensation.

The beach, crowded with trading vessels and piled up with merchandise, presents a lively picture. There are piles of Manchester cotton and boxes of English brandy—to warm outwardly and inwardly the natives of the Soudan—which are being loaded, for transport above the rapids, upon kneeling dromedaries which protest against the load in that most vulgar guttural of all animal sounds, more uncouth and less musical than the agonized bray of the donkey—a sort of grating menagerie-grumble which has neither the pathos of the sheep's bleat nor the dignity of the lion's growl; and bales of cinnamon and senna and ivory to go down the river. The wild Bisharee Arab attends his dromedaries; he has a clear-cut and rather delicate face, is bareheaded, wears his black hair in ringlets long upon his shoulders, and has for all dress a long strip of brown cotton cloth twisted about his body and his loins, leaving his legs and his right arm free. There are the fat, sleek Greek merchant, in sumptuous white Oriental costume, lounging amid his merchandise; the Syrian in gay apparel, with pistols in his shawl-belt, preparing for his journey to Kartoom; and the black Nubian sailors asleep on the sand. To add a little color to the picture, a Ghawazee, or dancing-girl, in striped flaming gown and red slippers, dark but comely, covered with gold and silver-gilt necklaces and bracelets, is walking about the shore, seeking whom she may devour.

At twelve o'clock we are ready to push off. The wind is strong from the north. The cataract men swarm on board, two or three sheykhs and thirty or forty men. They take command and possession of the vessel, and our reïs and crew give way. We have carefully closed the windows and blinds of our boat, for the cataract men are reputed to have long arms and fingers that crook easily. The Nubians run about like cats; four are at the helm, some are on the bow, all are talking and giving orders; there is an indescribable bustle and whirl as our boat is shoved off from the sand, with the chorus of "Hā! Yālēsah. Hā! Yalēsah!"* and takes the current. The great sail shaped like a bird's wing and a hundred feet long, is shaken out forward, and we pass swiftly on our way between the granite walls. The excited howadji are on deck feeling to their finger ends the thrill of expectancy.

The first thing the Nubians want is something to eat—a chronic complaint here in this land of romance. Squatting in circles all over the boat they dip their hands into the bowls of

---

*Yalesah (I spell the name according to the sound of the pronunciation) was, some say, one of the sons of Noah who was absent at the time the ark sailed, having gone down into Abyssinia. They pushed the ark in pursuit of him, and Noah called after his son, as the crew poled along, "Ha! Yalesah!" And still the Nile boatmen call Yalesah to come, as they push the poles and haul the sail, and urge the boat toward Abyssinia. Very likely "Ha! Yalesah!" (as I catch it) is only a corruption of "Halee! 'Eesà;" *Seyyidna 'Eesà* is the Moslem name for "Our Lord Jesus."

softened bread, cramming the food down their throats, and swallow all the coffee that can be made for them, with the gusto and appetite of simple men who have a stomach and no conscience.

While the Nubians are chattering and eating, we are gliding up the swift stream, the granite rocks opening a passage for us; but at the end of it our way seems to be barred. The only visible opening is on the extreme left, where a small stream struggles through the boulders. While we are wondering if that can be our course, the helm is suddenly put hard about, and we then shoot to the right, finding our way, amid whirlpools and boulders of granite, past the head of Elephantine island; and before we have recovered from this surprise we turn sharply to the left into a narrow passage, and the cataract is before us.

It is not at all what we have expected. In appearance this is a cataract without any falls and scarcely any rapids. A person brought up on Niagara or Montmorency feels himself trifled with here. The fisherman in the mountain streams of America has come upon many a scene that resembles this—a river-bed strewn with boulders. Only, this is on a grand scale. We had been led to expect at least high precipices, walls of lofty rock, between which we should sail in the midst of raging rapids and falls; and that there would be hundreds of savages on the rocks above dragging our boat with cables, and occasionally plunging into the torrent in order to carry a life-line to the top of some seagirt rock. All of this we did not see; but yet we have more respect for the cataract before we get through it than when it first came in sight.

What we see immediately before us is a basin, it may be a quarter of a mile, it may be half a mile broad, and two miles long; a wild expanse of broken granite rocks and boulders strewn hap-hazard, some of them showing the red of the syenite and others black and polished and shining in the sun; a field of rocks, none of them high, of fantastic shapes; and through this field the river breaks in a hundred twisting passages and chutes, all apparently small, but the water in them is foaming and leaping and flashing white; and the air begins to be pervaded by the multitudinous roar of rapids. On the east, the side of the land-passage between Assouan and Philæ, were high and jagged rocks in odd forms, now and then a palm-tree, and here and there a mud-village. On the west the basin of the cataract is hemmed in by the desert hills, and the yellow Libyan sand drifts over them in shining waves and rifts, which in some lights have the almost maroon color that we see in Gerome's pictures. To the south is an impassable barrier of granite and sand—mountains of them—beyond the glistening fields of rocks and water through which we are to find our way.

The difficulty of this navigation is not one cataract to be overcome by one heroic effort, but a hundred little cataracts or swift tortuous sluiceways, which are much more formidable when we get into them than they are when seen at a distance. The dahabeëhs which attempt to wind through them are in constant danger of having holes knocked in their hulls by the rocks.

The wind is strong, and we are sailing swiftly on. It is impossible to tell which one of the half-dozen equally uninviting channels we are to take. We guess, and of course point out the wrong one. We approach, with sails still set, a narrow passage through which the water pours in what is a very respectable torrent; but it is not a straight passage, it has a bend in it; if we get through it, we must make a sharp turn to the left or run upon a ridge of rocks, and even then we shall be in a boiling surge; and if we fail to make head against the current we shall go whirling down the caldron, bumping on the rocks—not a pleasant thing for a dahabeëh one hundred and twenty feet long with a cabin in it as large as a hotel. The passage of a boat of this size is evidently an event of some interest to the cataract people, for we see groups of them watching us from the rocks, and following along the shore. And we think that seeing our boat go up from the shore might be the best way of seeing it.

We draw slowly in, the boat trembling at the entrance of the swift water; it enters, nosing the current, feeling the tug of the sail, and hesitates. Oh, for a strong puff of wind! There are five watchful men at the helm; there is a moment's silence, and the boat still hesitates. At this critical instant, while we hold our breath, a naked man, whose name I am sorry I cannot give to an admiring American public, appears on the bow with a rope in his teeth; he plunges in and makes for the nearest rock. He swims hand over hand, swinging his arms from the shoulders out of water and striking them forward, splashing along like a side wheeler — the common way of swimming in the heavy water of the Nile. Two other black figures follow him and the rope is made fast to the point of the rock. We have something to hold us against the stream.

And now a terrible tumult arises on board the boat which is seen to be covered with men; one gang is hauling on the rope to draw the great sail close to its work; another gang is hauling on the rope attached to the rock, and both are singing that wild chanting chorus without which no Egyptian sailors pull an ounce or lift a pound; the men who are not pulling are shouting and giving orders; the sheykhs, on the upper deck where we sit with American serenity exaggerated amid the babel, in jumping up and down in a frenzy of excitement, screaming and gesticulating. We hold our own; we gain a little; we pull forward where the danger of a smash against the rocks is increased. More men appear on the rocks, whom we take to be spectators of our passage. No; they lay hold of the rope. With the additional help we still tremble in the jaws of the pass. I walk aft, and the stern is almost upon the rocks; it grazes them; but in the nick of time the bow swings round, we turn short off into an eddy; the great wing of a sail is let go, and our cat-like sailors are aloft, crawling along the slender yard, which is a hundred feet in length, and furling the tugging canvas. We breathe more freely, for the first danger is over. The first gate is passed.

In this lull there is a confab with the sheykhs. We are at the island of Sehèyl, and have accomplished what is usually the first day's journey of boats. It would be in harmony with the Oriental habit to stop here for the remainder of the day and the night. But our dragoman has in mind to accomplish, if not the impossible, what is synonymous with it in the East, the unusual. The result of the inflammatory stump-speeches on both sides is that two or three gold pieces are passed into the pliant hand of the head sheykh, and he sends for another sheykh and more men.

For some time we have been attended by increasing processions of men and boys on shore; they cheered us as we passed the first rapid; they came out from the villages, from the crevices of the rocks, their blue and white gowns flowing in the wind, and make a sort of holiday of our passage. Less conspicuous at first are those without gowns—they are hardly distinguishable from the black rocks amid which they move. As we lie here, with the rising roar of the rapids in our ears, we can see no further opening for our passage.

But we are preparing to go on. Ropes are carried out forward over the rocks. More men appear, to aid us. We said there were fifty. We count seventy; we count eighty; there are at least ninety. They come up by a sort of magic. From whence are they, these black forms? They seem to grow out of the rocks at the wave of the sheykh's hand; they are of the same color, shining men of granite. The swimmers and divers are simply smooth statues hewn out of the syenite or the basalt. They are not unbaked clay like the rest of us. One expects to see them disappear like stones when they jump into the water. The mode of our navigation is to draw the boat along, hugged close to the shore rocks, so closely that the current cannot get full hold of it, and thus to work it round the bends.

We are crawling slowly on in this manner, clinging to the rocks, when unexpectedly a passage opens to the left. The water before us runs like a mill race. If we enter it, nothing would seem to be able to hold the boat from dashing down amidst the breakers. But the bow is hardly let to feel the current before it is pulled short round, and we are swinging in the swift stream. Before we know it we are in the anxiety of another tug. Suppose the rope should break! In an instant the black swimmers are overboard striking out for the rocks; two ropes are sent out, and secured; and, the gangs hauling on them, we are working inch by inch through, everybody on board trembling with excitement. We look at our watches; it seems only fifteen minutes since we left Assouan; it is an hour and a quarter. Do we gain in the chute? It is difficult to say; the boat hangs back and strains at the cables; but just as we are in the pinch of doubt, the big sail unfurls its wing with exciting suddenness, a strong gust catches it, we feel the lift, and creep upward, amid an infernal din of singing and shouting and calling on the Prophet from the gangs who haul in the sail rope, who tug at the cables attached to the rocks, who are pulling at the hawsers on the shore. We forge ahead and are about to dash into a boiling caldron before us, from which there appears to be no escape, when a skilful turn of the great creaking helm once more throws us to the left, and we are again in an eddy with the stream whirling by us, and the sail is let go and is furled.

The place where we lie is barely long enough to admit our boat; its stern just clears the rocks, its bow is aground on hard sand. The number of men and boys on the rocks has increased; it is over one hundred, it is one hundred and thirty; on a recount it is one hundred and fifty. An anchor is now carried out to hold us in position when we make a new start; more ropes are taken to the shore, two hitched to the bow and one to the stern. Straight before us is a narrow passage through which the water comes in foaming ridges with extraordinary rapidity. It seems to be our way; but of course it is not. We are to turn the corner sharply, before reaching it; what will happen then we shall see.

There is a slight lull in the excitement, while the extra hawsers are got out and preparations are made for the next struggle. The sheykhs light their long pipes, and squatting on deck gravely wait. The men who have tobacco roll up cigarettes and smoke them. The swimmers come on board for reinforcement. The poor fellows are shivering as if they had an ague fit. The Nile may be friendly, though it does not offer a warm bath at this time of the year, but when they come out of it naked on the rocks the cold north wind sets their white teeth chattering. The dragoman brings out a bottle of brandy. It is none of your ordinary brandy, but must have cost over a dollar a gallon, and would burn a hole in a new piece of cotton cloth. He pours out a tumblerful of it, and offers it to one of the granite men. The granite man pours it down his throat in one flow, without moving an eye-winker, and holds the glass out for another. His throat must be lined with zinc. A second tumblerful follows the first. It is like pouring liquor into a brazen image.

I said there was a lull, but this is only in contrast to the preceding fury. There is still noise enough, over and above the roar of the waters, in the preparations going forward, the din of a hundred people screaming together, each one giving orders, and elaborating his opinion by a rhetorical use of his hands.

The waiting crowd scattered over the rocks disposes itself picturesquely, as an Arab crowd always does, and probably cannot help doing, in its blue and white gowns and white turbans. In the midst of these preparations, and unmindful of any excitement or confusion, a sheykh, standing upon a little square of sand amid the rocks, and so close to the deck of the boat that we can hear his "Alláhoo Akbar" (God is most Great), begins his kneelings and prostrations towards Mecca, and continues at his prayers, as undisturbed and as unregarded as if he were in a mosque, and wholly oblivious of the babel around him. So common has religion become in this land of its origin! Here is a half-clad sheykh of the desert stopping, in the midst of his contract to take the howadji up the cataract, to raise his forefinger and say, "I testify that there is no deity but God; and I testify that Mohammed is his servant and his apostle."

Judging by the eye, the double turn we have next to make is too short to admit our long hull. It does not seem possible that we can squeeze through; but we try. We first swing out and take the current as if we were going straight up the rapids. We are held by two ropes from the stern, while by four ropes from the bow, three on the left shore and one on an islet to the right, the cataract people are tugging to draw us up. As we watch almost breathless the strain on the ropes, look! there is a man in the tumultuous rapid before us swiftly coming down as if to his destruction. Another one follows, and then another, till there are half a dozen men and boys in this jeopardy, this situation of certain death to anybody not made of cork. And the singular thing about it is that the men are seated upright, sliding down the shining water like a boy, who has no respect for his trowsers, down a snow-bank. As they dash past us, we see that each man is seated on a round log about five feet long; some of them sit upright with their legs on the log, displaying the soles of their feet, keeping the equilibrium with their hands. These are smooth slimy logs that a white man would find it difficult to sit on if they were on shore, and in this water they would turn with him only once—the log would go one way and the man another. But these fellows are in no fear of the rocks below; they easily guide their barks out of the rushing floods, through the whirlpools and eddies, into the slack shore-water in the rear of the boat, and stand up like men and demand backsheesh. These logs are popular ferry-boats in the Upper Nile; I have seen a woman crossing the river on one, her clothes in a basket on her head—and the Nile is nowhere an easy stream to swim.

Far ahead of us the cataract people are seen in lines and groups, half-hidden by the rocks, pulling and stumbling along; black figures are scattered along, lifting the ropes over the jagged stones, and freeing them so that we shall not be drawn back, as we slowly advance; and severe as their toil is, it is not enough to keep them warm when the chilly wind strikes them. They get bruised on the rocks also, and have time to show us their barked shins and request backsheesh. An Egyptian is never too busy or too much in peril to forget to prefer that request at the sight of a traveller. When we turn into the double twist I spoke of above, the bow goes sideways upon a rock, and the stern is not yet free. The punt-poles are brought into requisition; half the men are in the water; there is poling and pushing and grunting, heaving, and "Yah Mohammed, Yah Mohammed," with all which noise and outlay of brute strength, the boat moves a little on and still is held close in hand. The current runs very swiftly. We have to turn almost by a right angle to the left and then by the same angle to the right; and the question is whether the boat is not too long to turn in the space. We just scrape along the rocks, the current growing every moment stronger, and at length get far enough to let the stern swing. I run back to see if it will go free. It is a close fit. The stern is clear; but if our boat had been four or five feet longer, her voyage would have ended then and there. There is now before us a straight pull up the swiftest and narrowest rapid we have thus far encountered.

Our sandal—the row-boat belonging to the dahabeëh, that becomes a felucca when a mast is stepped into it—which has accompanied us fitfully during the passage, appearing here and there tossing about amid the rocks, and aiding occasionally in the transport of ropes and men to one rock and another, now turns away to seek a less difficult passage. The rocks all about us are low, from three feet to ten feet high. We have one rope out ahead, fastened to a rock, upon which stand a gang of men, pulling. There is a row of men in the water under the left side of the boat, heaving at her with their broad backs, to prevent her smashing on the rocks. But our main dragging force is in the two long lines of men attached to the ropes on the left shore. They stretch out ahead of us so far that it needs an opera-glass to discover whether the leaders are pulling or only soldiering. These two long struggling lines are led and directed by a new figure who appears upon this operatic scene. It is a comical sheykh, who stands upon a high rock at one side and lines out the catch-lines of a working refrain, while the gangs howl and haul, in a surging chorus. Nothing could be wilder or more ludicrous, in the midst of this roar of rapids and strain of cordage. The sheykh holds a long staff which he swings like the baton of the leader of an orchestra, quite unconscious of the odd figure he cuts against the blue sky. He grows more and more excited, he swings his arms, he shrieks, but always in tune and in time with the hauling and the wilder chorus of the cataract men; he lifts up his right leg, he lifts up his left leg, he is in the very ecstasy of the musical conductor, displaying his white teeth, and raising first one leg and then the other in a delirious swinging motion, all the more picturesque on account of his flowing blue robe and his loose white cotton drawers. He lifts his leg with a gigantic pull, which is enough in itself to draw the boat onward, and every time he lifts it the boat gains on the current. Surely such an orchestra and such a leader was never seen before. For the orchestra is scattered over half an acre of ground, swaying and pulling and singing in rhythmic show, and there is a high wind and a blue sky, and rocks and foaming torrents, and an African village with palms in the background, amid the *débris* of the great convulsion of nature which has resulted in this chaos. Slowly we creep up against the stiff boiling stream, the good Moslems on deck muttering prayers and telling their beads, and finally make the turn and pass the worst eddies; and as we swing round into an ox-bow channel to the right, the big sail is again let out and hauled in, and with cheers we float on some rods and come into a quiet shelter, a stage beyond the journey usually made the first day. It is now three o'clock.

We have come to the real cataract, to the stiffest pull and the most dangerous passage.

A small freight dahabeëh obstructs the way, and while this

is being hauled ahead, we prepare for the final struggle. The chief cataract is called Bab (gate) Aboo Rabbia, from one of Mohammed Ali's captains, who some years ago vowed that he would take his dahabeëh up it with his own crew and without aid from the cataract people. He lost his boat. It is also sometimes called Bab Inglese from a young Englishman, named Cave, who attempted to swim down it early one morning, in imitation of the Nubian swimmers, and was drawn into the whirlpools, and not found for days after. For this last struggle in addition to the other ropes, an enormous cable is bent on, not tied to the bow, but twisted round the cross-beams of the forward deck, and carried out over the rocks. From the shelter where we lie we are to push out and take the current at a sharp angle. The water of this main cataract sucks down from both sides above through a channel perhaps one hundred feet wide, very rapid and with considerable fall, and with such force as to raise a ridge in the middle. To pull up this hill of water is the tug; if the ropes let go we shall be dashed into a hundred pieces on the rocks below and be swallowed in the whirlpools. It would not be a sufficient compensation for this fate to have this rapid hereafter take our name.

The preparations are leisurely made, the lines are laid along the rocks and the men are distributed. The fastenings are carefully examined. Then we begin to move. There are now four conductors of this gigantic orchestra (the employment of which as a musical novelty I respectfully recommend to the next Boston Jubilee), each posted on a high rock, and waving a stick with a white rag tied to it. It is now four o'clock. An hour has been consumed in raising the curtain for the last act. We are now carefully under way along the rocks which are almost within reach, held tight by the side ropes, but pushed off and slowly urged along by a line of half-naked fellows under the left side, whose backs are against the boat and whose feet walk along the perpendicular ledge. It would take only a sag of the boat, apparently, to crush them. It does not need our eyes to tell us when the bow of the boat noses the swift water. Our sandal has meantime carried a line to a rock on the opposite side of the channel, and our sailors haul on this and draw us ahead. But we are held firmly by the shore lines. The boat is never suffered, as I said, to get an inch the advantage, but is always held tight in hand.

As we appear at the foot of the rapid, men come riding down it on logs as before, a sort of horseback feat in the boiling water, steering themselves round the eddies and landing below us. One of them swims round to the rock where a line is tied, and looses it as we pass; another, sitting on the slippery stick and showing the white soles of his black feet, paddles himself about amid the whirlpools. We move so slowly that we have time to enjoy all these details, to admire the deep yellow of the Libyan sand drifted over the rocks at the right, and to cheer a sandal bearing the American flag which is at this moment shooting the rapids in another channel beyond us, tossed about like a cork. We see the meteor flag flashing out, we loose it behind the rocks, and catch it again appearing below. " O star spang "—but our own orchestra is in full swing again. The comical sheykh begins to swing his arms and his stick back and forth in an increasing measure, until his whole body is drawn into the vortex of his enthusiasm, and one leg after the other, by a sort of rhythmic hitch, goes up, displaying the white and baggy cotton drawers. The other three conductors join in, and a deafening chorus from two hundred men goes up along the ropes, while we creep slowly on amid the suppressed excitement of those on board, who anxiously watch the straining cables, and with a running fire of " backsheesh, backsheesh," from the boys on the rocks close at hand. The cable holds; the boat nags and jerks at it in vain; through all the roar and rush we go on, lifted, I think perceptibly, every time the sheykh lifts his leg.

At the right moment the sail is again shaken down; and the boat at once feels it. It is worth five hundred men. The ropes slacken; we are going by the wind against the current; haste is made to unbend the cable; line after line is let go until we are held by one alone; the crowd thins out, dropping away with no warning, and before we know that the play is played out, the cataract people have lost all interest in it, and are scattering over the black rocks to their homes. A few stop to cheer; the chief conductor is last seen on a rock, swinging the white rag, hurrahing and salaaming in grinning exultation; the last line is cast off, and we round the point and come into smooth but swift water, and glide into a calm wind. The noise, the struggle, the tense strain, the uproar of men and waves for four hours are all behind; and hours of keener excitement and enjoyment we have rarely known. At 12.20 we left Assouan; at 4.45 we swung round the rocky bend above the last and greatest rapid. I write these figures; for they will be not without a melancholy interest to those who have spent two or three days or a week in making this passage.

Turning away from the ragged mountains of granite which obstruct the straight course of the river, we sail by Mahatta, a little village of Nubians, a port where the trading and freight boats plying between the First and Second Cataract load and unload. There is a forest of masts and spars along the shore, which is piled with merchandise, and dotted with sunlit figures squatting in the sand, as if waiting for the goods to tranship themselves. With the sunlight slanting on our full sail, we glide into the shadow of high rocks, and enter, with the suddenness of a first discovery, into a deep winding river, the waters of which are dark and smooth, between lofty walls of granite. These historic masses, which have seen pass so many splendid processions and boastful expeditions of conquest in what seems to us the twilight of the world, and which excited the wonder of Father Herodotus only the other day, almost in our own time (for the Greeks belong to us and not to antiquity as it now unfolds itself), are piled in strange shapes, tottling rock upon rock, built up grotesquely, now in likeness of animal, or the gigantic profile of a human face, or temple walls and castle towers and battlements. We wind through the solemn highway, and suddenly, in the very gateway, Philæ! The lovely! Philæ, the most sentimental ruin in Egypt. There are the great pylon of the temple of Isis, the long colonnades of pillars, the beautiful square temple, with lofty columns and elongated capitals, misnamed Pharaoh's bed. The little oblong island, something like twelve hundred feet long, banded all round by an artificial wall, an island of rock completely covered with ruins, is set like the stone of a ring, with a circle of blue water about it, in the clasp of higher encircling granite peaks and ledges. On the left bank, as we turn to pass to the east of the island, is a gigantic rock, which some persons have imagined was a colossus once, perhaps in pre-Adamic times, but which now has no resemblance to human shape, except in a breast and left arm. Some Pharaoh cut his cartouche on the back—a sort of postage-stamp to pass the image along down the ages. The Pharaohs were a vulgar lot; they cut their names wherever they could find a conspicuous and smooth place.

While we are looking, distracted with novelty at every turn, and excited by a grandeur and loveliness opening upon us every moment, we have come into a quiet haven, shut in on all sides by broken ramparts,—alone with this island of temples. The sun is about to set, and its level light comes to us through the columns, and still gilds with red and yellow gold the Libyan sand sifted over the cliffs. We moor at once to a sand-bank which has formed under the broken walls, and at once step on shore. We climb to the top of the temple walls; we walk on the stone roof; we glance into the temple on the roof, where is sculptured the resurrection of Osiris. This cannot be called an old temple. It is a creation of the Ptolemies, though it doubtlessly replaced an older edifice. The temple of Isis was not begun more than three centuries before our era. Not all of these structures were finished—the priests must have been still carving on their walls these multitudes of sculptures, when Christ began his mission; and more than four centuries after that the mysterious rites of Isis were still celebrated in these dark chambers. It is silent and dead enough here now; and there lives nowhere upon the earth any man who can even conceive the state of mind that gave those rites vitality. Even Egypt has changed its superstitions.

Peace has come upon the earth after the strain of the last few hours. We can scarcely hear the roar of the rapids, in the beating of which we had been. The sun goes, leaving a changing yellow and faint orange on the horizon. Above in the west is the crescent moon; and now all the sky thereabout is rosy, even to the zenith, a delicate and yet deep colour, like that of the blush rose—a transparent colour that glows. A little later we see from our boat the young moon through the columns of the lesser temple. The January night is clear and perfectly dry; no dew is falling—no dew ever falls here—and the multiplied stars burn with uncommon lustre. When everything else is still, we hear the roar of the rapids coming steadily on the night breeze, sighing through the old and yet modern palace-temples of the *parvenu* Ptolemies, and of Cleopatra—a new race of conquerors and pleasure hunters, who in vain copied the magnificent works of the ancient Pharaohs.

Here on a pylon gate, General Dessaix has recorded the fact that in February (Ventose) in the seventh year of the Republic, General Bonaparte being then in possession of Lower Egypt, he pursued to this spot the retreating Memlooks. Egyptian kings, Ethiopian usurpers, Persians, Greeks, Romans, Nectanebo, Cambyses, Ptolemy, Philadelphus, Cleopatra, and her Roman lovers, Dessaix,—these are all shades now.

CHAPTER XX.

ON THE BORDERS OF THE DESERT.

IN PASSING the First Cataract of the Nile we pass an ancient boundary line; we go from the Egypt of old to the Ethiopia of old; we go from the Egypt proper of to-day into Nubia. We find a different country, a different river; the people are of another race; they have a different language. We have left the mild, lazy, gentle fellaheen—a mixed lot, but in general of Arabic blood—and come to Barábra, whose district extends from Philæ to the Second Cataract, a freer, manlier, sturdier people altogether. There are two tribes of them, the Kenóos and the Nooba; each has its own language.

Philæ was always the real boundary line, though the Pharaohs pushed their frontier now and again, down towards the equator, and built temples and set up their images, as at Aboo Simbel, as at Samneh, and raked the south land for slaves and ivory, concubines and gold. But the Ethiopians turned the tables now and again, and conquered Egypt, and reigned in the palaces of the Pharaohs, taking that title even, and making their names dreaded as far as Judea and Assyria.

The Ethiopians were cousins indeed of the old Egyptians, and of the Canaanites, for they were descendants of Cush, as the Egyptians were of Mizriam, and the Canaanites were of Canaan; three of the sons of Ham. The Cushites, or Ethiops, although so much withdrawn from the theatre of history, have done their share of fighting—the main business of man hitherto. Besides quarrels with their own brethren, they had often the attentions of the two chief descendants of Shem,—the Jews and the Arabs; and after Mohammed's coming, the Arabs descended into Nubia and forced the inhabitants into their religion at the point of the sword. Even the sons of Japhet must have their crack at these children of the "Sun-burned." It was a Roman prefect who, to avenge an attack on Syene by a warlike woman, penetrated as far south as El Berkel (of the present day), and overthrew Candace the queen of the Ethiopians in Napata, her capital; the large city, also called Meroë, of which Herodotus heard such wonders.

Beyond Ethiopia lies the vast, black cloud of Negroland. These negroes, with the crisp, woolly hair, did not descend from anybody, according to the last reports; neither from Shem, Ham nor Japhet. They have no part in the royal house of Noah. They are left out in the heat. They are the puzzle of ethnologists, the mystery of mankind. They are the real aristocracy of the world, their origin being lost in the twilight of time; no one else can trace his descent so far back and come to nothing. M. Lenormant says the black races have no tradition of the Deluge. They appear to have been passed over altogether, then. Where were they hidden? When we first know Central Africa they are there. Where did they come from? The great effort of ethnologists is to get them dry-shod round the Deluge, since derivation from Noah is denied them. History has no information how they came into Africa. It seems to me that, in history, whenever we hear of the occupation of a new land, there is found in it a primitive race, to be driven out or subdued. The country of the primitive negro is the only one that has never invited the occupation of a more powerful race. But the negro blood, by means of slavery, has been extensively distributed throughout the Eastern world.

These reflections did not occur to us the morning we left Philæ. It was too early. In fact, the sun was just gilding "Pharaoh's Bed," as the beautiful little Ptolemaic temple is called, when we spread sail and, in the shadow of the broken crags and savage rocks, began to glide out of the jaws of this wild pass. At early morning everything has the air of adventure. It was as if we were discoverers, about to come into a new African kingdom at each turn in the swift stream.

One must see, he cannot imagine, the havoc and destruction hereabout, the grotesque and gigantic fragments of rock, the islands of rock, the precipices of rock, made by the torrent when it broke through here. One of these islands is Biggeh— all rocks, not enough soft spot on it to set a hen. The rocks are piled up into the blue sky; from their summit we get the best view of Philæ—the jewel set in this rim of stone.

Above Philæ we pass the tomb of a holy man, high on the hill, and underneath it, clinging to the slope, the oldest mosque in Nubia, the Mosque of Belal, falling now into ruin, but the minaret shows in color no sign of great age. How should it in this climate, where you might leave a pair of white gloves upon the rocks for a year, and expect to find them unsoiled.

"How old do you suppose that mosque is, Abd-el-Atti?"

"I tink about twelve hundred years old. Him been built by the Friends of our Prophet when they come up here to make the people believe."

I like this euphuism. "But," we ask, "suppose they didn't believe, what then?"

"When thim believe, all right; when thim not believe, do away wid 'em."

"But they might believe something else, if not what Mohammed believed."

"Well, what our Prophet say? Mohammed, he say, find him anybody believe in God, not to touch him; find him anybody believe in the Christ, not to touch him; find him anybody believe in Moses, not to touch him; find him believe in the prophets, not to touch him; find him believe in bit wood, piece stone, do way wid him. Not so? Men worship something, wood, stone, I can't tell—I tink dis is nothing."

Abd-el-Atti always says the "Friends" of Mohammed, never followers or disciples. It is a pleasant word, and reminds us of our native land. Mohammed had the good sense that our politicians have. When he wanted anything, a city taken, a new strip of territory added, a "third term," or any trifle, he "put himself in the hands of his friends."

The Friends were successful in this region. While the remote Abyssinians retained Christianity, the Nubians all became Moslems, and so remain to this day.

"You think, then, Abd-el-Atti, that the Nubians believed?"

"Thim 'bliged. But I tink dese fellows, all of 'em, Musselmens as far as the throat; it don't go lower down."

The story is that this mosque was built by one of Mohammed's captains after the great battle here with the Infidels—the Nubians. Those who fell in the fight, it is also only tradition, were buried in the cemetery near Assouan, and they are martyrs: to this day the Moslems who pass that way take off their slippers and shoes.

After the battle, as the corpses of the slain lay in indistinguishable heaps, it was impossible to tell who were martyrs and who were unbelievers. Mohammed therefore ordered that they should bury as Moslems all those who had large feet, and pleasant faces, with the mark of prayer on the forehead. The bodies of the others were burned as infidels.

As we sweep along, the mountains are still high on either side, and the strips of verdure are very slight. On the east bank, great patches of yellow sand, yellow as gold, and yet reddish in some lights, catch the sun.

I think it is the finest morning I ever saw, for clearness and dryness. The thermometer indicates only 60°, and yet it is not too cool. The air is like wine. The sky is absolutely cloudless, and of wonderful clarity. Here is a perfectly pure and sweet atmosphere. After a little, the wind freshens, and it is somewhat cold on deck, but the sky is like sapphire; let the wind blow for a month, it will raise no cloud, nor any film of it.

Everything is wanting in Nubia that would contribute to the discomfort of a winter residence:—

It never rains;
There is never any dew above Philæ;
There are no flies;
There are no fleas;
There are no bugs, nor any insects whatever. The attempt to introduce fleas into Nubia by means of dahabeëhs has been a failure.

In fact there is very little animal life; scarcely any birds are seen; fowls of all sorts are rare. There are gazelles, however, and desert hares, and chameleons. Our chameleons nearly starved for want of flies. There are big crocodiles and large lizards.

In a bend a few miles above Philæ is a whirlpool called Shaymt el Wah, from which is supposed to be a channel communicating under the mountain to the great Oasis one hundred miles distant. The popular belief in these subterranean communications is very common throughout the East. The holy well, Zem-Zem, at Mecca has a connection with a spring at El Gebel in Syria. I suppose that is perfectly well known. Abd-el-Atti has tasted the waters of both; and they are exactly alike; besides, did he not know of a pilgrim who lost his drinking-cup in Zem-Zem and recovered it in El Gebel.

This Nubia is, to be sure, but a river with a colored border, but I should like to make it seem real to you and not a mere country of the imagination. People find room to live here; life goes on after a fashion, and every mile there are evidences of a mighty civilization and a great power which left its record in gigantic works. There was a time, before the barriers broke away at Silsilis, when this land was inundated by the annual rise; the Nile may have perpetually expanded above here into a lake, as Herodotus reports.

We sail between low ridges of rocky hills, with narrow banks of green and a few palms, but occasionally there is a village of square mud houses. At Gertassee, boldly standing out on a rocky platform, are some beautiful columns, the remains of a temple built in the Roman time. The wind is strong and rather colder with the turn of noon; the nearer we come to the tropics the colder it becomes. The explanation is that we get nothing but desert winds; and the desert is cool at this season; that is, it breeds at night cool air, although one does not complain of its frigidity who walks over it at midday.

After passing Tafa, a pretty-looking village in the palms, which boasts ruins both pagan and Christian, we come to rapids and scenery almost as wild and lovely as that at Philæ. The river narrows, there are granite rocks and black boulders in the stream; we sail for a couple of miles in swift and deep water, between high cliffs, and by lofty rocky islands—not without leafage and some cultivation, and through a series of rapids, not difficult but lively. And so we go cheerily on, through savage nature and gaunt ruins of forgotten history; past Kalábshe, where are remains of the largest temple in Nubia; past Bayt el Wellee—"the house of the saint"—where Rameses II. hewed a beautiful temple out of the rock; past Gerf Hossáyn, where Rameses II. hewed a still larger temple out of the rock and covered it with his achievements, pictures in which he appears twelve feet high, and slaying small enemies as a husbandman threshes wheat with a flail. I should like to see an ancient stone wall in Egypt, where this Barnum of antiquity wasn't advertising himself.

We leave him flailing the unfortunate; at eight in the evening we are still going on, first by the light of the crescent moon and then by starlight, which is like a pale moonlight, so many and lustrous are the stars; and last, about eleven o'clock, we go aground, and stop a little below Dakkeh, or seventy-one miles from Philæ, that being our modest run for the day.

Dakkeh, by daylight, reveals itself as a small mud-village attached to a large temple. You would not expect to find a temple here, but its great pylon looms over the town, and it is worth at least a visit. To see such a structure in America we would travel a thousand miles; the traveller on the Nile debates whether he will go ashore.

The bank is lined with the natives, who have something to sell, eggs, milk, butter in little greasy "pats," and a sheep. The men are, as to features and complexion, rather Arabic than Nubian. The women have the high cheek-bones and broad faces of our Indian squaws, whom they resemble in a general way. The little girls, who wear the Nubian costume (a belt with fringe) and strings of beads, are not so bad; some of them well formed. The morning is cool, and the women all wear some outer garment, so that the Nubian costume is not seen in its simplicity, except as it is worn by children. I doubt if it is at any season. So far as we have observed the Nubian women, they are as modest in their dress as their Egyptian sisters. Perhaps ugliness and modesty are sisters in their country. All the women and girls have their hair braided in a sort of plait in front, and heavily soaked with grease, so that it looks as if they had on a wig or a frontlet of leather; it hangs in small, hard, greasy curls, like leathern thongs, down each side. The hair appears never to be undone—only freshly greased every morning. Nose-rings and earrings abound.

This handsome temple was begun by Ergamenes, an Ethiopian king ruling at Meroë, at the time of the second Ptolemy, during the Greek period; and it was added to both by Ptolemies and Cæsars. This Nubia would seem to have been in possession of Ethiopians and Egyptians turn and turn about, and, both having the same religion, the temples prospered.

Ergamenes has gained a reputation by a change he made in

his religion, as it was practised in Meroë. When the priests thought a king had reigned long enough it was their custom to send him notice that the gods had ordered him to die; and the king, who would rather die than commit an impiety, used to die. But Ergamenes tried another method, which he found worked just as well; he assembled all the priests and slew them—a very sensible thing on his part.

You would expect such a man to build a good temple. The sculptures are very well executed, whether they are of his time or owe their inspiration to Berenice and Cleopatra; they show greater freedom and variety than those of most temples; the figures of lions, monkeys, cows, and other animals are excellent; and there is a picture of a man playing on a musical instrument, a frame with strings stretched over it, played like a harp, but not harp shaped—the like of which is seen nowhere else. The temple has the appearance of a fortification as well as a place of worship. The towers of the propylon are ascended by interior flights of stairs, and have, one above the other, four good-sized chambers. The stairways and the rooms are lighted by slits in the wall about an inch in diameter on the outside: but cut with a slant from the interior through some five feet of solid stone. These windows are exactly like those in European towers, and one might easily imagine himself in a Middle Age fortification. The illusion is heightened by the remains of Christian paintings on the walls, fresh in color, and in style very like those of the earliest Christian art in Italian churches. In the temple we are attended by a Nubian with a long and threatening spear, such as the people like to carry here; the owner does not care for blood, however; he only wants a little backsheesh.

Beyond Dakkeh the country opens finely; the mountains fall back, and we look a long distance over the desert on each side, the banks having only a few rods of green. Far off in the desert on either hand and in front, are sharp pyramidical mountains, in ranges, in groups, the resemblance to pyramids being very striking. The atmosphere as to purity is extraordinary. Simply to inspire it is a delight for which one may well travel thousands of miles.

We pass small patches of the castor-oil plant, and of a reddish-stemmed bush, bearing the Indian *bendigo*, Arabic *bahima*, the fruit a sort of bean in appearance and about as palatable. The

16

castor-oil is much used by the women as a hair-dressing, but they are not fastidious; they use something else if oil is wanting. The demand for butter for this purpose raised the price of it enormously this morning at Dakkeh.

In the afternoon, waiting for wind, we walk ashore and out upon the naked desert—the desert which is broken only by an occasional oasis, from the Atlantic to the Red Sea; it has a basis of limestone, strewn with sand like gold-dust, and a *detritus* of stone as if it had been scorched by fire and worn by water. There is a great pleasure in strolling over this pure waste blown by the free air. We visit a Nubian village, and buy some spurious scarabaei off the necks of the ladies of the town—alas, for rural simplicity! But these women are not only sharp, they respect themselves sufficiently to dress modestly, and even draw their shawls over their faces. The children take the world as they find it as to clothes.

The night here, there being no moisture in the air, is as brilliant as the day; I have never seen the moon and stars so clear elsewhere. These are the evenings that invite to long pipes and long stories. Abd-el-Atti opens his budget from time to time, as we sit on deck and while the time with anecdotes and marvels out of old Arab chronicles, spiced with his own ready wit and singular English. Most of them are too long for these pages; but here is an anecdote which, whether true or not, illustrates the character of old Mohammed Ali:—

"Mohammed Ali sent one of his captains, name of Walee Kasheef, to Derr, capital of Nubia (you see it by and by, very fashionable place, like I see 'em in Hydee Park, what you call Rotten Row). Walee when he come there, see the women, their hair all twisted up and stuck together with grease and castor-oil, and their bodies covered with it. He called the sheykhs together and made them present of soap, and told them to make the women clean the hair and wash themselves and make themselves fit for prayer. It was in accordin' to the Moslem religion so to do.

"The Nubians they not like this part of our religion, they not like it at all. They send the sheykhs down to have conversation with Mohammed Ali, who been stop at Esneh. They complain of what Walee done. Mohammed send for Walee, and say,

"'What this you been done in Nubia?'

"'Nothing, your highness, 'eept trying to make the Nubians conform to the religion.'

"'Well,' says old Mohammed, 'I not send you up there as priest; I send you up to get a little money. Don't you trouble the Nubians. We don't care if they go to Gennéh or Gehennem if you get the money.'"

So the Nubians were left in sin and grease, and taxed accordingly. And at this day the taxes are even heavier. Every date-palm and every sakiya is taxed. A sakiya sometimes pays three pounds a year, when there is not a piece of fertile land for it to water three rods square.

CHAPTER XXI.

ETHIOPIA.

IT IS a sparkling morning at Wady Saboóa; we have the desert and some of its high, scarred, and sandy pyramidal peaks close to us, but as is usual where a wady, or valley, comes to the river, there is more cultivated land. We see very little of the temple of Rameses II. in this "Valley of the Lions," nor of the sphinxes in front of it. The desert sand has blown over it and over it in drifts like snow, so that we walk over the buried sanctuary, greatly to our delight. It is a pleasure to find one *adytum* into which we cannot go and see this Rameses pretending to make offerings, but really, as usual, offering to show himself.

At the village under the ledges, many of the houses are of stone, and the sheykh has a pretentious stone enclosure with little in it, all to himself. Shadoofs are active along the bank, and considerable crops of wheat, beans, and corn are well forward. We stop to talk with a bright-looking Arab, who employs men to work his shadoofs, and lives here in an enclosure of cornstalks, with a cornstalk kennel in one corner, where he and his family sleep. There is nothing pretentious about this establishment, but the owner is evidently a man of wealth, and, indeed, he has the bearing of a shrewd Yankee. He owns a camel, two donkeys, several calves and two cows, and two young Nubian girls for wives, black as coal and greased, but rather pleasant-faced. He has also two good guns—appears to have duplicates of nearly everything. Out of the cornstalk shanty his wives bring some handsome rugs for us to sit on.

The Arab accompanies us on our walk, as a sort of host of the country, and we are soon joined by others, black fellows; some of them carry the long flint-lock musket, for which they seem to have no powder; and all wear a knife in a sheath on the left-arm; but they are as peaceable friendly folk as you would care to meet, and simple-minded. I show the Arab my field-glass, an object new to his experience. He looks through it, as I direct, and is an astonished man, making motions with his hand, to indicate how the distant objects are drawn towards him, laughing with a soft and childlike delight, and then lowering the glass, looks at it, and cries,

"Bismillah! Bismillah," an ejaculation of wonder, and also intended to divert any misfortune from coming upon him on account of his indulgence in this pleasure.

He soon gets the use of the glass and looks beyond the river and all about, as if he were discovering objects unknown to him before. The others all take a turn at it, and are equally astonished and delighted. But when I cause them to look through the large end at a dog near by, and they see him remove far off in the desert, their astonishment is complete. My comrade's watch interested them nearly as much, although they knew its use; they could never get enough of its ticking and of looking at its works, and they concluded that the owner of it must be a pasha.

The men at work dress in the slight manner of the ancient Egyptians; the women, however, wear garments covering them, and not seldom hide the face at our approach. But the material of their dress is not always of the best quality; an old piece of sacking makes a very good garment for a Nubian woman. Most of them wear some trinkets, beads, or bits of silver or carnelian round the neck, and heavy bracelets of horn. The boys have not yet come into their clothing, but the girls wear the leathern belt and fringe adorned with shells.

The people have little, but they are not poor. It may be that this cornstalk house of our friend is only his winter residence, while his shadoof is most active, and that he has another establishment in town. There are too many sakiyas in operation for this region to be anything but prosperous, apparently. They are going all night as we sail along, and the screaming is weird enough in the stillness. I should think that a prisoner was being tortured every eighth of a mile on the bank. We are never out of hearing of their shrieks. But the cry is not exactly that of pain; it is rather a song than a cry, with an impish squeak in it, and a monotonous iteration of one idea, like all the songs here. It always repeats one sentence, which sounds like *Iskander logheh-n-e-e-e-n*—whatever it is in Arabic; and there is of course a story about it. The king, Alexander, had concealed under his hair two horns. Unable to keep the secret to himself he told it in confidence to the sakiya; the sakiya couldn't hold the news, but shrieked out, "Alexander has two horns," and the other sakiyas got it; and the scandal went the length of the Nile, and never can be hushed.

The Arabs personify everything, and are as full of superstitions as the Scotch; peoples who have nothing in common except it may be that the extreme predestinationism of the one approaches the fatalism of the other—begetting in both a superstitious habit, which a similar cause produced in the Greeks. From talking of the sakiya we wander into stories illustrative of the credulity and superstition of the Egyptians. Charms and incantations are relied on for expelling diseases and warding off dangers. The snake-charmer is a person still in considerable request in towns and cities. Here in Nubia there is no need of his offices, for there are no snakes; but in Lower Egypt, where snakes are common, the mud-walls and dirt-floors of the houses permit them to come in and be at home with the family. Even in Cairo, where the houses are of brick, snakes are much feared, and the house that is reputed to have snakes in it cannot be rented. It will stand vacant like an old mansion occupied by a ghost in a Christian country. The snake-charmers take advantage of this popular fear.

Once upon a time when Abd-el-Atti was absent from the city, a snake-charmer came to his house, and told his sister that he divined that there were snakes in the house. "My sister," the story goes on, "never see any snake to house, but she woman, and much 'fraid of snakes, and believe what him say. She told the charmer to call out the snakes. He set to work his mumble, his conjor—('exorcism') yes, dat's it, exorcism 'em, and bring out a snake. She paid him one dollar.

"Then the conjuror say 'This the wife; the husband still in the house and make great trouble if he not got out.'"

"He want him one pound for get the husband out, and my sister gave it.

"When I come home I find my sister very sick, very sick

indeed, and I say what is it? She tell me the story that the house was full of snakes and she had a man call them out, but the fright make her a long time ill.

"I said, you have done very well to get the snakes out, what could we do with a house full of the nasty things? And I said, I must get them out of another house I have—house I let him since to machinery."

"Machinery! For what kind of machinery! Steam engines?"

"No, mishcenary—have a school in it."

"Oh, missionary."

"Yes, let 'em have it for 'bout three hundred francs less than I get before. I think the school good for Cairo. I send for the snake-charmer, and I say I have 'nother house I think has snakes in it, and I ask him to divine and see. He comes back and says, my house is full of snakes, but he can charm them out. I say, good, I will pay you well. We appointed early next morning for the operation, and I agreed to meet the charmer at my house. I take with me big black fellow I have in the house, strong like a bull. When we get there I find the charmer there in front of the house and ready to begin. But I propose that we go in the house, it might make disturbance to the neighborhood to call so many serpents out into the street. We go in and I say, tell me the room of the most snakes. The charmer say, and as soon as we go in there, I make him sign the black fellow and he throw the charmer on the ground, and we tie him with a rope. We find in his bosom thirteen snakes and scorpions. I tell him I had no idea there were so many snakes in my house. Then I had the fellow before the kadi: he had to pay back all the money he got from my sister and went to prison. But," added Abd-el-Atti, "the doctor did not pay back the money for my sister's illness."

Alexandria was the scene of another snake story. The owner of a house there had for tenants an Italian and his wife, whose lease had expired, but who would not vacate the premises. He therefore hired a snake-charmer to go to the house one day when the family were out, and leave snakes in two of the rooms. When the lady returned and found a snake in one room she fled into another, but there another serpent raised his head and hissed at her. She was dreadfully frightened, and sent for the charmer, and had the snakes called out but she declared that she wouldn't occupy such a house another minute. And the family moved out that day of their own accord. A novel writ of ejectment.

In the morning we touched bottom as to cold weather, the thermometer at sunrise going down to 47°; it did, indeed, as we heard afterwards, go below 40° at Wady Halfa the next morning; but the days were sure to be warm enough. The morning is perfectly calm, and the depth of the blueness of the sky, especially as seen over the yellow desert sand and the blackened surface of the sandstone hills, is extraordinary. An artist's representation of this color would be certain to be called an exaggeration. The skies of Lower Egypt are absolutely pale in comparison.

Since we have been in the tropics, the quality of the sky has been the same day and night—sometimes a turquoise blue, such as on rare days we get in America through a break in the clouds, but exquisitely delicate for all its depth. We passed the Tropic of Cancer in the night, somewhere about Dendoór, and did not see it. I did not know, till afterwards, that there had been any trouble about it. But it seems that it has been moved from Assouan, where Strabo put it and some modern atlases still place it, southward, to a point just below the ruins of the temple of Dendoór, where Osiris and Isis were worshipped. Probably the temple, which is thought to be of the time of Augustus and consequently is little respected by an antiquarian, was not built with any reference to the Tropic of Cancer; but the point of the turning of the sun might well have been marked by a temple to the mysterious deity who personified the sun and who was slain and rose again.

Our walk on shore to-day reminds us of a rugged path in Switzerland. Before we come to Kalkeh (which is of no account, except that it is in the great bend below Korosko) the hills of sandstone draw close to the east bank, in some places in sheer precipices, in others leaving a strip of sloping sand. Along the cliff is a narrow donkey-path, which travel for thousands of years has worn deep; and we ascend along it high above the river. Wherever at the foot of the precipices there was a chance to grow a handful of beans or a hill of corn, we found the ground occupied. In one of these lonely recesses we made the acquaintance of an Arab family.

Walking rapidly, I saw something in the path, and held my foot just in time to avoid stepping upon a naked brown baby, rather black than brown, as a baby might be who spent his time outdoors in the sun without any umbrella.

"By Jorge! a nice plumpee little chile," cried Abd-el-Atti, who is fond of children, and picks up and shoulders the boy, who shows no signs of fear and likes the ride.

We come soon upon his parents. The man was sitting on a rock smoking a pipe. The woman, dry and withered, was picking some green leaves and blossoms, of which she would presently make a sort of *purée*, that appears to be a great part of the food of these people. They had three children. Their farm was a small piece of the sloping bank, and was in appearance exactly like a section of sandy railroad embankment grown to weeds. They had a few beans and some squash or pumpkin vines, and there were remains of a few hills of doora which had been harvested.

While the dragoman talked with the family, I climbed up to their dwelling, in a ravine in the rocks. The house was of the simplest architecture—a circular stone enclosure, so loosely laid up that you could anywhere put your hand through it. Over a segment of this were laid some cornstalks, and under these the piece of matting was spread for the bed. That matting was the only furniture of the house. All their clothes the family had on them, and those were none too many—they didn't hold out to the boy. And the mercury goes down to 47° these mornings! Before the opening of this shelter was a place for a fire against the rocks, and a saucepan, water-jar, and some broken bottles. The only attraction about this is its simplicity. Probably this is the country-place of the proprietor, where he retires for "shange of air" during the season when his crops are maturing, and then moves into town under the palm-trees during the heat of summer.

Talking about Mohammed (we are still walking by the shore) I found that Abd-el-Atti had never heard the legend of the miraculous suspension of the Prophet's coffin between heaven and earth; no Moslem ever believed any such thing: no Moslem ever heard of it.

"Then there isn't any tradition or notion of that sort among Moslems?"

"No, sir. Who said it?"

"Oh, it's often alluded to in English literature—by Mr. Carlyle for one, I think."

"What for him say that? I tink he must put something in his book to make it sell. How could it? Every year since Mohammed died, pilgrims been make to his grave, where he buried in the ground; shawl every year carried to cover it; always buried in that place. No Moslem think that."

"Once a good man, a welee of Fez, a friend of the Prophet, was visited by a vision and by the spirit of the Prophet, and he was gecited (excited) to go to Mecca and see him. When he was come near in the way, a messenger from the Prophet came to the welee, and told him not to come any nearer; that he should die and be buried in the spot where he then was. And it was so. His tomb you see it there now before you come to Mecca.

"When Mohammed was asked the reason why he would not permit the welee to come to his tomb to see him, he said that the welee was a great friend of his, and if he came to his tomb, he should feel bound to rise and see him; and he ought not to do that, for the time of the world was not yet fully come; if he rose from his tomb, it would be finish, the world would be at an end. Therefore he was 'bliged to refuse his friend.

"Nobody doubt he buried in the ground. But Ali, different. Ali, the son-in-law of Mohammed (married his daughter Fat'meh, his sons Hasan and Hoseyn,) died in Medineh. When he died he ordered that he should be put in a coffin, and said that in the morning there would come from the desert a man with a dromedary; that his coffin should be bound upon the back of the dromedary, and let go. In the morning, as was foretold, the man appeared, leading a dromedary; his head was veiled except his eyes. The coffin was bound upon the back of the beast, and the three went away into the desert; and no man ever saw either of them more, or knows, to this day, where Ali is buried. Whether it was a man or an angel with the dromedary, God knows."

Getting round the great bend at Korosko and Amada is the most vexatious and difficult part of the Nile navigation. The distance is only about eight miles, but the river takes a freak here to run south-south east, and as the wind here is usually north-north west, the boat has both wind and current against it. But this is not all; it is impossible to track on the west bank on account of the shallows and sandbars, and the channel on the east side is beset with dangerous rocks. We thought ourselves fortunate in making these eight miles in two days, and one of them was a very exciting day. The danger was in stranding the dahabeëh on the rocks, and being compelled to leave her; and our big boat was handled with great difficulty.

Traders and travellers going to the Upper Nile leave the river at Korosko. Here begins the direct desert route—as utterly waste, barren and fatiguing as any in Africa—to Aboo Hamed, Sennaar and Kartoom. The town lies between a fringe of palms on the river, and backed by high and savage desert mountains. As we pass we see on the high bank piles of merchandise and the white tents of the caravans.

This is still the region of slavery. Most of the Arabs, poor as they appear, own one or two slaves, got from Sennaar or Darfoor—though called generally Nubians. We came across a Sennaar girl to-day of perhaps ten years of age, hoeing alone in the field. The poor creature, whose ideas were as scant as her clothing, had only a sort of animal intelligence; she could speak a little Arabic, however (much more than we could—speaking of intelligence!) and said she did not dare come with us for fear her mistress would beat her. The slave trade is, however, greatly curtailed by the expeditions of the Khedive. The bright Abyssinian boy, Ahmed, whom we have on board, was brought from his home across the Red Sea by way of Mecca. This is one of the ways by which a few slaves still sift into Cairo.

We are working along in sight of Korosko all day. Just above it, on some rocks in the channel, lies a handsome dahabeëh belonging to a party of English gentlemen, which went on a week ago; touched upon concealed rocks in the evening as the crew were tracking, was swung further on by the current, and now lies high and almost dry, the Nile falling daily, in a position where she must wait for the rise next summer. The boat is entirely uninjured, and no doubt might have been got off the first day if there had only been mechanical skill in the crew. The governor at Derr sent down one hundred and fifty men, who hauled and heaved at it two or three days, with no effect. Half a dozen Yankees, with a couple of jack-screws, and probably with only logs for rollers, would have set it afloat. The disaster is exceedingly annoying to the gentlemen, who have, however, procured a smaller boat from Wady Halfa in which to continue their voyage. We are several hours in getting past these two boats, and accomplish it not without a tangling of rigging, scraping off of paint, smashing of deck rails, and the expenditure of a whole dictionary of Arabic. Our Arabs never see but one thing at a time. If they are getting the bow free, the stay-ropes and stern must take care of themselves. If, by simple heedlessness, we are letting the yard of another boat rip into our rigging, God wills it. While we are in this confusion and excitement, the dahabeëh of General McClellan and half a dozen in company, sweep down past us, going with wind and current.

It is a bright and delicious Sunday morning that we are still tracking above Korosko. To-day is the day the pilgrims to Mecca spend upon the mountain of Arafat. To-morrow they sacrifice; our crew will celebrate it by killing a sheep and eating it—and it is difficult to see where the sacrifice comes in for them. The Moslems along this shore lost their reckoning, mistook the day, and sacrificed yesterday.

This is not the only thing, however, that keeps this place in our memory. We saw here a pretty woman. Considering her dress, hair, the manner in which she had been brought up, and her looks, a tolerably pretty woman; a raving beauty in comparison with her comrades. She has a slight cast in one eye, that only shows for a moment occasionally, and then disappears. If these feeble tributary lines ever meet that eye, I beg her to know that, by reason of her slight visual defect, she is like a revolving light, all the more brilliant when she flashes out.

We lost time this morning, were whirled about in eddies and drifted on sandbars, owing to contradictory opinions among our navigators, none of whom seem to have the least sconce. They generally agree, however, not to do anything that the pilot orders. Our pilot from Philæ to Wady Halfa and back, is a Barábra, and one of the reïses of the Cataract, a fellow very tall, and thin as a hop-pole, with a withered face and a high forehead. His garments, a white cotton nightgown, without sleeves, a brown overgown with flowing sleeves, both reaching to the ankles, and a white turban. He is barefooted and barelegged, and, in his many excursions into the river to explore sandbars, I have noticed a hole where he has stuck his knee through his nightgown. His stature and his whole bearing have in them something, I know not what, of the theatrical air of the Orient.

He had a quarrel to-day with the crew, for the reason mentioned above, in which he was no doubt quite right, a quarrel conducted as usual with an extraordinary expense of words and vituperation. In his inflamed remarks, he at length threw out doubts about the mother of one of the crew, and probably got something back that enraged him still more. While the wrangle went on, the crew had gathered about their mess-dish on the forward deck, squatting in a circle round it, and dipping out great mouthfuls of the *purée* with the right hand. The pilot paced the upper deck, and his voice, which is like that of many waters, was lifted up in louder and louder lamentations, as the other party grew more quiet and were occupied with their dinner—throwing him a loose taunt now and then, followed by a chorus of laughter. He strode back and forth, swinging his arms, and declaring that he would leave the boat, that he would not stay where he was so treated, that he would cast himself into the river.

"When you do, you'd better leave your clothes behind," suggested Abd-el-Atti.

Upon this cruel sarcasm he was unable to contain himself longer. He strode up and down, raised high his voice, and tore his hair and rent his garments—the supreme act of Oriental desperation. I had often read of this performance, both in the Scriptures and in other Oriental writings, but I had never seen it before. The manner in which he tore his hair and rent his garments was as follows, to wit:—He almost entirely unrolled his turban, doing it with an air of perfect recklessness; and then he carefully wound it again round his smoothly shaven head. That stood for tearing his hair. He then swung his long arms aloft, lifted up his long garment above his head, and, with desperate force, appeared to be about to rend it in twain. But he never started a seam nor broke a thread. The nightgown wouldn't have stood much nonsense.

In the midst of his most passionate outburst, he went forward and filled his pipe, and then returned to his tearing and rending and his lamentations. The picture of a strong man in grief is always touching.

The country along here is very pretty, the curved shore for miles being a continual palm-grove, and having a considerable strip of soil which the sakiya irrigation makes very productive. Beyond this rise mountains of rocks in ledges; and when we climb them we see only a waste desert of rock strewn with loose shale, and, further inland, black hills of sandstone, which thickly cover the country all the way to the Red Sea.

Under the ledges are the habitations of the people, square enclosures of stone and clay of considerable size, with interior courts and kennels. One of them—the only sign of luxury we have seen in Nubia, had a porch in front of it covered with palm boughs. The men are well-made and rather prepossessing in appearance, and some of them well-dressed—they had no doubt made the voyage to Cairo; the women are hideous without exception. It is no pleasure to speak thus continually of woman: and I am sometimes tempted to say that I see here the brown and bewitching maids, with the eyes of the gazelle and the form of the houri, which gladden the sight of more fortunate voyagers through this idle land; but when I think of the heavy amount of misrepresentation that would be necessary to give any one of these creatures a reputation for good looks abroad, I shrink from the undertaking.

They are decently covered with black cotton mantles, which they make a show of drawing over the face; but they are perhaps wild rather than modest, and have a sort of animal shyness. Their heads are sights to behold. The hair is all braided in strings, long at the sides and cut off in front, after the style adopted now-a-days for children (and women) in civilised countries, and copied from the young princes, prisoners in the Tower. Each round strand of hair has a dab of clay on the end of it. The whole is drenched with castor-oil, and when the sun shines on it, it is as pleasant to one sense as to another. They have flattish noses, high cheek-bones, and always splendid teeth; and they all, young girls as well as old women, hold tobacco in their under lip, and squirt out the juice with placid and scientific accuracy. They wear two or three strings of trumpery beads and necklaces, bracelets of horn and of greasy leather, and occasionally a finger-ring or two. Nose-rings they wear if they have them; if not, they keep the bore open for one by inserting a kernel of doora.

In going back to the boat we met a party of twenty or thirty of these attractive creatures, who were returning from burying a boy of the village. They came striding over the sand, chattering in shrill and savage tones. Grief was not so weighty on them that they forgot to demand backsheesh, and (unrestrained by the men in the town) their clamor for it was like the cawing of crows; and their noise, when they received little from us, was worse. The tender and loving woman, stricken in grief by death, is, in these regions, when denied backsheesh, an enraged, squawking bird of prey. They left us with scorn in their eyes and abuse on their tongues.

At a place below Korosko we saw a singular custom, in which the women appeared to better advantage. A whole troop of women, thirty or forty of them, accompanied by children, came in a rambling procession down to the Nile, and brought a baby just forty days old. We thought at first that they were about to dip the infant into Father Nile, as an introduction to the fountain of all the blessings of Egypt. Instead of this, however, they sat down on the bank, took kohl and daubed it in the little fellow's eyes. They perform this ceremony by the Nile when the boy is forty days old, and they do it that he may have a fortunate life. Kohl seems to enlarge the pupil, and doubtless it is intended to open the boy's eyes early.

At one of the little settlements to-day the men were very hospitable, and brought us out plates (straw) of sweet dried dates. Those that we did not eat, the sailor with us stuffed into his pocket; our sailors never let a chance of provender slip, and would, so far as capacity "to live on the country" goes, make good soldiers. The Nubian dates are called the best in Egypt. They are longer than the dates of the Delta, but hard and quite dry. They take the place of coffee here in the complimentary hospitality. Whenever a native invites you to take "coffee," and you accept, he will bring you a plate of dates and probably a plate of popped doora, like our popped corn. Coffee seems not to be in use here; even the governors entertain us with dates and popped corn.

We are working up the river slowly enough to make the acquaintance of every man, woman, and child on the banks; and a precious lot of acquaintances we shall have. I have no desire to force them upon the public, but it is only by these details that I can hope to give you any idea of the Nubian life.

We stop at night. The moon and starlight is something superb. From the high bank under which we are moored, the broad river, the desert opposite, and the mountains, appear in a remote African calm—a calm only broken by the shriek of the sakiyas which pierce the air above and below us.

In the sakiya near us, covered with netting to keep off the north wind, is a little boy, patient and black, seated on the pole of the wheel, urging the lean cattle round and round. The little chap is alone and at some distance from the village, and this must be for him lonesome work. The moonlight, through the chinks of the palm-leaf, touches tenderly his pathetic figure, when we look in at the opening, and his small voice utters the one word of Egypt—"backsheesh."

Attracted by a light—a rare thing in a habitation here—we walk over to the village. At the end of the high enclosure of a dwelling there is a blaze of fire, which is fed by doora-stalks, and about it squat five women, chattering; the fire lights up their black faces and hair shining with the castor-oil. Four of them are young; and one is old and skinny, and with only a piece of sacking for all clothing. Their husbands are away in Cairo, or up the river with a trading dahabeëh (so they tell our guide); and these poor creatures are left here (it may be for years, it may be for ever) to dig their own living out of the ground. It is quite the fashion husbands have in this country; but the women are attached to their homes; they have no desire to go elsewhere. And I have no doubt that in Cairo they would pine for the free and simple life of Nubia.

These women all want backsheesh, and no doubt will quarrel over the division of the few piastres they have from us. Being such women as I have described, and using tobacco as has been sufficiently described also, crouching about these embers, this group composes as barbaric a picture as one can anywhere see. I need not have gone so far to see such a miserable group; I could have found one as wretched in Pigville (every city has its Pigville). Yes, but this is characteristic of the country.

These people are as good as anybody here. (We have been careful to associate only with the first families.) These women have necklaces and bracelets, and rings in their ears, just like any woman, and rings in the hair, twisted in with the clay and castor-oil. And in Pigville one would not have the range of savage rocks, which tower above these huts, whence the jackals, wolves, and gazelles come down to the river, nor the row of palms, nor the Nile, and the sands beyond, yellow in the moonlight.

CHAPTER XXII.

LIFE IN THE TROPICS.—WADY HALFA.

OURS is the crew to witch the world with noble seamanship. It is like a first-class orchestra, in which all the performers are artists. Ours are all captains. The reïs is merely an elder brother. The pilot is not heeded at all. With so many intentions on board, it is an hourly miracle that we get on at all.

We are approaching the capital of Nubia, trying to get round a sharp bend in the river, with wind adverse, current rapid, sandbars on all sides. Most of the crew are in the water ahead, trying to haul us round the point of a sand-spit on which the stream foams, and then swirls in an eddy below. I can see now the Pilot, the long Pilot, who has gone in to feel about for deep water, in his white nightgown, his shaven head, denuded of its turban, shining in the sun, standing in two feet of water, throwing his arms wildly above his head, screaming entreaties, warnings, commands, imprecations upon the sailors in the river and the commanders on the boat. I can see the crew, waist deep, slacking the rope which they have out ahead, stopping to discuss the situation. I can see the sedate reïs on the bow arguing with the raving pilot, the steersman, with his eternal smile, calmly regarding the peril, and the boat swinging helplessly about and going upon the shoals. "Stupids," mutters Abd-el-Atti, who is telling his beads rapidly, as he always does in exciting situations.

When at length we pass the point, we catch the breeze so suddenly and go away with it, that there is no time for the men to get on board, and they are obliged to scamper back over the sand-spits to the shore and make a race of it to meet us at

Derr. We can see them running in file, dodging along under the palms by the shore, stopping to grab occasionally a squash or a handful of beans for the pot.

The capital of Nubia is the New York of this region, not so large, nor so well laid out, nor so handsomely built, but the centre of fashion and the residence of the *ton*. The governor lives in a whitewashed house, and there is a sycamore here eight hundred years old, which is, I suppose, older than the Stuyvesant Pear in New York. The houses are not perched up in the air like tenement buildings for the poor, but aristocratically keep to the ground in one-story rooms; and they are beautifully moulded of a tough clay. The whole town lies under a palm-grove. The elegance of the capital, however, is not in its buildings, but in its women; the ladies who come to the river to fill their jars are arrayed in the height of the mode. Their hair is twisted and clayed and castor-oiled, but, besides this and other garments, they wear an outer robe of black which sweeps the ground for a yard behind, and gives them the grace and dignity that court-robes always give. You will scarcely see longer skirts on Broadway or in a Paris *salon*. I have, myself, no doubt that the Broadway fashions came from Derr, all except the chignons. Here the ladies wear their own hair.

Making no landing in this town so dangerous to one susceptible to the charms of fashion, we went on, and stopped at night near Ibreen, a lofty precipice, or range of precipices, the southern hill crowned with ruins and fortifications which were last occupied by the Memlooks, half a century and more ago. The night blazed with beauty; the broad river was a smooth mirror, in which the mountains and the scintillating hosts of heaven were reflected. And we saw a phenomenon which I have never seen elsewhere. Not only were the rocky ledges reproduced in a perfect definition of outline, but even in the varieties of shade, in black and reddish-brown color.

Perhaps it needs the affidavits of all the party to the more surprising fact, that we were all on deck next morning before five o'clock, to see the SOUTHERN CROSS. The moon had set, and these famous stars of the southern sky flashed color and brilliancy like enormous diamonds. "Other worlds than ours"? I should think so! All these myriads of burning orbs only to illuminate our dahabeëh and a handful of Nubians, who are asleep! The Southern Cross lay just above the horizon and not far from other stars of the first quality. There are, I believe, only three stars of the first magnitude and one of the second, in this constellation, and they form, in fact, not a cross but an irregular quadrilateral. It needs a vivid imagination and the aid of small stars to get even a semblance of a cross out of it. But if you add to it, as we did, for the foot of the cross, a brilliant in a neighboring constellation, you have a noble cross.

This constellation is not so fine as Orion, and for all we saw, we would not exchange our northern sky for the southern; but this morning we had a rare combination. The Morning Star was blazing in the east; and the Great Bear (who has been nightly sinking lower and lower, until he dips below the horizon) having climbed high up above the Pole in the night, filled the northern sky with light. In this lucid atmosphere the whole heavens from north to south seemed to be crowded with stars of the first size.

During the morning we walked on the west bank through a castor-oil plantation; many of the plants were good-sized trees, with boles two and a half to three inches through, and apparently twenty-five feet high. They were growing in the yellow sand which had been irrigated by sakiyas, but was then dry, and some of the plants were wilting. We picked up the ripe seeds and broke off some of the fat branches; and there was not water enough in the Nile to wash away the odor afterwards.

Walking back over the great sand-plain towards the range of desert mountains, we came to an artificial mound—an ash-heap, in fact—fifty or sixty feet high. At its base is a habitation of several compartments, formed by sticking the stalks of castor-oil plants into the ground, with a roof of the same. Here we found several women with very neat dabs of clay on the ends of their hair-twists, and a profusion of necklaces, rings in the hair and other ornaments—among them, scraps of gold. The women were hospitable, rather modest than shy, and set before us plates of dried dates; and no one said "backsheesh." A better class of people than those below, and more purely Nubian.

It would perhaps pay to dig open this mound. Near it are

three small oases, watered by sakiyas, which draw from wells that are not more than twenty feet deep. The water is clear as crystal but not cool. These are ancient Egyptian wells, which have been re-opened within a few years; and the ash-mound is no doubt the *débris* of a village and an old Egyptian settlement.

At night we are a dozen miles from Aboo Simbel (Ipsamboul), the wind—which usually in the winter blows with great and steady force from the north in this part of the river—having taken a fancy to let us see the country.

A morning walk takes us over a rocky desert; the broken shale is distributed as evenly over the sand as if the whole had once been under water, and the shale were a dried mud, cracked in the sun. The miserable dwellings of the natives are under the ledges back of the strip of arable land. The women are shy and wild as hawks, but in the mode; they wear a profusion of glass beads and trail their robes in the dust.

It is near this village that we have an opportunity to execute justice. As the crew were tracking, and lifting the rope over a sakiya, the hindmost sailor saw a sheath-knife on the bank, and thrust it into his pocket as he walked on. In five minutes the owner of the knife discovered the robbery, and came to the boat to complain. The sailor denied having the knife, but upon threat of a flogging gave it up. The incident, however, aroused the town, men and women came forth discussing it in a high key, and some foolish fellows threatened to stone our boat. Abd-el-Atti replied that he would stop and give them a chance to do it. Thereupon they apologized; and, as there was no wind, the dragoman asked leave to stop and do justice.

A court was organized on shore. Abd-el-Atti sat down on a lump of earth, grasping a marline-spike, the crew squatted in a circle in the high beans, and the culprit was arraigned. The owner testified to his knife, a woman swore she saw the sailor take it. Abd-el-Atti pronounced sentence, and rose to execute it with his stake. The thief was thrown upon the ground and held by two sailors. Abd-el-Atti, resolute and solemn as an executioner, raised the club and brought it down with a tremendous whack—not however upon the back of the victim, he had at that instant squirmed out of the way. This conduct greatly enraged the minister of justice, who thereupon came at his object with fury, and would no doubt have hit him, if the criminal had not got up and run, screaming, with the sailors and Abd-el-Atti after him. The ground was rough, the legs of Abd-el-Atti are not long and his wind is short. The fellow was caught, and escaped again and again, but the punishment was a mere scrimmage; whenever Abd-el-Atti, in the confusion, could get a chance to strike he did so, but generally hit the ground, sometimes the fellow's gown and perhaps once or twice the man inside, but never to his injury. He roared all the while that he was no thief, and seemed a good deal more hurt by the charge that he was, than by the stick. The beating was, in short, only a farce laughable from beginning to end, and not a bad sample of Egyptian justice. And it satisfied everybody.

Having put ourselves thus on friendly relations with this village, one of the inhabitants brought down to the boat a letter for the dragoman to interpret. It had been received two weeks before from Alexandria, but no one had been able to read it until our boat stopped here. Fortunately we had the above little difficulty here. The contents of the letter gave the village employment for a month. It brought news of the death of two inhabitants of the place, who were living as servants in Alexandria, one of them a man eighty years old and his son aged sixty.

I never saw grief spread so fast and so suddenly as it did with the uncorking of this vial of bad news. Instantly a lamentation and wild mourning began in all the settlement. It wasn't ten minutes before the village was buried in grief. And, in an incredible short space of time, the news had spread up and down the river, and the grief-stricken began to arrive from other places. Where they came from, I have no idea; it did not seem that we had passed so many women in a week as we saw now. They poured in from all along the shore, long strings of them, striding over the sand, throwing up their garments, casting dust on their heads (and all of it stuck), howling, flocking like wild geese to a rendezvous, and filling the air with their clang. They were arriving for an hour or two.

The men took no part in this active demonstration. They were seated gravely before the house in which the bereaved relatives gathered; and there I found Abd-el-Atti, seated also, and holding forth upon the inevitable coming of death, and saying that there was nothing to be regretted in this case, for the time of these men had come. If it hadn't come, they wouldn't have died. Not so?

The women crowded into the enclosure and began mourning in a vigorous manner. The chief ones grouping themselves in an irregular ring, cried aloud: "O that he had died here!" "O that I had seen his face when he died;" repeating these lamentations over and over again, throwing up the arms and then the legs in a kind of barbaric dance as they lamented, and uttering long and shrill ululations at the end of each sentence.

To-day they kill a calf and feast, and to-morrow the lamentations and the African dance will go on, and continue for a week. These people are all feeling. It is a heathen and not a Moslem custom however; and whether it is of negro origin or of ancient Egyptian I do not know, but probably the latter. The ancient Egyptian women are depicted in the tombs mourning in this manner; and no doubt the Jews also so bewailed, when they "lifted up their voices" and cast dust on their heads, as we saw these Nubians do. It is an unselfish pleasure to an Eastern woman to "lift up the voice." The heavy part of the mourning comes upon the women, who appear to enjoy it. It is their chief occupation, after the carrying of water and the grinding of doora, and probably was so with the old race; these people certainly keep the ancient customs; they dress the hair, for one thing, very much as the Egyptians did, even to the castor-oil.

At this village, as in others in Nubia, the old women are the corn-grinders. These wasted skeletons sit on the ground before a stone with a hollow in it; in this they bruise the doora with a smaller stone; the flour is then moistened and rubbed to a paste. The girls and younger women, a great part of the time, are idling about in their finery. But, then, they have the babies and the water to bring; and it must be owned that some of them work in the field—grubbing grass and stuff for "greens" and for fuel, more than the men. The men do the heavy work of irrigation.

But we cannot stay to mourn with those who mourn a week in this style; and in the evening, when a strong breeze springs up, we spread our sail and go, in the "daylight of the moon," flying up the river, by black and weird shores; and before midnight pass lonesome Aboo Simbel, whose colossi sit in the moonlight with the impassive mien they have held for so many ages.

In the morning, with an easy wind, we are on the last stage of our journey. We are almost at the limit of dahabeëh navigation. The country is less interesting than it was below. The river is very broad, and we look far over the desert on each side. The strip of cultivated soil is narrow and now and again disappears altogether. To the east are seen, since we passed Aboo Simbel, the pyramid hills, some with truncated tops, scattered without plan over the desert. It requires no stretch of fancy to think that these mathematically built hills are pyramids erected by races anterior to Menes, and that all this waste that they dot is a necropolis of that forgotten people.

The sailors celebrate the finishing of the journey by a ceremony of state and dignity. The chief actor is Farrag, the wit of the crew. Suddenly he appears as the Governor of Wady Halfa, with horns on his head, face painted, a long beard, hair sprinkled with flour, and dressed in shaggy sheepskin. He has come on board to collect his taxes. He opens his court, with the sailors about him, holding a long marline-spike which he pretends to smoke as a chibook. His imitation of the town dignitaries along the river is very comical, and his remarks are greeted with roars of laughter. One of the crew acts as his bailiff and summons all the officers and servants of the boat before him, who are thrown down upon the deck and bastinadoed, and released on payment of backsheesh. The travellers also have to go before the court and pay a fine for passing through the Governor's country. The Governor is treated with great deference till the end of the farce, when one of his attendants sets fire to his beard, and another puts him out with a bucket of water.

The end of our journey is very much like the end of everything else—there is very little in it. When we follow anything to its utmost, we are certain to be disappointed—simply because it is the nature of things to taper down to a point. I suspect it must always be so with the traveller, and that the farther he penetrates into any semi-savage continent, the meaner and ruder will he find the conditions of life. When we come to the end, ought we not to expect the end?

We have come a thousand miles not surely to see Wady Halfa but to see the thousand miles. And yet Wady Halfa, figuring as it does on the map, the gate of the great Second Cataract, the head of navigation, the destination of so many eager travellers, a point of arrival and departure of caravans, might be a little less insignificant than it is. There is the thick growth of palm-trees under which the town lies, and beyond it, several miles, on the opposite west bank, is the cliff of Aboosir, which looks down upon the cataract; but for this noble landmark, this dominating rock, the traveller could not feel that he had arrived anywhere, and would be so weakened by the shock of arriving nowhere at the end of so long a journey (as a man is by striking a blow in the air) that he would scarcely have strength to turn back.

At the time of our arrival, however, Wady Halfa, has some extra life. An expedition of the government is about to start for Darfoor. When we moor at the east bank, we see on the west bank the white tents of a military encampment set in right lines on the yellow sand; near them the government storehouse and telegraph-office, and in front a mounted howitzer and a Gatlin gun. No contrast could be stronger. Here is Wady Halfeh, in the doze of an African town, a collection of mud-huts under the trees, listless, apathetic, sitting at the door of a vast region, without either purpose or ambition. There, yonder, is a piece of life out of our restless age. There are the tents, the guns, the instruments, the soldiers and servants of a new order of things for Africa. We hear the trumpet call to drill. The flag which is planted in the sand in front of the commander's tent is to be borne to the equator.

But this is not a military expedition. It is a corps of scientific observation, simply. Since the Sultan of Darfoor is slain and the Khedive's troops have occupied his capital, and formally attached that empire to Egypt, it is necessary to know something of its extent, resources, and people, concerning all of which we have only the uncertain reports of traders. It is thought by some that the annexation of Darfoor adds five millions to the population of the Khedive's growing empire. In order that he may know what he has conquered, he has sent out exploring expeditions, of which this is one. It is under command of Purdy Bey assisted by Lieutenant-Colonel Mason, two young American officers of the Khedive, who fought on opposite sides in our civil war. They are provided with instruments for making all sorts of observations, and are to report upon the people and the physical character and capacity of the country. They expect to be absent three years, and after surveying Darfoor, will strike southward still, and perhaps contribute something to the solution of the Nile problem. For escort they have a hundred soldiers only, but a large train of camels and attendants. In its purpose it is an expedition that any civilized ruler might be honored for setting on foot. It is a brave overture of civilization to barbarism. The nations are daily drawing nearer together. As we sit in the telegraph-office here, messages are flashed from Cairo to Kartoom.

CHAPTER XXIII.

APPROACHING THE SECOND CATARACT.

THERE are two ways of going to see the Second Cataract and the cliff of Aboosir, which is about six miles above Wady Halfa; one is by small boat, the other by dromedary over the desert. We chose the latter, and the American officers gave us a mount and their company also. Their camp presented a lively scene when we crossed over to it in the morning. They had by requisition pressed into their service three or four hundred camels, and were trying to select out of the lot half a dozen fit to ride. The camels were, in fact, mostly burden camels, and not trained to the riding-saddle; besides, half of them were poor, miserable rucks of bones, half-starved to death; for the Arabs, whose business it had been to feed them, had stolen the Government supplies. An expedition which started south two weeks ago lost more than a hundred camels from starvation, before it reached Semdeh, thirty-five miles up the river. They had become so weak that they wilted and died on the first hard march. For his size and knotty appearance the camel is the most disappointing of beasts. He is a sheep as to endurance. As to temper, he is vindictive.

Authorities differ in regard to the distinction between the camel and the dromedary. Some say that there are no camels in Egypt, that they are all dromedaries, having one hump; and that the true camel is the Bactrian, which has two humps. It is customary here, however, to call those camels which are beasts of burden, and those dromedaries which are trained to ride; the distinction being that between the cart-horse and the saddle-horse.

The camel-drivers, who are as wild Arabs as you will meet

anywhere, select a promising beast and drag him to the tent. He is reluctant to come; he rebels against the saddle; he roars all the time it is being secured on him, and when he is forced to kneel, not seldom he breaks away from his keepers and shambles off into the desert. The camel does this always; and every morning on a march he receives his load only after a struggle. The noise of the drivers is little less than the roar of the beasts, and with their long hair, shaggy breasts and bare legs, they are not less barbarous in appearance.

Mounting the camel is not difficult, but it has some sweet surprises for the novice. The camel lies upon the ground with all his legs shut up under him like a jackknife. You seat yourself in the broad saddle, and cross your legs in front of the pommel. Before you are ready something like a private earthquake begins under you. The camel raises his hindquarters suddenly, and throws you over upon his neck; and, before you recover from that, he straightens up his knees and gives you a jerk over his tail; and, while you are not at all certain what has happened, he begins to move off with that dislocated walk which sets you into a see-saw motion, a weaving backwards and forwards in the capacious saddle. Not having a hinged back fit for this movement, you lash the beast with your koorbásh to make him change his gait. He is nothing loth to do it, and at once starts into a high trot which sends you a foot into the air at every step, bobs you from side to side, drives your backbone into your brain, and makes castanets of your teeth. Capital exercise. When you have enough of it, you pull up, and humbly enquire what is the heathen method of riding a dromedary.

It is simple enough. Shake the loose halter-rope (he has neither bridle nor bit) against his neck as you swing the whip, and the animal at once swings into an easy pace; that is, a pretty easy pace, like that of a rocking-horse. But everything depends upon the camel. I happened to mount one that it was a pleasure to ride, after I brought him to the proper gait. We sailed along over the smooth sand, with level keel, and (though the expression is not nautical) on cushioned feet. But it is hard work for the camel, this constant planting of his spongy feet in the yielding sand.

Our way lay over the waste and rolling desert (the track of the southern caravans) at some little distance from the river; and I suppose six miles of this travel are as good as a hundred. The sun was blazing hot, the yellow sand glowed in it, and the far distance of like sand and bristling ledges of black rock shimmered in waves of heat. No tree, no blade of grass, nothing but blue sky bending over a sterile land. Yet, how sweet was the air, how pure the breath of the desert, how charged with electric life the rays of the sun!

The rock Aboosir, the *ultima Thule* of pleasure travel on the Nile, is a sheer precipice of perhaps two to three hundred feet above the Nile; but this is high enough to make it one of the most extensive lookouts in Egypt. More desert can be seen here than from almost anywhere else. The Second Cataract is spread out beneath us. It is less a "fall" even than the First. The river is from a half mile to a mile in breadth, and for a distance of some five miles is strewn with trap-rock, boulders and shattered fragments, through which the Nile swiftly forces itself in a hundred channels. There are no falls of any noticeable height. Here, on the flat rock, where we eat our luncheon, a cool breeze blows from the north. Here, on this eagle's perch, commanding a horizon of desert and river for a hundred miles, fond visitors have carved their immortal names, following an instinct of ambition that is well-nigh universal, in the belief no doubt that the name will have for us, who come after, all the significance it has in the eyes of him who carved it. But I cannot recall a single name I read there; I am sorry that I cannot, for it seems a pitiful and cruel thing to leave them there in their remote obscurity.

From this rock we look with longing to the southward, into vast Africa, over a land we may not further travel, which we shall probably never see again; on the far horizon the blue peaks of Dongola are visible, and beyond these we know are the ruins of Meroë, that ancient city, the capital of that Ethiopian queen Candace, whose dark face is lighted up by a momentary gleam from the Scriptures. On the beach at Wady Halfa are half a dozen trading vessels, loaded with African merchandise for Cairo, and in the early morning there is a great hubbub among the merchants and the caravan owners. A sudden dispute arises among a large group around the ferry-boat, and there ensues that excited war, or movement, which always threatens to come to violence in the East, but never does; Niagaras of talk are poured out; the ebb and flow of the parti-colored crowd, and the violent and not ungraceful gestures make a singular picture.

Bales of merchandise are piled on shore, cases of brandy and cottons from England, to keep the natives of Soudan warm inside and out; Greek merchants, splendid in silk attire, are lounging amid their goods, slowly bargaining for their transportation. Groups of camels are kneeling on the sand with their Bedaween drivers. These latter are of the Bisharee Arabs, and free sons of the desert. They wear no turban, and their only garment is a long strip of brown cotton thrown over the shoulder so as to leave the right arm free, and then wound about the waist and loins. The black hair is worn long, braided in strands which shine with oil, and put behind the ears. This sign of effeminacy is contradicted by their fine athletic figures, by a bold strong eye, and a straight resolute nose.

Wady Halfa (*wady* is valley, and *halfa* is a sort of coarse grass) has a post-office and a mosque, but no bazaar, nor any centre of attraction. Its mud-houses are stretched along the shore for a mile and a half, and run back into the valley, under the lovely palm-grove; but there are no streets and no roads through the deep sand. There is occasionally a sign of wealth in an extensive house, that is, one consisting of several enclosed courts and apartments within one large mud wall; and in one we saw a garden, watered by a sakiya, and two latticed windows in a second story looking on it, as if some one had a harem here which was handsome enough to seclude.

We called on the kadi, the judicial officer of this district, whose house is a specimen of the best, and as good as is needed in this land of the sun. On one side of an open enclosure is his harem; in the other is the reception-room where he holds court. This is a mud-hut, with nothing whatever in it except some straw mats. The kadi sent for rugs, and we sat on the mud-bench outside, while attendants brought us dates, popped corn, and even coffee; and then they squatted in a row in front of us and stared at us, as we did at them. The ladies went into the harem and made the acquaintance of the judge's one wife and his dirty children. Not without cordiality and courtesy of manner these people; but how simple are the terms of life here; and what a thoroughly African picture this is, the mud-huts, the sand, the palms, the black-skinned groups.

The women here are modestly clad, but most of them frightfully ugly and castor-oily; yet we chanced upon two handsome girls, or rather married women, of fifteen or sixteen. One of them had regular features and a very pretty expression, and evidently knew she was a beauty, for she sat apart on the ground, keeping her head covered most of the time, and did not join the women who thronged about us to look with wonder at the costume of our ladies and to beg for backsheesh. She was loaded with necklaces, bracelets of horn and ivory, and had a ring on every finger. There was in her manner something of scorn and resentment at our intrusion; she no doubt had her circle of admirers and was queen in it. Who are these pale creatures who come to stare at my charms? Have they no dark pretty women in their own land? And she might well have asked, what would she do—a beauty of New York city, let us say—when she sat combing her hair on the marble doorsteps of her father's palace in Madison Square, if a lot of savage, impolite Nubians, should come and stand in a row in front of her and stare?

The only shops here are the temporary booths of traders, birds of passage to or from the equatorial region. Many of them have pitched their gay tents under the trees, making the scene still more like a fair or an encampment for the night. In some are displayed European finery and trumpery, manufactured for Africa, calico in striking colors, glass beads and cotton cloth; others are coffee-shops, where men are playing at a sort of draughts—the checker-board being holes made in the sand and the men pebbles. At the door of a pretty tent stood a young and handsome Syrian merchant, who cordially invited us in, and pressed upon us the hospitality of his house. He was on his way to Darfoor, and might remain there two or three years, trading with the natives. We learned this by the interpretation of his girl-wife, who spoke a little barbarous French. He had married her only recently, and this was their bridal tour, we inferred. Into what risks and perils was this pretty woman going? She was Greek, from one of the islands, and had the *naïveté* and freshness of both youth and ignorance. Her fair complexion was touched by the sun and ruddy with health.

Her blue eyes danced with the pleasure of living. She wore her hair natural, with neither oil nor ornament, but cut short and pushed behind the ears. For dress she had a simple calico gown of pale yellow, cut high in the waist, *à la Grecque*, the prettiest costume woman ever assumed. After our long regimen of the hideous women of the Nile, plastered with dirt, soaked in oil, and hung with tawdry ornaments, it may be imagined how welcome was this vision of a woman, handsome, natural, and clean; with neither the shyness of an animal nor the brazenness of a Ghawazee.

Our hospitable entertainers hastened to set before us what they had; a bottle of Maraschino was opened, very good European cigars were produced, and a plate of pistachio nuts, to eat with the cordial. The artless Greek beauty cracked the nuts for us with her shining teeth, laughing all the while; urging us to eat, and opening her eyes in wonder that we would not eat more and would not carry away more. It must be confessed that we had not much conversation, but we made it up in constant smiling, and ate our pistachios and sipped our cordial in great glee. What indeed could we have done more with words, or how have passed a happier hour? We perfectly understood each other; we drank each other's healths; we were civilized beings, met by chance in a barbarous place; we were glad to meet, and we parted in the highest opinion of each other, with gay salaams, and not in tears. What fate I wonder had these handsome and adventurous merchants among the savages of Darfoor and Kordofan?

The face of our black boy, Gohah, was shining with pleasure when we walked away, and he said with enthusiasm, pointing to the tent, "*Sitt tyeb, quéi-is.*" Accustomed as he was to the African beauties of Soudan, I do not wonder that Gohah thought this "lady" both "good" and "beautiful."

We have seen Wady Halfa. The expedition to Darfoor is packing up to begin its desert march in the morning. Our dahabeëh has been transformed and shorn of a great part of its beauty. We are to see no more the great bird-wing sail. The long yard has been taken down and is slung above us the whole length of the deck. The twelve big sweeps are put in place; the boards of the forward deck are taken up, so that the rowers will have place for their feet as they sit on the beams. They sit fronting the cabin, and rise up and take a step forward at each stroke, settling slowly back to their seats. On the mast is rigged the short stern-yard and sail, to be rarely spread. Hereafter we are to float, and drift, and whirl, and try going with the current and against the wind.

At ten o'clock of a moonlight night, a night of summer heat, we swing off, the rowers splashing their clumsy oars and setting up a shout and chorus in minor, that sound very much like a wail, and would be quite appropriate if they were ferrymen of the Styx. We float a few miles, and then go aground and go to bed.

The next day we have the same unchanging sky, the same groaning and creaking of the sakiyas, and in addition the irregular splashing of the great sweeps as we slide down the river. Two crocodiles have the carelessness to show themselves on a sand-island, one a monstrous beast, whose size is magnified every time we think how his great back sunk into the water when our sandal was yet beyond rifle-shot. Of course he did not know that we carried only a shot-gun and intended only to amuse him, or he would not have been in such haste.

The wind is adverse, we gain little either by oars or by the current, and at length take to the shore, where something novel always rewards us. This time we explore some Roman ruins, with round arches of unburned bricks, and find in them also the unmistakable sign of Roman occupation, the burnt bricks—those thin slabs, eleven inches long, five wide, and two thick, which were a favourite form with them, bricks burnt for eternity, and scattered all over the East wherever the Roman legions went.

Beyond these is a village, not a deserted village, but probably the laziest in the world. Men, and women for the most part too, were lounging about and in the houses, squatting in the dust, in absolute indolence, except that the women, all of them, were suckling their babies, and occasionally one of them was spinning a little cotton-thread on a spindle whirled in the hand. The men are more cleanly than the women, in every respect in better condition, some of them bright, fine-looking fellows. One of them showed us through his house, which was one of the finest in the place, and he was not a little proud of it. It was a large mud-wall enclosure. Entering by a rude door we came into an open space, from which opened several doors, irregular breaks in the wall, closed by shackling doors of wood. Stepping over the sill and stooping, we entered the living-rooms. First, is the kitchen; the roof of this is the sky—you are always liable to find yourself outdoors in these houses—and the fire for cooking is built in one corner. Passing through another hole in the wall we come to a sleeping-room, where were some jars of dates and doora, and a mat spread in one corner to lie on. Nothing but an earth-floor, and dust and grime everywhere. A crowd of tittering girls were flitting about, peeping at us from doorways, and diving into them with shrill screams, like frightened rabbits, if we approached.

Abd-el-Atti raises a great laugh by twisting a piastre into the front lock of hair of the ugliest hag there, calling her his wife, and drawing her arm under his to take her to the boat. It is an immense joke. The old lady is a widow and successfully conceals her reluctance. The tying the piece of silver in the hair is a sign of marriage. All the married women wear a piastre or some scale of silver on the forehead; the widows leave off this ornament from the twist; the young girls show, by the hair plain, except always the clay dabs, that they are in the market. The simplicity of these people is noticeable. I saw a woman seated on the ground, in dust three inches thick, leaning against the mud-bank in front of the house, having in her lap a naked baby; on the bank sat another woman, braiding the hair of the first, wetting it with muddy water, and working into it sand, clay, and tufts of dead hair. What a way to spend Sunday!

This is, on the whole, a model village. The people appear to have nothing, and perhaps they want nothing. They do nothing and I suppose they would thank no one for coming to increase their wants and set them to work. Nature is their friend.

I wonder what the staple of conversation of these people is, since the weather offers nothing, being always the same, and always fine.

A day and a night and a day we fight adverse winds, and make no headway. One day we lie at Farras, a place of no consequence, but having, almost as a matter of course, ruins of the time of the Romans and the name Rameses II. cut on a rock. In a Roman wall we find a drain-tile exactly like those we use now. In the evening, after moon-rise, we drop down to **Aboo Simbel.**

CHAPTER XXIV.

GIANTS IN STONE.

WHEN daylight came, the Colossi of Aboo Simbel (or Ipsamboul) were looking into our windows; greeting the sunrise as they have done every morning for three thousand five hundred years; and keeping guard still over the approach to the temple, whose gods are no longer anywhere recognized, whose religion disappeared from the earth two thousand years ago:—vast images, making an eternity of time in their silent waiting.

The river here runs through an unmitigated desert. On the east the sand is brown, on the west the sand is yellow; that is the only variety. There is no vegetation, there are no habitations, there is no path on the shore, there are no footsteps on the sand, no one comes to break the spell of silence. To find such a monument of ancient power and art as this temple in such a solitude enhances the visitor's wonder and surprise. The Pyramids, Thebes, and Aboo Simbel are the three wonders of Egypt. But the great temple of Amboo Simbel is unique. It satisfies the mind. It is complete in itself, it is the projection of one creative impulse of genius. Other temples are growths, they have additions, afterthoughts, we can see in them the workings of many minds and many periods. This is a complete thought, struck out, you would say, at a heat.

In order to justify this opinion, I may be permitted a little detail concerning this temple, which impressed us all as much as anything in Egypt. There are two temples here, both close to the shore, both cut in the mountain of rock which here almost overhangs the stream. We need not delay to speak of the smaller one, although it would be wonderful, if it were not for the presence of the larger. Between the two was a rocky gorge.

This is now nearly filled up, to the depth of one hundred feet, by the yellow sand that has drifted and still drifts over from the level of the desert hills above.

This sand, which drifts exactly like snow, lies in ridges like snow, and lies loose and sliding under the feet, or packs hard like snow, once covered the façade of the big temple altogether, and now hides a portion of it. The entrance to the temple was first cleared away in 1817 by Belzoni and his party, whose gang of laborers worked eight hours a day for two weeks with the thermometer at 112° to 116° Fahrenheit in the shade—an almost incredible endurance when you consider what the heat must have been in the sun beating upon this dazzling wall of sand in front of them.

The rock in which the temple is excavated was cut back a considerable distance, but in this cutting the great masses were left which were to be fashioned into the four figures. The façade thus made, to which these statues are attached, is about one hundred feet high. The statues are seated on thrones with no intervening screens, and, when first seen, have the appearance of images in front of and detached from the rock of which they form a part. The statues are all tolerably perfect, except one, the head of which is broken and lies in masses at its feet; and at the time of our visit the sand covered the two northernmost to the knees. The door of entrance, over which is a hawk-headed figure of Re, the titular divinity, is twenty feet high. Above the Colossi, and as a frieze over the curve of the cornice, is a row of monkeys (there were twenty-one originally, but some are split away), like a company of negro minstrels, sitting and holding up their hands in the most comical manner. Perhaps the Egyptians, like the mediæval cathedral builders, had a liking for grotesque effects in architecture; but they may have intended nothing comic here, for the monkey had sacred functions; he was an emblem of Thoth, the scribe of the under-world, who recorded the judgments of Osiris.

These Colossi are the largest in the world*; they are at least

---

* The following are some of the measurements of one of these giants:—height of figure, sixty-six feet; pedestal on which it sits, ten; leg from knee to heel, twenty; great toe, one and a half feet thick; ear, three feet five inches long; fore-finger, three feet; from inner side of elbow-joint to end of middle finger, fifteen feet.

fifteen feet higher than the wonders of Thebes, but it is not their size principally that makes their attraction. As works of art they are worthy of study· Seated, with hands on knees, in that eternal, traditional rigidity of Egyptian sculpture, nevertheless the grandeur of the head and the noble beauty of the face take them out of the category of mechanical works. The figures represent Rameses II. and the features are of the type which has come down to us as the perfection of Egyptian beauty.

I climbed up into the lap of one of the statues; it is there only that you can get an adequate idea of the size of the body. What a roomy lap! Nearly ten feet between the wrists that rest upon the legs! I sat comfortably in the navel of the statue, as in a niche, and mused on the passing of the nations. To these massive figures the years go by like the stream. With impassive, serious features, unchanged in expression in thousands of years, they sit listening always to the flowing of the unending Nile, that fills all the air and takes away from that awful silence which would else be painfully felt in this solitude.

The interior of this temple is in keeping with its introduction. You enter a grand hall supported by eight massive Osiride columns, about twenty-two feet high as we estimated them. They are figures of Rameses become Osiris—to be absorbed into Osiris is the end of all the transmigrations of the blessed soul. The expression of the faces of such of these statues as are uninjured, is that of immortal youth—a beauty that has in it the promise of immortality. The sides of this hall are covered with fine sculptures, mainly devoted to the exploits of Rameses II.; and here is found again, cut in the stone, the long Poem of the poet Pentaour, celebrating the single-handed exploit of Rameses against the Khitas on the river Orontes. It relates that the king, whom his troops dared not follow, charged with his chariot alone into the ranks of the enemy and rode through them again and again, and slew them by hundreds. Rameses at that time was only twenty-three; it was his first great campaign. Pursuing the enemy, he overtook them in advance of his troops, and, rejecting the councils of his officers, began the fight at once. "The footmen and the horsemen then," says the poet (the translator is M. de Rougé), "recoiled before the enemy who were masters of Kadesh, on the left bank of the Orontes.

.... Then his majesty, in the pride of his strength, rising up like the god Mauth, put on his fighting dress. Completely armed, he looked like Baal in the hour of his might. Urging on his chariot, he pushed into the army of the vile Khitas; he was alone, no one was with him. He was surrounded by 2,500 chariots, and the swiftest of the warriors of the vile Khitas, and of the numerous nations who accompanied them, threw themselves in his way.... Each chariot bore three men, and the king had with him neither princes nor generals, nor his captains of archers nor of chariots."

Then Rameses calls upon Amun; he reminds him of the obelisk he has raised to him, the bulls he has slain for him:— "Thee, I invoke, O my Father! I am in the midst of a host of strangers, and no man is with me. My archers and horsemen have abandoned me; when I cried to them, none of them has heard, when I called for help. But I prefer Amun to thousands of millions of archers, to millions of horsemen, to millions of young heroes all assembled together. The designs of men are nothing, Amun overrules them."

Needless to say the prayer was heard, the king rode slashing through the ranks of opposing chariots, slaying, and putting to rout the host. Whatever basis of fact the poem may have had in an incident of battle or in the result of one engagement, it was like one of Napoleón's bulletins from Egypt. The Khitas were not subdued and, not many years after, they drove the Egyptians out of their land and from nearly all Palestine, forcing them out of all their conquests, into the valley of the Nile itself. During the long reign of this Rameses, the power of Egypt steadily declined, while luxury increased and the nation was exhausted in building the enormous monuments which the king projected. The close of his pretentious reign has been aptly compared to that of Louis XIV.—a time of decadence; in both cases the great fabric was ripe for disaster.

But Rameses liked the poem of Pentaour. It is about as long as a book of the Iliad, but the stone-cutters of his reign must have known it by heart. He kept them carving it and illustrating it all his life, on every wall he built where there was room for the story. He never, it would seem, could get enough of it. He killed those vile Khitas a hundred times; he pursued them over all the stone walls in his kingdom. The story is told here at Ipsambool; it is carved in the Rameseum; the poem is graved on Luxor and Karnak.

Out of this great hall open eight other chambers, all more or less sculptured, some of them covered with well-drawn figures on which the color is still vivid. Two of these rooms are long and very narrow, with a bench running round the walls, the front of which is cut out so as to imitate seats with short pillars. In one are square niches, a foot deep, cut in the wall. The sculptures in one are unfinished, the hieroglyphics and figures drawn in black but not cut—some event having called off the artists and left their work incomplete. We seem to be present at the execution of these designs, and so fresh are the colors of those finished, that it seems it must have been only yesterday that the workman laid down the brush. (A small chamber in the rock outside the temple, which was only opened in 1874, is wonderful in the vividness of its colors; we see there better than anywhere else the colors of vestments).

These chambers are not the least mysterious portion of this temple. They are in absolute darkness, and have no chance of ventilation. By what light was this elaborate carving executed? If people ever assembled in them, and sat on these benches, when lights were burning, how could they breathe? If they were not used, why should they have been so decorated? They would serve very well for the awful mysteries of the Odd Fellows. Perhaps they were used by the Free Masons in Solomon's time.

Beyond the great hall is a transverse hall (having two small chambers off from it) with four square pillars, and from this a corridor leads to the adytum. Here, behind an altar of stone, sit four marred gods, facing the outer door, two hundred feet from it. They sit in a twilight that is only brightened by rays that find their way in at the distant door; but at morning they can see, from the depth of their mountain cavern, the rising sun.

We climbed, up the yielding sand-drifts, to the top of the precipice in which the temple is excavated, and walked back to a higher ridge. The view from these is perhaps the best desert view on the Nile, more extensive and varied than that of Aboosir. It is a wide sweep of desolation. Up and down the river we see vast plains of sand and groups of black hills; to the west and north the Libyan desert extends with no limit to an horizon fringed with sharp peaks, like aiguilles of the Alps, that have an exact resemblance to a forest.

At night, we give the ancient deities a sort of Fourth of July, and illumirate the temple with colored lights. A blue light burns upon the altar in the adytum before the four gods, who may seem in their penetration to receive again the worship to which they were accustomed three thousand years ago. A green flame in the great hall brings out mysteriously the features of the gigantic Osiride, and revives the midnight glow of the ancient ceremonies. In the glare of torches and colored lights on the outside, the Colossi loom in their gigantic proportions and cast grotesque shadows.

Imagine this temple as it appeared to a stranger initiated into the mysteries of the religion of the Pharaohs—a *cultus* in which the mathematical secrets of the Pyramid and the Sphinx, art and architecture, were wrapped in the same concealment with the problem of the destiny of the soul ; when the colors on these processions of gods and heroes, upon these wars and pilgrimages sculptured in large on the walls, were all brilliant ; when these chambers were gorgeously furnished, when the heavy doors that then hung in every passage, separating the different halls and apartments, only swung open to admit the neophyte to new and deeper mysteries, to halls blazing with light, where he stood in the presence of these appalling figures, and of hosts of priests and acolytes.

The temple of Aboo Simbel was built early in the reign of Rameses II., when art, under the impulse of his vigorous predecessors, was in its flower, and before the visible decadence which befel it later under a royal patronage and "protection," and in the demand for a wholesale production, which always reduces any art to mechanical conditions. It seemed to us about the finest single conception in Egypt. It must have been a genius of rare order and daring who evoked in this solid mountain a work of such grandeur and harmony of proportion, and then executed it without a mistake. The first blow on the exterior, that began to reveal the Colossi, was struck with the same certainty and precision as that which brought into being the gods who are seated before the altar in the depth of the mountain. A bolder idea was never more successfully wrought out.

Our last view of this wonder was by moonlight and by sunrise. We arose and went forth over the sand-bank at five o'clock. Venus blazed as never before. The Southern Cross was paling in the moonlight. The moon, in its last half, hung over the south-west corner of the temple rock, and threw a heavy shadow across a portion of the sitting figures. In this dimness of the half-light their proportions were supernatural. Details were lost.

These might be giants of pre-historic times, or the old fabled gods of antediluvian eras, outlined largely and majestically, groping their way out of the hills.

Above them was the illimitable, purplish blue of the sky. The Moon, one of the goddesses of the temple, withdrew more and more before the coming of Re, the sun-god to whom the temple is dedicated, until she cast a shadow on the façade. The temple, even the interior, caught the first glow of the reddening east. The light came, as it always comes at dawn, in visible waves, and these passed over the features of the Colossi, wave after wave, slowly brightening them into life.

In the interior the first flush was better than the light of many torches, and the Osiride figures were revealed in their hiding-places. At the spring equinox the sun strikes squarely in, two hundred feet, upon the faces of the sitting figures in the adytum. That is their annual salute! Now it only sent its light to them; but it made rosy the Osiride faces on one side of the great hall.

The morning was chilly, and we sat on a sand-drift, wrapped up against the cutting wind, watching the marvellous revelation. The dawn seemed to ripple down the gigantic faces of the figures outside, and to touch their stony calm with something like a smile of gladness; it almost gave them motion, and we would hardly have felt surprised to see them arise and stretch their weary limbs, cramped by ages of inaction, and sing and shout at the coming of the sun-god. But they moved not, the strengthening light only revealed their stony impassiveness; and when the sun, rapidly clearing the eastern hills of the desert, gilded first the row of grinning monkeys, and then the light crept slowly down over faces and forms to the very feet, the old heathen helplessness stood confessed.

And when the sun swung free in the sky, we silently drew away and left the temple and the guardians alone and unmoved. We called the reïs and the crew; the boat was turned to the current, the great sweeps dipped into the water, and continued our voyage down the eternal river, which still sings and flows in this lonely desert place, where sit the most gigantic figures man ever made.

CHAPTER XXV.

FLITTING THROUGH NUBIA.

E HAVE been learning the language. The language consists merely of *tyeb*. With *tyeb* in its various accents and inflections, you can carry on an extended conversation. I have heard two Arabs talking for a half hour, in which one of them used no word for reply or response except *tyeb* "good."

Tyeb is used for assent, agreement, approval, admiration, both interrogatively and affectionately. It does the duty of the Yankee "all right" and the vulgarism " that's so" combined; it has as many meanings as the Italian *va bene*, or the German *So!* or the English girl's yes! yes? ye-e-s, ye-e-as? yes (short), 'n ye-e-es in doubt and really a negative—ex.:—" How lovely Blanche looks to night!" "'n ye-e-es." You may hear two untutored Americans talking, and one of them, through a long interchange of views will utter nothing except " that's so," " that's so "? " *that's* so" "that's *so*." I think two Arabs meeting could come to a perfect understanding with,

" *Tyeb?* "
" *Tyeb.* "
" *Tyeb?* " (both together).
" *Tyeb?* " (showing something).
" *Tyeb* " (emphatically, in admiration).
" *Tyeb* " (in approval of the other's admiration).
" *Tyeb Keteér* " ("good much").
" *Tyeb Keteér?* "
" *Tyeb.* "
" *Tyeb.* " (together, in ratification of all that has been said).

I say *tyeb* in my satisfaction with you; you say *tyeb* in pleasure at my satisfaction; I say *tyeb* in my pleasure at your pleasure. The servant says *tyeb* when you give him an order; you say *tyeb* upon his comprehending it. The Arabic is the richest of languages. I believe there are three hundred names for earth, a hundred for lion, and so on. But the vocabulary of the common people is exceedingly limited. Our sailors talk all day with the aid of a very few words.

But we have got beyond *tyeb*. We can say *eiwa* ("yes")—or *nām*, when we wish to be elegant—and *la* ("no"). The universal negative in Nubia, however, is simpler than this—it is a cluck of the tongue in the left cheek and a slight upward jerk of the head. This cluck and jerk makes "no," from which there is no appeal. If you ask a Nubian the price of anything —*be-kám dee!*—and he should answer *khámsa* ("five"), and you should offer *thelátu* ("three"), and he should *keh* and jerk up his head, you might know the trade was hopeless; because the *keh* expresses indifference as well as a negative. The best thing you could do would be to say *bookra* ("to-morrow"), and go away—meaning in fact to put off the purchase forever, as the Nubian very well knows when he politely adds *tyeb*.

But there are two other words necessary to be mastered before the traveller can say he knows Arabic. To the constant call for "backsheesh" and the obstructing rabble of beggars and children, you must be able to say *mafeesh* ("nothing"), and *im'shee* ("get away," "clear out," "scat.") It is my experience that this *im'shee* is the most necessary word in Egypt.

We do nothing all day but drift, or try to drift, against the north wind, not making a mile an hour, constantly turning about, floating from one side of the river to the other. It is impossible to row, for the steersman cannot keep the boat's bow to the current.

There is something exceedingly tedious, even to a lazy and resigned man, in this perpetual drifting hither and thither. To float, however slowly, straight down the current, would be quite another thing. To go sideways, to go stern first, to waltz around so that you never can tell which bank of the river you are looking at, or which way you are going, or what the points of the compass are, is confusing and unpleasant. It is the one serious annoyance of a dahabeëh voyage. If it is calm, we go on delightfully with oars and current; if there is a southerly breeze we travel rapidly, and in the most charming way in the world. But our high-cabined boats are helpless monsters in this wind, which continually blows; we are worse than becalmed, we are badgered.

However, we might be in a worse winter country, and one less entertaining. We have just drifted in sight of a dahabeëh, with the English flag, tied up to the bank. On the shore is a picturesque crowd; an awning is stretched over high poles; men are busy at something under it—on the rock near sits a group of white people under umbrellas. What can it be? Are they repairing a broken yard? Are they holding a court over some thief? Are they performing some mystic ceremony? We take the sandal and go to investigate.

An English gentleman has shot two crocodiles, and his people are skinning them, stuffing the skin, and scraping the flesh from the bones, preparing the skeletons for a museum. Horrible creatures they are, even in this butchered condition. The largest is twelve feet long; that is called a big crocodile here; but last winter the gentleman killed one that was seventeen feet long; that was a monster.

In the stomach of one of these he found two pairs of bracelets, such as are worn by Nubian children, two "cunning" little leathern bracelets ornamented with shells—a most useless ornament for a crocodile. The animal is becoming more and more shy every year, and it is very difficult to get a shot at one. They come out in the night, looking for bracelets. One night we nearly lost Ahmed, one of our black boys; he had gone down upon the rudder, when an enquiring crocodile came along and made a snap at him—when the boy climbed on deck he looked white even by starlight.

The invulnerability of the crocodile hide is exaggerated. One of these had two bullet-holes in his back. His slayer says he has repeatedly put bullets through the hide on the back. When we came away we declined steaks, but the owner gave us some eggs, so that we might raise our own crocodiles.

Gradually we drift out of this almost utterly sterile country, and come to long strips of palm-groves, and to sakiyas innumerable, shrieking on the shore every few hundred feet. We have time to visit a considerable village, and see the women at their other occupation (besides lamentation), braiding each other's hair; sitting on the ground, sometimes two at a head, patiently twisting odds and ends of loose hair into the snaky braids, and muddling the whole with sand, water, and clay, preparatory to the oil. A few women are spinning with a hand-spindle, and producing very good cotton-thread. All appear to have time on their hands. And what a busy place this must be in summer, when the heat is like that of an oven! The men loaf about like the women, and probably do even less. Those at work are mostly slaves, boys and girls in the slightest clothing; and even these do a great deal of "standing round." Wooden hoes are used.

The desert over which we walked beyond the town was very different from the Libyan with its drifts and drifts of yellow sand. We went over swelling undulations (like our rolling prairies), cut by considerable depressions, of sandstone with a light sand cover, but all strewn with shale or shingle. This black shale is sometimes seen adhering like a layer of glazing to the coarse rock; and, though a part of the rock, it has the queer appearance of having been a deposit solidified upon it and subsequently broken off. On the tops of these hills we found everywhere holes scooped out by the natives in search of nitre; the holes showed evidence, in dried mud, of the recent presence of water.

We descended into a deep gorge, in which the rocks were broken squarely down the face, exhibiting strata of red, white, and variegated sandstone; the gorge was a wady that ran far back into the country among the mountains; we followed it down to a belt of *sont* acacias and palms on the river. This wady was full of rocks, like a mountain stream at home; a great torrent running long in it, had worn the rocks into fantastic shapes, cutting punch-bowls and the like, and water had recently dried in the hollows. But it had not rained on the river.

This morning we are awakened by loud talking and wrangling on deck, that sounds like a Paris revolution. We have only stopped for milk! The forenoon we spend among the fashionable ladies of Derr, the capital of Nubia, studying the modes, in order that we may carry home the latest. This is an aristocratic place. One of the eight-hundred-years-old sycamore trees, of which we made mention, is still vigorous and was bearing the sycamore fig. The other is in front of a grand mud-house with latticed windows, the residence of the Kashefs of Sultan Selim, whose descendants still occupy it, and, though shorn of authority, are said to be proud of their Turkish origin. One of them, Hassan Kashef, an old man in the memory of our dragoman, so old that he had to lift up his eyelids with his finger when he wanted to see, died only a few years ago. This patriarch had seventy-two wives as his modest portion in this world; and as the Koran allows only four, there was some difficulty in settling the good man's estate. The matter was referred to the Khedive, but he wisely refused to interfere. When the executor came to divide the property among the surviving children, he found one hundred and five to share the inheritance.

The old fellow had many other patriarchal ways. On his death-bed he left a legacy of both good and evil wishes, requests to reward this friend, and to "serve out" that enemy, quite in the ancient style, and in the Oriental style, recalling the last recorded words of King David, whose expiring breath was an expression of a wish for vengeance upon one of his enemies, whom he had sworn not to kill. It reads now as if it might have been spoken by a Bedawee sheykh to his family only yesterday :—"And, behold, thou hast with thee Shimei the son of Gera, a Benjamite of Bahurim, which cursed me with a grievous curse in the day when I went to Mahanaim : but he came down to meet me at Jordan, and I sware to him by the Lord, saying, I will not put thee to death with the sword. Now, therefore, hold him not guiltless : for thou art a wise man, and knowest that thou oughtest to do unto him ; but his hoar head bring thou down to the grave with blood. So David slept with his fathers, and was buried in the city of David."

We call at the sand-covered temple at A'mada, and crawl into it; a very neat little affair, with fresh color and five sculptures, and as old as the time of Osirtasen III. (the date of the obelisk of Heliopolis, of the Tombs of Beni Hassan, say about fifteen hundred years before Rameses II.); and then sail quickly down to Korosko, passing over in an hour or so a distance that required a day and a half on the ascent.

At Korosko there are caravans in from Kartoom; the camel-drivers wear monstrous silver rings, made in the interior, the crown an inch high and set with blood-stone. I bought from the neck of a pretty little boy a silver "charm," a flat plate with the name of Allah engraved on it. Neither the boy nor the charm had been washed since they came into being.

The caravan had brought one interesting piece of freight, which had just been sent down the river. It was the *head* of the Sultan of Darfoor, preserved in spirits, and forwarded to the Khedive as a present. This was to certify that the Sultan was really killed, when Darfoor was captured by the army of the Viceroy; though I do not know that there is any bounty on the heads of African Sultans. It is an odd gift to send to a ruler who wears the European dress and speaks French, and whose chief military officers are Americans.

The desolate hills behind Korosko rise a thousand feet, and we climbed one of the peaks to have a glimpse of the desert route and the country towards Kartoom. I suppose a more savage landscape does not exist. The peak of black disintegrated rocks on which we stood was the first of an assemblage of such as far as we could see south; the whole horizon was cut by these sharp peaks; and through these thickly clustering hills the caravan trail made its way in sand and powdered dust. Shut in from the breeze, it must be a hard road to travel, even with a winter sun multiplying its rays from all these hot rocks; in the summer it would be frightful. But on these summits, or on any desert swell, the air is an absolute elixir of life; it has a quality of lightness but not the rarity that makes respiration difficult.

At a village below Korosko we had an exhibition of the manner of fighting with the long Nubian war-spear and the big round shield made of hippopotamus-hide. The men jumped about and uttered frightening cries, and displayed more agility than fight, the object being evidently to terrify by a threatening aspect; but the scene was as barbarous as any we see in African pictures. Here also was a pretty woman (pretty for her) with beautiful eyes, who wore a heavy nose-ring of gold, which she said she put on to make her face beautiful; nevertheless she would sell the ring for nine dollars and a half. The people along here will sell anything they have, ornaments, charms to protect them from the evil-eye,—they will part with anything for money. At this village we took on a crocodile ten feet long, which had been recently killed, and lashed it to the horizontal yard. It was Abd-el-Atti's desire to present it to a friend in Cairo, and perhaps he was not reluctant, when we should be below the cataract, to have it take the appearance, in the eyes of spectators, of having been killed by some one on this boat.

We obtained above Korosko one of the most beautiful animals in the world—a young gazelle—to add to our growing menagerie; which consists of a tame duck, who never gets away when his leg is tied; a timid desert hare, who has lived for a long time in a tin box in the cabin, trembling like an aspen leaf night and day; and a chameleon.

The chameleon ought to have a chapter to himself. We have reason to think that he has the soul of some transmigrating Egyptian. He is the most uncanny beast. We have made him a study, and find very little good in him. His changeableness of color is not his worst quality. He has the nature of a spy, and he is sullen and snappish besides. We discovered that his color is not a purely physical manifestation, but that it depends upon his state of mind, upon his temper. When everything is serene, he is green as a May morning, but anger changes him instantly for the worse. It is however true that he takes his color mainly from the substance upon which he dwells, not from what he eats; for he eats flies and allows them to make no impression upon his exterior. When he was taken off an acacia-tree, this chameleon was of the bright-green color of the leaves. Brought into our cabin, his usual resting-place was on the reddish maroon window curtains, and his green changed muddily into the color of the woollen. When angry, he would become mottled with dark spots, and have a thick cloudy color. This was the range of his changes of complexion; it is not enough (is it?) to give him his exaggerated reputation.

I confess that I almost hated him, and perhaps cannot do him justice. He is a crawling creature at best, and his mode of getting about is disagreeable; his feet have the power of clinging to the slightest roughness, and he can climb anywhere; his feet are like hands; besides, his long tail is like another hand; it is prehensile like the monkey's. He feels his way along very carefully, taking a turn with his tail about some support, when he is passing a chasm, and not letting go until his feet are firmly fixed on something else. And, then, the way he uses his eye is odious. His eye-balls are stuck upon the end of protuberances on his head, which protuberances work like ball-and-socket joints—as if you had your eye on the end of your finger. When he wants to examine anything, he never turns his head; he simply swivels his eye round and brings it to bear on the object. Pretending to live in cold isolation on the top of a window curtain, he is always making clammy excursions round the cabin, and is sometimes found in our bed-chambers. You wouldn't like to feel his cold tail dragging over you in the night.

The first question every morning, when we come to breakfast, is,

"Where is that chameleon?"

He might be under the table, you know, or on the cushions, and you might sit on him. Commonly he conceals his body behind the curtain, and just lifts his head above the roller. There he sits, spying us, gyrating his evil eye upon us, and never stirring his head; he takes the colour of the curtain so nearly that we could not see him if it was not for that swivel eye. It is then that he appears malign, and has the aspect of a wise but ill-disposed Egyptian, whose soul has had ill-luck in getting into any respectable bodies for three or four thousand years. He lives upon nothing,—you would think he had been raised in a French *pension*. Few flies happen his way; and, perhaps he is torpid out of the sun so much of the time, he is not active to catch those that come. I carried him a big one the other day, and he repaid my kindness by snapping my finger. And I am his only friend.

Alas, the desert hare, whom we have fed with corn, and greens, and tried to breed courage in for a long time, died this morning at an early hour; either he was chilled out of the world by the cold air on deck, or he died of palpitation of the heart; for he was always in a flutter of fear, his heart going like a trip-hammer, when anyone approached him. He only rarely elevated his long silky ears in a serene enjoyment of society. His tail was too short, but he was, nevertheless, an animal to become attached to.

Speaking of Hassan Kashef's violation of the Moslem law, in taking more than four wives, is it generally known that the women in Mohammed's time endeavoured also to have the privileges of men? Forty women, who had cooked for the soldiers who were fighting the infidels and had done great service in the campaign, were asked by the Prophet to name their reward. The chief lady, who was put forward to prefer the request of the others, asked that as men were permitted four wives, women might be allowed to have four husbands. The Prophet gave them a plain reason for refusing their petition, and it has never been renewed. The legend shows that long ago women protested against their disabilities.

The strong north wind, with coolish weather, continues. On Sunday we are nowhere in particular, and climb a high sandstone peak, and sit in the shelter of a rock, where wandering men have often come to rest. It is a wild, desert place, and there is that in the atmosphere of the day which leads to talk of the end of the world.

Like many other Moslems, Abd-el-Atti thinks that these are the last days, bad enough days, and that the end draws near. We have misunderstood what Mr. Lane says about Christ coming to "judge" the world. The Moslems believe that Christ, who never died, but was taken up into heaven away from the Jews,—a person in his likeness being crucified in his stead,—will come to rule, to establish the Moslem religion and a reign of justice (the Millennium); and that after this period Christ will die, and be buried in Medineh, not far from Mohammed. Then the world will end, and Azrael, the angel of death, will be left alone on the earth for forty days. He will go to and fro, and find no one; all will be in their graves. Then Christ and Mohammed and all the dead will rise. But the Lord God will be the final judge of all.

"Yes, there have been many false prophets. A man came before Haroun e' Rasheed pretending to be a prophet.

"'What proof have you that you are one? What miracle can you do?'"

"'Anything you like.'"

"'Christ, on whom be peace, raised men from the dead.'"

"'So will I.' This took place before the king and the chief-justice. 'Let the head of the chief-justice be cut off,' said the pretended prophet, 'and I will restore him to life.'"

"'Oh,' cried the chief-justice, 'I believe that the man is a real prophet. Anyone who does not believe can have his head cut off, and try it.'"

"A woman also claimed to be a prophetess. 'But,' said the Khalif Haroun e' Rasheed, 'Mohammed declared that he was the last man who should be a prophet.'"

"'He didn't say that a *woman* shouldn't be,' the woman she answer."

The people vary in manners and habits here from village to village, much more than we supposed they would. Walking this morning for a couple of miles through the two villages of Maharraka—rude huts scattered under palm-trees—we find the inhabitants partly Arab, partly Barabra, and many negro slaves, more barbaric than any we have seen; boys and girls, till the marriageable age, in a state of nature, women neither so shy nor so careful about covering themselves with clothing as in other places, and the slaves wretchedly provided for. The heads of the young children are shaved in streaks, with long tufts of hair left; the women are loaded with tawdry necklaces, and many of them, poor as they are, sport heavy hoops of gold in the nose, and wear massive silver bracelets.

The slaves, blacks and mulattoes, were in appearance like those seen formerly in our southern cotton-fields. I recall a picture, in abolition times, representing a colored man standing alone, and holding up his arms, in a manner beseeching the white man passing by, to free him. To-day I saw the picture realized. A very black man, standing nearly naked in the midst of a bean-field, raised up both his arms, and cried aloud to us as we went by. The attitude had all the old pathos in it. As the poor fellow threw up his arms in a wild despair, he cried "Backsheesh, backsheesh, O! howadji!"

For the first time we found the crops in danger. The country was overrun with reddish-brown locusts, which settled in clouds upon every green thing; and the people in vain attempted to frighten them from their scant strip of grain. They are not, however, useless. The attractive women caught some, and, pulling off the wings and legs, offered them to us to eat. They said locusts were good; and I suppose they are such as John the Baptist ate. We are not Baptists.

As we go down the river we take in two or three temples a day, besides these ruins of humanity in the village,—Dakkeh,

Gerf Hossáyn, Dendoor. It is easy to get enough of these second-class temples. That at Gerf Hossáyn is hewn in the rock, and is in general arrangement like Ipsambool—it was also made by Rameses II.—but is in all respects inferior, and lacks the Colossi. I saw sitting in the adytum four figures whom I took to be Athos, Parthos, Aramis, and D'Artignan—though this edifice was built long before the day of the "Three Guardsmen."

The people in the village below have such a bad reputation that the dragoman, in great fright sent sailors after us, when he found we were strolling through the country alone. We have seen no natives so well off in cattle, sheep, and cooking-utensils, or in nose-rings, beads, and knives; they are, however, a wild, noisy tribe, and the whole village followed us for a mile, hooting for backsheesh. The girls wear a nose-ring and a girdle; the boys have no rings or girdles. The men are fierce and jealous of their wives, perhaps with reason, stabbing and throwing them into the river on suspicion, if they are caught talking with another man. So they say. At this village we saw pits dug in the sand (like those described in the Old Testament), in which cattle, sheep and goats were folded; it being cheaper to dig a pit than to build a stone fence.

At Kalábshee are two temples, ruins on a sufficiently large scale to be imposing; sculptures varied in character and beautifully colored; propylons with narrow staircases, and concealed rooms, and deep windows bespeaking their use as fortifications and dungeons as well as temples; and columns of interest to the architect; especially two, fluted (time of Rameses II.) with square projecting abacus like the Doric, but with broad bases. The inhabitants are the most pestilent on the river, crowding their curiosities upon us, and clamoring for money. They have for sale gazelle-horns, and the henna (which grows here), in the form of a green powder.

However, Kalábshee has educational facilities. I saw there a boys' school in full operation. In the open air, but in the sheltering angle of a house near the ruins, sat on the ground the schoolmaster. Behind him leaned his gun against the wall; before him lay an open Koran; and in his hand he held a thin palm rod with which he enforced education. He was dictating sentences from the book to a scrap of a scholar, a boy who sat on the ground, with an inkhorn beside him, and wrote the sentences on a board slate, repeating the words in a loud voice as he wrote. Near by was another urchin, seated before a slate leaning against the angle of the wall, committing the writing on it to memory, in a loud voice also. When he looked off, the stick reminded him to attend to his slate. I do not know whether he calls this a private or a public school.

Quitting these inhospitable savages as speedily as we can, upon the springing up of a south wind, we are going down stream at a spanking rate, leaving a rival dahabeëh, belonging to an English lord, behind, when the adversary puts it into the head of our pilot to steer across the river, and our prosperous career is suddenly arrested on a sandbar. We are fast, and the English boat, keeping in the channel, shows us her rudder and disappears round the bend.

Extraordinary confusion follows; the crew are in the water, they are on deck, the anchor is got out, there are as many opinions, as people, and no one obeys. The long pilot is a spectacle, after he has been wading about in the stream and comes on deck. His gown is off and his turban also; his head is shaved; his drawers are in tatters like lace-work. He strides up and down beating his breast, his bare poll shining in the sun like a billiard ball. We are on the sand nearly four hours, and the accident, causing us to lose this wind, loses us, it so happens, three days. By dark we tie up near the most excruciating sakiya in the world. It is suggested to go on shore and buy the property and close it out. But the boy who is driving will neither sell nor stop his cattle.

At Gertassee we have more ruins and we pass a beautiful, single column, conspicuous for a long distance over the desert, as fine as the once "nameless column" in the Roman forum. These temples, or places of worship, are on the whole depressing. There was no lack of religious privileges if frequency of religious edifices gave them. But the people evidently had no part in the ceremonies, and went never into these dark chambers, which are now inhabited by bats. The old religion does not commend itself to me. Of what use would be one of these temples on Asylum Hill, in Hartford, and how would the Rev. Mr. Twichell busy himself in its dark recesses, I wonder, even with the help of the deacons and the committee? The Gothic is quite enough for us.

This morning—we have now entered upon the month of February—for the first time in Nubia, we have early a slight haze, a thin veil of it; and passing between shores rocky and high and among granite breakers, we are reminded of the Hudson river on a June morning. A strong north wind, however, comes soon to puff away this illusion, and it blows so hard that we are actually driven up-stream.

The people and villages under the crumbling granite ledges that this delay enables us to see, are the least promising we have encountered; women and children are more nearly barbarians in dress and manners; for the women, a single strip of brown cotton, worn *à la* Bedawee, leaving free the legs, the right arm and breast, is a common dress. And yet, some of these women are not without beauty. One pretty girl sitting on a rock, the sun glistening on the castor-oil of her hair, asked for backsheesh in a sweet voice, her eyes sparkling with merriment. A flower blooming in vain in this desert!

Is it a question of "converting" these people? Certainly, nothing but the religion of the New Testament, put in practice here, bringing in its train, industry, self-respect, and a desire to know, can awaken the higher nature, and lift these creatures into a respectable womanhood. But the task is more difficult than it would be with remote tribes in Central Africa. These people have been converted over and over again. They have had all sorts of religions during the last few thousand years, and they remain essentially the same. They once had the old Egyptian faith, whatever it was; and subsequently they varied that with the Greek and Roman shades of heathenism. They then accepted the early Christianity, as the Abyssinians did, and had for hundreds of years, opportunity of Christian worship, when there were Christian churches all along the Nile from Alexander to Meroë, and holy hermits in every eligible cave and tomb. And then came Mohammed's friends, giving them the choice of belief or martyrdom, and they embraced the religion of Mecca as cordially as any other.

They have remained essentially unchanged through all their changes. This hopelessness of their condition is in the fact that in all the shiftings of religions and of dynasties, the women have continued to soak their hair in castor-oil. The fashion is as old as the Nile world. Many people look upon castor-oil as an excellent remedy. I should like to know what it has done for Africa.

At Dabód is an interesting ruin, and a man sits there in front of his house, weaving, confident that no rain will come to spoil his yarn. He sits and works the treadle of his loom in a hole in the ground, the thread being stretched out twenty or thirty feet on the wall before him. It is the only industry of the village, and a group of natives are looking on. The poor weaver asks backsheesh, and when I tell him I have nothing smaller than an English sovereign, he says he can change it!

Here we find also a sort of Holly-Tree Inn, a house for charitable entertainments, such as is often seen in Moslem villages. It is a square mud-structure, entered by two doors, and contains two long rooms with communicating openings. The dirt-floors are cleanly swept and fresh mats are laid down at intervals. Any stranger or weary traveller, passing by, is welcome to come in and rest or pass the night, to have a cup of coffee and some bread. There are two cleanly dressed attendants, and one of them is making coffee, within, over a handful of fire, in a tiny coffee-pot. In front, in the sun, on neat mats, sit half a dozen turbaned men, perhaps tired wanderers and pilgrims in this world, who have turned aside to rest for an hour, for a day, or for a week. They appear to have been there forever. The establishment is maintained by a rich man of the place; but signs of an abode of wealth we failed to discover in any of the mud-enclosures.

When we are under way again, we express surprise at finding here such an excellent charity.

"You no think the Lord he take care for his own?" says Abd-el-Atti. "When the kin' [king] of Abyssinia go to 'stroy the Kaabeh in Mecca"—

"Did you ever see the Kaabeh?"

"Many times. Plenty times I been in Mecca."

"In what part of the Kaabeh is the Black Stone?"

"So. The Kaabeh is a building like a cube, about, I think him, thirty feet high, built in the middle of the mosque at Mecca. It was built by Abraham, of white marble. In the outside the east wall, near the corner, 'bout so (four feet) high you find him, the Black Stone, put there by Abraham, call him *haggeh el ashad*, the lucky, the fortunatestone. It is opposite the sunrise. Where Abraham get him? God knows. If any one sick, he touch this stone, be made so well as he was. So I *hun*derstand. The Kaabeh is in the centre of the earth, and has fronts to the four quarters of the globe, Asia, Hindia, Egypt, all places, toward which the Moslem kneel in prayer. Near the Kaabeh is the well, the sacred well Zem-Zem, has clear water, beautiful, so lifely. One time a year, in the month before Ramadán, Zem-Zem spouts up high in the air, and people come to drink of it. When Hagar left Ishmael, to look for water, being very thirsty, the little fellow scratched with his fingers in the sand, and a spring of water rushed up; this is the well Zem-Zem. I told you the same water is in the spring in Syria, El Gebel; I find him just the same; come under the earth from Zem-Zem."

"When the kin' of Abyssinia, who not believe, what you call infidel, like that Englishman, yes, Mr. Buckle, I see him in Sinai and Petra—very wise man, know a great deal, very nice gentleman, I like him very much, but I think he not believe—when the kin' of Abyssinia came with all his great army and his elephants to fight against Mecca, and to 'stroy the Kaabeh as well the same time to carry off all the cattle of the people, then the people they say, 'the cattle are ours, but the Kaabeh is the Lord's, and he will have care over it; the Kaabeh is not ours.' There was one of the elephants of the kin' of Abyssinia, the name of Mahmoud, and he was very wise, more wise than anybody else. When he came in sight of Mecca, he turned back and went the other way, and not all the spears and darts of the soldiers could stop him. The others went on. Then the Lord sent out of the hell very small birds, with very little stones, taken out of hell, in their claws, no larger than mustard seeds; and the birds dropped these on the heads of the soldiers that rode on the elephants—generally three or four on an elephant. The little seeds went right down through the men and through the elephants, and killed them, and by this the army was 'stroyed.

"When the kin', after that, come into the mosque, some power outside himself made him to bow down in respect to the Kaabeh. He went away and did not touch it. And it stands there the same now."

CHAPTER XXVI.

MYSTERIOUS PHIL.E.

WE are on deck early to see the approach to Philæ, which is through a gateway of high rocks. The scenery is like parts of the Rhine; and as we come in sight of the old mosque perched on the hillside, and the round tomb on the pinnacle above, it is very like the Rhine, with castle ruins. The ragged and rock island of Biggeh rises before us and seems to stop the way, but at a turn in the river, the little temple, with its conspicuous columns, then the pylon of the great temple, and at length the mass of ruins, that cover the little island of Philæ, open on the view.

In the narrows we meet the fleet of government boats conveying the engineer expedition going up to begin the railway from Wady Halfa to Berber. Abd-el-Atti does not like the prospect of Egypt running deeper and deeper in debt, with no good to come of it, he says; he believes that the Khedive is acting under the advice of England, which is entirely selfish, and only desires a short way to India, in case the French should shut the Suez Canal against them (his view is a very good example of a Moslem's comprehension of affairs). Also thinking, with all Moslems, that it is best to leave the world and its people as the Lord has created and placed them, he replied to an enquiry about his opinion of the railroad, with this story of Jonah:—

"When the prophet Jonah came out of the whale and sat down on the bank to dry under a tree (I have seen the tree) in Syria, there was a blind man sitting near by, who begged the prophet to give him sight. Then Jonah asked the Lord for help, and the blind man was let to see. The man was eating dates at the same time, and the first thing he did when he got his eyes open was to snap the hard seeds at Jonah, who you know was very tender from being so long in the whale. Jonah was stung on his skin, and bruised by the stones, and he cry out,

"O! Lord, how is this?"

And the Lord said, "Jonah, you not satisfied to leave things as I placed 'em; and now you must suffer for it."

One muses and dreams at Philæ, and does not readily arouse himself to the necessity of exploring and comprehending the marvels and the beauties that insensibly lead him into sentimental reveries. If ever the spirit of beauty haunted a spot, it is this. Whatever was harsh in the granite ledges, or too sharp in the granite walls, whatever is repellant in the memory concerning the uses of these temples of a monstrous theogony, all is softened now by time, all asperities are worn away; nature and art grow lovely together in a gentle decay, sunk in a repose too beautiful to be sad. Nowhere else in Egypt has the grim mystery of the Egyptian's *cultus* softened into so harmless a memory.

The oval island contains perhaps a hundred acres. It is a rock, with only a patch or two of green, and a few scattered palms, just enough to give it a lonely, poetic, and not a fruitful aspect, and, as has been said, is walled all round from the water's edge. Covered with ruins, the principal are those of the temple of Isis. Beginning at the southern end of the island, where a flight of steps lead up to it, it stretches along, with a curved and broadening colonnade, giant pylons, great courts and covered temples. It is impossible to imagine a structure or series of structures more irregular in the lines or capricious in the forms. The architects gave free play to their fancy, and we find here the fertility and variety, if not the grotesqueness of imagination of the mediæval cathedral buildings. The capitals of the columns of the colonnade are sculptured in rich variety; the walls of the west cloister are covered with fine carvings, the color on them still fresh and delicate; and the ornamental designs are as beautiful and artistic as the finest Greek work, which some of it suggests: as rich as the most lovely Moorish patterns, many of which seem to have been copied from these living creations —diamond-work, birds, exquisite medallions of flowers, and sphinxes.

Without seeing this mass of buildings, you can have no notion of the labor expended in decorating them. All the surfaces of the gigantic pylons, of the walls and courts, exterior and interior, are covered with finely and carefully cut figures and hieroglyphics, and a great deal of the work is minute and delicate chiselling. You are lost in wonder if you attempt to estimate the time and the number of workmen necessary to accomplish all this. It seems incredible that men could ever have had patience or leisure for it. A great portion of the figures, within and without, have been, with much painstaking, defaced; probably it was done by the early Christians, and this is the only impress they have left of their domination in this region.

The most interesting sculptures, however, at Philæ are those in a small chamber, or mortuary chapel, on the roof of the main temple, touching the most sacred mystery of the Egyptian religion, the death and resurrection of Osiris. This myth, which took many fantastic forms, was no doubt that forbidden topic upon which Herodotus was not at liberty to speak. It was the growth of a period in the Egyptian theology when the original revelation of one God grew weak and began to disappear under a monstrous symbolism. It is possible that the priests, who held their religious philosophy a profound secret from the vulgar (whose religion was simply a gross worship of symbols), never relinquished the belief expressed in their sacred texts, which say of God "that He is the sole generator in heaven and earth, and that He has not been begotten. . . That He is the only living and true God, who was begotten by Himself. . . He who has existed from the beginning. . . . who has made all things and was not Himself made." It is possible that they may have held to this and still kept in the purity of its first conception the myth of the manifestation of Osiris, however fantastic the myth subsequently became in mythology and in the popular worship.

Osiris, the personification of the sun, the life-giving, came upon the earth to benefit men, and one of his titles was the "manifester of good and truth." He was slain in a conflict with Set, the spirit of evil and darkness; he was buried; he was raised from the dead by the prayers of his wife, Isis; he became the judge of the dead; he was not only the life-giving but the saving deity; "himself the first raised from the dead, he assisted to raise those who were justified, after having aided them to overcome all their trials."

But whatever the priests and the initiated believed, this myth is here symbolized in the baldest forms. We have the mummy of Osiris passing through its interment and the successive stages of the under-world; then his body is dismembered and scattered, and finally the limbs and organs are reassembled and joined together, and the resurrection takes place before our eyes. It reminds one of a pantomime of the Ravels, who used to chop up the body of a comrade and then put him together again as good as new, with the *insouciance* of beings who lived in a world where such transactions were common. The whole temple indeed, would be a royal place for the tricks of a conjurer or the delusions of a troop of stage wizards. It is full of dark chambers and secret passages, some of them in the walls and some subterranean, the entrances to which are only disclosed by removing a close-fitting stone.

The great pylons, ascended by internal stairways, have habitable chambers in each story, lighted by deep slits of windows, and are like palace fortresses. The view from the summit of one of them is fascinating, but almost grim; that is, your surroundings are huge masses of granite mountains and islands, only relieved by some patches of green and a few palms on the east shore. But time has so worn and fashioned the stones of the overtopping crags, and the color of the red granite is so warm, and the *contours* are so softened that under the brilliant sky the view is mellowed and highly poetical, and ought not to be called grim.

This little island, gay with its gorgeously colored walls, graceful colonnades, garden-roofs, and spreading terraces, set in its rim of swift water, protected by these granite fortresses, bent over by this sky, must have been a dear and sacred place to the worshippers of Isis and Osiris, and we scarcely wonder that the celebration of their rites was continued so long in our era. We do not need, in order to feel the romance of the place, to know that it was a favorite spot with Cleopatra, and that she moored her silken-sailed dahabeëh on the sandbank where ours now lies. Perhaps she was not a person of romantic nature. There is a portrait of her here (the authenticity of which rests upon I know not what authority) stiffly cut in the stone, in which she appears to be a resolute woman with full sensual lips and a determined chin. Her hair is put up in decent simplicity. But I half think that she herself was like her other Egyptian sisters and made her silken locks to shine with the juice of the castor-oil plant. But what were these mysteries in which she took part, and what was this worship, conducted in these dark and secret chambers? It was veiled from all vulgar eyes; probably the people were scarcely allowed to set foot upon the sacred island.

Sunday morning was fresh and cool, with fleecy clouds, light and summer-like. Instead of Sabbath bells, when I rose late, I heard the wild chant of a crew rowing a dahabeëh down the echoing channel. And I wondered how church bells, rung on the top of these pylons, would sound reverberating among these granite rocks and boulders. We climbed, during the afternoon, to the summit of the island of Biggeh, which overshadows Philæ, and is a most fantastic pile of crags. You can best understand this region by supposing that a gigantic internal explosion lifted the granite strata into the air, and that the fragments fell hap-hazard. This Biggeh might have been piled up by the giants who attempted to scale heaven, when Zeus blasted them and their work with his launched lightning.

From this summit, we have in view the broken, rock-strewn field called the Cataract, and all the extraordinary islands of rock above, that almost dam the river; there, over Philæ, on the north shore, is the barrack-like Austrian Mission, and near it the railway that runs through the desert waste, round the hills of the Cataract, to Assouan. These vast piled-up fragments and splintered ledges, here and all about us, although of red granite and syenite, are all disintegrating and crumbling into fine atoms. It is this decay that softens the hardness of the outlines, and harmonizes with the ruins below. Wild as the convulsion was that caused this fantastic wreck, the scene is not without a certain peace now, as we sit here this Sunday afternoon, on a high crag, looking down upon the pagan temples, which resist the tooth of time almost as well as the masses of granite rock that are in position and in form their sentinels.

Opposite, on the hill, is the mosque, and the plastered dome of the sheykh's tomb with its prayer-niche, a quiet and commanding place of repose. The mosque looks down upon the ever-flowing Nile, upon the granite desolation, upon the decaying temple of Isis,—converted once into a temple of the true God, and now merely the marvel of the traveller. The mosque itself, representative of the latest religion, is falling to ruin. What will come next? What will come to break up this civilized barbarism?

"Abd-el-Atti, why do you suppose the Lord permitted the old heathens to have such a lovely place as this Philæ for the practice of their superstitions?"

"Do' know, be sure. Once there was a stranger, I reckon him travel without any dragoman, come to the tent of the prophet Abraham, and ask for food and lodging; he was a kind of infidel, not believe in God, not to believe in anything but a bit of stone. And Abraham was very angry, and sent him away without any dinner. Then the Lord, when he saw it, scolded Abraham.

"'But,' says Abraham, 'the man is an infidel, and does not believe in Thee.'

"'Well,' the Lord he answer to Abraham, 'he has lived in my world all his life, and I have suffered him, and taken care of him, and prospered him, and borne his infidelity; and you could not give him a dinner, or shelter for one night in your house!'

"Then Abraham ran after the infidel, and called him back, and told him all that the Lord he say. And the infidel when he heard it, answer,

"'If the Lord says that, I believe in him; and I believe that you are a prophet.'"

"And do you think, Abd-el-Atti, that men have been more tolerant, the Friends of Mohammed, for instance, since then?"

"Men pretty nearly always the same; I see 'em all 'bout alike. I read in our books a little, what you call 'em?—yes, anecdote, how a Moslem 'ulama, and a Christian priest, and a Jewish rabbi, were in a place together, and had some conversation, and they agreed to tell what each would like best to happen.

"The priest he began:—'I should like,' says he, 'as many Moslems to die as there are animals sacrificed by them on the day of sacrifice.'

"'And I,' says the 'ulama, 'would like to see put out of the way so many Christians as they eat eggs on Easter.'

"Now it is your turn, says they both to the rabbi:—'Well, I should like you both to have your wishes.' I think the Jew have the best of it. Not so?"

The night is soft and still, and envelopes Philæ in a summer warmth. The stars crowd the blue-black sky with scintillant points, obtrusive and blazing in startling nearness; they are all repeated in the darker blue of the smooth river, where lie also, perfectly outlined, the heavy shadows of the granite masses. Upon the silence suddenly break the notes of a cornet, from a dahabeëh moored above us, in pulsations, however, rather to emphasize than to break the hush of the night.

"Eh! that's Mr. Fiddle," cries Abd-el-Atti, whose musical nomenclature is not very extensive, "that's a him."

Once on a moonless night in Upper Nubia, as we lay tied to the bank, under the shadow of the palms, there had swept past us, flashing into sight an instant and then gone in the darkness, an upward-bound dahabeëh, from the deck of which a cornet-à-piston flung out, in salute, the lively notes of a popular American air. The player (whom the dragoman could never call by any name but "Mr. Fiddle"), as we came to know later, was an Irish gentleman, Anglicized and Americanized, and indeed cosmopolitan, who has a fancy for going about the world and awaking here and there remote and commonly undisturbed echoes with his favorite brass horn. I daresay that moonlight voyagers on the Hudson have heard its notes dropping down from the Highlands; it has stirred the air of every land on the globe except India; our own Sierras have responded to its invitations, and Mount Sinai itself has echoed its strains. There is a prejudice against the cornet, that it is not exactly a family instrument; and not more suited to assist in morning and evening devotions than the violin, which a young clergyman, whom I knew, was endeavoring to learn, in order to play it, gently, at family prayers.

This traveled cornet, however, begins to play, with deliberate pauses between the bars, the notes of that glorious hymn, "How firm a foundation, ye saints of the Lord," following it with the Prayer from Der Freischutz, and that, again, with some familiar Scotch airs (a transition perfectly natural in home-circles on Sunday evening), every note of which, leisurely floating out into the night, is sent back in distant echoes. Nothing can be lovelier than the scene,—the tropical night, the sentimental island, the shadows of columns and crags, the mysterious presence of a brooding past,—and nothing can be sweeter than these dulcet, lingering, re-echoing strains, which are the music of our faith, of civilization, of home. From these old temples did never come, in the days of the flute and the darabooka, such melodies. And do the spirits of Isis and Osiris, and of Berenice, Cleopatra, and Antoninus, who worshipped them here, listen, and know perhaps that a purer and better spirit has come into the world?

In the midst of this echoing melody, a little boat, its sail noiselessly furled, its gunwales crowded with gowned and white-turbaned Nubians, glides out of the shadow and comes alongside, as silently as a ferry-boat of the under-world bearing the robed figures of the departed, and the venerable Reïs of the Cataract steps on board, with *es-salaäm 'aleykum;* and the negotiation for shooting the rapids in the morning begins.

The reïs is a Nubian of grave aspect, of a complexion many shades darker than would have been needed to disqualify its possessor to enjoy civil rights in our country a few years ago, and with watchful and shrewd black eyes which have an occasional gleam of humor; his robe is mingled black and white, his turban is a fine camels'-hair shawl; his legs are bare, but he wears pointed red-morocco slippers. There is a long confab between him and the dragoman, over pipes and coffee, about the down trip. It seems that there is a dahabeëh at Assouan, carrying the English Prince Arthur and a Moslem prince, which has been waiting for ten days the whim of the royal scion, to make the ascent. Meantime no other boat can go up or down. The cataract business is at a standstill. The government has given orders that no other boat shall get in the way; and many travellers' boats have been detained from one to two weeks; some of them have turned back, without seeing Nubia, unable to spend any longer time in a vexatious uncertainty. The prince has signified his intention of coming up the cataract to-morrow morning, and consequently we cannot go down, although the descending channel is not the same as the ascending. A considerable fleet of boats is now at each end of the cataract, powerless to move.

The cataract people express great dissatisfaction at this interference in their concerns by the government, which does not pay them as much as the ordinary traveller does for passing the cataract. And yet they have their own sly and mysterious method of dealing with boats that is not less annoying than the government favoritism. They will very seldom take a dahabeëh through in a day; they have delight in detaining it in the rapids and showing their authority.

When, at length, the reïs comes into the cabin, to pay us a visit of courtesy, he is perfect in dignity and good-breeding, in spite of his bare legs; and enters into a discourse of the situation with spirit and intelligence. In reply to a remark, that, in America we are not obliged to wait for princes, his eyes sparkle, as he answers, with much vivacity of manner,

"You quite right. In Egypt we are in a mess. Egypt is a ewe sheep from which every year they shear the wool close off; the milk that should go to the lamb they drink; and when the poor old thing dies, they give the carcass to the people — the skin they cut up among themselves. This season," he goes on, "is to the cataracts like what the pilgrimage is to Mecca and to Jerusalem—the time when to make the money from the traveller. And when the princes they come, crowding the traveller to one side, and the government makes everything done for them for nothing, and pays only one dollar for a turkey for which the traveller pays two, 'bliges the people to sell their provisions at its own price,"—the sheykh stopped.

"The reïs, then, Abd-el-Atti, doesn't fancy this method of doing business?"

"No, him say he not like it at all."

And the reïs kindled up, "You may call the prince anything you like, you may call him king; but the real sultan is the man who pays his money and does not come here at the cost of the government. Great beggars some of these big nobility; all the great people want the Viceroyal to do 'em charity, and take 'em up the Nile, into Abyssinia, I don't know where all. I think the greatest beggars always those who can best afford to pay."

With this philosophical remark the old sheykh concludes a long harangue, the substance of which is given above, and takes his leave with a hundred complimentary speeches.

Forced to wait, we employed Monday advantageously in exploring the land-route to Assouan, going to Mahatta, where the trading boats lie, and piles of merchandise lumber the shore. It is a considerable village, and full of most persistent beggars and curiosity vendors. The road, sandy and dusty, winds through hills of granite boulders—a hot and desolate though not deserted highway, for strings of camels, with merchandise, were in sight the whole distance. We passed through the ancient cemetery, outside of Assouan, a dreary field of sand and rocks, the leaning grave stones covered with inscriptions in old Arabic (or Cuffic), where are said to rest the martyred friends of the prophet who perished in the first battle with the infidels above Philæ.

Returning we made a *détour* to the famous syenite quarries, the openings of several of which are still visible. They were worked from the sides, and not in pits, and offer little to interest the ordinary sight-seer. Yet we like to see where the old workmen chipped away at the rocks; there are frequent marks of the square holes that they drilled, in order to split off the stone with wet wedges of wood. The great obelisk which lies in the quarry, half covered by sand, is unfinished; it is tapered from the base to its tip, ninety-eight feet, but it was doubtless, as the marks indicate, to be worked down to the size of the big obelisk at Karnak; the part which is exposed measures ten to eleven feet square. It lies behind ledges of rock, and it could only have been removed by cutting away the enormous mass in front of it, or by hoisting it over. The suggestion of Mr. Wilkinson that it was to be floated out by a canal, does not commend itself to one standing on the ground.

We came back by the long road, the ancient travelled way, along which, on the boulders, are rudely-cut sculptures and hieroglyphics, mere scratchings on the stone, but recording the passage of kings and armies as long ago as the twelfth dynasty. Nearly all the way from Assouan to Philæ are remains of a huge wall of unburnt bricks, ten to fifteen feet broad and probably fifteen to twenty feet high, winding along the valley and over the low ridges. An apparently more unnecessary wall does not exist; it is said by people here to have been thrown up by the Moslems as a protection against the Nubians when they first traversed this desert; but it is no doubt Roman. There are indications that the Nile once poured its main flood through this opening.

We emerge not far from the south end of the railway track, and at the deserted Austrian Mission. A few Nubian families live in huts on the bank of the stream. Among the bright-eyed young ladies, with shining hair, who entreat backsheesh, while we are waiting for our sandal, is the daughter of our up-river pilot. We should have had a higher opinion of his dignity and rank if we had not seen his house and his family.

After sunset the dahabeës of the Prince came up and were received with salutes by the waiting boats, which the royal craft did not return. Why the dragoman of the arriving dahabeëh came to ours with the prince's request, as he said, for our cards, we were not informed; we certainly intended no offence by the salute; it was, on the part of the other boats, a natural expression of pleasure that the royal boat was at last out of the way.

At dark we loose from lovely Philæ, in order to drop down to Mahatta and take our station for running the cataract in the morning. As we draw out from the little fleet of boats, Irish, Hungarian, American, English, rockets and blue lights illumine the night, and we go off in a blaze of glory. Regardless of the Presence, the Irish gentleman responds on his cornet with the Star-Spangled Banner, the martial strains of which echo from all the hills.

In a moment, the lights are out, the dahabeëhs disappear and the enchanting island is lost to sight. We are gliding down the swift and winding channel, through granite walls, under the shadow of giant boulders, immersed in the gloom of a night which the stars do not penetrate. There is no sound save the regular, chopping fall of the heavy sweeps, which steady the timorous boat, and are the only sign, breaking the oppressive silence, that we are not a phantom ship in a world of shades. It is a short but ghostly voyage, and we see at length with a sigh of relief the lines of masts and spars in the port of Mahatta. Working the boat through the crowd that lie there we moor for the night, with the roar of the cataract in our ears.

CHAPTER XXVII.

RETURNING.

WE are on deck before sunrise. A film is over the sky and a light breeze blows out our streamer—a bad omen for the passage.

The downward run of the Cataract is always made in the early morning, that being the time when there is least likely to be any wind. And a calm is considered absolutely necessary to the safety of the boat. The north wind, which helps the passage up, would be fatal going down. The boat runs with the current, and any exterior disturbance would whirl her about and cast her upon the rocks.

If we are going this morning, we have no time to lose, for it is easy to see that this breeze, which is now uncertainly dallying with our colours, will before long strengthen. The Cataract people begin to arrive; there is already a blue and white row of them squatting on the bank above us, drawing their cotton robes about them, for the morning is a trifle chilly. They come loitering along the bank and sit down as if they were merely spectators, and had no interest in the performance.

The sun comes, and scatters the cloud-films; as the sun rises we are ready to go; everything has been made snug and fast above and below; and the breeze has subsided entirely. We ought to take instant advantage of the calm; seconds count, now. But we wait for the Reïs of the Cataract, the head reïs, without whose consent no move can be made. It is the sly old sheykh with whom we have already negotiated, and he has his reasons for delaying. By priority of arrival at Philæ our boat is entitled to be first taken down; but the dragoman of another boat has been crossing the palms of the guileless patriarch with gold pieces, and he has agreed to give the other boat the preference. It is not probable that the virtuous sheykh ever intended to do so, but he must make some show of keeping his bargain. He would like to postpone our voyage, and take the chances of another day.

But here he comes, mounted on a donkey, in state, wrapped about the head and neck in his cashmere, and with a train of attendants—the imperturbable, shrewd old man. He halts a moment on the high bank, looks up at our pennant, mutters something about "wind, not good day, no safe," and is coolly about to ride by.

Our dragoman in an instant is at his side, and with half-jocular but firm persistence invites him to dismount. It is in vain that the sheykh invents excuse after excuse for going on. There is a neighbor in the village whose child is dead, and he must visit him. The consolation, Abd-el-Atti thinks, can be postponed an hour or two. Allah is all-merciful. He is chilly, his fingers are cold, he will just ride to the next house and warm his hands, and by that time we can tell whether it is to be a good morning. Abd-el-Atti is sure that he can warm his fingers much better on our boat, in fact he can get warm all through there.

"I'll warm him if he won't come," continues the dragoman, turning to us; "if I let him go by, the old rascal, he slip down to Assouan, and that become the last of him."

Before the patriarch knows exactly what has happened, or the other dragoman can hinder, he is gently hustled down the steep bank aboard our boat. There is a brief palaver, and then he is seated, with a big bowl of coffee and bread; we are still waiting, but it is evident that the decisive nod has been given. The complexion of affairs has changed!

The people are called from the shore; before we interpret rightly their lazy stir, they are swarming on board. The men are getting their places on the benches at the oars—three stout fellows at each oar; it looks like "business." The three principal reïses are on board; there are at least a dozen steersmen; several heads of families are present, and a dozen boys. More than seventy-five men have invaded us—and they may all be needed to get ropes ashore in case of accident. This unusual swarm of men and the assistance of so many sheykhs, these extra precautions, denote either fear, or a desire to impress us with the magnitude of the undertaking. The head reïs shakes his head at the boat and mutters "much big." We have aboard almost every skilful pilot of the rapids.

The Cataract flag, two bands of red and yellow with the name of "Allah" worked on it in white, is set up by the cabin stairs.

There is a great deal of talking, some confusion, and a little nervousness. Our dragoman cheerfully says, "we will hope for the better," as the beads pass through his fingers. The reïses are audibly muttering their prayers. The pilots begin to strip to their work. A bright boy of twelve years, squat on deck by the tiller, is loudly and rapidly reciting the Koran.

At the last moment the most venerable reïs of the cataract comes on board, as a great favor to us. He has long been superannuated, his hair is white, his eye-sight is dim, but when he is on board all will go well. Given a conspicuous seat in a chair on the cabin deck, he begins at once prayers for our safe passage. This sheykh is very distinguished, tracing his ancestry back beyond the days of Abraham; his family is very large— seven hundred is the number of his relations; this seems to be a favorite number: Ali Moorad at Luxor has also seven hundred relations. The sheykh is treated with great deference; he seems to have had something to do with designing the cataract, and opening it to the public.

The last rope is hauled in; the crowd on shore cheer; our rowers dip the oars, and in a moment we are sweeping along in the stiff current, avoiding the boulders on either side. We go swiftly. Everybody is muttering prayers now; two venerable reïses seated on a box in front of the rudder increase the speed of their devotions; and the boy chants the Koran with a freer swing.

Our route down is not the same as it was up. We pass the head of the chief rapid—in which we struggle—into which it would need only a wink of the helm to turn us—and sweep away to the west side; and even appear to go a little out of our way to run near a precipice of rock. A party of ladies and gentlemen who have come down from their dahabeëh above, to see us make the chûte, are standing on the summit, and wave handkerchiefs and hats as we rush by.

Before us, we can see the great rapids—a down-hill prospect. The passage is narrow, and so crowded is the hurrying water that there is a ridge down the centre. On this ridge, which is broken and also curved, we are to go. If it were straight, it would be more attractive, but it curves short to the right near the bottom of the rapid, and, if we do not turn sharp with it, we shall dash against the rocks ahead, where the waves strike in curling foam. All will depend upon the skill and strength of the steersmen, and the sheer at the exact instant.

There is not long to think of it, however, and no possibility now of evading the trial. Before we know it, the nose of the boat is in the rapid, which flings it up in the air; the next second we are tossed on the waves. The bow dips, and a heavy wave deluges the cook's domain; we ship a ton or two of water, the dragoman, who stands forward, is wet to his breast; but the boat shakes it off and rises again, tossed like an egg-shell. It is glorious. The boat obeys her helm admirably, as the half-dozen pilots, throwing their weight upon the tiller, skilfully veer it slightly or give it a broad sweep.

It is a matter of only three or four minutes, but they are minutes of intense excitement. In the midst of them, the reïs of our boat, who has no command now and no responsibility, and is usually imperturbably calm, becomes completely unmanned by the strain upon his nerves, and breaks forth into convulsive shouting, tears and perspiration running down his cheeks. He has "the power," and would have hysterics if he were not a man. A half-dozen people fly to his rescue, snatch off his turban, hold his hands, mop his face, and try to call him out of his panic. By the time he is somewhat composed, we have shunned the rocks and made the turn, and are floating in smoother but still swift water. The reïses shake hands and come to us with salaams and congratulations. The chief pilot desires to put my fez on his head in token of great joy and amity. The boy stops shouting the Koran, the prayers cease, the beads are put up. It is only when we are in a tight place that it is necessary to call upon the name of the Lord vigorously.

"You need not have feared," said a reïs of the Cataract to ours, pointing to the name on the red and yellow flag, "Allah would bring us through."

That there was no danger in this passage we cannot affirm.

The dahabeëhs that we left at Mahatta, ready to go down, and which might have been brought through that morning, were detained four or five days upon the whim of the reïses. Of the two that came first, one escaped with a slight knock against the rocks, and the other was dashed on them, her bottom staved in, and half filled with water immediately. Fortunately, she was fast on the rock; the passengers, luggage, and stores were got ashore; and after some days the boat was rescued and repaired.

For a mile below this chûte we have rapid going, rocks to shun, short turns to make, and quite uncertainty enough to keep us on the *qui vive*, and finally, another lesser rapid, where there is infinitely more noise by the crew, but less danger from the river than above.

As we approach the last rapid, a woman appears in the swift stream, swimming by the help of a log—that being the handy ferry-boat of the country; her clothes are all in a big basket, and the basket is secured on her head. The sandal, which is making its way down a side channel, with our sheep on board, is signalled to take this lady of the lake in, and land her on the opposite shore. These sheep of ours, though much tossed about, seem to enjoy the voyage, and look about upon the raging scene with that indifference which comes of high breeding. They are black, but that was not to their prejudice in their Nubian home. They are comely animals in life, and in death are the best mutton in the East; it is said that they are fed on dates, and that this diet imparts to their flesh its sweet flavour. I think their excellence is quite as much due to the splendid air they breathe. While we are watching the manœuvring of the boat, the woman swims to a place where she can securely lodge her precious log in the rocks and touch bottom with her feet. The boat follows her and steadies itself against the same rocks, about which the swift current is swirling. The water is up to the woman's neck, and the problem seems to be to get the clothes out of the basket which is on her head, and put them on, and not wet the clothes. It is the old myth of Venus rising from the sea, but under changed conditions, and in the face of modern sensitiveness. How it was accomplished, I cannot say, but when I look again the aquatic Venus is seated in the sandal, clothed, dry, and placid.

We were an hour passing the rapids, the last part of the time with a strong wind against us; if it had risen sooner, we should have had serious trouble. As it was, it took another hour with three men at each oar, to work down to Assouan through the tortuous channel, which is full of rocks and whirlpools. The men at each bank of oars belonged to different tribes, and they fell into a rivalry of rowing, which resulted in an immense amount of splashing, spurting, yelling, chorusing, and calling on the Prophet. When the contest became hot, the oars were all at sixes and sevens, and in fact the rowing gave way to vituperation and a general scrimmage. Once, in one of the most ticklish places in the rapids, the rowers had fallen to quarrelling, and the boat would have gone to smash, if the reïs had not rushed in and laid about him with a stick. These artless children of the sun! However, we came down to our landing in good form, exchanging salutes with the fleet of boats waiting to make the ascent.

At once four boats, making a gallant show with their spread wings, sailed past us, bound up the cataract. The passengers fired salutes, waved their handkerchiefs, and exhibited the exultation they felt in being at last under way for Philæ; and well they might, for some of them had been waiting here fifteen days.

But alas for their brief prosperity. The head reïs was not with them; that autocrat was still upon our deck, leisurely stowing away coffee, eggs, cold meat, and whatever provisions were brought him, with the calmness of one who has a good conscience. As the dahabeëhs swept by he shook his head and murmured, "not much go."

And they did "not much go." They stopped indeed, and lay all day at the first gate, and all night. The next morning, two dahabeëhs, carrying persons of rank, passed up, and were given the preference, leaving the first-comers still in the rapids; and two days after, they were in mid-passage, and kept day after day in the roar and desolation of the cataract, at the pleasure of its owners. The only resource they had was to write indignant letters, in remonstrance to the governor at Assouan.

This passage of the cataract is a mysterious business, the secrets of which are only mastered by patient study. Why the reïses should desire to make it so vexatious is the prime mystery. The traveller who reaches Assouan often finds himself entangled in an invisible web of restraints. There is no opposition to his going on; on the contrary the governor, the reïses, and everyone overflow with courtesy and helpfulness. But, somehow, he does not go on, he is played with from day to day. The old sheykh, before he took his affectionate leave of us that morning, let out the reason of the momentary hesitation he had exhibited in agreeing to take our boat up the cataract when we arrived. The excellent owners, honest Aboo Yoosef and the plaintive little Jew of Bagdad, had sent him a bribe of a whole piece of cotton cloth, and some money to induce him to prevent our passage. He was not to refuse, not by any means, for in that case the owners would have been liable to us for the hundred pounds forfeit named in the contract in case the boat could not be taken up; but he was to amuse us, and encourage us, and delay us, on various pretexts, so long that we should tire out and freely choose not to go any farther.

The integrity of the reïs was proof against the seduction of this bribe; he appropriated it, and then earned the heavy fee for carrying us up, in addition. I can add nothing by way of eulogium upon this clever old man, whose virtue enabled him to withstand so much temptation.

We lay for two days at the island Elephantine, opposite Assouan, and have ample time to explore its two miserable villages, and to wander over the heaps on heaps, the *débris* of so many successive civilizations. All day long, women and children are clambering over these mounds of ashes, pottery, bricks, and fragments of stone, unearthing coins, images, beads, and bits of antiquity, which the strangers buy. There is nothing else on the island. These indistinguishable mounds are almost the sole evidence of the successive occupation of ancient Egyptians, Canaanites, Ethiopians, Persians, Greeks, Romans, Christians, and conquering Arabs. But the grey island has an indefinable charm. The northern end is green with wheat and palms; but if it were absolutely naked, its fine granite outlines would be attractive under this splendid sky. The days are lovely, and the nights enchanting. Nothing more poetic could be imagined than the silvery reaches of river at night, with their fringed islands and shores, the stars and the new moon, the uplifted rocks, and the town reflected in the stream.

Of Assouan itself, its palm-groves and dirty huddle of dwellings, we have quite enough in a day. Curiosity leads us to visit the jail, and we found there, by chance, one of our sailors, who is locked up for insubordination, and our venerable reïs keeping him company, for being inefficient in authority over his crew. In front of the jail, under the shade of two large acacia trees, the governor has placed his divan and holds his *levées* in the open air, transacting business, and entertaining his visitors with coffee and cigars. His excellency is a very "smartish," big black fellow, not a negro nor a Nubian exactly, but an Ababdeh, from a tribe of desert Arabs; a man of some aptitude for affairs and with very little palaver. The jail has an outer guard-room, furnished with divans and open at both ends, and used as a court of justice. A not formidable door leads to the first room, which is some twenty feet square; and here, seated upon the ground with some thirty others, we are surprised to recognize our reïs. The respectable old incapable was greatly humiliated by the indignity. Although he was speedily released, his incarceration was a mistake; it seemed to break his spirit, and he was sullen and uncheerful ever afterwards. His companions were in for trivial offences: most of them for not paying the government taxes, or for debt to the Khedive, as the phrase was. In an adjoining, smaller room, were the great criminals, the thieves and murderers. Three murderers were chained together by enormous iron cables attached to collars about their necks, and their wrists were clamped in small wooden stocks. In this company were five decent-looking men, who were also bound together by heavy chains from neck to neck; we were told that these were the brothers of men who had run away from the draft, and that they would be held until their relations surrendered themselves. They all sat glumly on the ground. The jail does not differ in comfort from the ordinary houses; and the men are led out once a day for fresh air; we saw the murderers taking an airing, and exercise also in lugging their ponderous irons.

We departed from Assouan early in the morning, with water and wind favorable for a prosperous day. At seven o'clock our worthy steersman stranded us on a rock. It was a little difficult to do it, for he had to go out of his way and to leave the broad and plainly staked-out channel. But he did it very neatly. The rock was a dozen feet out of water, and he laid the boat, without injury, on the shelving upper side of it, so that the current would constantly wash it further on, and the falling river would desert it. The steersman was born in Assouan and knows every rock and current here, even in the dark. This accident no doubt happened out of sympathy with the indignity to the reïs. That able commander is curled up on the deck ill, and no doubt was greatly grieved when he felt the grating of the bottom upon the rock; but he was not too ill to exchange glances with the serene and ever-smiling steersman. Three hours after the stranding, our crew have succeeded in working us a little further on than we were at first, and are still busy; surely there are in all history no such navigators as these.

It is with some regret that we leave, or are trying to leave, Nubia, both on account of its climate and its people. The men, various sorts of Arabs as well as the Nubians, are better material than the fellaheen below, finer looking, with more spirit and pride, more independence and self-respect. They are also more barbarous; they carry knives and heavy sticks universally, and guns if they can get them, and in many places have the reputation of being quarrelsome, turbulent, and thieves. But we have rarely received other than courteous treatment from them. Some of the youngest women are quite pretty, or would be but for the enormous nose and ear-rings, the twisted hair and the oil; the old women are all unnecessarily ugly. The children are apt to be what might be called free in apparel, except that the girls wear fringe, but the women are as modest in dress and manner as those of Egypt. That the highest morality invariably prevails, however, one cannot affirm, notwithstanding the privilege of husbands, which we are assured is sometimes exercised, of disposing of a wife (by means of the knife and river) who may have merely incurred suspicion by talking privately with another man. This process is evidently not frequent, for women are plenty, and we saw no bodies in the river.

But our chief regret at quitting Nubia is on account of the climate. It is incomparably the finest winter climate I have ever known; it is nearly perfect. The air is always elastic and inspiring; the days are full of sun; the nights are cool and refreshing; the absolute dryness seems to counteract the danger from changes of temperature. You may do there what you cannot in any place in Europe in the winter—get warm. You may also there have repose with langour.

We went on the rock at seven and got off at two. The governor of Assouan was asked for help and he sent down a couple of boat-loads of men, who lifted us off by main strength and the power of their lungs. We drifted on, but at sunset we were not out of sight of the mosque of Assouan. Strolling ashore we found a broad and rich plain, large palm-groves and wheat-fields, and a swarming population—in striking contrast to the country above the Cataract. The character of the people is wholly different; the women are neither so oily, nor have they the wild shyness of the Nubians; they mind their own business and belong to a more civilized society; slaves, negroes as black as night, abound in the fields. Some of the large wheat-fields are wholly enclosed by substantial unburnt brick walls, ten feet high.

Early in the evening our serene steersman puts us hard aground again on a sandbar. I suppose it was another accident. The wife and children of the steersman live at a little town opposite the shoal upon which we have so conveniently landed, and I suppose the poor fellow wanted an opportunity to visit them. He was not permitted leave of absence while the boat lay at Assouan, and now the dragoman says that, so far as he is concerned, the permission shall not be given from here, although the village is almost in sight; the steersman ought to be punished for his conduct, and he must wait till he comes up next year before he can see his wife and children. It seems a hard case, to separate a man from his family in this manner.

"I think it's a perfect shame," cries Madame, when she hears of it, "not to see his family for a year!"

"But one of his sons is on board, you know, as a sailor. And the steersman spent most of his time with his wife, the boy's mother, when we were at Assouan."

"I thought you said his wife lived opposite here?"

"Yes, but this is a newer one, a younger one; that is his old wife, in Assouan."

"Oh!"

"The poor fellow has another in Cairo."

"Oh!"

"He has wives, I daresay, at proper distances along the Nile, and whenever he wants to spend an hour or two with his family, he runs us aground."

"I don't care to hear anything more about him."

The Moslem religion is admirably suited to the poor mariner, and especially to the sailor on the Nile through a country that is all length and no width.

CHAPTER XXVIII.

MODERN FACTS AND ANCIENT MEMORIES.

ON a high bluff stands the tottering temple of Kom Ombo, conspicuous from a distance, and commanding a dreary waste of desert. Its gigantic columns are of the Ptolemaic time, and the capitals show either Greek influence or the relaxation of the Egyptian hieratic restraint.

The temple is double, with two entrances and parallel suites of apartments, a happy idea of the builders, impartially to split the difference between good and evil. One side is devoted to the worship of Horus, the embodiment of the principle of Light, and the other to that of Savak, the crocodile-headed god of Darkness. I fear that the latter had here the more worshippers; his title was Lord of Ombos, and the fear of him spread like night. On the sand-bank, opposite, the once-favored crocodiles still lounge in the sun, with a sharp eye out for the rifle of the foreigner, and, no doubt, wonder at the murderous spirit which has come into the world to supplant the peaceful heathenism.

These ruins are an example of the jealousy with which the hierarchy guarded their temples from popular intrusion. The sacred precincts were enclosed by a thick and high brick wall, which must have concealed the temple from view except on the river side; so formidable was this wall, that although the edifice stands upon an eminence, it lies in a basin formed by the ruins of the enclosure. The sun beating in it at noon converted it into a reverberating furnace—a heat sufficient to melt any image not of stone, and not to be endured by persons who do not believe in Savak.

We walked a long time on the broad desert below Ombos, over sand as hard as a sea-beach pounded by the waves, looking for the bed of pebbles mentioned in the handbook, and found it a couple of miles below. In the soft bank an enormous mass of pebbles has been deposited, and is annually added to—sweepings of the Nubian deserts, flints and agates, bits of syenite from Assouan, and colored stones in great variety. There is a tradition that a sailor once found a valuable diamond here, and it seems always possible that one may pick some precious jewel out of the sand. Some of the desert pebbles, polished by ages of sand-blasts, are very beautiful.

Every day when I walk upon the smooth desert away from the river, I look for colored stones, pebbles, flints, chalcedonies, and agates. And I expect to find, some day, the *ewige* pebble, the stone translucent, more beautiful than any in the world—perhaps, the lost seal of Solomon, dropped by some wandering Bedawee. I remind myself of one looking always in the desert for the pearl of great price, which all the markets and jewelers of the world wait for. It seems possible, here under this serene sky, on this expanse of sand, which has been trodden for thousands of years by all the Oriental people in turn, by caravans, by merchants and warriors and wanderers, swept by so many geologic floods and catastrophes, to find it. I never tire of looking, and curiously examine every bit of translucent and variegated flint that sparkles in the sand. I almost hope, when I find it, that it will not be cut by hand of man, but that it will be changeable in color, and be fashioned in a cunning manner by nature herself. Unless, indeed, it should be, as I said, the talismanic ring of Solomon, which is known to be somewhere in the world.

In the early morning we have drifted down to Silsilis, one of the most interesting localities on the Nile. The difference in the level of the land above and below and the character of the rocky passage at Silsilis teach that the first cataract was here before the sandstone dam wore away and transferred it to Assouan. Marks have been vainly sought here for the former height of the Nile above; and we were interested in examining the upper strata of rocks laid bare in the quarries. At a height of perhaps sixty feet from the floor of the quarry, we saw *between* two strata of sandstone a layer of other material that had exactly the appearance of the deposits of the Nile which so closely resemble rock along the shore. Upon reaching it we found that it was friable and, in fact, a sort of hardened earth. Analysis would show whether it is a Nile deposit, and might contribute something to the solution of the date of the catastrophe here.

The interest at Silsilis is in these vast sandstone quarries, and very little in the excavated grottoes and rock-temples on the east shore, with their defaced and smoke-obscured images. Indeed, nothing in Egypt, not even the temples and pyramids, has given us such an idea of the immense labor the Egyptians expended in building, as these vast excavations in the rock. We have wondered before where all the stone came from that we have seen piled up in buildings and heaped in miles of ruins; we wonder now what use could have been made of all the stone quarried from these hills. But we remember that it was not removed in a century, nor in ten centuries, but that for great periods of a thousand years workmen were hewing here, and that much of the stone transported and scattered over Egypt has sunk into the soil out of sight.

There are half a dozen of these enormous quarries close together, each of which has its communication with the river. The method of working was this:—a narrow passage was cut in from the river several hundred feet into the mountain, or until the best-working stone was reached, and then the excavation was broadened out without limit. We followed one of these passages, the sides of which are evenly-cut rock, the height of the hill. At length we came into an open area, like a vast cathedral in the mountain, except that it wanted both pillars and roof. The floor was smooth, the sides were from fifty to seventy-five feet high, and all perpendicular, and as even as if dressed down with chisel and hammer. This was their general character, but in some of them steps were left in the wall and platforms, showing perfectly the manner of working. The quarrymen worked from the top down perpendicularly, stage by stage. We saw one of these platforms, a third of the distance from the top, the only means of reaching which was by nicks cut in the face of the rock, in which one might plant his feet and swing down by a rope. There was no sign of splitting by drilling, or by the use of plugs, or of any explosive material. The walls of the quarries are all cut down in fine lines that run from top to bottom slantingly and parallel. These lines have every inch or two round cavities, as if the stone had been bored by some flexible instrument that turned in its progress. The workmen seem to have cut out the stone always of the shape and size they wanted to use; if it was for a statue, the place from which it came in the quarry is rounded, showing the *contour* of the figure taken. They took out every stone by the most patient labor. Whether it was square or round, they cut all about it a channel four to five inches wide, and then separated it from the mass underneath by a like broad cut. Nothing was split away; all was carefully chiseled out, apparently by small tools. Abandoned work, unfinished, plainly shows this. The ages and the amount of labor required to hew out such enormous quantities of stone are heightened in our thought, by the recognition of this slow process. And what hells these quarries must have been for the workmen, exposed to the blaze of a sun intensified by the glaring reflection from the light-colored rock, and stifled for want of air. They have left the marks of their unending task in these little chiselings on the face of the sandstone walls. Here and there some one has rudely sketched a figure or outlined a hieroglyphic. At intervals places are cut in the rock through which ropes could be passed, and these are worn deeply, showing the use of ropes, and no doubt of derricks, in handling the stones.

These quarries are as deserted now as the temples which were taken from them; but nowhere else in Egypt was I more impressed with the duration, the patience, the greatness of the race that accomplished such prodigies of labor.

The grottoes, as I said, did not detain us; they are common calling places, where sailors and wanderers often light fires at night, and where our crew slept during the heat of this day. We saw there nothing more remarkable than the repeated figure of the boy Horus taking nourishment from the breast of his mother, which provoked the irreverent remark of a voyageur that Horus was more fortunate than his dragoman had been in finding milk in this stony region.

Creeping on, often aground and always expecting to be, the weather growing warmer as we went north, we reached Edfoo. It was Sunday, and the temperature was like that of a July day, a south wind, and the mercury at 85°.

In this condition of affairs it was not unpleasant to find a temple, entire, clean, perfectly excavated, and a cool retreat from the glare of the sun. It was not unlike entering a cathedral. The door by which we were admitted was closed and guarded; we were alone; and we experienced something of the sentiment of the sanctuary, that hush and cool serenity which is sometimes mistaken for religion, in the presence of ecclesiastical architecture.

Although this is a Ptolemaic temple, it is, by reason of its nearly perfect condition, the best example for study. The propylon, which is two hundred and fifty feet high, and one hundred and fifteen long, contains many spacious chambers, and confirms our idea that these portions of the temples were residences. The roof is something enormous, being composed of blocks of stone, three feet thick, by twelve wide, and twenty-two long. Upon this roof are other chambers. As we wandered through the vast pillared courts, many chambers, and curious passages, peered into the secret ways and underground and intermural alleys, and emerged upon the roof, we thought what a magnificent edifice it must have been for the gorgeous processions of the old worship, which are sculptured on the walls.

But outside this temple, and only a few feet from it, is a stone wall of circuit, higher than the roof of the temple itself. Like every inch of the temple walls, this wall outside and inside is covered with sculptures, scenes in river life, showing a free fancy, and now and then a dash of humor; as, when a rhinoceros is made to tow a boat—recalling the western sportiveness of David Crockett with the alligator. Not only did this wall conceal the temple from the vulgar gaze, but outside it was again an *enceinte* of unbaked brick, effectually excluding and removing to a safe distance all the populaces. Mariette Bey is of the opinion that all the imposing ceremonies of the old ritual had no witnesses except the privileged ones of the temple; and that no one except the king could enter the *adytum*.

It seems to us also that the king, who was high priest and king, lived in these palace-temples, the pylons of which served him for fortresses as well as residences. We find no ruins of palaces in Egypt, and it seems not reasonable that the king, who had all the riches of the land at his command, would have lived in a hut of mud.

From the summit of this pylon we had an extensive view of the Nile and the fields of ripening wheat. A glance into the squalid town was not so agreeable. I know it would be a severe test of any village if it were unroofed, and one could behold its varied domestic life. We may from such a sight as this have some conception of the appearance of this world to the angels looking down. Our view was into filthy courts and roofless enclosures, in which were sorry women and unclad children, sitting in the dirt; where old people, emaciated and feeble, and men and women ill of some wasting disease, lay stretched upon the ground, uncared for, stifled by the heat and swarmed upon by flies.

The heated day lapsed into a delicious evening, a half-moon over head, the water glassy, the shores fringed with palms, the air soft. As we came to El Kab, where we stopped, a carawan was whistling on the opposite shore—a long, shrill whistle, like that of a mocking-bird. If we had known, it was a warning to us that the placid appearances of the night were deceitful, and that violence was masked under this smiling aspect. The barometer indeed had been falling rapidly for two days. We were about to have our first experience of what may be called a simoon.

Towards nine o'clock, and suddenly, the wind began to blow from the north, like one of our gusts in summer, preceding a thunderstorm. The boat took the alarm at once, and endeavoured to fly, swinging to the wind and tugging at her moorings. With great difficulty she was secured by strong cables fore and aft, anchored in the sand, but she trembled and shook and rattled, and the wind whistled through the rigging as if we had been on the Atlantic—any boat loose upon the river that night must have gone to inevitable wreck. It became at once dark, and yet it was a ghastly darkness; the air was full of fine sand that obscured the sky, except directly overhead, where there were the ghost of a wan moon and some spectral stars. Looking upon the river, it was like a Connecticut fog—but a sand fog; and the river itself roared, and high waves ran against the current. When we stepped from the boat, eyes, nose, and mouth, were instantly choked with sand, and it was almost impossible to stand. The wind increased, and rocked the boat like a storm at sea; for three hours it blew with much violence, and in fact did not spend itself in the whole night.

"The worser storm, God be merciful," says Abd-el-Atti, "ever I saw in Egypt."

When it somewhat abated, the dragoman recognized a divine beneficence in it; "it show that God 'member us."

It is a beautiful belief of devout Moslems that personal afflictions and illnesses are tokens of a heavenly care. Often when our dragoman has been ill, he has congratulated himself that God was remembering him.

"Not so! A friend of me in Cairo was never in his life ill, never any pain, toothache, headache, nothing. Always well. He begin to have fear that something should happen, mebbe God forgot him. One day I meet him in the Mooskee very much pleased; all right now, he been broke him the arm; God 'member him."

During the gale we had a good specimen of Arab character. When it was at its height, and many things about the attacked vessel needed looking after, securing and tightening, most of the sailors rolled themselves up, drawing their heads into their burnouses, and went sound asleep. The after-sail was blown loose and flapping in the wind; our reïs sat composedly looking at it, never stirring from his haunches, and let the canvas whip to rags; finally a couple of men were aroused and secured the shreds. The Nile crew is a marvel of helplessness in an emergency; and considering the dangers of the river to these top-heavy boats, it is a wonder that any accomplish the voyage in safety. There is no more discipline on board than in a district school meeting at home. The boat might as well be run by ballot.

It was almost a relief to have an unpleasant day to talk about. The forenoon was like a mixed fall and spring day in New England, strong wind, flying clouds, but the air full of sand instead of snow; there was even a drop of rain, and we heard a peal or two of feeble thunder—evidently an article not readily manufactured in this country; but the afternoon settled back into the old pleasantness.

Of the objects of interest at Eilethyas I will mention only two, the famous grottoes, and a small temple of Amunoph III., not often visited. It stands between two and three miles from the river, in a desolate valley, down which the Bisharee Arabs used to come on marauding excursions. What freak placed it in this remote solitude? It contains only one room, a few paces square, and is, in fact, only a chapel, but it is full of capital pieces of sculptures of a good period of art. The architect will find here four pillars, which clearly suggest the Doric style. They are fourteen-sided, but one of the planes is broader than the others and has a raised tablet of sculptures which terminate above in a face, said to be that of Lucina, to whom the temple is dedicated, but resembling the cow-headed Isis. These pillars, with the sculptures on one side finished at the top with a head, may have suggested the Osiride pillars.

The grottoes are tombs in the sandstone mountain, of the time of the eighteenth dynasty, which began some thirty-five hundred years ago. Two of them have remarkable sculptures, the coloring of which is still fresh; and I wish to speak of them a little, because it is from them (and some of the same character) that Egyptologists have largely reconstructed for us the common life of the ancient Egyptians. Although the work is somewhat rude, it has a certain veracity of execution which is pleasing.

We assume this tomb to have been that of a man of wealth. This is the ante-chamber; the mummy was deposited in a pit let into a small excavation in the rear. On one wall are sculptured agricultural scenes: ploughing, sowing, reaping wheat and pulling doora (the color indicates the kind of grain), hatchelling the latter, while oxen are treading out the wheat, and the song of the threshers encouraging the oxen is written in hieroglyphics above; the winnowing and storing of the grain; in a line under these, the various domestic animals of the deceased are brought forward to a scribe, who enumerates them and notes the numbers on a roll of papyrus. There are river-scenes:—grain is loaded into freight-boats; pleasure-dahabeëhs are on the stream, gayly painted, with one square sail amidships, rowers along the sides, and windows in the cabin; one has a horse and chariot on board, the reïs stands at the bow, the overseer, kurbash in hand, is threatening the crew, a sailor is falling overboard. Men are gathering grapes, and treading out the wine with their feet; others are catching fish and birds in nets, and dressing and curing them. At the end of this wall, offerings are made to Osiris. In one compartment a man is seated holding a boy on his lap.

On the opposite wall are two large figures, supposed to be the occupant of the tomb and his wife, seated on a *fauteuil;* men and women, in two separate lines, facing the large figures, are seated, one leg bent under them, each smelling a lotus flower. In the rear, men are killing and cutting up animals as if preparing for a feast. To the leg of the *fauteuil* is tied a monkey; and Mr. Wilkinson says that it was customary at entertainments for the hosts to have a "favorite monkey" tied to the leg of the chair. Notwithstanding the appearance of the monkey here in that position, I do not suppose that he would say that an ordinary entertainment is represented here. For, although there are preparations for a feast, there is a priest standing between the friends and the principal personages, making offerings, and the monkey may be present in his character of emblem of Thoth. It seems to be a funeral and not a festive representation. The pictures apparently tell the story of the life of the deceased and his occupations, and represent the mourning at his tomb. In other grottoes, where the married pair are seated as here, the arm of the woman on the shoulder of the man, and the "favorite monkey" tied to the chair, friends are present in the act of mourning, throwing dust on their heads, and accompanied by musicians; and the mummy is drawn on a sledge to the tomb, a priest standing on the front, and a person pouring oil on the ground that the runners may slip easily.

The setting sun strikes into these chambers, so carefully prepared for people of rank, of whom not a pinch of dust now remains, and lights them up with a certain cheer and hope. We cannot make anything melancholy out of a tomb so high and with such a lovely prospect from its front door. The former occupants are unknown, but not more unknown than the peasants we see on the fields below, still at the tasks depicted in these sculptures. Thirty-five hundred years is not so very long ago! Slowly we pick our way down the hill and regain our floating home; and, bidding farewell forever to El Kab, drift down in the twilight. In the morning we are at Esneh.

In Esneh the sound of the grinding is never low. The town is full of primitive ox-power mills in which the wheat is ground, and there are always dahabeëhs staying here for the crew to bake their bread. Having already had one day of Esneh, we are tired of it, for it is exactly like all other Egyptian towns of its size; we know all the possible combinations of mud-hovels, crooked lanes, stifling dust, nakedness, squalor. We are so accustomed to picking our way in the street amid women and children sprawling in the dirt, that the scene has lost its strangeness; it is even difficult to remember that in other countries women usually keep in-doors and sit on chairs.

The town is not without liveliness. It is half Copt, and beggars demand backsheesh on the ground that they are Christians, and have a common interest with us. We wander through the bazaars where there is nothing to buy, and into the market-place, always the most interesting study in an unknown city. The same wheat lies on the ground in heaps; the same roots and short stalks of the doora are tied in bundles and sold for fuel, and cakes of dried manure for the like use; people are lying about in the sun in all picturesque attitudes, some curled up and some on their backs fast asleep; more are squatting before little heaps of corn or beans or some wilted "greens," or dried tobacco-leaves and pipe-bowls; children swarm and tumble about everywhere; donkeys and camels pick their way through the groups.

I spent half an hour in teaching a handsome young Copt how to pronounce English words in his Arabic-English primer. He was very eager to learn and very grateful for assistance. We had a large and admiring crowd about us, who laughed at every successful and still more at every unsuccessful attempt on the part of the pupil, and repeated the English words themselves when they could catch the sound,—an exceedingly good-natured lot of idlers. We found the people altogether pleasant, some in the ingrained habit of begging, quick to take a joke and easily excited. While I had my scholar, a *fantasia* of music on two tambourines was performed for the amusement of my comrade, which had also its ring of spectators watching the effect of the monotonous thumping, upon the grave howadji; he was seated upon the mastabah of a shop, with all formality, and enjoyed all the honors of the entertainment, as was proper, since he bore the entire expense alone,—about five cents.

The coffee-shops of Esneh are many, some respectable and

others decidedly otherwise. The former are the least attractive, being merely long and dingy mud-apartments, in which the visitors usually sit on the floor and play at draughts. The coffee-houses near the river have porticoes and pleasant terraces in front, and look not unlike some picturesque Swiss or Italian wine-shops. The attraction there seems to be the Ghawazees or dancing-girls, of whom there is a large colony here, the colony consisting of a tribe. All the family act as procurers for the young women, who are usually married. Their dress is an extraordinary combination of stripes and colors, red and yellow being favorites, which harmonize well with their dark, often black, skin, and eyes heavily shaded with kohl. I suppose it must be admitted, in spite of their total want of any womanly charm of modesty, that they are the finest-looking women in Egypt, though many of them are ugly; they certainly are of a different type from the Egyptians, though not of a pure type; they boast that they have preserved themselves without admixture with other peoples or tribes from a very remote period; one thing is certain, their profession is as old as history and their antiquity may entitle them to be considered an aristocracy of vice. They say that their race is allied in origin to that of the people called gypsies, with whom many of their customs are common. The men are tinkers, blacksmiths, or musicians, and the women are the ruling element in the band; the husband is subject to the wife. But whatever their origin, it is admitted that their dance is the same as that with which the dancing-women amused the Pharaohs, the same that the Phœnicians carried to Gades and which Juvenal describes, and, Mr. Lane thinks, the same by which the daughter of Herodias danced off the head of John the Baptist. Modified here and there, it is the immemorial dance of the Orient.

Esneh has other attractions for the sailors of the Nile; there are the mahsheshehs, or shops where hasheesh is smoked; an attendant brings the "hubble-bubble" to the guests who are lolling on the mastabah; they inhale their portion, and then lie down in a stupor, which is at every experiment one remove nearer idiocy.

Still drifting, giving us an opportunity to be on shore all the morning. We visit the sugar establishment at Mutánch, and walk along the high bank under the shade of the acacias for a couple of miles below it. Nothing could be lovelier in this sparkling morning—the silver-grey range of mountains across the river and the level smiling land on our left. This is one of the Viceroy's possessions, bought of one of his relations at a price fixed by his highness. There are ten thousand acres of arable land, of which some fifteen hundred is in sugar-cane, and the rest in grain. The whole is watered by a steam-pump, which sends a vast stream of water inland, giving life to the broad fields and the extensive groves, as well as to a village the minaret of which we can see. It is a noble estate. Near the factory are a palace and garden, somewhat in decay, as is usual in this country, but able to offer us roses and lemons.

The works are large, modern, with improved machinery for crushing and boiling, and apparently well managed; there is said to be one of the sixteen sugar-factories of the Khedive which pays expenses; perhaps this is the one. A great quantity of rum is distilled from the refuse. The vast field in the rear, enclosed by a whitewashed wall, presented a lively appearance, with camels bringing in the cane and unloading it and arranging it upon the endless trough for the crushers. In the factory, the workmen wear little clothing, and are driven to their task; all the overseers march among them kurbash in hand; the sight of the black fellows treading about in the crystallized sugar, while putting it up in sacks, would decide a fastidious person to take her tea unsweetened.

The next morning we pass Erment without calling, satisfied to take the word of others that you may see there a portrait of Cleopatra; and by noon come to our old mooring-place at Luxor, and add ours to the painted dahabeëhs lounging in this idle and gay resort.

During the day we enjoyed only one novel sensation. We ate of the ripe fruit of the dôm-palm. It tastes and smells like stale gingerbread, made of sawdust instead of flour.

I do not know how long one could stay contentedly at Thebes; certainly a winter, if only to breathe the inspiring air, to bask in the sun, to gaze, never sated, upon plains and soft mountains, which climate and association clothe with hues of beauty and romance, to yield for once to a leisure that is here rebuked by no person and by no urgency of affairs; perhaps for years, if one seriously attempted a study of antiquity.

The habit of leisure is at least two thousand years old here; at any rate, we fell into it without the least desire to resist its spell. This is one of the eddies of the world in which the modern hurry is unfelt. If it were not for the coughing steamboats and the occasional glimpse one has of a whisking file of Cook's tourists, Thebes would be entirely serene, and an admirable place of retirement.

It has a reputation, however, for a dubious sort of industry. All along the river from Geezeh to Assouan, whenever a spurious scarabæus or a bogus image turned up, we would hear, "Yes, make 'em in Luxor." As we drew near to this great mart of antiquities, the specification became more personal—"Can't tell edzactly whether that make by Mr. Smith or by that Moslem in Goorneh, over the other side."

The person named is well known to all Nile voyagers as Antiquity Smith, and he has, though I cannot say that he enjoys, the reputation hinted at above. How much of it is due to the enmity of rival dealers in relics of the dead, I do not know; but it must be evident to anyone that the very clever forgeries of antiquities, which one sees, could only be produced by skilful and practised workmen. We had some curiosity to see a man who has made the American name so familiar the length of the Nile, for Mr. Smith is a citizen of the United States. For seventeen years he has been a voluntary exile here, and most of the time the only foreigner resident in the place; long enough to give him a good title to the occupation of any grotto he may choose.

In appearance Mr. Smith is somewhat like a superannuated agent of the Tract Society, of the long, thin, shrewd, learned Yankee type. Few men have enjoyed his advantages for sharpening the wits. Born in Connecticut, reared in New Jersey, trained for seventeen years among the Arabs and antiquity-mongers of this region, the sharpest in the Orient, he ought to have not only the learning attached to the best wrapped mummy, but to be able to read the hieroglyphics on the most inscrutable human face among the living.

Mr. Smith lives on the outskirts of the village, in a house, surrounded by a garden, which is a kind of museum of the property, not to say the bones, of the early Egyptians.

"You seem to be retired from society here Mr. Smith," we ventured to say.

"Yes, for eight months of the year, I see nobody, literally nobody. It is only during the winter that strangers come here."

"Isn't it lonesome?"

"A little, but you get used to it."

"What do you do during the hottest months?"

"As near nothing as possible."

"How hot is it?"

"Sometimes the thermometer goes to 120° Fahrenheit. It stays a long time at 100°. The worst of it is that the nights are almost as hot as the days."

"How do you exist?"

"I keep very quiet, don't write, don't read anything that requires the least thought. Seldom go out, never in the daytime. In the early morning I sit a while on the veranda, and about ten o'clock get into a big bath-tub, which I have on the ground-floor, and stay in it nearly all day, reading some very mild novel, and smoking the weakest tobacco. In the evening I find it rather cooler outside the house than in. A white man can't do anything here in the summer."

I did not say it to Mr. Smith, but I should scarcely like to live in a country where one is obliged to be in water half the year, like a pelican. We can have, however, from his experience some idea what this basin must have been in summer, when its area was a crowded city, upon which the sun, reverberated from the incandescent limestone hills, beat in unceasing fervor.

CHAPTER XXIX.

THE FUTURE OF THE MUMMY'S SOUL.

I SHOULD like to give you a conception, however faint, of the Tombs of the ancient Egyptians, for in them is to be found the innermost secret of the character, the belief, the immortal expectation of that accomplished and wise people. A barren description of these places of sepulchre would be of small service to you, for the key would be wanting, and you would be simply confused by a mass of details and measurements, which convey no definite idea to a person who does not see them with his own eyes. I should not indeed be warranted in attempting to say anything about these great Tombs at Thebes, which are so completely described in many learned volumes, did I not have the hope that some readers, who have never had access to the works referred to, will be glad to know something of that which most engaged the educated Egyptian mind.

No doubt the most obvious and immediate interest of the Tombs of old Egypt is in the sculptures that depict so minutely the life of the people, represent all their occupations and associations, are, in fact, their domestic and social history written in stone. But it is not of this that I wish to speak here; I want to write a word upon the tombs and what they contain, in their relation to the future life.

A study of the tombs of the different epochs, chronologically pursued, would show, I think, pretty accurately, the growth of the Egyptian theology, its development, or rather its departure from the primitive revelation of one God, into the monstrosities of its final mixture of coarse polytheistic idolatry and the vaguest pantheism. These two extremes are represented by the beautiful places of sepulchre of the fourth and fifth dynasties at Geezeh and Memphis, in which all the sculptures relate to the life of the deceased and no deities are represented; and the tombs of the twenty-fourth dynasty at Thebes which are so largely covered with the gods and symbols of a religion become wholly fantastic. It was in the twenty-sixth dynasty (just before the conquest of Egypt by the Persians) that the Funeral Ritual received its final revision and additions—the sacred chart of the dead which had grown, paragraph by paragraph, and chapter by chapter, from its brief and simple form in the earliest times.

The Egyptians had a considerable, and also a rich literature, judging by the specimens of it preserved and by the value set upon it by classical writers; in which no department of writing was unrepresented. The works which would seem of most value to the Greeks were doubtless those on agriculture, astronomy, and geometry; the Egyptians wrote also on medicine, but the science was empirical then as it is now. They had an enormous bulk of historical literature, both in verse and prose, probably as semi-fabulous and voluminous as the thousand great volumes of Chinese history. They did not lack, either, in the department of *belles lettres*; there were poets, poor devils no doubt who were compelled to celebrate in grandiose strains achievements they did not believe; and essayists and letter-writers, graceful, philosophic, humorous. Nor was the field of fiction unoccupied; some of their lesser fables and romances have been preserved; they are however of a religious character, myths of doctrine, and it is safe to say, different from our Sunday-school tales. The story of Cinderella was a religious myth. No one has yet been fortunate enough to find an Egyptian novel, and we may suppose that the *quid-nuncs*, the critics of Thebes, were all the time calling upon the writers of that day to make an effort and produce The Great Egyptian Novel.

The most important part, however, of the literature of Egypt was the religious, and of that we have, in the Ritual or Book of the Dead, probably the most valuable portion. It will be necessary to refer to this more at length. A copy of the Funeral Ritual, or "The Book of the Manifestation to Light" as it was entitled, or some portion of it—probably according to the rank or wealth of the deceased, was deposited with every mummy.

In this point of view, as this document was supposed to be of infinite service, a person's wealth would aid him in the next world; but there came a point in the peregrination of every soul where absolute democracy was reached, and every man stood for judgment on his character. There was a foreshadowing of this even in the ceremonies of the burial. When the mummy, after the lapse of the seventy days of mourning, was taken by the friends to the sacred lake of the nome (district), across which it must be transported in the boat of Charon before it could be deposited in the tomb, it was subjected to an ordeal. Forty-two judges were assembled on the shore of the lake, and if anyone accused the deceased, and could prove that he led an evil life, he was denied burial. Even kings were subjected to this trial, and those who had been wicked, in the judgment of their people, were refused the honors of sepulchre. Cases were probably rare where one would dare to accuse even a dead Pharaoh.

Debts would sometimes keep a man out of his tomb, both because he was wrong in being in debt, and because his tomb was mortgaged. For it was permitted a man to mortgage not only his family tomb but the mummy of his father,—a kind of mortmain security that could not run away, but a ghastly pledge to hold. A man's tomb, it would seem, was accounted his chief possession; as the one he was longest to use. It was prepared at an expense never squandered on his habitation in life.

You may see as many tombs as you like at Thebes, you may spend weeks underground roaming about in vast chambers or burrowing in zig-zag tunnels, until the upper-world shall seem to you only a passing show; but you will find little, here or elsewhere, after the Tombs of the Kings, to awaken your keenest interest; and the exploration of a very few of these will suffice to satisfy you. We visited these gigantic mausoleums twice; it is not an easy trip to them, for they are situated in wild ravines or gorges that lie beyond the western mountains which circle the plain and ruins of Thebes. They can be reached by a footpath over the crest of the ridge behind Medeenet Haboo; the ancient and usual road to them is up a valley that opens from the north.

The first time we tried the footpath, riding over the blooming valley and leaving our donkeys at the foot of the ascent. I do not know how high this mountain backbone may be, but it is not a pleasant one to scale. The path winds, but it is steep; the sun blazes on it; every step is in pulverized limestone, that seems to have been calcined by the intense heat, and rises in irritating powder; the mountain-side is white, chalky, glaring, reflecting the solar rays with blinding brilliancy, and not a breath of air comes to temper the furnace temperature. On the summit, however, there was a delicious breeze, and we stood long looking over the great basin, upon the temples, the villages, the verdant areas of grain, the patches of desert, all harmonized by the wonderful light, and the purple eastern hills —a view unsurpassed. The descent to the other side was steeper than the ascent, and wound by precipices, on narrow ledges, round sharp turns, through jagged gorges, amid rocks stricken with the ashy hue of death, into the bottoms of intersecting ravines, a region scarred, blasted, scorched, a grey Gehenna, more desolate than imagination ever conceived.

Another day we rode to it up the valley from the river, some three miles. It is a winding, narrow valley, little more than the bed of a torrent; but as we advanced, windings became shorter, the sides higher, fantastic precipices of limestone frowned on us, and there was evidence of a made road and of rocks cut away to broaden it. The scene is wilder, more freakishly savage, as we go on, and knowing that it is a funeral way and that only, and that it leads to graves and to nothing else, our procession imperceptibly took on the sombre character of an expedition after death, relieved by I know not what that is droll in the impish forms of the crags, and the reaction of our natures against this unnecessary accumulation of grim desolation. The sun overhead was like a dish from which poured liquid heat. I could feel the waves, I thought I could see it running in streams down the crumbling ashy slopes; but it was not unendurable, for the air was pure and elastic and we had no sense of weariness; indeed, now and then a puff of desert air suddenly greeted us as we turned a corner. The slender strip of sky seen above the grey limestone was of astonishing depth and color—a purple, almost like a night sky, but of unimpeachable delicacy.

Up this strange road were borne in solemn state, as the author of Job may have seen, "*the kings and counsellors of the earth, which built desolate places for themselves;*" the journey was a fitting prelude to an entry into the depths of these frightfull hills. It must have been an awful march, awful in its errand, awful in the desolation of the way; and, in the heat of summer, a mummy passing this way might have melted down in his *cercueuil* before he could reach his cool retreat.

When we came to the end of the road, we see no tombs. There are paths winding in several directions, round projecting ridges and shoulders of powdered rock, but one might pass through here and not know that he was in a cemetery. Above the rubbish here and there we see, when they are pointed out, holes in the rock. We climb one of these heaps, and behold the entrance, maybe half-filled up, of one of the great tombs. This entrance may have been laid open so as to disclose a portal cut in the face of the rock and a smoothed space in front. Originally the tomb was not only walled up and sealed, but rocks were tumbled down over it, so as to restore that spot in the hill to its natural appearance. The chief object of every tomb was to conceal the mummy from intrusion forever. All sorts of misleading devices were resorted to for this purpose.

Twenty-five tombs (of the nineteenth and twentieth dynasties) have been opened in this locality, but some of them belonged to princes and other high functionaries; in a valley west of this are tombs of the eighteenth dynasty, and in still another gorge are the tombs of the queens. These tombs all differ in plan, in extent, in decoration; they are alike in not having, as many others elsewhere have, an exterior chamber where friends could assemble to mourn; you enter all these tombs by passing through an insignificant opening, by an inclined passage, directly into the heart of the mountain, and there they open into various halls, chambers, and grottoes. One of them, that of Sethi I., into whose furthermost and most splendid halls Belzoni broke his way, extends horizontally four hundred and seventy feet into the hill, and descends to a depth of one hundred and eighty feet below the opening. The line of direction of the excavation is often changed, and the continuation skilfully masked, so that the explorer may be baffled. You come by several descents and passages, through grand chambers and halls, to a hall vast in size and magnificently decorated; here is a pit, here is a granite sarcophagus; here is the fitting resting-place of the royal mummy. But it never occupied this sarcophagus.

Somewhere in this hall is a concealed passage. It was by breaking through a wall of solid masonry in such a room, smoothly stuccoed and elaborately painted with a continuation of the scenes on the side-walls, that Belzoni discovered the magnificent apartment beyond, and at last a chamber that was never finished, where one still sees the first draughts of the figures for sculpture on the wall, and gets an idea of the bold freedom of the old draughtsmen, in the long, graceful lines, made at a stroke by the Egyptian artists. Were these inner chambers so elaborately concealed, by walls and stucco and painting, *after* the royal mummy was somewhere hidden in them? Or was the mummy deposited in some obscure lateral pit, and was it the fancy of the king himself merely to make these splendid and highly decorated inner apartments private?

It is not uncommon to find rooms in the tombs unfinished. The excavation of the tomb was begun when the king began to reign; it was a work of many years and might happen to be unfinished at his death. He might himself become so enamoured of his enterprise, and his ideas might expand in regard to his requirements, as those of builders always do, that death would find him still excavating and decorating. I can imagine that if one thought he were building a house for eternity—or cycles beyond human computation,—he would, up to his last moment, desire to add to it new beauties and conveniences. And he must have had a certain humorous satisfaction in his architectural tricks, for putting posterity on a false scent about his remains.

It would not be in human nature to leave undisturbed tombs containing so much treasure as was buried with a rich or royal mummy. The Greeks walked through all these sepulchres; they had already been rifled by the Persians; it is not unlikely that some of them had been ransacked by Egyptians, who could appreciate jewelry and fine-work in gold as much as we do that found by M. Mariette on the cold person of Queen Aahhotep. This dainty lady might have begun to flatter herself, having escaped through so many ages of pillage, that danger was over, but she had not counted upon there coming an age of science. It is believed that she was the mother of Amosis, who expelled the Shepherds, and the wife of Kamès, who long ago went to his elements. After a repose here at Thebes, not far from the temple of Koorneh, of about thirty-five hundred years, Science one day cried, "Aah-hotep of Drah-Aboo-l-neggah! we want you for an Exposition of the industries of all nations at Paris ; put on your best things and come forth."

I suppose there is no one living who would not like to be the first to break into an Egyptian tomb (and there are doubtless still some undisturbed in this valley), to look upon its glowing paintings before the air had impaired a tint, and to discover a sweet and sleeping princess, simply encrusted in gems, and cunning work in gold, of priceless value—in order that he might add something to our knowledge of ancient art!

But the government prohibits all excavations by private persons. You are permitted, indeed, to go to the common pits and carry off an armful of mummies, if you like; but there is no pleasure in the disturbance of this sort of mummy; he may perhaps be a late Roman ; he has no history, no real antiquity, and probably not a scarabæus of any value about him.

When we pass out of the glare of the sun and descend the incline down which the mummy went, we feel as if we had begun his awful journey. On the walls are sculptured the ceremonies and liturgies of the dead, the grotesque monsters of the under-world, which will meet him and assail him on his pilgrimage, the deities friendly and unfriendly, the tremendous scenes of cycles of transmigration. Other sculptures there are, to be sure, and in some tombs these latter predominate, in which astronomy, agriculture, and domestic life are depicted. In one chamber are exhibited trades, in another the kitchen, in another arms, in another the gay boats and navigation of the Nile, in another all the vanities of elegant house-furniture. But all these only emphasize the fact that we are passing into another world, and one of the grimmest realities. We come at length, whatever other beauties or wonders may detain us, to the king, the royal mummy, in the presence of the deities, standing before Osiris, Athor, Phtah, Isis, Horus, Anubis, and Nofre-Atmoo.

Somewhere in this vast and dark mausoleum the mummy has been deposited; he has with him the roll of the Funeral Ritual ; the sacred scarabæus is on his breast ; in one chamber bread and wine are set out; his bearers withdraw, the tomb is closed, sealed, all trace of its entrance effaced. The mummy begins his pilgrimage.

THE FUTURE OF THE MUMMY'S SOUL. 341

The Ritual * describes all the series of pilgrimage of the soul in the lower-world; it contains the hymns, prayers, and formula for all funeral ceremonies and the worship of the dead; it embodies the philosophy and religion of Egypt; the basis of it is the immortality of the soul, that is of the souls of the justified, but a clear notion of the soul's personality apart from the body it does not give.

The book opens with a grand dialogue, at the moment of death, in which the deceased, invoking the god of the lower world, asks entrance to his domain; a chorus of glorified souls interposes for him; the priest implores the divine clemency; Osiris responds, granting permission, and the soul enters Kar-Neter, the land of the dead; and then renews his invocations. Upon his entry he is dazzled by the splendor of the sun (which is Osiris) in this subterranean region, and sings to it a magnificent hymn.

The second part traces the journeys of the soul. Without knowledge, he would fail, and finally be rejected at the tribunal. Knowledge is in Egyptian *sbo*, that is, "food in plenty"; knowledge and food are identified in the Ritual; "the knowledge of religious truths is the mysterious nourishment that the soul must carry with it to sustain it in its journeys and trials." This necessary preliminary knowledge is found in the statement of the Egyptian faith in the Ritual; other information is given him from time to time on his journey. But although his body is wrapped up, and his soul instructed, he cannot move, he has not the use of his limbs: and he prays to be restored to his faculties that he may be able to walk, speak, eat, fight; the prayer granted, he holds his scarabæus over his head, as a passport, and enters Hades.

His way is at once beset by formidable obstacles; monsters, servants of Typhon, assail him; slimy reptiles, crocodiles, serpents seek to devour him; he begins a series of desperate combats, in which the hero and his enemies hurl long and insulting speeches at each other. Out of these combats he comes victorious, and sings songs of triumph; and after rest and refreshment from the Tree of Life, given him by the goddess Nu, he begins a dialogue with the personification of the divine

---
*Lenormant's Epitome.

Light, who instructs him, explaining the sublime mysteries of nature. Guided by this new Light, he advances, and enters into a series of transformations, identifying himself with the noblest divine symbols: he becomes a hawk, an angel, a lotus, the god Ptah, a heron, etc.

Up to this time the deceased has been only a shade, an *eidolon*, the simulacrum of the appearance of his body. He now takes his body, which is needed for the rest of the journey; it was necessary therefore that it should be perfectly preserved by the embalming process. He goes on to new trials and dangers, to new knowledge, to severer examinations of his competence; he shuns wiles and delusions; he sails down a subterranean river and comes to the Elysian Fields, in fact, to a reproduction of Egypt with its camels and its industries, when the soul engages in agriculture, sowing and reaping divine fruit for the bread of knowledge which he needs now more than ever.

At length he comes to the last and severest trial, to the judgment-hall where Osiris awaits him, seated on his throne, accompanied by the forty-two assessors of the dead. Here his knowledge is put to the test; here he must give an account of his whole life. He goes on to justify himself by declaring at first, negatively, the crimes that he has not committed. " I have not blasphemed," he says in the Ritual; "I have not stolen; I have not smitten men privily; I have not treated any person with cruelty; I have not stirred up trouble; I have not been idle; I have not been intoxicated; I have not made unjust commandments; I have shown no improper curiosity; I have not allowed my mouth to tell secrets; I have not wounded any-one; I have not put anyone in fear; I have not slandered any-one; I have not let envy gnaw my heart; I have spoken evil neither of the king nor of my father; I have not falsely accused anyone; I have not withheld milk from the mouths of suck-lings; I have not practised any shameful crime; I have not calumniated a slave to his master."

The deceased then speaks of the good he has done in his life-time; and the positive declarations rise to a higher morality than the negative; among them is this wonderful sentence:—
" *I have given food to the hungry, drink to the thirsty, and clothes to the naked.*"

The heart of the deceased, who is now called Osiris, is then weighed in the balance against "truth," and (if he is just) is not found wanting; the forty-two assessors decide that his knowledge is sufficient, the god Osiris gives sentence of justification, Thoth, (the Hermes of the Greeks, the conductor of souls, the scribe of Osiris, and also the personification of literature or letters) records it, and the soul enters into bliss.

In a chamber at Dayr el Medeeneh you may see this judgment-scene. Osiris is seated on his throne waiting the introduction of souls into Amenti; the child Harpocrates, with his finger on his lip, sits upon his crook; behind are the forty-two assessors. The deceased humbly approaches; Thoth presents his good deeds, written upon papyrus; they are weighed in the balance against an ostrich-feather, the symbol of truth; on the beam sits a monkey, the emblem of Thoth. The same conceit of weighing the soul in judgment scenes was common to the mediaeval church; it is very quaintly represented in a fresco in the porch of the church of St. Lawrence at Rome.

Sometimes the balance tipped the wrong way; in the tomb of Rameses VI. is sculptured a wicked soul, unjustified, retiring from the presence of Osiris in the ignoble form of a pig.

The justified soul retired into bliss. What was this bliss? The third part of the Ritual is obscure. The deceased is Osiris, identified with the sun, traversing with him, and as him, the various houses of heaven; afterwards he seems to pass into an identification with all the deities of the pantheon. This is a poetical flight. The justified soul was absorbed into the intelligence from which it emanated. For the wicked there was annihilation; they were destroyed, decapitated by the evil powers. In these tombs you will see pictures of beheadings at the block, of dismembered bodies. It would seem that in some cases the souls of the wicked returned to the earth and entered unclean animals. We always had a suspicion, a mere idle fancy, that a chameleon, which we had on our boat, which had a knowing and wicked eye, had been somebody.

The visitor's first astonishment here is to find such vast and rich tombs, underground temples in fact, in a region so unutterably desolate, remote from men, to be reached only by a painful pilgrimage. He is bewildered by the variety and beauty of the decorations, the grace and freedom of art, the minute finish of birds and flowers, the immortal loveliness of faces here and there; and he cannot understand that all this was not made for exhibition, that it was never intended to be seen, that it was not seen except by the workmen and the funeral attendants, and that it was then sealed away from human eyes forever. Think of the years of labor expended, the treasure lavished in all this gorgeous creation, which was not for men to see! Has human nature changed? Expensive monuments and mausoleums are built now as they have been in all the Christian era; but they are never concealed from the public view. I cannot account for these extraordinary excavations, not even for one at the Assasecf, which extends over an acre and a quarter of ground, upon an ostentation of wealth, for they were all closed from inspection, and the very entrances masked. The builders must have believed in the mysteries of the under-world, or they would not have expended so much in enduring representations of them; they must have believed also that the soul had need of such a royal abode. Did they have the thought that money lavished in this pious labor would benefit the soul, as much as now-a-days legacies bequeathed to missions and charities.

On our second visit to these tombs we noticed many details that had escaped us before. I found sculptured a cross of equal arms, three or four inches long, among other sacred symbols. We were struck by the peculiar whiteness of the light, the sort of chalkiness of the sunshine as we saw it falling across the entrance of a tomb from which we were coming, and by the lightness of the shadows. We illuminated some of the interiors, lighting up the vast sculptured and painted halls and corniced chambers, to get the *tout ensemble* of colours and figures. The colours came out with startling vividness on the stuccoed, white walls, and it needed no imagination, amidst these awful and *bizarre* images and fantastic scenes, to feel that we were in a real under-world. And all this was created for darkness!

But these chambers could neither have been cut nor decorated without light, and bright light. The effect of the rich ceiling and sides could not have been obtained without strong light. I believe that these rooms, as well as the dark and decorated chambers in the temples, must have been brilliantly illuminated on occasion; the one at the imposing funeral ceremonies, the other at the temple services. What light was used? The sculptures give us no information. But the light must have been not only a very brilliant but a pure flame, for these colours were fresh and unsullied when the tombs were opened. However these chambers were lighted, some illuminating substance was used that produced no smoke, nor formed any gas that could soil the whiteness of the painted lotus.

In one of these brilliant apartments, which is finished with a carved and painted cornice, and would serve for a drawing-room with the addition of some furniture, we almost had a feeling of comfort and domesticity—as long as the illumination lasted. When that flashed out, and we were left in that thick darkness of the grave which one can feel gathering itself in folds about him, and which the twinkling candles in our hands punctured but did not scatter, and we groped our way, able to see only a step ahead and to examine only a yard square of wall at a time, there was something terrible in this subterranean seclusion. And yet, this tomb was intended as the place of abode of the deceased owner during the long ages before soul and body, united, should be received into bliss; here were buried with him no doubt some portions of his property, at least jewels and personal ornaments of value; here were pictured his possessions and his occupations while on earth; here were his gods, visibly cut in stone; here were spread out, in various symbols and condensed writing, the precepts of profound wisdom and the liturgies of the book of the dead. If at any time he could have awakened (as no doubt he supposed he should), and got rid of his heavy granite sarcophagus (if his body ever lay in it) and removed the myrrh and pitch from his person, he would have found himself in a most spacious and gay mansion, of which the only needs were food, light, and air.

While remembering, however, the grotesque conception the Egyptians had of the next world, it seems to me that the decorators of these tombs often let their imaginations run riot, and that not every fantastic device has a deep signification. Take the elongated figures on the ceiling, stretching fifty feet across, the legs bent down on one side and the head the other; or such a picture as this:—a sacred boat having a crocodile on the deck, on the back of the crocodile a human head, out of the head a long stick protruding which bears on its end the crown of Lower Egypt; or this conceit:—a small boat ascending a cataract, bearing a huge beetle (scarabæus) having a ram's head, and sitting on each side of it a bird with a human head. I think much of this work is pure fancy.

In these tombs the snake plays a great part, the snake purely coiled or extended, carried in processions, his length borne on the shoulders of scores of priests, crawling along the walls in hideous convolutions; and, again, the snake with two, three, and four heads, with two and six feet; the snake with wings; the snake coiled about the statues of the gods, about the images of the mummies, and in short everywhere. The snake is the most conspicuous figure.

The monkey is also numerous, and always pleasing; I think he is the comic element of hell, though perhaps gravely meant. He squats about the lower-world of the heathen, and gives it an almost cheerful and *débonnair* aspect. It is certainly refreshing to meet his self-possessed, grave, and yet friendly face amid all the serpents, crocodiles, hybrids, and chimerical monsters of the Egyptian under-world.

Conspicuous in ceremonies represented in the tombs and in the temples is the sacred boat or *ark*, reminding one always, in its form and use and the sacredness attached to it, of the Jewish Ark of the Covenant. The arks contain the sacred emblems, and sometimes the beetle of the sun, overshadowed by the wings of the goddess of Thmei or Truth, which suggest the cherubim of the Jews. Mr. Wilkinson notices the fact, also, that Thmei, the name of the goddess who was worshipped under the double character of Truth and Justice, is the origin of the Hebrew *Thummim*—a word implying "truth"; this Thummim (a symbol perfectly comprehensible now that we know its origin) which was worn only by the high priest of the Jews, was, like the Egyptian figure, which the archjudge put on when he sat at the trial of a case, studded with precious stones of various colors.

Before we left the valley we entered the tomb of Menephtah (or Merenphtah), and I broke off a bit of crumbling limestone from the inner cave as a memento of the Pharaoh of the Exodus. I used to suppose that this Pharaoh was drowned in the Red Sea; but he could not have been if he was buried here; and here certainly is his tomb. It is the opinion of scholars that Menephtah long survived the Exodus. There is nothing to conflict with this in the Biblical description of the disaster to the Egyptians. It says that all Pharaoh's host was drowned, but it does not say that the king was drowned; if he had been, so important a fact, it is likely, would have been emphasized. Joseph came into Egypt during the reign of one of the usurping Shepherd Kings, Apepi probably. Their seat of empire was at Tanis, where their tombs had been discovered. The Israelites were settled in that part of the Delta. After some generations, the Shepherds were expelled, and the ancient Egyptian race of kings was reinstated in the dominion of all Egypt. This is probably the meaning of the passage, " now there arose up a new king over Egypt, which knew not Joseph." The narrative of the Exodus seems to require that the Pharaoh should be at Memphis. The kings of the nineteenth dynasty, to which Menephtah belonged, had the seat of their empire at Thebes; he alone of that dynasty established his court at Memphis. But it was natural that he should build his tomb at Thebes.

We went again and again to the temples on the west side and to the tombs there. I never wearied of the fresh morning ride across the green plain, saluting the battered Colossi as we passed under them, and galloping (don't, please, remember that we were mounted on donkeys) out upon the desert. Not all the crowd of loping Arabs with glittering eyes and lying tongues, who attended us, offering their dead merchandise, could put me out of humor. Besides, there were always slender, pretty, and cheerful little girls running beside us with their water-koollehs. And may I never forget the baby Charon on the vile ferry-boat that sets us over one of the narrow streams. He is the cunningest specimen of a boy in Africa. His small brothers pole the boat, but he is steersman, and stands aft, pushing about the tiller, which is level with his head. He is a mere baby as to stature, and is in fact only four years old, but he is a perfect beauty, even to the ivory teeth which his engaging smile discloses. And such self-possession and self-respect. He is a man of business, and minds his helm, " the dear little scrap," say the ladies. When we give him some evidently unexpected coppers, his eyes and whole face beam with pleasure, and in the sweetest voice he says, *Kêt'ther kháyrak, keteér* ("Thank you very much indeed").

I yield myself to, but cannot account for, the fascination of this vast field of desolation, this waste of crumbled limestone, gouged into ravines and hills, honeycombed with tombs and mummy-pits, strewn with the bones of ancient temples, brightened by the glow of sunshine on elegant colonnades and sculptured walls, saddened by the mud-hovels of the fellaheen. The dust is abundant, and the glare of the sun reflected from the high, white precipices behind is something unendurable.

Of the tombs of the Assaseef, we went far into none, except that of the priest Petamunoph, the one which occupies, with its many chambers and passages, an acre and a quarter of underground. It was beautifully carved and painted throughout, but the inscriptions are mostly illegible now, and so fouled by bats as to be uninteresting. Our guide said truly, "bats not too much good for 'scriptions." In truth, the place smells horribly of bats—an odor that will come back to you with sickening freshness days after—and a strong stomach is required for the exploration.

Even the chambers of some of the temples here were used in later times as receptacles for mummies. The novel and most interesting temple of Dayr el Bahree did not escape this indignity. It was built by Amun-noo-het, or Hatasoo as we more familiarly call her, and like everything else that this spirited woman did, it bears the stamp of originality and genius. The structure rises up the side of the mountain in terraces, temple above temple, and is of a most graceful architecture; its varied and brilliant sculptures must be referred to a good period of art. Walls that have recently been laid bare shine with extraordinary vividness of color. The last chambers in the rock are entered by arched doorways, but the arch is in appearance, not in principle. Its structure is peculiar. Square stones were laid up on each side, the one above lapping over the one beneath until the last two met at the top; the interior corners were then cut away, leaving a perfect round arch; but there is no lateral support or keystone. In these interior rooms were depths on depths of mummy-wrappings and bones, and a sickening odor of dissolution.

There are no tombs better known than those of Sheykh el Koorneh, for it is in them that so much was discovered revealing the private life, the trades, the varied pursuits of the Egyptians. We entered those called the most interesting, but they are so smoked, and the paintings are so defaced, that we had small satisfaction in them. Some of them are full of mummy-cloths and skeletons, and smell of mortality to that degree that it needs all the wind of the desert to take the scent of death out of our nostrils.

All this plain and its mounds and hills are dug over and pawed over for remnants of the dead, scarabæi, beads, images, trinkets, sacred and profane. It is the custom of some travellers to descend into the horrible and common mummy-pits, treading about among the dead, and bring up in their arms the body of some man, or some woman, who may have been, for aught the traveller knows, not a respectable person. I confess to an uncontrollable aversion to all of them, however well preserved they are. The present generation here (I was daily beset by an Arab who wanted always to sell me an arm or a foot, from whose eager, glittering eyes I seemed to see a ghoul looking out,) lives by plundering the dead. A singular comment upon our age and upon the futile hope of security for the body after death, even in the strongest house of rock.

Old Petamunoph, with whom be peace, builded better than he knew; he excavated a vast hotel for bats. Perhaps he changed into bats himself in the course of his transmigrations, and in this state is only able to see dimly, as bats do, and to comprehend only partially, as an old Egyptian might, our modern civilization.

CHAPTER XXX.

FAREWELL TO THEBES.

SOCIAL life at Thebes, in the season, is subject to peculiar conditions. For one thing, you suspect a commercial element in it. Back of all the politeness of native consuls and resident effendis, you see spread out a collection of antiques, veritable belongings of the ancient Egyptians, the furniture of their tombs, the ornaments they wore when they began their last and most solemn journey, the very scarabæus, cut on the back in the likeness of the mysterious eye of Osiris, which the mummy held over his head when he entered the ominously silent land of Kar-Neter, the intaglio seal which he always used for his signature, the "charms" that he wore at his guard-chain, the necklaces of his wife, the rings and bracelets of his daughter.

These are very precious things, but you may have them — such is the softening influence of friendship — for a trifle of coined gold, a mere trifle, considering their value and the impossibility of replacing them. What are two, five, even ten pounds for a genuine bronze figure of Isis, for a sacred cat, for a bit of stone, wrought four thousand years ago by an artist into the likeness of the immortal beetle, carved exquisitely with the name of the Pharaoh of that epoch, a bit of stone that some Egyptian wore at his chain during his life, and which was laid upon his breast when he was wrapped up for eternity! Here in Thebes, where the most important personage is the mummy and the Egyptian past is the only real and marketable article, there comes to be an extraordinary value attached to these trinkets of mortality. But when the traveller gets away, out of this charmed circle of enthusiasm for antiquity, away from this fictitious market in sentiment, among the cold people of the world who know not Joseph, and only half believe in Potiphar, and think the little blue images of Osiris ugly, and the mummy-beads trash, and who never heard of the scarabæus, when, I say, he comes with his load of *antiques* into this air of scepticism, he finds that he has invested in a property no longer generally current, objects of *vertu* for which Egypt is actually the best market. And if he finds, as he may, that a good part of his purchases are only counterfeits of the antique, manufactured and doctored to give them an appearance of age, he experiences a sinking of the heart mingled with a lively admiration of the adroitness of the smooth and courtly Arabs of Luxor.

Social life is also peculiar in the absence of the sex that is thought to add a charm to it in other parts of the world. We receive visits of ceremony or of friendship from the chief citizens of the village, we entertain them at dinner, but they are never accompanied by their wives or daughters; we call at their houses and are *fêted* in turn, but the light of the harem never appears. Dahabeëhs of all nations are arriving and departing, there are always several moored before the town, some of them are certain to have lovely passengers, and the polite Arabs are not insensible to the charm of their society: there is much visiting constantly on the boats; but when it is returned at the houses of the natives, at an evening entertainment, the only female society offered is that of the dancing-girls.

Of course, when there is so much lingual difficulty in intercourse, the demonstrations of civility must be mainly overt, and in fact they are mostly illuminations and "fantasias." Almost every boat once in the course of its stay, and usually upon some natal day or in honor of some arrival, will be beautifully illuminated and display fireworks. No sight is prettier than a dahabeëh strung along its decks and along its masts and yards with many colored lanterns. The people of Luxor respond with illuminations in the houses, to which they add barbarous music and the kicking and posturing of the Ghawazees. In this consists the gayety of the Luxor season.

Perhaps we reach the high water-mark of this gayety in an entertainment given us by Ali Moorad Effendi, the American consular agent, in return for a dinner on the dahabeëh. Ali is of good Bedawee blood; and has relations at Karnak enough to fill an opera-house; we esteemed him one of the most trustworthy Arabs in the country, and he takes great pains and pleasure in performing all the duties of his post, which are principally civilities to American travellers. The entertainment consisted of a dinner and a "fantasia." It was understood that it was to be a dinner in Arab style.

We go at sunset when all the broad surface of the Nile is like an opal in the reflected light. The consul's house is near the bank of the river, and is built against the hill, so that we climb two or three narrow stairways before we get to the top of it. The landing-places of the stairways are terraces overlooking the river; and the word terrace has such a grand air that it is impossible to describe this house without making it appear better than it is. The consul comes down to the bank to receive us; we scramble up its crumbling face. We ascend a stairway to the long consular reception-room, where we sit for half an hour, during which coffee is served, and we get the last of the glowing sunset from the windows.

We are then taken across a little terrace, up another flight of steps to the main house, which is seen to consist of a broad hall with small rooms on each side. No other members of the consul's family appear, and, regarding Arab etiquette, we make no enquiry for them. We could not commit a greater breach of good-breeding than to ask after the health of any members of the harem. Into one of the little rooms we are shown for dinner. It is very small, only large enough to contain a divan and a round table capable of seating eight persons. The only ornaments of the room are an American flag, and a hand-mirror hung too high for anyone to see herself in it. The round table is of metal, hammered out and turned at the edge,—a little barrier that prevents anything rolling off. At each place are a napkin and a piece of bread—no plate or knives or forks.

Deference is so far paid to European prejudice that we sit in chairs, but I confess that when I am to eat with my fingers I prefer to sit on the ground—the position in a chair is too formal for what is to follow. When we are seated, a servant brings water in a basin and ewer, and a towel, and we wash our right hands—the left hand is not to be used. Soup is first served. The dish is placed in the middle of the table, and we are given spoons with which each one dips in, and eats rapidly or slowly according to habit; but there is necessarily some deliberation about it, for we cannot all dip at once. The soup is excellent, and we praise it, to the great delight of our host, who shows his handsome teeth and says *tyeb ;* all that we have hitherto said was *tyeb,* we now add *kateer.* More smiles; and claret is brought in—another concession to foreign tastes.

After the soup, we rely upon our fingers, under the instructions of Ali and an Arab guest. The dinner consists of many courses, each article served separately, but sometimes placed upon the table in three or four dishes for the convenience of the convive in reaching it. There are meats and vegetables of all sorts procurable, fish, beef, mutton, veal, chickens, turkeys, quails and other small birds, pease, beans, salad, and some compositions which defied such analysis as one could make with his thumb and finger. Our host prided himself upon having a Turkish artist in the kitchen, and the cooking was really good and toothsome, even to the pastry and sweetmeats; we did not accuse him of making the champagne.

There is no difficulty in getting at the meats; we tear off strips, mutually assisting each other in pulling them asunder; but there is more trouble about such dishes as peas and a *purée* of something. One hesitates to make a scoop of his four fingers, and plunge in; and then it is disappointing to an unskilled person to see how few peas he can convey to his mouth at a time. I sequester and keep by me the breast-bone of a chicken, which makes an excellent scoop for small vegetables and gravies, and I am doing very well with it, until there is a universal protest against the unfairness of the device.

Our host praises everything himself in the utmost simplicity, and urges us to partake of each dish; he is continually picking out nice bits from the dish and conveying them to the mouth of his nearest guest. My friend, who sits next to Ali, ought to be grateful for this delicate attention, but I fear he is not. The fact is that Ali, by some accident, in fishing, hunting, or war, has lost the tip of the index finger of his right hand, the very hand that conveys the delicacies to my friend's mouth. And he told me afterwards that he felt each time he was fed that he had swallowed that piece of the consul's finger.

During the feast there is music by performers in the adjoining hall, music in minor, barbaric strains insisted on with the monotonous *nonchalance* of the Orient, and calculated, I should say, to excite a person to ferocity, and to make feeding with his fingers a vent to his aroused and savage passions. At the end of the courses water is brought for us to lave our hands, and coffee and chibooks are served.

"Dinner very nice, very fine," says Ali, speaking the common thought which most hosts are too conventional to utter.

"A splendid dinner, O! consul; I have never seen such an one in America."

The Ghawazees have meantime arrived; we hear a burst of singing occasionally with the wail of the instruments. The dancing is to be in the narrow hall of the house, which is lighted as well as a room can be with so many dusky faces in it. At the far end are seated on the floor the musicians, with two stringed instruments, a tambourine and a darabooka. That which answers for a violin has two strings of horsehair, stretched over a cocoanut-shell; the bowstring, which is tightened by the hand as it is drawn, is of horsehair. The music is certainly exciting, harassing, plaintive, complaining; the very monotony of it would drive one wild in time. Behind the musicians is a dark cloud of turbaned servants and various privileged retainers of the house. In front of the musicians sit the Ghawazees, six girls, and an old woman with parchment skin and twinkling eyes, who has been a famous dancer in her day. They are waiting a little wearily, and from time to time one of them throws out the note or two of a song, as if the music were beginning to work in her veins. The spectators are grouped at the entrance of the hall and seated on chairs down each side, leaving but a narrow space for the dancers between; and there are dusky faces peering in at the door.

Before the dance begins we have an opportunity to see what these Ghawazees are like, a race which prides itself upon preserving a pure blood for thousands of years, and upon an ancestry that has always followed the most disreputable profession. These girls are aged say from sixteen to twenty; one appears much older and looks exactly like an Indian squaw, but, strange to say, her profile is also exactly that of Rameses, as we see it in the sculptures. The leading dancer is dressed in a flaring gown of red and figured silk, a costly Syrian dress; she is fat, rather comely, but coarsely uninteresting, although she is said to have on more jewelry than any other dancing-girl in Egypt; her abundant black hair is worn long and in strands thickly hung with gold coins; her breast is covered with necklaces of gold-work and coins; and a mass of heavy twinkling silver ornaments hangs about her waist. A third dancer is in an almost equally striking gown of yellow, and wears also much coin; she is a Pharaonic beauty, with a soft skin and the real Oriental eye and profile. The dresses of all are plainly cut, and straight-waisted, like an ordinary calico gown of a milkmaid. They wear no shawls or any other Oriental wrappings, and dance in their stocking-feet.

At a turn in the music, the girl in red and the girl in yellow stand up; for an instant they raise their castanets till the time of the music is caught, and then start forward, with less of languor and a more skipping movement than we expected; and they are not ungraceful as they come rapidly down the hall, throwing the arms aloft and the feet forward, to the rattle of the castanets. These latter are small convex pieces of brass, held between the thumb and finger, which have a click like the rattle of the snake. In mid-advance they stop, face each other, *chassee*, retire, and again come further forward, stop, and the peculiar portion of the dance begins, which is not dancing at all, but a quivering, undulating motion given to the body, as the girl stands with feet planted wide apart. The feet are still, the head scarcely stirs, except with an almost imperceptible snake-like movement, but the muscles of the body to the hips quiver in time to the monotonous music, in muscular thrills, in waves running down, and at intervals extending below the waist. Sometimes one side of the body quivers while the other is perfectly still, and then the whole frame, for a second, shares in the ague. It is certainly an astonishing muscular performance, but you could not call it either graceful or pleasing. Some people see in the intention of the dance a deep symbolic meaning, something about the Old Serpent of the Nile, with its gliding, quivering movement and its fatal fascination. Others see in it only the common old Snake that was in Eden. I suppose in fact that it is the old and universal Oriental dance, the chief attraction of which never was its modesty.

After standing for a brief space, with the body throbbing and quivering, the castanets all the time held above the head in sympathetic throbs, the dancers start forward, face each other, pass, pirouette, and take some dancing steps, retire, advance, and repeat the earthquake performance. This is kept up a long time, and with wonderful endurance, without change of figure; but sometimes the movements are more rapid, when the music hastens, and more passion is shown. But five minutes of it is as good as an hour. Evidently the dance is nothing except with a master, with an actress who shall abandon herself to the tide of feeling which the music suggests, and throw herself into the full passion of it; who knows how to tell a story by pantomime, and to depict the woes of love and despair. All this needs grace, beauty, and genius. Few dancing-girls have either. An old resident of Luxor complains that the dancing is not at all what it was twenty years ago; that the old fire and art seem to be lost.

"The old hag, sitting there on the floor, was asked to exhibit the ancient style; she consented, and danced marvelously for a time, but the performance became in the end too shameful to be witnessed."

I fancy that if the dance has gained anything in propriety, which is hard to believe, it has lost in spirit. It might be passionate, dramatic, tragic. But it needs genius to make it anything more than a suggestive and repulsive vulgarity.

During the intervals, the girls sing to the music; the singing is very wild and barbaric. The song is in praise of the Night, a love-song consisting of repeated epithets:—

> "O the Night! nothing is so lovely as the Night!
> O my heart! O my soul! O my liver;
> My love he passed my door, and saw me not;
> O the night! How lovely is the night!"

The strain is minor, and there is a wail in the voices which stridently chant to the twanging strings. Is it only the echo of ages of sin in these despairing voices? How melancholy it all becomes! The girl in yellow, she of the oblong eyes, straight nose and high type of Oriental beauty, dances down alone; she is slender, she has the charm of grace, her eyes never wander to the spectators. Is there in her soul any faint contempt for herself or for the part she plays? Or is the historic consciousness of the antiquity of both her profession and her sin strong enough to throw yet the lights of illusion over such a performance? Evidently the fat girl in red is a prey to no such misgiving, as she comes bouncing down the line, and flings herself into her ague fit.

"Look out, the hippopotamus!" cries Abd-el-Atti, " I 'fraid she kick me."

While the dance goes on, pipes, coffee, and brandy are frequently passed; the dancers swallow the brandy readily. The house is illuminated, and the entertainment ends with a few rockets from the terrace. This is a full-blown "fantasia."

As the night is still young and the moon is full, we decide to efface, as much as may be, the vulgarities of modern Egypt, by a vision of the ancient, and, taking donkeys, we ride to Karnak.

For myself I prefer day to night, and abounding sunshine to the most generous moonlight; there is always some disappointment in the night effect in ruins, under the most favorable conditions. But I have great deference to that poetic yearning for half-light, which leads one to grope about in the heavy night-shadows of a stately temple; there is no bird more worthy of respect than the round-eyed attendant of Pallas-Athene.

And it cannot be denied that there is something mysterious and almost ghostly in our silent night ride. For once, our attendants fall into the spirit of the adventure, keep silent, and are only shades at our side. Not a word or a blow is heard as we emerge from the dark lanes of Luxor and come out into the yellow light of the plain; the light seems strong and yet the plain is spectral, small objects become gigantic, and although the valley is flooded in radiance, the end of our small procession is lost in dimness. Nothing is real, all things take fantastic forms, and all proportions are changed. One moves as in a sort of spell, and it is this unreality which becomes painful. The old Egyptians had need of little imagination to conjure up the phantasmagoria of the under world; it is this without the sun.

So far as we can see it, the great mass of stone is impressive as we approach—I suspect because we know how vast and solid it is; and the pylons never seemed so gigantic before. We do our best to get into a proper frame of mind, by wandering apart, and losing ourselves in the heavy shadows. And for moments we succeed. It would have been the shame of our lives not to have seen Karnak by moonlight. The Great Hall, with its enormous columns planted close together, it is more difficult to see by night than by day, but such glimpses as we have of it, the silver light slanting through the stone forest and the heavy shadows, are profoundly impressive. I climb upon a tottering pylon where I can see over the indistinct field and chaos of stone, and look down into the weird and half-illumined Hall of Columns. In this isolated situation I am beginning to fall into the classical meditation of Marius at Carthage, when another party of visitors arrives, and their donkeys, meeting our donkeys in the centre of the Great Hall, begin (it is their donkeys that begin) such a braying as never was heard before; the challenge is promptly responded to, and a duet ensues and is continued and runs into a chorus, so hideous, so unsanctified, so wretchedly attuned, and out of harmony with history, romance, and religion, that sentiment takes wings with silence and flies from the spot.

We can pick up again only some scattered fragments of emotion by wandering alone in the remotest nooks. But we can go nowhere that an Arab, silent and gowned, does not glide from behind a pillar or step out of the shade, staff in hand, and stealthily accompany us. Even the donkey-boys have cultivated their sensibilities by association with other nocturnal pilgrims, and encourage our gush of feeling by remarking in a low voice, "Karnak very good." One of them, who had apparently attended only the most refined and appreciative, keeps repeating at each point of view, "Exquisite!"

As I am lingering behind the company, a shadow glides up to me in the gloom of the great columns, with "good evening;" and, when I reply, it draws nearer, and, in confidential tones, whispers, as if it knew that the moonlight visit was different from that by day, "Backsheesh."

There is never wanting something to do at Luxor, if all the excursions were made. There is always an exchange of courtesies between dahabeëhs, calls are made and dinners given. In the matter of visits the naval etiquette prevails, and the last comer makes the first call. But if you do not care for the society of travellers, you can at least make one of the picturesque idlers on the bank; you may chance to see a display of Arab horsemanship; you may be entertained by some new device of the curiosity-mongers; and there always remain the "collections" of the dealers to examine. One of the best of them is that of the German consul, who rejoices in the odd name of Todrous Paulos, which reappears in his son as Moharb Todrous; a Copt who enjoys the reputation among Moslems of a trustworthy man—which probably means that a larger proportion of his antiquities are genuine than of theirs. If one were disposed to moralize there is abundant field for it here in Luxor. I wonder if there is an insatiable demoralization connected with the dealing in antiquities, and especially in the relics of the departed. When a person, as a business, obtains his merchandise from the unresisting clutch of the dead, in violation of the firman of his ruler, does he add to his wickedness by manufacturing imitations and selling them as real? And what of the traveller who encourages both trades by buying?

One night the venerable Mustapha Aga gave a grand entertainment, in honor of his reception of a firman from the Sultan, who sent him a decoration of diamonds set in silver. Nothing in a Moslem's eyes could exceed the honor of this recognition by the Khalif, the successor of the prophet. It was an occasion of religious as well as social demonstration of gratitude. There was service, with the reading of the Koran in the mosque, for the faithful only; there was a slaughter of sheep with a distribution of the mutton among the poor; and there was a fantasia at the residence of Mustapha (the house built into the columns of the temple of Luxor), to which everybody was bidden. There had been an arrival of Cook's Excursionists by steamboat, and there must have been as many as two hundred foreigners at the entertainment in the course of the evening.

The way before the house was arched with palms and hung with colored lanterns; bands of sailors from the dahabeëhs sat in front, strumming the darabooka and chanting their wild refrains; crowds of Arabs squatted in the light of the illumination and filled the steps and the doorway. Within were feasting, music and dancing, in Oriental abandon. In the hall, which was lined with spectators, was to be seen the stiff-legged sprawling-about and quivering of the Ghawazees, to the barbarous tum-tum, thump-thump, of the musicians; in each side-room also dancing was extemporized, until the house was pervaded with the monotonous vulgarity, which was more pronounced than at the house of Ali.

In the midst of these strange festivities, the grave Mustapha received congratulations upon his newly-conferred honor, with the air of a man who was responding to it in the finest Oriental style. Nothing grander than this entertainment could be conceived in Luxor.

Let us try to look at it also with Oriental eyes. How fatal it would be to it *not* to look at it with Oriental eyes, we can conceive by transferring the scene to New York. A citizen, from one of the oldest families, has received from the President, let us suppose, the decoration of the Grand Order of Inspector of Consulates. In order to do honor to the occasion, he throws open his residence at Gramercy Park, procures a lot of sailors to sit on his steps and sing nautical ditties, and drafts a score of girls from Central-street to entertain his guests with a style of dancing which could not be worse if it had three thousand years of antiquity.

I prefer not to regard this Luxor entertainment in such a light; and although we hasten from it as soon as we can with civility, I am haunted for a long time afterwards by I know not what there was in it of fantastic and barbaric fascination.

The last afternoon at Luxor we give to a long walk to Karnak and beyond, through the wheat and barley fields now vocal with the songs of birds. We do not, however, reach the conspicuous pillars of a temple on the desert far to the north-east; but, returning, climb the wall of circuit and look our last upon these fascinating ruins. From this point the relative vastness of the Great Hall is apparent. The view this afternoon is certainly one of the most beautiful in the world. You know already the elements of it.

Late at night, after a parting dinner of ceremony, and with a pang of regret, although we are in bed, the dahabeëh is loosed from Luxor, and we quietly drop down below old Thebes.

CHAPTER XXXI.

LOITERING BY THE WAY.

WE are at home again. Our little world, which has been somewhat disturbed by the gayety of Thebes, and is already as weary of tombs as of temples and of the whole incubus of Egyptian civilization, readjusts itself and settles into its usual placid enjoyment.

We have now two gazelles on board, and a most disagreeable lizard, nearly three feet long; I dislike the way his legs are set on his sides; I dislike his tail, which is a fat continuation of his body; and the "feel" of his cold, creeping flesh is worse than his appearance; he is exceedingly active, darting rapidly about in every direction to the end of his rope. The gazelles chase each other about the deck, frolicking in the sun, and their eyes express as much tenderness and affection as any eyes can, set like theirs. If they were mounted in a woman's head, and properly shaded with long lashes, she would be the most dangerous being in existence.

Somehow there is a little change in the atmosphere of the dahabeëh. The jester of the crew, who kept them alternately laughing and grumbling, singing and quarreling, turbulent with hasheesh or sulky for want of it, was left in jail at Assouan. The reïs has never recovered the injury to his dignity inflicted by his brief incarceration, and gives us no more a cheerful good-morning. The steersman smiles still, with the fixed look of enjoyment that his face assumed when it first came into the world, but he is listless; I think he has struck a section of the river in which there is a dearth of his wives; he has complained that his feet were cold in the fresh mornings, but the stockings we gave him he does not wear, and probably is reserving for a dress occasion. Abd-el-Atti meditates seriously upon a misunderstanding with one of his old friends at Luxor; he likes to tell us about the diplomatic and sarcastic letter he addressed him on leaving: "I wrote it," he says, "very grammatick, the meaning of him very deep; I think he feel it." There is no language like the Arabic for the delivery of courtly sarcasm, in soft words at which no offence can be taken—for administering a smart slap in the face, so to say, with a feather.

It is a ravishing sort of day, a slight haze, warm but life-giving air, and we row a little and sail a little down the broadening river, by the palms, and the wheat-fields growing yellow, and the soft chain of Libyan hills,—the very *dolce far niente* of life. Other dahabeëhs accompany us, and we hear the choruses of their crews responding to ours. From the shore comes the hum of labor and of idleness, men at the shadoofs, women at the shore for water; there are flocks of white herons and spoonbills on the sandbars; we glide past villages with picturesque pigeon-houses; a ferry-boat ever and anon puts across, a low black scow, its sides banked up with clay, a sail all patches and tatters, and crowded in it three or four donkeys and a group of shawled women and turbaned men, silent and sombre. The country through which we walk, towards night, is a vast plain of wheat, irrigated by canals, with villages in all directions; the peasants are shabbily dressed, as if taxes ate up all their labor, but they do not beg.

The city of Keneh, to which we come next morning, is the nearest point of the Nile to the Red Sea, the desert route to Kosseir being only one hundred and twenty miles; it is the Neapolis of which Herodotus speaks, near which was the great city of Chemmis, that had a temple dedicated to Perseus. The Chemmitæ declared that this demi-god often appeared to them on earth, and that he was descended from citizens of their country who had sailed into Greece; there is no doubt that Perseus came here when he made the expedition into Libya to bring the Gorgon's head.

Keneh is now a thriving city, full of evidences of wealth, and of well-dressed people, and there are handsome houses and bazaars like those of Cairo. From time immemorial it has been famous for its *koollehs*, which are made of a fine clay found only in this vicinity, of which ware is manufactured almost as thin as paper. The process of making them has not changed since the potters of the Pharaohs' time. The potters of to-day are very skilful at the wheel. A small mass of moistened clay, mixed with sifted ashes of halfeh-grass and kneaded like bread, is placed upon a round plate of wood which whirls by a treadle. As it revolves, the workman with his hands fashions the clay into vessels of all shapes, graceful and delicate, with a sleight of hand that is wonderful. He makes a koolleh, or a drinking-cup, or a vase with a slender neck, in a few seconds, fashioning it as truly as if it were cast in a mould. It was like magic to see the fragile forms grow in his hands. We sat for a long time in one of the cool rooms where two or three potters were at work, shaded from the sun by palm-branches, which let the light flicker upon the earth-floor, upon the freshly made vessels and the spinning wheels of the turbaned workmen, whose deft fingers wrought out unceasingly these beautiful shapes from the revolving clay.

At the house of the English consul we have coffee; he afterwards lunches with us and insists, but in vain, that we stay and be entertained by a Ghawazee dance in the evening. It is a kind of amusement of which a very little satisfies one. At his house, Prince Arthur and his suite were also calling; a slender, pleasant appearing young gentleman, not noticeable anywhere, and with a face of no special force, but bearing the family likeness. As we have had occasion to remark more than once, Princes are so plenty on the Nile this year as to be a burden to the officials,—especially German princes, who, however, do not count any more. The private, unostentatious traveller, who asks no favor of the Khedive, is becoming almost a rarity. I hear the natives complain that almost all the Englishmen of rank who come to Egypt, beg, or shall we say accept ? substantial favors of the Khedive. The nobility appear to have a new rendering of *noblesse oblige*. This is rather humiliating to us Americans, who are, after all, almost blood-relations of the English ; and besides, we are often taken for *Inglese*, in villages where few strangers go. It cannot be said that all Americans are modest, unassuming travellers ; but we are glad to record a point or two in their favor :—they pay their way, and they do not appear to cut and paint their names upon the ruins in such numbers as travellers from other countries ; the French are the greatest offenders in this respect, and the Germans next.

We cross the river in the afternoon and ride to the temple of Athor or Venus at Denderah. This temple, although of late construction, is considered one of the most important in Egypt. But it is incomplete, smaller, and less satisfactory than that at Edfoo. The architecture of the portico and succeeding hall is on the whole noble, but the columns are thick and ungraceful, and the sculptures are clumsy and ungraceful. The myth of the Egyptian Venus is worked out everywhere with the elaboration of a later Greek temple. On the ceiling of several rooms her gigantic figure is bent round three sides, and from a globe in her lap rays proceed in the vivifying influence of which trees are made to grow.

Everywhere in the temple are subterranean and intramural passages, entrance to which is only had by a narrow aperture, once closed by a stone. For what were these perfectly dark alleys intended? Processions could not move in them, and if they were merely used for concealing valuables, why should their inner sides have been covered with such elaborate sculptures?

The most interesting thing at Denderah is the small temple of Osiris, which is called the "lying-in-temple," the subjects of sculptures being the mystical conception, birth, and babyhood of Osiris. You might think from the pictures on the walls, of babes at nurse and babes in arms, that you had obtruded into one of the institutions of charity called a Day Nursery. We are glad to find here, carved in large, the image of the four-headed, ugly little creature we have been calling Typhon, the spirit of evil; and to learn that it is not Typhon but is the god Bes, a jolly promoter of merriment and dancing. His appearance is very much against him.

Mariette Bey makes the great mystery of the *adytum* of the large temple, which the king alone could enter, the golden *sistrum* which was kept there. The *sistrum* was the mysterious emblem of Venus; it is sculptured everywhere in this building —although it is one of the sacred symbols found in all temples. This sacred instrument *par excellence* of the Egyptians played as important a part in their worship, says Mr. Wilkinson, as the tinkling bell in Roman Catholic services. The great privilege of holding it was accorded to queens, and ladies of rank who were devoted to the service of the deity. The *sistrum* is a strip of gold, or bronze, bent in a long loop, and the ends, coming together, are fastened in an ornamented handle. Through the loop bars are run upon which are rings, and when the instrument is shaken the rings move to and fro. Upon the sides of the handle were sometimes carved the faces of Isis and of Nephthys, the sister goddesses, representing the beginning and the end.

It is a little startling to find, when we get at the inner secret of the Egyptian religion, that it is a rattle! But it is the symbol of eternal agitation, without which there is no life. And the Egyptians profoundly knew this great secret of the universe.

We pass next day, quietly, to the exhibition of a religious devotion which is trying to get on without any *sistrum* or any agitation whatever. Towards sunset, below Höw, we come to a place where a holy man, called Sheykh Saleem, roosts forever on a sloping bank, with a rich country behind him; beyond, on the plain, hundreds of men and boys are at work throwing up an embankment against the next inundation; but he does not heed them. The holy man is stark naked and sits upon his haunches, his head, a shock of yellow hair, upon his knees. He is of that sickly, whitey-black color which such holy skin as his gets by long exposure. Before him on the bank is a row of large water-jars; behind him is a little kennel of mud, into which he can crawl if it ever occurs to him to go to bed. About him, seated on the ground, is a group of his admirers. Boys run after us along the bank begging backsheesh for Sheykh Saleem. A crowd of hangers-on, we are told, always surround him, and live on the charity that his piety evokes from the faithful. His own wants are few. He spends his life in this attitude principally, contemplating the sand between his knees. He has sat here for forty years.

People pass and repass, camels swing by him, the sun shines, a breeze as of summer moves the wheat behind him, and our great barque, with its gay flags and a dozen rowers rowing in time, sweeps before him, but he does not raise his head. Perhaps he has found the secret of perfect happiness. But his example cannot be widely imitated. There are not many climates in the world in which a man can enjoy such a religion out of doors at all seasons of the year.

We row on and by sundown are opposite Farshoot and its

sugar-factories; the river broadens into a lake, shut in to the north by limestone hills rosy in this light, and it is perfectly still at this hour. But for the palms against the sky, and the cries of men at the shadoofs, and the clumsy native boats with their freight of immobile figures, this might be a glassy lake in the remote Adirondack forest, especially when the light has so much diminished that the mountains no longer appear naked.

The next morning, as we were loitering along, wishing for a breeze to take us quickly to Bellianeh, that we might spend the day in visiting old Abydus, a beautiful wind suddenly arose according to our desire.

"You always have good fortune," says the dragoman.

"I thought you didn't believe in luck?"

"Not to call him luck. You think the wind to blow 'thout the Lord know it?"

We approach Bellianeh under such fine headway that we fall almost into the opposite murmuring, that this helpful breeze should come just when we were obliged to stop and lose the benefit. We half incline to go on, and leave Abydus in its ashes, but the absurdity of making a journey of seven thousand miles and then passing near to, but unseen, the spot most sacred to the old Egyptians, flashes upon us, and we meekly land. But our inclination to go on was not so absurd as it seems; the mind is so constituted that it can contain only a certain amount of old ruins, and we were getting a mental indigestion of them. Loathing is perhaps too strong a word to use in regard to a piece of sculpture, but I think that a sight at this time, of Rameses II. in his favorite attitude of slicing off the heads of a lot of small captives, would have made us sick.

By eleven o'clock we were mounted for the ride of eight miles, and it may give some idea of the speed of the donkey under compulsion, to say that we made the distance in an hour and forty minutes. The sun was hot, the wind fresh, the dust considerable,—a fine sandy powder that, before night, penetrated clothes and skin. Nevertheless, the ride was charming. The way lay through a plain extending for many miles in every direction, every foot of it green with barley (of which here and there a spot was ripening), with clover, with the rank, dark Egyptian bean. The air was sweet, and filled with songs of the birds that glanced over the fields or poised in the air on even wing like the lark. Through the vast, unfenced fields were narrow well-beaten roads in all directions, upon which men women, and children, usually poorly and scantily clad, donkeys and camels, were coming and going. There was the hum of voices everywhere, the occasional agonized blast of the donkey and the caravan bleat of the camel. It often seems to us that the more rich and broad the fields and the more abundant the life, the more squalor among the people.

We had noticed, at little distances apart in the plain, mounds of dirt five or six feet high. Upon each of these stood a solitary figure, usually a naked boy—a bronze image set up above the green.

"What are these?" we ask.

"What you call scarecrows, to frighten the birds; see that chile throw dirt at 'em!"

"They look like sentries; do the people here steal?"

"Everybody help himself, if nobody watch him."

At length we reach the dust-swept village of Arábat, on the edge of the desert, near the ruins of the ancient Thinis (or Abydus), the so-called cradle of the Egyptian monarchy. They have recently been excavated. I cannot think that this ancient and most important city was originally so far from the Nile; in the day of its glory the river must have run near it. Here was the seat of the first Egyptian dynasty, five thousand and four years before Christ, according to the chronology of Mariette Bey. I find no difficulty in accepting the five thousand but I am puzzled about the *four* years. It makes Menes four years older than he is generally supposed to have been. It is the accuracy of the date that sets one pondering. Menes, the first-known Egyptian king, and the founder of Memphis, was born here. If he established his dynasty here six thousand eight hundred and seventy-nine years ago, he must have been born some time before that date; and to be a ruler he must have been of noble parents, and no doubt received a good education. I should like to know what sort of a place, as to art, say, and literature, and architecture, Thinis was seven thousand and four years ago. It is chiefly sand-heaps now.

Not only was Menes born here, in the grey dawn of history, but Osiris, the manifestation of Light on earth, was buried here in the greyer dawn of a mythic period. His tomb was venerated by the Pharaonic worshippers as the Holy Sepulchre is by Christians, and for many ages. It was the last desire of the rich and noble Egyptians to be buried at Thinis, in order that they might lie in the same grave with Osiris; and bodies were brought here from all parts of Egypt to rest in the sacred earth. Their tombs were heaped up one above another, about the grave of the god. There are thousands of mounds here, clustering thickly about a larger mound; and, by digging, M. Mariette hopes to find the reputed tomb of Osiris. An enclosure of crude brick marks the supposed site of this supposed most ancient city of Egypt.

From these prehistoric ashes, it is like going from Rome to Peoria, to pass to a temple built so late as the time of Sethi I., only about thirty-three hundred years ago. It has been nearly all excavated and it is worth a long ride to see it. Its plan differs from that of all other temples, and its varied sculpture ranks with the best of temple carving; nowhere else have we found more life and grace of action in the figures and more expressive features; in number of singular emblems and devices and in their careful and beautiful cutting, and brilliant coloring, the temple is unsurpassed. The non-stereotyped plan of the temple beguiled us into a hearty enjoyment of it. Its numerous columns are pure Egyptian of the best style—lotus capitals; and it contains some excellent specimens of the Doric column, or of its original, rather. The famous original tablet of kings, seventy-six, from Menes to Sethi, a partial copy of which is in the British Museum, has been re-covered with sand for its preservation. This must have been one of the finest of the old temples. We find here the novelty of vaulted roofs, formed by a singular method. The roof stones are not laid flat, as elsewhere, but on edge, and the roof, thus having sufficient thickness, is hollowed out on the under side, and the arch is decorated with stars and other devices. Of course, there is a temple of Rameses II., next door to this one, but it exists now only in its magnificent foundations.

We rode back through the village of Arábat in a whirlwind of dust, amid cries of "backsheesh," hailed from every door, and pursued by yelling children. One boy, clad in the loose gown that passes for a wardrobe in these parts, in order to earn his money, threw a somersault before us, and, in a flash, turned completely out of his clothes, like a new-made Adam! Nothing was ever more neatly done; except it may have been a feat of my donkey a moment afterwards, executed perhaps in rivalry of the boy. Pretending to stumble, he went on his head, and threw a somersault also. When I went back to look for him, his head was doubled under his body so that he had to be helped up.

When we returned, we found six other dahabeëhs moored near ours. Out of the seven, six carried the American flag—one of them in union with the German—and the seventh was English. The American flags largely outnumber all others on the Nile this year; in fact, Americans and various kinds of princes appear to be monopolizing this stream. A German, who shares a boat with Americans, drops in for a talk. It is wonderful how much more space in the world every German needs, now that there is a Germany. Our visitor expresses the belief that the Germans and the Americans are to share the dominion of the world between them. I suppose that this means that we are to be permitted to dwell on our present possessions in peace, if we don't make faces; but one cannot contemplate the extinction of all the other powers without regret.

Of course we have outstayed the south wind; the next morning we are slowly drifting against the north wind. As I look from the window before breakfast, a Nubian trader floats past, and on the bow deck is crouched a handsome young lion, honest of face and free of glance, little dreaming of the miserable menagerie life before him. There are two lions and a leopard, and a cargo of cinnamon, senna, elephants' tusks, and ostrich-feathers, on board; all Central Africa seems to float beside us, and the coal-black crew do not lessen the barbaric impression.

It is after dark when we reach Girgeh, and are guided to our moorage by the lights of other dahabeëhs. All that we see of this decayed but once capital town, are four minarets, two of them surrounding picturesque ruins and some slender columns of a mosque, the remainder of the building having been washed into the river. As we land, a muëzzin sings the evening call to prayer in a sweet, high tenor voice; and it sounds like a welcome.

Decayed, did we say of Girgeh? What is not decayed, or

decaying, or shifting, on this aggressive river? How age laps back on age and one religion shuffles another out of sight. In the hazy morning we are passing Menshéeh, the site of an old town that once was not inferior to Memphis; and then we come to Ekhmeem—ancient Panopolis. You never heard of it? A Roman visitor called it the oldest city of all Egypt; it was in fact founded by Ekhmeem, the son of Misraim, the offspring of Cush, the son of Ham. There you are, almost personally present at the Deluge. Below here are two Coptic convents, probably later than the time of the Empress Helena. On the shore are walking some Coptic Christians, but they are in no way superior in appearance to other natives; a woman, whom we hail, makes the sign of the cross, and then demands backsheesh.

We had some curiosity to visit a town of such honorable foundation. We found in it fine mosques and elegant minarets, of a good Saracenic epoch. Upon the lofty stone top of one sat an eagle, who looked down upon us unscared; the mosque was ruinous and the door closed, but through the windows we could see the gaily decorated ceiling; the whole was in the sort of decay that the traveller learns to think Moslemism itself.

We made a pretence of searching for the remains of a temple of Pan—though we probably care less for Pan than we do for Rameses. Making known our wants, several polite gentlemen in turbans offered to show us the way—the gentlemen in these towns seem to have no other occupation than to sit on the ground and smoke the chibook—and we were attended by a procession, beyond the walls, to the cemetery. There in a hollow, we saw a few large stones, some of them showing marks of cutting. This was the temple spoken of in the hand-book. Our hosts then insisted upon dragging us half a mile further through the dust of the cemetery mounds, in the glare of the sun, and showed us a stone half buried, with a few hieroglyphics on one end. Never were people so polite. A grave man here joined us, and proposed to show us some *quei-is antéeka* ("beautiful antiquities"); and we followed this obliging person half over town; and finally, in the court of a private house, he pointed to the torso of a blue granite statue. All this was done out of pure hospitality; the people could not have been more attentive if they had had something really worth seeing. The town has handsome, spacious coffee-houses and shops, and an appearance of Oriental luxury.

One novelty the place offered, and that was in a drinking-fountain. Under a canopy, in a wall-panel, in the street, was inserted a copper nipple, which was worn, by constant use, as smooth as the toe of St. Peter at Rome. When one wishes to drink, he applies his mouth to this nipple and draws; it requires some power of suction to raise the water, but it is good and cool when it comes. As Herodotus would remark, now I have done speaking about this nipple.

We walked on interminably, and at length obtained a native boat, with a fine assortment of fellahs and donkeys for passengers, to set us over to Soohag, the capital of the province, a busy, and insupportably dirty town, with hordes of free-and-easy natives loafing about, and groups of them, squatting by little dabs of tobacco, or candy, or doora, or sugar-cane, making what they are pleased to call a market.

It seemed to be a day for hauling us about. Two bright boys seized us, and urged us to go with them and see something marvellously beautiful. One of them was an erect, handsome lad, with courtly and even elegant dignity, a high and yet simple bearing, which I venture to say not a king's son in Europe is possessed of. They led us a chase, through half the sprawling town, by lanes and filthy streets, under bazaars, into the recesses of domestic poverty, among unknown and inquisitive natives, until we began to think that we should never see our native dahabeëh again. At last we were landed in a court where sat two men, adding up columns of figures. It was an Oriental picture, but scarcely worth coming so far to see.

The men looked at us in wondering query, as if demanding what we wanted.

We stood looking at them, but couldn't tell them what we wanted, since we did not know. And if we had known, we could not have told them. We only pointed to the boys who had brought us. The boys pointed to the ornamental portals of a closed door.

After a long delay, and the most earnest posturing and professions of our young guides, and evident suspicion of us, a key was brought, and we were admitted into a cool and clean Coptic church, which had fresh matting and an odor of incense.

Ostrich-eggs hung before the holy places, as in mosques; an old clock, with a long and richly inlaid dial-case, stood at one end; and there were paintings in the Byzantine style of "old masters." One of them represented the patron saint of the Copts, St. George, slaying the dragon; the conception does equal honor to the saint and the artist; the wooden horse, upon which St. George is mounted, and its rider, fill nearly all the space of the canvas, leaving very little room for the landscape with its trees, for the dragon, for the maiden, and for her parents looking down upon her from the castle window. And this picture perfectly represents the present condition of art in the whole Orient.

At Soohag a steamboat passed down towing four barges, packed with motley loads of boys and men, impressed to work in the Khedive's sugar-factory at Rhodes. They are seized, so many from a village, like the recruits for the army. They receive from two to two and a half piastres (ten to twelve and a half cents) a day wages, and a couple of pounds of bread each.

I suspect the reason the Khedive's agricultural operations and his sugar-factories are unprofitable, is to be sought in the dishonest agents and middle-men—a kind of dishonesty that seems to be ingrained in the Eastern economy. The Khedive loses both ways:—that which he attempts to expend on a certain improvement is greatly diminished before it reaches its object; and the returns from the investment, on their way back to his Highness, are rubbed away, passing through so many hands, to the vanishing point. It is the same with the taxes; the fellah pays four times as much as he ought, and the Khedive receives not the government due. The abuse is worse than it was in France with the farmers-general in the time of Louis XIV. and Louis XV. The tax apportioned to a province is required of its governor. He adds a lumping per cent. to the total, and divides the increased amount among his sub-governors for collection; they add a third to their levy and divide it among the tax-gatherers of sections of the district; these again swell their quota before apportioning it among the sheykhs or actual collectors, and the latter take the very life-blood out of the fellah.

As we sail down the river in this approaching harvest-season we are in continual wonder at the fertility of the land; a fertility on the slightest cultivation, the shallowest ploughing, and without fertilization. It is customary to say that the soil is inexhaustible, that crop after crop of the same kind can be depended on, and the mud (*limon*) of the overflowing Nile will repair all wastes.

And yet, I somehow get an impression of degeneracy, of exhaustion, both in Upper and Lower Egypt, in the soil; and it extends to men and to animals; horses, cattle, donkeys, camels, domestic fowls look impoverished—we have had occasion to say before that the hens lay ridiculously small eggs—they put the contents of one egg into three shells. (They might not take this trouble if eggs were sold by weight, as they should be.) The food of the country does not sufficiently nourish man or beast. Its quality is deficient. The Egyptian wheat does not make wholesome bread; most of it has an unpleasant odor—it tends to speedy corruption, it lacks certain elements, phosphorus probably. The bread that we eat on the dahabeëh is made from foreign wheat. The Egyptian wheat is at a large discount in European markets. One reason of this inferiority is supposed to be the succession of a wheat crop year after year upon the same field; another is the absolute want of any fertilizer except the Nile mud; and another the use of the same seed forever. Its virtue has departed from it, and the most hopeless thing in the situation is the unwillingness of the fellah to try anything new, in his contented ignorance. The Khedive has made extraordinary efforts to introduce improved machinery and processes, and he has set the example on his own plantations. It has no effect on the fellah. He will have none of the new inventions or new ways. It seems as hopeless to attempt to change him as it would be to convert a pyramid into a Congregational meeting-house.

For the political economist and the humanitarian, Egypt is the most interesting and the saddest study of this age; its agriculture and its people are alike unique. For the ordinary traveller the country has not less interest, and I suppose he may be pardoned if he sometimes loses sight of the misery in the strangeness, the antique barbarity, the romance by which he is surrounded.

As we lay, windbound, a few miles below Soohag, the Nubian trading-boat I had seen the day before was moored near; and we improved this opportunity for an easy journey to Central Africa, by going on board. The forward-deck was piled with African hides so high that the oars were obliged to be hung on outriggers; the cabin-deck was loaded with bags of gums, spices, medicines; and the cabin itself was stored so full, that when we crawled down into it there was scarcely room to sit upright on the bags. Into this penetralia of barbaric merchandise, the ladies preceded us, upon the promise of the sedate and shrewd-eyed traveller to exhibit his ostrich-feathers. I suppose nothing in the world of ornament is so fascinating to a woman as an ostrich-feather; and to delve into a mine of them, to be able to toss about handfuls, sheafs of them, to choose any size and shape and any color, glossy black, white, grey, and white with black tips,—it makes one a little delirious to think of it! There is even a mild enjoyment in seeing a lady take up a long, drooping plume, hold it up before her dancing, critical eyes, turning the head a little one side, shaking the feathered curve into its most graceful fall—"Isn't it a beauty?" Is she thinking how it will look upon a hat of the mode? Not in the least. The ostrich-feather is the symbol of truth and justice; things that are equal to the same thing are equal to each other—it is also the symbol of woman. In the last judgment before Osiris, the ostrich-feather is weighed in the balance against all the good deeds of a man's life. You have seen many a man put all his life against the pursuit of an ostrich-feather in a woman's hat —the plume of truth in beauty's bonnet.

While the ostrich-trade is dragging along its graceful length, other curiosities are produced; the short, dangerous tusks of the wild boar; the long tusks of the elephant—a beast whose enormous strength is only made a show of, like that of Samson; and pretty silver-work from Soudan.

"What is this beautiful tawny skin, upon which I am sitting?"

"Lion's; she was the mother of one of the young lions out yonder. And this," continued the trader, drawing something from the corner, "is her skull." It gave a tender interest to the orphan outside, to see these remains of his mother. But sadness is misplaced on her account; it is better that she died than to live to see her child in a menagerie.

"What's that thick stuff in a bottle there behind you?"

"That's lion's oil, some of *her* oil." Unhappy family, the mother skinned and boiled, the offspring dragged into slavery.

I took the bottle. To think that I held in my hand the oil of a lion! Bear's oil is vulgar. But this is different; one might anoint himself for any heroic deed with this royal ointment.

"And is that another bottle of it?"

"*Mais*, no; you don't get a lion every day for oil; that is ostrich oil. This is good for rheumatism."

It ought to be. There is nothing rheumatic about the ostrich. When I have tasted sufficiently the barbaric joys of the cabin I climb out upon the deck to see more of this strange craft.

Upon the narrow and dirty bow, over a slow fire, on a shallow copper dish, a dark and slender boy is cooking flap-jacks as big as the flap of a leathern apron. He takes the flap-jack up by the edge in his fingers and turns it over, when one side is cooked, as easily as if it were a sheepskin. There is a pile of them beside him, enough to make a whole suit of clothes, burnous and all, and very durable it would prove. Near him is tied, by a cotton cord, a half-grown leopard, elegantly spotted, who has a habit of running out his tongue, giving a side-lick to his chops, and looking at you in the most friendly manner. If I were the boy I wouldn't stand with my naked back to a leopard which is tied with a slight string.

On shore, on the sand and in the edge of the wheat, are playing in the sun a couple of handsome young lions, gentle as kittens. After watching their antics for some time, and calculating the weight of their paws as they cuff each other, I satisfy a long ungratified Van Amburgh ambition, by patting the youngest on the head and putting my hand (for an exceedingly brief instant) into his mouth, experiencing a certain fearful pleasure, remembering that although young he is a lion!

The two play together very prettily, and when I leave them they have lain down to sleep, face to face, with their arms round each other's necks, like the babes in the wood. The lovely leopard occasionally rises to his feet and looks at them and then lies down again, giving a soft sweep to his long and rather vicious tail. His countenance is devoid of the nobility of the lion's. The lion's face inspires you with confidence; but I can see little to trust in the yellow depths of his eyes. The lion's eyes, like those of all untamed beasts, have the repulsive trait of looking at you without any recognition in them—the dull glare of animality.

The next morning, when the wind falls, we slip out from our cover, like the baffled mariners of Jason, and row past the bold, purplish-grey cliff of Gebel Sheykh Hereedee, in which are grottoes and a tomb of the sixth dynasty, and on to Tahta, a large town, almost as picturesque, in the distance, with its tall minarets and one great, red-colored building, as Venice from the Lido. Then the wind rises, and we are again tantalized with no progress. One likes to dally and eat the lotus by his own will; but when the elements baffle him, and the wind blows contrary to his desires, the old impatience, the free will of ancient Adam, arises, and man falls out of his paradise. We are tempted to wish to be hitched (just for a day, or to get round a bend), to one of these miserable steamboats that go swashing by, frightening all the game-birds, and fouling the sweet air of Egypt with the black smoke of their chimneys.

In default of going on, we climb a high spur of the Mokattam, which has a vast desert plain on each side, and in front, and up and down the very crooked river (the wind would need to change every five minutes to get us round these bends), an enormous stretch of green fields, dotted with villages, flocks of sheep and cattle, and strips of palm-groves. Whenever we get in Egypt this extensive view over mountains, desert, arable land and river, it is always both lovely and grand. There was this afternoon on the bare limestone precipices a bloom as of incipient spring verdure. There is always some surprise of color for the traveller who goes ashore, or looks from his window, on the Nile,—either in the sky, or in the ground which has been steeped in color for so many ages that even the brown earth is rich.

The people hereabouts have a bad reputation, perhaps given them by the government, against which they rebelled on account of excessive taxes; the insurrection was reduced by knocking a village or two into the original dust with cannon balls. We, however, found the inhabitants very civil. In the village was one of the houses of entertainment for wanderers—a half-open cow-shed it would be called in less favored lands. The interior was decorated with the rudest designs in bright colors, and sentences from the Koran; we were told that any stranger could lodge in it and have something to eat and drink; but I should advise the coming traveller to bring his bed, and board also.

We were offered the fruit of the nabbek tree (something like a sycamore), a small apple, a sort of cross between the thorn and the crab, with the disagreeable qualities of both. Most of the vegetables and fruits of the valley we find insipid; but the fellaheen seem to like neutral flavors as they do neutral colors. The almost universal brown of the gowns in this region harmonizes with the soil, and the color does not show dirt; a great point for people who sit always on the ground.

The next day we still have need of patience; we start, meet an increasing wind, which whirls us about and blows us up stream. We creep under a bank and lie all day, a cold March day, and the air dark with dust.

After this Sunday of rest, we walk all the following morning through fields of wheat and lentils, along the shore. The people are uninteresting, men gruff; women ugly; clothes scarce; fruit, the nabbek, which a young lady climbs a tree to shake down for us. But I encountered here a little boy who filled my day with sunshine.

He was a sort of shepherd boy, and I found him alone in a field, the guardian of a donkey which was nibbling coarse grass. But his mind was not on his charge, and he was so much absorbed in his occupation that he did not notice my approach. He was playing, for his own delight and evidently with intense enjoyment, upon a reed pipe—an instrument of two short reeds, each with four holes, bound together, and played like a clarionet.

Its compass was small, and the tune ran round and round in it, accompanied by one of the most doleful drones imaginable. Nothing could be more harrowing to the nerves. I got the boy to play it a good deal. I saw that it was an antique instrument (it was in fact Pan's pipe unchanged in five thousand years), and that the boy was a musical enthusiast—a gentle Mozart who lived in an ideal world which he created for himself in the midst of the most forlorn conditions. The little fellow had the knack of inhaling and blowing at the same time, expanding his cheeks, and using his stomach like the bellows of the Scotch bagpipe, and producing the same droning sound as that delightful instrument. But I would rather hear this boy half a day than the bagpipe a week.

I talked about buying the pipe, but the boy made it himself, and prized it so highly that I could not pay him what he thought it was worth, and I had not the heart to offer its real value. Therefore I left him in possession of his darling, and gave him half a silver piastre. He kissed it and thanked me warmly, holding the unexpected remuneration for his genius in his hand, and looking at it with shining eyes. I feel an instant pang, and I am sorry that I gave it to him. I have destroyed the pure and ideal world in which he played to himself, and tainted the divine love of sweet sounds with the idea of gain and the scent of money. The serenity of his soul is broken up, and he will never again be the same boy, exercising his talent merely for the pleasure of it. He will inevitably think of profit, and will feverishly expect something from every traveller. He may even fall so far as to repair to landings where boats stop, and play in the hope of blacksheesh.

At night we came to Assiout, greeted from afar by the sight of its slender and tall minarets and trees, on the rosy background of sunset.

CHAPTER XXXII

JOTTINGS.

LETTING our dahabeëh drift on in the morning, we spend the day at Assiout, intending to overtake it by a short cut across the oxbow which the river makes here. We saw in the city two examples, very unlike, of the new activity in Egypt. One related to education, the other to the physical developement of the country and to conquest.

After paying our respects to the consul, we were conducted by his two sons to the Presbyterian Mission-school. These young men were educated at the American College in Beyrout. Nearly everywhere we have been in the East, we have found a graduate of this school, that is as much as to say, a person intelligent and anxious and able to aid in the regeneration of his country. It would not be easy to overestimate the services that this one liberal institution of learning is doing in the Orient.

The mission-school was under the charge of the Rev. Dr. John Hogg and his wife (both Scotch), with two women-teachers and several native assistants. We were surprised to find an establishment of about one hundred and twenty scholars, of whom over twenty were girls. Of course the majority of the students were in the primary studies, and some were very young; but there were classes in advanced mathematics, in logic, history, English, etc. The Arab young men have a fondness for logic and metaphysics, and develop easily an inherited subtlety in such studies. The text-books in use are Arabic, and that is the medium of teaching.

The students come from all parts of upper Egypt, and are almost all the children of Protestant parents, and they are, with an occasional exception, supported by their parents, who pay at least their board while they are at school. There were few Moslems among them, I think only one Moslem girl. I am bound to say that the boys and young men in their close rooms did not present an attractive appearance; an ill-assorted assembly, with the stamp of physical inferiority and dullness —an effect partially due to their scant and shabby apparel, for some of them had bright, intelligent faces.

The school for girls, small as it is, impressed us as one of the most hopeful things in Egypt. I have no confidence in any scheme for the regeneration of the country, in any development of agriculture, or extension of territory, or even in education, that does not reach woman and radically change her and her position. It is not enough to say that the harem system is a curse to the East; woman herself is everywhere degraded. Until she becomes totally different from what she now is, I am not sure but the Arab is right in saying that the harem is a necessity; the woman is secluded in it (and in the vast majority of harems there is only one wife) and has a watch set over her, because she cannot be trusted. One hears that Cairo is full of intrigue, in spite of locked doors and eunuchs. The large towns are worse than the country; but I have heard it said that woman is the evil and plague of Egypt—though I don't know how the country could go on without her. Sweeping generalizations are dangerous, but it is said that the sole education of most Egyptian women is in arts to stimulate the passion of men. In the idleness of the most luxurious harem, in the grim poverty of the lowest cabin, woman is simply an animal.

What can you expect of her? She is literally uneducated, untrained in every respect. She knows no more of domestic economy than she does of books, and she is no more fitted to make a house attractive or a room tidy than she is to hold an intelligent conversation. Married when she is yet a child, to a person she may have never seen, and a mother at an age when she should be in school, there is no opportunity for her to become anything better than she is.

A primary intention in this school is to fit the girls to become good wives, who can set an example of tidy homes economically managed, in which there shall be something of social life and intelligent companionship between husband and wife. The girls are taught the common branches, sewing, cooking, and housekeeping—as there is opportunity for learning it in the family of the missionaries. This house of Dr. Hogg's, with its books, music, civilized *ménage*, is a school in itself, and the girl who has access to it for three or four years will not be content with the inconvenience, the barren squalor of her parental hovel; for it is quite as much ignorance as poverty that produces miserable homes. Some of the girls now here expect to become teachers; some will marry young men who are also at this school. Such an institution would be of incalculable service if it did nothing else than postpone the marriage of women a few years. This school is a small seed in Egypt, but it is, I believe, the germ of a social revolution. It is, I think, the only one in Upper Egypt. There is a mission school of similar character in Cairo, and the Khedive also has undertaken schools for the education of girls.

In the last room we came to the highest class, a dozen girls, some of them mere children in appearance, but all of marriageable age. I asked the age of one pretty child, who showed uncommon brightness in her exercises.

"She is twelve," said the superintendent, "and no doubt would be married, if she were not here. The girls become marriageable from eleven years, and occasionally they marry younger; if one is not married at fifteen she is in danger of remaining single."

"Do the Moslems oppose your school?"

"The heads of the religion endeavor to prevent Moslem children coming to it; we have had considerable trouble; but generally the mothers would like to have their girls taught here, they become better daughters and more useful at home."

"Can you see that you gain here?"

"Little by little. The mission has been a wonderful success. I have been in Egypt eighteen years; since the ten years that we have been at Assiout, we have planted, in various towns in Upper Egypt, ten churches."

"What do you think is your greatest difficulty?"

"Well, perhaps the Arabic language."

"The labor of mastering it?"

"Not that exactly, although it is an unending study. Arabic is an exceedingly rich language, as you know—a tongue that has often a hundred words for one simple object has almost infinite capabilities for expressing shades of meaning. To know Arabic grammatically is the work of a lifetime. A man says, when he has given a long life to it, that he knows a little Arabic. My Moslem teacher here, who was as learned an Arab as I ever knew, never would hear me in a grammatical lesson upon any passage he had not carefully studied beforehand. He begged me to excuse him, one morning, from hearing me (I think we were reading from the Koran) because he had not had time to go over the portion to be read. Still, the difficulty of which I speak, is that Arabic and the Moslem religion are one and the same thing, in the minds of the faithful. To know Arabic is to learn the Koran, and that is the learning of a learned Arab. He never gets to the end of the deep religious meaning hidden in the grammatical intricacies. Religion and grammar thus become one."

"I suppose that is what our dragoman means, when he is reading me something out of the Koran, and comes to a passage that he calls too deep."

"Yes. There is room for endless differences of opinion in the rendering of almost any passage, and the disagreement is important, because it becomes a religious difference. I had an example of the unity of the language and the religion in the Moslem mind. When I came here the learned thought I must be a Moslem because I knew the grammatical Arabic; they could not conceive how else I should know it."

When we called upon his excellency, Shakeer Pasha, the square in front of his office and the streets leading to it were so covered with sitting figures that it was difficult to make a way amidst them. There was an unusual assembly of some sort, but its purport we could not guess. It was hardly in the nature of a popular convention, although its members sat at their ease, smoking, and a babel of talk arose. Nowhere else in Egypt have I seen so many fine and even white-looking men gathered together. The centre of every group was a clerk, with inkhorn and reed, going over columns of figures.

The governor's quarters were a good specimen of Oriental style and shabbiness; spacious whitewashed apartments, with dirty faded curtains. But we were received with a politeness that would have befitted a palace, and with the cordial ease of old friends. The Pasha was heartbroken that we had not notified him of our coming, and that now our time would not permit us to stay and accept a dinner—had we not promised to do so on our return? He would send couriers and recall our boat, he would detain us by force. Allowing for all the exaggeration of Oriental phraseology, it appeared only too probable that the Pasha would die if we did not stay to dinner and spend the night. But we did not.

This great concourse? Oh, they were sheykhs and head men of all the villages in the country round, whom he had summoned to arrange for the purchase of dromedaries. The government has issued orders for the purchase of a large number, which it wants to send to Darfoor. The Khedive is making a great effort to open the route to Darfoor (twenty-eight days by camel) to regular and safe travel, and to establish stations on the road. That immense and almost unknown territory will thus be brought within the commercial world.

During our call we were served with a new beverage in place of coffee; it was a hot and sweetened tea of cinnamon, and very delicious.

On our return to the river, we passed the new railway station building, which is to be a handsome edifice of white limestone. Men, women, and children are impressed to labor on it, and, an intelligent Copt told us, without pay. Very young girls were the mortar-carriers, and as they walked to and fro, with small boxes on their heads, they sang, the precocious children, an Arab love-song:—

"He passed by my door, he did not speak to me."

We have seen little girls, quite as small as these, forced to load coal upon the steamers, and beaten and cuffed by the overseers. It is a hard country for women. They have only a year or two of time, in which all-powerful nature and the wooing sun sing within them the songs of love, then a few years of married slavery, and then ugliness, old age, and hard work.

I do not know a more melancholy subject of reflection than the condition, the lives of these women we have been seeing for three months. They have neither any social nor any religious life. If there were nothing else to condemn the system of Mohammed, this is sufficient. I know what splendours of art it has produced, what achievements in war, what benefits to literature and science in the dark ages of Europe. But all the culture of a race that in its men has borne accomplished scholars, warriors, and artists, has never touched the women. The condition of woman in the Orient is the conclusive verdict against the religion of the Prophet.

I will not contrast that condition with the highest; I will not compare a collection of Egyptian women, assembled for any purpose, a funeral or a wedding, with a society of American ladies in consultation upon some work of charity, nor with an English drawing-room. I chanced once to be present at a representation of Verdi's Grand Mass, in Venice, when all the world of fashion, of beauty, of intelligence, assisted. The *coup d'œil* was brilliant. Upon the stage, half a hundred of the chorus-singers were ladies. The leading solo-singers were ladies. I remember the freshness, the beauty even, the vivacity, the gay decency of the toilet, of that group of women who contributed their full share in a most intelligent and at times profoundly pathetic rendering of the Mass. I recall the sympathetic audience, largely composed of women, the quick response to a noble strain nobly sung, the cheers, the tears even which were not wanting in answer to the solemn appeal; in fine, the highly civilized sensitiveness to the best product of religious art. Think of some such scene as that, and of the women of an European civilization; and then behold the women who are the product of this,—the sad, dark fringe of water-drawers and baby-carriers, for eight hundred miles along the Nile.

We have a row in the sandal of nine miles before we overtake our dahabeëh, which the wind still baffles. However, we slip along under the cover of darkness, for, at dawn, I hear the muëzzin calling to prayer at Manfaloot, trying in vain to impress a believing but drowsy world, that prayer is better than sleep. This is said to be the place where Lot passed the period of his exile. Near here, also, the Holy Family sojourned when it spent a winter in Egypt. (The Moslems have appropriated and localized everything in our Scriptures which is picturesque, and they plant our Biblical characters where it is convenient.) It is a very pretty town, with minarets and gardens.

It surprises us to experience such cool weather towards the middle of March; at nine in the morning the thermometer marks 55°; the north wind is cold, but otherwise the day is royal. Having nothing better to do we climb the cliffs of Gebel Aboofeyda, at least a thousand feet above the river; for ten miles it presents a bold precipice, unscalable except at intervals. We find our way up a ravine. The rocks *surface* the river and in the ravine are worn exactly as the sea wears rock, honeycombed by the action of water, and excavated into veritable sea-caves near the summit. The limestone is rich in fossil shells.

The plain on top presented a singular appearance. It was strewn with small boulders, many of them round and as shapely as cannon balls, all formed no doubt before the invention of the conical missiles. While we were amusing ourselves with the thousand fantastic freaks of nature in hardened clay, two sinister Arabs approached us from behind and cut off our retreat. One was armed with a long gun, and the other with a portentous spear. We saluted them in the most friendly manner, and hoped that they would pass on; but, no, they attached themselves to us. I tried to think of cases of travellers followed into the desert on the Nile and murdered, but none occurred to me. There seemed to be no danger from the gun so long as we kept near its owner, for the length of it would prevent his bringing it into action close at hand. The spear appeared to be the more effective weapon of the two; it was so, for I soon ascertained that the gun was not loaded and that its bearer had neither powder nor balls. It turned out that this was a detachment of the local guard, sent out to protect us; it would have been a formidable party in case of an attack.

Continuing our walk over the stone-clad and desolate swells, it suddenly occurred to us that we had become so accustomed to this sort of desert-walking, with no green or growing thing in sight, that it had ceased to seem strange to us. It gave us something like a start, therefore, shortly after, to see, away to the right, blue water forming islands out of the hill-tops along the horizon; there was an appearance of verdure about the edge of the water, and dark clouds sailed over it. There was, however, when we looked steadily, about the whole landscape a shimmer and a shadowy look that taught us to know that it was a *mirage*; the rich Nile valley below us, with the blue water, the green fields, the black lines of palms, was dimly mirrored in the sky and thrown upon the desert hills in the distance. We stood where we could compare the original picture with the blurred copy.

Making our way down the face of the cliff, along some ledges, we came upon many grottoes and mummy-pits cut in the rock, all without sculptures, except one; this had on one side an arched niche and pilasters from which the arch sprung. The vault of the niche had been plastered and painted, and a Greek cross was chiseled in each pilaster; but underneath the pilaster the rock was in ornamental squares, lozenges and curves in Saracenic style, although it may have been ancient Egyptian. How one religion has whitewashed, and lived on the remains of another here; the tombs of one age become the temples of another and the dwellings of a third. On these ledges, and on the desert above, we found bits of pottery. Wherever we have wandered, however far into the desert from the river, we never get beyond the limit of broken pottery; and this evidence of man's presence everywhere, on the most barren of these high or low plains of stone and sand, speaks of age and of human occupation as clearly as the temples and monuments. There is no virgin foot of desert even; all is worn and used. Human feet have trodden it in every direction for ages. Even on high peaks where the eagles sit, men have piled stones and made shelters, perhaps lookouts for enemies, it may be five hundred, it may be three thousand years ago. There is nowhere in Egypt a virgin spot.

By moonlight we are creeping under the frowning cliffs of Aboofeyda, and voyage on all night in a buccaneerish fashion; the next day sail by Hadji Kandell, where travellers disembark for Tel el Amarna. The remains of a once vast city strew the plain, but we only survey it through a field-glass. What, we sometimes say in our more modern moments, is one spot more than another? The whole valley is a sepulchre of dead civilizations; its inhabitants were stowed away, tier on tier, shelf on shelf, in these ledges.

However, respect for age sent us in the afternoon to the grottoes on the north side of the cliff of Sheykh Saïd. This whole curved ranged, away round to the remains of Antinoë, is full on tombs. Some that we visited are large and would be very comfortable dwellings; they had been used for Christian churches, having been plastered and painted. Traces of one painting remain—trees and a comical donkey, probably part of the story of the flight of the Holy Family into Egypt. We found in one of the ovals Cheops, the builder of the great pyramid, and much good sculpture in the best old manner—agricultural scenes, musicians, dancers, beautifully cut, with careful details and also with spirit. This is very old work, and, even abused as it has been, it is as good as any the traveller will find in Egypt. This tomb no doubt goes back to the fourth dynasty, and its drawing of animals, cows, birds, and fish are better than we usually see later. In a net in which fish is taken, many kinds are represented, and so faithfully that the species are recognizable; in a marsh is seen a hippopotamus, full of life and viciousness, drawn with his mouth stretched asunder wide enough to serve for a menagerie show-bill. There are some curious false doors and architectural ornaments, like those of the same epoch in the tombs at the pyramids.

At night we were at Rhoda, where is one of the largest of the Khedive's sugar-factories; and the next morning at Beni Hassan, famed, next to Thebes, for its grottoes, which have preserved to us, in painted scenes, so much of the old Egyptian life. Whoever has seen pictures of these old paintings and read the vast amount of description and inferences concerning the old Egyptian life, based upon them, must be disappointed when he sees them to-day. In the first place they are only painted, not cut, and in this respect are inferior to those in the grottoes of Sheykh Saïd; in the second place, they are so defaced, as to be with difficulty deciphered, especially those depicting the trades.

Some of the grottoes are large—sixty feet by forty feet; fine apartments in the rock, high and well lighted by the portal. Architecturally, no tombs are more interesting; some of the ceilings are vaulted, in three sections; they are supported by fluted pillars, some like the Doric, and some in the beautiful lotus style; the pillars are architraves; and there are some elaborately wrought false doorways. And all this goes to show that, however ancient these tombs are, they imitated stone buildings already existing in a highly developed architecture.

Essentially the same subjects are represented in all the tombs; these are the trades, occupations, amusements of the people. Men are blowing glass, working in gold, breaking flax, tending herds (even doctoring animals that are ill), chiselling statues, painting, turning the potter's wheel; the barber shaves his customer; two men play at draught; the games most in favor are wrestling and throwing balls, and in the latter women play. But what one specially admires is the honesty of the decorators, which conceals nothing from posterity; the punishment of the bastinado is again and again represented, and even women are subject to it; but respect was shown for sex; the woman was not cast upon the ground, she kneels and takes the flagellation on her shoulders.

We saw in these tombs no horses among the many animals; we have never seen the horse in any sculptures except harnessed in a war-chariot; "the horse and his rider" do not appear.

There is a scene here which was the subject of a singular mistake, that illustrates the needless zeal of early explorers to find in everything in Egypt confirmation of the Old Testament narratives. A procession, painted on the wall, now known to represent the advent of an Asiatic tribe into Egypt, perhaps the Shepherds, in a remote period, was declared to represent the arrival of Joseph's brethren. The tomb, however, was made several centuries before the advent of Joseph himself. And even if it were of later date than the event named, we should not expect to find in it a record of an occurrence of such little significance at that time. We ought not to be surprised at the absence in Egypt of traces of the Israelitish sojourn, and we should not be, if we looked at the event from the Egyptian point of view and not from ours. In a view of the great drama of the ancient world in the awful Egyptian perspective, the Jewish episode is relegated to its proper proportion in secular history. The whole Jewish history, as a worldly phenomenon, occupies its narrow limits. The incalculable effect upon desert tribes of a long sojourn in a highly civilized state, the subsequent development of law and of a literature unsurpassed in after-times, and the final flower into Christianity,—it is in the light of all this that we read the smaller incidents of Jewish history, and are in the habit of magnifying its contemporary relations. It was the slenderest thread in the days of Egyptian puissance. In the ancient atmosphere of Egypt, events purely historical fall into their proper proportions. Many people have an idea that the ancient world revolved round the Jews, and even hold it as a sort of religious faith.

It is difficult to believe that the race we see here are descendants of the active, inventive, joyous people who painted their lives upon these tombs. As we lie all the afternoon before a little village opposite Beni Hassan, I wonder for the hundredth time what it is that saves such miserable places from seeming to us as vile as the most wretched abodes of poverty in our own land. Is it because, with an ever-cheerful sun and a porous soil, the village is not so filthy as a like abode of misery would be with us? Is it that the imagination invests the foreign and the Orient with its own hues; or is it that our reading, prepossessing our minds, gives the lie to all our senses? I cannot understand why we are not more disgusted with such a scene as this. Not to weary you with a repetition of scenes sufficiently familiar, let us put the life of the Egyptian fellah, as it appears at the moment, into a paragraph.

Here is a jumble of small mud-hovels, many of them only roofed with cornstalks, thrown together without so much order as a beaver would use in building a village, distinguishable only from dog-kennels in that they have wooden doors—not distinguishable from them when the door is open and a figure is seen in the aperture. Nowhere any comfort or cleanliness, except that sometimes the inner kennel, of which the woman guards the key, will have its floor swept and clean matting in one corner. The court about which there are two or three of these kennels, serves the family for all purposes; there the fire for cooking is built, there are the water-jars, and the stone for grinding corn; there the chickens and the dogs are; there crouch in the dirt women and men, the women spinning, making bread, or nursing children, the men in vacant idleness. While the women stir about and go for water, the men will sit still all day long. The amount of sitting down here in Egypt is inconceivable; you might almost call it the feature of the country. No one in the village knows anything, either of religion or of the world; no one has any plans; no one exhibits any interest in anything; can any of them have any hopes? From this life nearly everything but the animal is eliminated. Children, and pretty children, swarm, tumbling about everywhere; besides, nearly every woman has one in her arms.

We ought not to be vexed at this constant north wind which baffles us, for they say it is necessary to the proper filling out of the wheat heads. The boat drifts about all day in a mile square, having passed the morning on a sand-spit where the stupidity and laziness of the crew placed it; and we have leisure to explore the large town of Menich, which lies prettily along the river. Here is a costly palace, which I believe has never been occupied by the Khedive, and a garden attached, less slovenly in condition than those of country palaces usually are. The sugar-factory is furnished with most costly machinery, which could not have been bought for less than half a million of dollars. Many of the private houses give evidences of wealth in their highly ornamented doorways and Moorish arches, but the mass of the town is of the usual sort here—tortuous lanes in which weary hundreds of people sit in dirt, poverty, and resignation. We met in the street and in the shops many coal-black Nubians and negroes, smartly dressed in the recent European style, having an impudent air, who seemed to be persons of wealth and consideration here. In the course of our wanderings I came to a large public building, built in galleries about an open court, and unwittingly in my examination of it, stumbled into the apartment of the Governor, Osman Bey, who was giving audience to all comers. Justice is still administered in patriarchal style; the door is open to all; rich and poor were crowding in, presenting petitions and papers of all sorts, and among them a woman preferred a request. Whether justice was really done did not appear, but Oriental hospitality is at least unfailing. Before I could withdraw, having discovered my blunder, the Governor welcomed me with all politeness and gave me a seat beside him. We smiled at each other in Arabic and American, and came to a perfect understanding on coffee and cigarettes.

The next morning we were slowly passing the Copt convent of Gebel e' Tyrr, and expecting the appearance of the swimming Christians. There is a good opportunity to board us, but no one appears. Perhaps because it is Sunday, and these Christians do not swim on Sunday. No. We learn from a thinly clad and melancholy person who is regarding us from the rocks that the Khedive has forbidden this disagreeable exhibition of muscular Christianity. It was quite time. But thus, one by one, the attractions of the Nile vanish.

What a Sunday! But not an exceptional day. "Oh dear," says madame, in a tone of injury, "here's another fine day!" Although the north wind is strong, the air is soft, caressing, elastic.

More and more is forced upon us the contrast of the scenery of Upper and Lower Egypt. Here it is not simply that the river is wider and the mountains more removed and the arable land broader; the lines are all straight and horizontal, the mountain ranges are level-topped, parallel to the flat prairies— at sunset a low level of white limestone hills in the east looked exactly like a long line of fence whitewashed. In Upper Egypt, as we have said, the plains roll, the hills are broken, there are pyramidal mountains, and evidences of upheaval and disorder. But these wide sweeping and majestic lines have their charm; the sunsets and sunrises are in some respects finer than in Nubia; the tints are not so delicate, the colors not so pure, but the moister atmosphere and clouds make them more brilliant and various. The dawn, like the after-glow, is long; the sky burns half round with rose and pink, the color mounts high up. The sunsets are beyond praise, and always surprises. Last night the reflection in the east was of a color unseen before— almost a purple below and a rose above; and the west glowed for an hour in changing tints. The night was not less beautiful —we have a certain comfort in contrasting both with March in New England. It was summer; the Nile slept, the moon half full, let the stars show; and as we glided swiftly down, the oars rising and falling to the murmured chorus of the rowers, there were deep shadows under the banks, and the stately palms, sentinelling the vast plain of moonlight over which we passed,—the great silence of an Egyptian night—seemed to remove us all into dreamland. The land was still, except for the creak of an occasional shadoof worked by some wise man who thinks it easier to draw water in the night than in the heat of the day, or an aroused wolfish dog, or a solitary bird piping on the shore.

Thus we go, thus we stay, in the delicious weather, encouraged now and again by a puff of southern wind, but held back from our destination by some mysterious angel of delay. But one day the wind comes, the sail is distended, the bow points down-stream, and we move at the dizzy rate of five miles an hour.

It is a day of incomparable beauty. We see very little labor along the Nile; the crops are maturing. But the whole population comes to the river, to bathe, to sit in the shallows, to sit on the bank. All the afternoon we pass groups, men, women, children, motionless, the picture of idleness. There they are, hour after hour, in the sun. Women, coming for water, put down their jars, and bathe and frolic in the grateful stream. In some distant reaches of the river there are rows of women along the shore, exactly like the birds which stand in the shallow places or sun themselves on the sand. There are more than twenty miles of bathers, of all sexes and ages.

When at last we come to a long sand-reef, dotted with storks, cranes and pelicans, the critic says he is glad to see something with feathers on it.

We are in full tide of success and puffed up with confidence; it is perfectly easy to descend the Nile. All the latter part of the afternoon we are studying the False Pyramid of Maydoon, that structure, older than Cheops, built, like all the primitive monuments, in degrees as the Tower of Babel was, as the Chaldean temples were. It lifts up, miles away from the river, only a broken mass from the *débris* at its base. We leave it behind. We shall be at Bedreshayn, for Memphis, before daylight. As we turn in, the critic says:

"We've got the thing in our hands now."

Alas! the Lord reached down and took it out. The wind chopped suddenly, and blew a gale from the north. At breakfast time we were waltzing round opposite the pyramids of Dashoor, liable to go aground on islands, and sandbars, and unable to make the land. Determined not to lose the day, we anchored, took the sandal, had a long pull, against the gale, to Bedreshayn, and mounted donkeys for the ruins of ancient Memphis.

When Herodotus visited Memphis, probably about four hundred and fifty years before Christ, it was a great city. He makes special mention of its temple of Vulcan, whose priests gave him a circumstantial account of the building of the city by Menes, the first Pharaoh. Four hundred years later, Diodorus found it magnificent; about the beginning of the Christian era, Strabo says it was next in size to Alexandria.

Although at the end of the twelfth century it had been systematically despoiled to build Cairo, an Arab traveller says that "its ruins occupy a space half a day's journey every way," and that its wonders could not be described. Temples, palaces, gardens, villas, acres of common dwellings—the city covered this vast plain with its splendor and its squalor.

The traveller now needs a guide to discover a vestige, a stone here and there, of this once most magnificent capital. Here came Moses and Aaron, from the Israelitish settlement in the Delta, from Zoan (Tanis) probably, to beg Menephtah to let the Jews depart; here were performed the miracles of the Exodus. This is the Biblical Noph, against which burned the wrath of the prophets. "No, (Heliopolis, or On) shall be rent asunder, and Noph shall have distresses daily." The decree was "published in Noph":—"Noph shall be waste and desolate without an inhabitant;" "I will cause their images to cease out of Noph."

The images have ceased, the temples have either been removed or have disappeared under the deposits of inundations; you would ride over old Memphis without knowing it, but the inhabitants have returned to this fertile and exuberant plain. It is only in the long range of pyramids and the great necropolis in the desert that you can find old Memphis.

The superabundant life of the region encountered us at once. At Bedreshayn is a ferry, and its boats were thronged, chiefly by women, coming and going, and always with a load of grain or other produce on the head. We rode round the town on an elevated dyke, lined with palms, and wound onward over a flat, rich with wheat and barley, to Mitrahenny, a little village in a splendid palm-grove. This marks the central spot of the ruins of old Memphis. Here are some mounds, here are found fragments of statues and cut stones, which are preserved in a temporary shelter. And here, lying on its side, in a hollow from which the water was just subsiding, is a polished colossal statue of Rameses II.—the Pharaoh who left more monuments of less achievements than any other "swell" of antiquity. The face is handsome, as all his statues are, and is probably conventionalized like our pictures of George Washington, or Napoleon's busts of himself. I confess to a feeling of perfect satisfaction at seeing his finely chiseled nose rooting in the mud.

This—some mounds, some fragments of stone, and the statue, —was all we saw of Memphis. But I should like to have spent a day in this lovely grove, which was carpeted with the only turf I saw in Egypt; reclining upon the old mounds in the shade, and pretending to think of Menes and Moses and Menephtah; and of Rhampsinitus, the king who "descended alive into the place which the Greeks call Hades, and there played at dice with Ceres, and sometimes won, and other times lost," and of the treasure-house he built here; and whether, as Herodotus believed, Helen, the beautiful cause of the Iliad, really once dwelt in a palace here, and whether Homer ever recited his epic in these streets.

We go on over the still rich plain to the village of Sakkarah —chiefly babies and small children. The cheerful life of this prairie fills us with delight—flocks of sheep, herds of buffaloes, trains of dromedaries, hundreds of laborers of both sexes in the fields, children skylarking about; on every path are women, always with a basket on the head, their blue cotton gown (the only article of dress except a head-shawl,) open in front, blowing back so as to show their figures as they walk.

When we reach the desert we are in the presence of death— perhaps the most mournful sight on this earth is a necropolis in the desert, savage, sand-drifted, plundered, all its mounds dug over and over. We ride along at the bases of the pyramids. I stop at one, climb over the *débris* at its base, and break off a fragment of stone. The pyramid is of crumbling limestone, and, built in stages or degrees, like that of Maydoon; it is slowly becoming an unsightly heap. And it is time. This is believed to be the oldest structure in the world, except the tower of Babel. It seems to have been the sepulchre of Keken, a king of the second dynasty. At this period hieroglyphic writing was developed, but the construction and ornamentation of the doorway of the pyramid exhibit art in its infancy. This would seem to show that the Egyptians did not emigrate from Asia with the developed and highly perfected art found in the sculptures of the tombs of the fourth, fifth, and sixth dynasties, as some have supposed, but that there was a growth, which was arrested later.

But no inference in regard to old Egypt is safe; a discovery to-morrow may upset it. Statues recently found, representing persons living in the third dynasty, present a different type of race from that shown in statues of the fourth and fifth dynasties. So that, in that period in which one might infer a growth of art, there may have been a change of the dominating race.

The first great work of Mariette Bey in Egypt—and it is a monument of his sagacity, enthusiasm, and determination,—was the unearthing, in this waste of Memphis, the lost Serapeum and the Apis Mausoleum, the tombs of the sacred bulls. The remains of the temple are again covered with sand; but the visitor can explore the Mausoleum. He can walk, taper in hand, through endless galleries, hewn in the rock, passing between rows of gigantic granite sarcophagi, in which once rested the mummies of the sacred bulls. Living, the bull was daintily fed—the Nile water unfiltered was thought to be too fattening for him—and devotedly worshipped; and dying, he was entombed in a sepulchre as magnificent as that of kings, and his adorers lined the walls of his tomb with votive offerings. It is partly from these stelæ, or slabs with inscriptions, that Mariette Bey has added so much to our knowledge of Egyptian history.

Near the Serapeum is perhaps the most elegant tomb in Egypt, the tomb of Tih, who lived in the fifth dynasty, some time later than Cheops, but when hippopotami abounded in the river in front of his farm. Although Tih was a priest, he was a gentleman of elegant tastes, an agriculturist, a sportsman. He had a model farm, as you may see by the buildings and by the thousand details of good management he carved. His tomb does him great credit. In all the work of later times there is nothing so good as this sculpture, so free, so varied, so beautiful; it promises everything. Tih even had, what we do not expect in people of that early time, humor; you are sure of it from some of the pictures here. He must have taken delight in decorating his tomb, and have spent, altogether, some pleasant years in it before he occupied it finally; so that he had become accustomed to staying here.

But his rule was despotic, it was that of the "stick." Egyptians have never changed in this respect, as we have remarked before. They are now, as then, under the despotism of some notion of governance—divine or human—despotic and fateful. The "stick" is as old as the monarchy; it appears in these tombs; as to-day, nobody then worked or paid taxes without its application.

The sudden arrest of Egyptian art was also forced upon us next day, in a second visit to the pyramids of Geezeh. We spent most of the day in the tombs there. In some of them we saw the ovals of all the kings of the fourth dynasty, many of them perfect and fresh in color. As to drawing, cutting, variety, liveliness of attitude and color, there is nothing better, little so good, in tombs of recent date. We find almost every secular subject in the early tombs that is seen in the latest. In thousands of years, the Egyptians scarcely changed or made any progress. The figures of men and animals are better executed in these old tombs than in the later. Again, these tombs are free from the endless repetitions of gods and of offerings to them. The life of the people represented is more natural, less superstitious; common events are naïvely portrayed, with the humorous unconsciousness of a simple age; art has thought it not unworthy its skill to represent the fact in one tomb, that men acted as mid-wives to cows, in the dawn of history.

While we lay at Geezeh we visited one of the chicken-hatching establishments for which the Egyptians have been famous from a remote period. It was a very unpretending affair, in a dirty suburb of the town. We were admitted into a low mud-building, and into a passage with ovens on each side. In these ovens the eggs are spread upon mats, and the necessary fire is made underneath. The temperature is at 100° to 108° Fahrenheit. Each oven has a hole in the centre, through which the naked attendant crawls to turn the eggs from time to time. The process requires usually twenty-one days, but some eggs hatch on the twentieth. The eggs are supplied by the peasants who usually receive, without charge, half as many chickens as they bring eggs. About one third of the eggs do not hatch. The hatching is only performed about three months in the year, during the spring.

In the passage, before one of the ovens, was a heap of soft chickens, perhaps half a bushel, which the attendant scraped together whenever they attempted to toddle off. We had the pleasure of taking up some handfuls of them. We also looked into the ovens, where there was a stir of life, and were permitted to hold some eggs while the occupants kicked off the shell.

I don't know that a plan will ever be invented by which eggs, as well as chickens, will be produced without the intervention of the hen. If one could be, it would leave the hen so much more time to scratch—it would relieve her from domestic cares so that she could take part in public affairs. The hen in Egypt is only partially emancipated. But since she is relieved from setting, I do not know that she is any better hen. She lays very small eggs.

This ends what I have to say about the hen. We have come to Cairo, and the world is again before us.

CHAPTER XXXIII.

THE KHEDIVE.

WHAT excitement there is in adjacency to a great city! To hear its inarticulate hum, to feel the thrill of its myriads, the magnetism of a vast society! How the pulse quickens at the mere sight of multitudes of buildings, and the overhanging haze of smoke and dust that covers a little from the sight of the angels the great human struggle and folly. How impatient one is to dive into the ocean of his fellows.

The stir of life has multiplied every 'hour in the past two days. The river swarms with boats, the banks are vocal with labor, traffic, merriment. This morning early we are dropping down past huge casernes full of soldiers—the bank is lined with them, thousands of them, bathing and washing their clothes, their gabble filling the air. We see again the lofty mosque of Mohammed Ali, the citadel of Saladin, the forest of minarets above the brown roofs of the town. We pass the isle of Rhoda and the ample palaces of the Queen-Mother. We moor at Gezereh amid a great shoal of dahabeëhs, returned from High Egypt, deserted of their passengers, flags down, blinds closed—a spectacle to fill one with melancholy that so much pleasure is over.

The dahabeëhs usually discharge their passengers at Gezereh, above the bridge. If the boat goes below with baggage, it is subject to a port-duty, as if it were a traveller,—besides the tax for passing the draw-bridge. We decide to remain some days on our boat, because it is comfortable, and because we want to postpone the dreaded breaking up of housekeeping, packing up our scattered effects, and moving. Having obtained permission to moor at the government dock below Kasr-el-Nil, we drop down here.

The first person to greet us there is Aboo Yusef, the owner. Behind him comes Habib Bagdadli, the little Jew partner. There is always that in his mien which says, "I was really born in Bagdad, but I know you still think I am a Jew from Algiers. No, gentlemens, you wrong a man to whom reputation is everything." But he is glad to see his boat safe; he expresses as much pleasure as one can throw from an eye with a cast in it. Aboo Yusef is radiant. He is attired gorgeously, in a new suit, from fresh turban to red slippers, on the profits of the voyage. His robe is silk, his sash is cashmere. He overflows with complimentary speech.

"Allah be praised, I see you safe."

"We have reason to be grateful."

"And that you had a good journey."

"A perfect journey."

"We have been made desolate by your absence; thank God, you have enjoyed the winter."

"I suppose you are glad to see the boat back safe also?"

"That is nothing, not to mention it, I not think of it; the return of the boat safe, that is nothing. I only think that you are safe. But it is a good boat. You will say it is the first-class of boats? And she goes up the cataract all right. Did I not say she go up the cataract? Abd-el-Atti he bear me witness."

"You did. You said so. Habib said so also. Was there any report here in Cairo that we could not go up?"

"Mashallah. Such news. The boat was lost in the cataract; the reïs was drowned. For the loss of the boat I did not care; only if you were safe."

"Did you hear that the cataract reïses objected to take us up?"

"What rascals! They always make the traveller some trouble. But, Allah forgive us all, the head reïs is dead. Not so, Abd-el-Atti?"

"What, the old reïs that we said good-bye to only a little while ago at Assouan?"

"Him dead," says Abd-el-Atti. "I have this morning some conversation with a tradin' boat from the Cataract. Him dead shortly after we leave."

It was the first time it had ever occurred to me that one of these tough old Bedaween could die in the ordinary manner.

But alas, his spirit was too powerful for his frame. We have not in this case the consolation of feeling that his loss is our gain; for there are plenty more like him at the First Cataract. He took money from Aboo Yusef for *not* taking us up the Cataract, and he took money from us *for* taking us up. His account is balanced. He was an impartial man. Peace to his colored ashes.

Aboo Yusef and the little Jew took leave with increased demonstrations of affection, and repeated again and again their joy that we had ascended the Cataract and returned safe. The Jew, as I said, had a furtive look, but Aboo is open as the day. He is an Arab you would trust. I can scarcely believe that it was he and his partner who sent the bribe to the reïs of the Cataract to prevent our going up.

As we ride to town through the new part, the city looks exceedingly bright and attractive; the streets are very broad; the handsome square houses—ornamented villas, with balconies, pillared piazzas, painted with lively figures and in *bizarre* patterns—stand behind walls overgrown with the convolvulus, and in the midst of gardens; plats in the centre of open spaces, and at the angles of streets are gay with flowers in bloom—chiefly scarlet geraniums. The town wears a spring aspect, and would be altogether bright but for the dust which overlays everything, houses, streets, foliage. No amount of irrigation can brighten the dust-powdered trees.

When we came to Cairo last fall, fresh from European cities, it seemed very shabby. Now that we come from Upper Egypt, with our eyes trained to eight hundred miles of mud-hovels, Cairo is magnificent. But it is Cairo. There are just as many people squatting in the dust of the highways as when we last saw them, and they have the air of not having moved in three months. We ride to Shepherd's Hotel, there are twenty dragomans for every tourist who wants to go to Syria, there is the usual hurry of arrival and departure, and no one to be found; we call at the consul's, it is not his hour; we ride through the blindest ways to the bankers, in the Rosetti Gardens (don't imagine there is any garden there), they do no business from twelve to three. It is impossible to accomplish anything in

Cairo without calm delay. And, falling into the mode, we find ourselves sauntering through one of the most picturesque quarters, the bazaar of Khán Khaléel, feasting the eye on the Oriental splendors of silks, embroidered stuffs, stiff with gold and silver, sown with pearls, antique Persian brasses, old arms of the followers of Saladin. How cool, how quiet it is. All the noises are soft. Noises enough there are, a babel of traffic, jostling, pushing, clamoring; and yet we have a sense of quiet in it all. There is no rudeness, no angularity, no glare of sun. At times you feel an underflow of silence. I know no place so convenient for meditation as the recesses of these intricate bazaars. Their unlikeness to the streets of other cities is mainly in the absence of any hard pavement. From the moment you come into the Mooskee, you strike a silent way, no noise of wheels or hoofs, nor footfalls of the crowd. It is this absence of foot-fall patter, which is always heard in our streets, that gives us the impression here of the underflow of silence.

Returning through the Ezbekeëh Park, and through the new streets, we are glad we are not to judge the manhood of Egypt by the Young Egypt we meet here, nor the future of Egypt by the dissolute idlers of Cairo and Alexandria. From Cairo to Wady Halfeh we have seen men physically well developed, fine specimens of their race, and better in Nubia than in Egypt Proper; but these youths are feeble, and of unclean appearance, even in their smart European dress. They are not unlike the effeminate and gilded youth of Italy that one sees in the cities, or Parisians of the same class. Egypt, which needed a different importation, has added most of the vices of Europe to its own; it is noticeable that the Italians, who emigrate elsewhere little, come here in great numbers, and men and women alike take kindly to this loose feebleness. French as well as Italians adapt themselves easily to Eastern dissoluteness. The French have never shown in any part of the globe any prejudice against a mingling of races. The mixture here of the youths of the Latin races and the worn-out Orientals, who are a little polished by a lacquer of European vice, is not a good omen for Egypt. Happily such youths are feeble, and, I trust, not to be found outside the two large cities.

The great question in Egypt, among foreigners and observers (there *is* no great question among the common people) is about the Khedive, Ismaïl Pasha, his policy and his real intentions with regard to the country. You will hear three distinct opinions; one from devout Moslems, another from the English, and a third from the Americans. The strict and conservative Moslems like none of the changes and innovations, and express not too much confidence in the Khedive's religion. He has bought pictures and statues for his palaces, he has marble images of himself, he has set up an equestrian statue in the street; all this is contrary to the religion. He introduces European manners and costumes, every government *employé* is obliged to wear European dress, except the tarboosh. What does he want with such a great army; why are the taxes so high, and growing higher every day?

With the Americans in Cairo, as a rule, the Khedive is popular; they sympathize with his ambition, and think that he has the good of Egypt at heart; almost uniformly they defend him. The English, generally, distrust the Khedive and criticise his every movement. Scarcely ever have I heard Englishmen speak well of the Khedive and his policy. They express a want of confidence in the sincerity of his efforts to suppress the slave-trade, for one thing. How much the fact that American officers are preferred in the Khedive's service has to do with the English and American estimate, I do not know; the Americans are naturally preferred over all others, for in case of a European complication over Egypt they would have no entangling alliances.

The Americans point to what has actually been accomplished by the present Viceroy, the radical improvements in the direction of a better civilization, improvements which already change the aspect of Egypt to the most casual observer. There are the railroads, which intersect the Delta in all directions, and extend over two hundred and fifty miles up the Nile, and the adventurous iron track which is now following the line of the telegraph to distant Kartoom. There are the canals, the Sweet-Water that runs from Cairo and makes life on the Isthmus possible, and the network of irrigating canals and system of ditches, which have not only transformed the Delta, but have changed its climate, increasing enormously the rainfall. No one who has not seen it can have any conception of the magnitude of this irrigation by canals which all draw water from the

Nile, nor of the immense number of laborers necessary to keep the canals in repair. Talk of the old Pharaohs, and their magnificent canals, projected or constructed, and their vaunted expeditions of conquest into Central Africa! Their achievements, take them all together, are not comparable to the marvels the Khedive is producing under our own eyes, in spite of a people ignorant, superstitious, reluctant. He does not simply make raids into Africa; he occupies vast territories, he has absolutely stopped the Nile slave-trade, he has converted the great slave-traders into his allies, by making it more their interest to develope legitimate commerce than to deal in flesh and blood; he has permanently opened a region twice as large as Egypt to commercial intercourse; he sends explorers and scientific expeditions into the heart of Africa. It is true that he wastes money, that he is robbed and cheated by his servants, but he perseveres, and behold the results. Egypt is waking out of its sleep, it is annexing territory, and population by millions, it is becoming a power. And Ismaïl Pasha is the centre and spring of the whole movement.

Look at Cairo! Since the introduction of gas, the opening of broad streets, the tearing down of some of the worst rookeries, the admission of sun and air, Cairo is exempt from the old epidemics, the general health is improved, and even that scourge, ophthalmia, has diminished. You know his decree forbidding early marriages; you know he has established and encourages schools for girls; you see what General Stone is doing in the education of the common soldiers, and in his training of those who show any aptitude in engineering, draughting, and the scientific accomplishments of the military profession.

Thus the warmest admirers of the Khedive speak. His despotism, which is now the most absolute in the world, perhaps, and least disputed, is referred to as a "personal government." And it is difficult to see how under present circumstances it could be anything else. There is absolutely in Egypt no material for anything else. The Khedive has annually summoned, for several years, a sort of parliament of the chief men of Egypt, for information and consultation. At first it was difficult to induce the members to say a word, to give any information or utter an opinion. It is a new thing in a despotic government, the shadow even of a parliament.

An English gentleman in Cairo, and a very intelligent man, gives the Khedive credit for nothing but a selfish desire to enrich himself, to establish his own family, and to enjoy the traditional pleasures of the Orient.

"But he is suppressing the slave-trade."

"He is trying to make England believe so. Slaves still come to Cairo; not so many down the Nile, but by the desert. I found a slave-den in some desert tombs once over the other side the river; horrible treatment of women and children; a caravan came from Darfoor by way of Assiout."

"But that route is cut off by the capture of Darfoor."

"Well, you'll see; slaves will come if they are wanted. Why, look at the Khedive's harem!"

"He hasn't so many wives as Solomon, who had seven hundred; the Khedive has only four."

"Yes, but he has more concubines; Solomon kept only three hundred; the Khedive has four hundred and fifty, and perhaps nearer five hundred. Some of them are beautiful Circassians for whom it is said he paid as much as £2000 and even £3000 sterling."

"I suppose that is an outside price."

"Of course, but think of the cost of keeping them. Then, each of his four wives has her separate palace and establishment. Rather an expensive family."

"Almost as costly as the royal family of England."

"That's another affair; to say nothing of the difference of income. The five hundred, more or less, concubines are under the charge of the Queen-mother, but they have *carte blanche* in indulgence in jewels, dress, and all that. They wear the most costly Paris modes. They spend enormous sums in pearls and diamonds. They have their palaces re-furnished whenever the whim seizes them, re-decorated in European style. Where does the money come from? You can see that Egypt is taxed to death. I heard to-day that the Khedive was paying seventeen per cent. for money, money borrowed to pay the interest on his private debts. What does he do with the money he raises?"

"Spends a good deal of it on his improvements, canals, railroads, on his army."

"I think he runs in debt for his improvements. Look again at his family. He has something like forty palaces, costing from one half-million to a million dollars each; some of them, which he built, he has never occupied, many of them are empty, many of those of his predecessors, which would lodge a thousand people, are going to decay; and yet he is building new ones all the time. There are two or three in process of erection on the road to the pyramids."

"Perhaps they are for his sons or for his high officers. Victor Emanuel, whose treasury is in somewhat the condition of the Khedive's, has a palace in every city of Italy, and yet he builds more."

"If the Khedive is building for his children, I give it up. He has somewhere between twenty and thirty acknowledged children. But he does give away palaces and houses. When he has done with a pretty slave, he may give her, with a palace or a fine house here in town, to a favorite officer. I can show you houses here that were taken away from their owners, at a price fixed by the Khedive and not by the owner, because the Viceroy wanted them to give away with one or another of his concubines."

"I suppose that is Oriental custom."

"I thought you Americans defended the Khedive on account of his progressive spirit."

"He is a man who is accomplishing wonders, trammelled as he is by usages thousands of years old, which appear monstrous to us, but are to him as natural as any Oriental condition. Yet I confess that he stands in very contradictory lights. If he knew it, he could do the greatest service to Egypt by abolishing his harem of concubines, converting it into—I don't know what—a convent or a boarding-school, or a milliner's shop, or an establishment for canning fruit—and then set the example of living, openly, with one wife."

"Wait till he does. And you talk about the condition of Egypt! Every palm-tree, and every sakiya is taxed, and the tax has doubled within a few years. The taxes are now from one pound and a half to three pounds an acre on all lands not owned by him."

"In many cases, I know this is not a high tax (compared with taxes elsewhere) considering the yield of the land, and the enormous cost of the irrigating canals."

"It is high for such managers as the fellahs. But they will

not have to complain long. The Khedive is getting into his own hands all the lands of Egypt. He owns I think a third of it now, and probably half of it is in his family; and this is much the better land."

"History repeats itself in Egypt. He is following the example of Joseph who, you know, taking advantage of the famine, wrung all the land, except that in possession of the priests, from the people, and made it over to Pharaoh. By Joseph's management the king owned, before the famine was over, not only all the land, but all the money, all the cattle, and all the people of Egypt. And he let the land to them for a fifth of its increase."

"I don't know that it is any better because Egypt is used to it. Joseph was a Jew. The Khedive pretends to be influenced by the highest motives, the elevation of the condition of the people, the regeneration of Egypt."

"I think he is sincerely trying to improve Egypt and the Egyptians. Of course a despot, reared in Oriental prejudices, is slow to see that you can't make a nation except by making men; that you can't make a rich nation unless individuals have free scope to accumulate property. I confess that the chief complaint I heard up the river was that no one dared to show that he had any money, or to engage in extensive business, for fear he would be 'squeezed.'"

"So he would be. The Khedive has some sixteen sugar-factories, worked by forced labour, very poorly paid. They ought to be very profitable."

"They are not."

"Well, he wants more money, at any rate. I have just heard that he is resorting to a forced loan, in the form of bonds. A land-owner is required to buy them in the proportion of one dollar and a half for each acre he owns; and he is to receive seven per cent. interest on the bonds. In Cairo a person is required to take these bonds in a certain proportion on his personal property. And it is said that the bonds are not transferable, and that they will be worthless to the heirs. I heard of this new dodge from a Copt."

"I suppose the Khedive's friends would say that he is trying to change Egypt in a day, whereas it is the work of generations."

When we returned to the dahabeëh we had a specimen of "personal government." Abd-el-Atti was standing on the deck, slipping his beads, and looking down.

"What has happened?"

"Ahman, been took him."

"Who took him?"

"Police, been grab him first time he go 'shore, and lock him up."

"What had he been doing?"

"Nothing he been done; I send him up town of errand; police catch him right out there."

"What for?"

"Take him down to Soudan to work; the vice-royal he issue an order for the police to catch all the black fellows in Cairo, and take 'em to the Soudan, down to Gondokora for what I know, to work the land there."

"But Ahman is our servant; he can't be seized."

"Oh, I know, Ahman belong to me; he was my slave till I gave him liberty; I go to get him out directly. These people know me, I get him off."

"But if you had no influence with the police, Ahman would be dragged off to Soudan to work in a cotton or rice field?"

"Lots of black fellows like him sent of. But I get him back, don't you have worry. What the vice-royal to do with my servant—I don't care if he Kin' of Constantinople!"

Sure enough, early in the evening the handsome Abyssinian boy came back, none the worse, except for a thorough scare, eyes and teeth shining, and bursting into his usual hearty laugh upon allusion to his capture.

"Police *tyeb?*"

"*Moosh-tyeb*" ("bad"), with an explosion of merriment.

The boy hadn't given himself much uneasiness, for he regards his master as his Providence.

We are moored at the dock and below the lock of the Sweet-water Canal which runs to Ismailia. A dredge-boat lies in the entrance, and we have an opportunity of seeing how government labour is performed; we can understand why it is that so many labourers are needed, and that the great present want of Egypt is stout and willing arms.

In the entrance of the canal and in front of the lock is a flatboat upon which are fifteen men. They have two iron scoops, which would hold about a gallon each; to each is attached a long pole and a rope. Two men jab the pole down and hold the pot on the bottom, while half a dozen pull leisurely on the rope, with a "*yah-sah*" or other chorus, and haul in the load; when it comes up, a man scrapes out the mud with his hand, sometimes not getting more than two quarts. It is very restful to watch their unexhausting soil. It takes several minutes to capture a pot of sand. There are fifteen men at this spoon-work, but one scoop is only kept going at a time. After it is emptied, the men stop and look about, converse a little, and get ready for another effort, standing meantime in liquid mud, ankle-deep. When they have rested, over goes the scoop again, and the men stand to the rope, and pull feebly, but only at intervals, that is when they sing the response to the line of the leader. The programme of singing and pulling is something like this:

Salee ah nadd (voice of the leader).
Yalee, halee (chorus, pull altogether).
Salee ah nadd.
Yalee, halee (pull).
Salee ah nadd.
Yalee halee (pull).

And the outcome of three or four minutes of hauling and noise enough to raise a ton, is about a quart of mud!

The river panorama is always varied and entertaining, and we are of a divided mind between a lazy inclination to sit here and watch the busy idleness of the population, or address ourselves to the much that still remains to be seen in Cairo. I ought to speak, however, of an American sensation on the river. This is a little steam-yacht, fifty feet long by seven and a half broad—which we saw up the Nile, where it attracted more attention along the banks than anything else this season. I call it American, because it carries the American flag and is owned by a New York art student, Mr. Anderson, and an English-American, Mr. Medler; but the yacht was built in London, and shipped on a large steamboat to Alexandria. It is the first steam vessel, I believe, carrying anything except Egyptian (or Turkish) colours that has ever been permitted to ascend the Nile. We took a trip on it one fine morning up to Helwán, and enjoyed the animation of its saucy speed. When put to its best, it makes eighteen miles an hour; but life would not be as long on it as it is on a dahabeëh. At Helwán are some hot sulphur-springs, famous and much resorted to in the days of the Pharaohs, and just now becoming fashionable again.

Our days pass we can hardly say how, while we wait for the proper season for Syria, and regard the invincible obstacles that debar us from the longed-for desert journey to Sinai and Arabia Petrea. The bazaars are always a refuge from the heat, a never-failing entertainment. We spend hours in lounging through them. We lunch at the shops of the sweetmeat makers, on bread, pistachio nuts, conserve of roses, I know not what, and Nile-water, with fingans of coffee fetched hot and creamy from the shop near by. We give a copper to an occasional beggar: for beggars are few in the street, and these are either blind or very poor, or derweeshes; and to all these, being regarded as Allah's poor, the Moslems give cheerfully, for charity is a part of their religion. We like also to stand at the doors of the artisans. There is a street where all the workmen are still making the old flint-lock guns and pistols, and the firearms with the flaring blunderbuss muzzles, as if the object were to scatter the charge, and hit a great many people but to kill none. I think the Peace Society would do well to encourage this kind of gun. There are shops also where a man sits before a heap of flint-chalk, chipping the stone with a flat iron mallet, and forming the flints for the antiquated locks.

We happen to come often in our wanderings, the distinction being a matter of luck, upon a very interesting old city gate of one of the quarters. The gate itself is a wooden one of two leaves, crossed with iron bands fastened with heavy spikes, and not remarkable except as an illustration of one of the popular superstitions of the Arabs. The wood is driven full of nails, bits of rags flutter on it, and human teeth are crowded under the iron bands. It is believed that if a person afflicted with headache will drive a nail into this door he will never have the headache again. Other ills are relieved by other offerings, bits of rag, teeth, etc. It would seem to be a pretty sure cure for toothache to leave the tooth in this gate. The Arabs are called the most superstitious of peoples, they wear charms against the evil-eye ("charm from the eye of girl, sharper than a spike;

charm from the eye of boy, more painful than a whip"), and they have a thousand absurd practices. Yet we can match most of them in Christian communities.

How patiently all the people work, and wait. Complaints are rare. The only reproof I ever received was from a donkey-boy, whom I had kept waiting late one evening at the Hotel Nil. When I roused him from his sleep on the ground, he asked, with an accent of weariness, "how much clock you got?"

By the twenty-third day of March it is getting warm; the thermometer is 81°. It is not simply the heat, but the Khámaseen, the south wind, the smoky air, the dust in the city, the languor. To-day it rained a few drops, and looked threatening, just as it does in a hot summer day at home. The outskirts of Cairo are enveloped in dust, and the heat begins to simmer over the palaces and gardens. The travellers are leaving. The sharp traders, Jews from Bagdad, Syrians, Jews from Constantinople, Greeks, Armenians from Damascus, all sorts, are packing up their goods, in order to meet the traveller and fleece him again in Jerusalem, in Beyrout, in Damascus, in Smyrna, on the Golden Horn. In the outskirts, especially on the open grounds by the canal, are the coffee-booths and dance-shanties—rows of the disreputable. The life, always out of doors even in the winter, is now more flamboyantly displayed in these open and verandahed dwellings; there is a yielding to the relaxation of summer. We hear at night, as we sit on the deck of our dahabeëh, the throbbing of the darabookah-drum and the monotonous songs of the dissolute ones.

CHAPTER XXXIV.

THE WOODEN MAN.

THE Khedive and his court, if it may be so called, are not hedged in by any formidable barriers; but there are peculiarities of etiquette. When his Highness gives a grand ball and public reception, of course only the male members of his household are present, only the men of the Egyptian society; it would in fact be a male assembly but for the foreign ladies visiting or residing in the city. Of course there cannot be any such thing as "society" under such circumstances; and as there are no women to regulate the ball invitations, the assembly is "mixed." There is no such thing as reciprocity with the Arabs and Turks; they are willing to meet the wives or the female friends of all foreigners; they never show their own.

If a lady visiting Cairo wishes to visit one of the royal harems, it is necessary that her husband or some gentleman of her party should first be presented to the Khedive. After this ceremony, notice is received through the chamberlain of the Viceroy that the lady will be received on such a day and hour, in a palace named, by her Highness So-So. Which Highness? That you can never tell before the notice is received. It is a matter of royal convenience at the time. In a family so large and varied as that of the Khedive, you can only be presented to a fragment of it. You may be received by one of his wives; it may please the Queen-mother, who is in charge of his largest harem, to do the honours; or the wife of the heir-apparent, or of one of the younger sons, may open her doors to you. I suppose it is a good deal a matter of whim with the inmates of the harem; sometimes they are tired of seeing strangers and of dressing for them. Usually they are eager to break the monotony of their lives with a visit that promises to show them a new costume. There is only one condition made as to the dress of the lady who is to be received at a royal harem; she must not wear black. There is a superstition connected with a black dress, it puts the inmates of the harem in low spirits. Gentlemen presented to the Khedive wear the usual evening dress.

The Khedive's winter-residence is the Palace of Abdeen, not far from the Ezbekeëh, and it was there that Dr. Lamborn and myself were presented to his Highness by Mr. Beardsley, our consul-general. Nothing regal could be more simple or less ceremonious. We arrived at the door at the moment fixed, for the Khedive is a man of promptness, and I imagine has his entire day parcelled out in engagements. We first entered a spacious entrance-hall, from which a broad stairway leads to the first story; here were thirty or forty janizaries, gentlemen-in-waiting, and eunuchs, standing motionless, at the sides, and guarding the approach to the stairway, in reception attitudes. Here we were received by an attendant who conducted us to a room on the left, where we were introduced to the chamberlain, and deposited our outer coats and hats. The chamberlain then led us to the foot of the stairs, but accompanied us no further; we ascended to the first landing, and turning to another broad stairway saw the Khedive awaiting us at the head of it. He was unattended; indeed we saw no officer or servant on this floor. The furniture above and below was European, except the rich, thick carpets of Turkey and Persia.

His Highness, who wore a dress altogether European except the fez, received us cordially, shaking hands and speaking with simplicity, as a private gentleman might, and, wasting no time in Oriental compliments, led the way to a small reception-room furnished in blue satin. We were seated together in a corner of the apartment, and an animated talk at once began. Dr. Lamborn's special errand was to ascertain whether Egypt would be represented in our Centennial, about which the Khedive was well informed. The conversation then passed to the material condition of Egypt, the development of its resources, its canals and railroads, and especially the new road into Soudan, and the opening of Darfour. The Khedive listened attentively to any practical information, either about railroads, factories, or agriculture, that my companions were able to give him, and had the air of a man eager to seize any idea that might be for the advancement of Egypt; when he himself spoke, it was with vivacity, shrewdness, and good sense. And he is not without a gleam of humour now and then,—a very hopeful quality in a sovereign and especially in an Oriental ruler.

The Khedive, in short, is a person to inspire confidence; he appears to be an able, energetic man of affairs, quick and resolute; there is not the slightest stiffness or "divine right" pretence in his manner. He is short, perhaps five feet seven or eight inches in height, and stout. He has a well-proportioned, solid head, good features, light complexion, and a heavy, strong jaw, which his closely-trimmed beard does not conceal. I am not sure that the penetration of his glance does not gain a little from a slight defect in one eye—the result of ophthalmia in his boyhood.

When the interview had lasted about fifteen minutes, the Khedive ended it by rising; at the head of the stairs we shook hands and exchanged the proper speeches; at the bottom of the first flight we turned and bowed, his Highness still standing and bowing, and then we saw him no more. As we passed out an order had come from above which set the whole household in a flurry of preparation, a running hither and thither as for speedy departure—the sort of haste that is mingled with fear, as for the command of a power that will not brook an instant's delay.

Exaggerated notions are current about harems and harem-receptions, notions born partly of the seclusion of the female portion of the household in the East. Of course the majority of harems in Egypt are simply the apartment of the one wife and her children. The lady who enters one of them pays an ordinary call, and finds no mystery whatever. If there is more than one wife, a privileged visitor, able to converse with the inmates, might find some skeletons behind the screened windows. It is also true that a foreign lady may enter one of the royal harems and be received with scarcely more ceremony than would attend an ordinary call at home. The receptions at which there is great display, at which crowds of beautiful or ugly slaves line the apartments, at which there is music and dancing by almehs, an endless service of sweets and pipes and coffee, and a dozen changes of dress by the hostess during the ceremony, are not frequent, are for some special occasion, the celebration of a marriage, or the entertainment of a visitor of high rank. One who expects, upon a royal invitation to the harem, to wander into the populous dove-cote of the Khedive, where languish the beauties of Asia, the sisters from the Gardens of Gul, pining for a new robe of the mode from Paris, will be most cruelly disappointed.

But a harem remains a harem, in the imagination. The ladies went one day to the house—I suppose it is a harem—of Hussein, the waiter who has served us with unremitting fidelity and cleverness. The house was one of the ordinary sort of unburnt brick, very humble, but perfectly tidy and bright. The secret of its cheerfulness was in a nice, cheery, happy little wife, who made a home for Hussein such as it was a pleasure to see in Egypt. They had four children, the eldest a daughter, twelve years old and very good-mannered and pretty. As she was of marriageable age, her parents were beginning to think of settling her in life.

"What a nice girl she is, Hussein," says Madame.

"Yes'm," says Hussein, waving his hands in his usual struggle with the English language, and uttering the longest speech ever heard from him in that tongue, but still speaking as if about something at table, "yes'm; good man have it; bad man, drinkin' man, smokin' man, eatin' man not have it."

I will describe briefly two royal presentations, one to the favorite wife of the Khedive, the other to the wife of Mohammed Tufik Pasha, the eldest son and heir-apparent, according to the late revolution in the rules of descent. French, the court language, is spoken not only by the Khedive but by all the ladies of his family who receive foreigners. The lady who was presented to the Khedive's wife, after passing the usual guard of eunuchs in the palace, was escorted through a long suite of showy apartments. In each one she was introduced to a maid of honor who escorted her to the next, each lady-in-waiting being more richly attired than her predecessor, and the lady was always thinking that *now* this one must be the princess herself. Female slaves were in every room, and a great number of them waited in the hall where the princess received her visitor. She was a strikingly handsome woman, dressed in pink satin and encrusted with diamonds. The conversation consisted chiefly of the most exaggerated and barefaced compliments on both sides, both as to articles of apparel and personal appearance. Coffee, cigarettes, and sweets without end, in cups of gold set with precious stones, were served by the female slaves. The wife was evidently delighted with the impression made by her beauty, her jewels, and her rich dress.

The wife of Tufik Pasha received at one of the palaces in the suburbs. At the door eunuchs were in waiting to conduct the visitors up the flight of marble steps, and to deliver them to female slaves in waiting. Passing up several broad stairways, they were ushered into a grand reception-hall furnished in European style, except the divans. Only a few servants were in attendance, and they were white female slaves. The princess is *petite*, pretty, intelligent, and attractive. She received her visitors with entire simplicity, and without ceremony, as a lady would receive callers in America. The conversation ran on the opera, the travel on the Nile, and topics of the town. Coffee and cigarettes were offered, and the sensible interview ended like an accidental visit. It is a little disenchanting, all this adoption of European customs; but the wife of Tufik Pasha should ask him to go a little further, and send all the eunuchs out of the palace.

We had believed that summer was come. But we learned that March in Cairo is, like the same month the world over, treacherous. The morning of the twenty-sixth was cold, the thermometer 60°. A north wind began to blow, and by afternoon increased to a gale, such as had not been known here for years. The town was enveloped in a whirldwind of sand; everything loose was shaking and flying; it was impossible to see one's way, and people scudding about the streets with their heads drawn under their robes continually dashed into each other. The sun was wholly hidden. From our boat we could see only a few rods over the turbulent river. The air was so thick with sand that it had the appearance of a yellow canvas. The desert had invaded the air—that was all. The effect of the light through this was extremely weird; not like a dark day of clouds and storm in New England, but a pale, yellowish-greenish, phantasmagoric light, which seemed to presage calamity. Such a light as may be at the Judgment Day. Cairo friends who dined with us said they had never seen such a day in Egypt. Dahabeëhs were torn from their moorings; trees were blown down in the Ezbekïeh Gardens.

We spent the day, as we had spent other days, in the Museum of Antiquities at Boulak. This wonderful collection, which is the work of Mariette Bey, had a thousand times more interest for us now than before we made the Nile voyage and acquired some knowledge of ancient Egypt through its monuments. Everything that we saw had meaning—statues, mummy-cases, images, scarabæi, seals, stelæ, gold jewelry, and the simple articles in domestic use.

It must be confessed that to a person uninformed about Egypt and unaccustomed to its ancient art, there is nothing in the world so dreary as a collection of its antiquities. The endless repetition of designs, the unyielding rigidity of form, the hideous mingling of the human and the bestial, the dead formality, are insufferably wearisome. The mummy is thoroughly disagreeable. You can easily hate him and all his belongings; there is an air of infinite conceit about him; I feel it in the exclusive box in which he stands, in the smirk of his face painted on his case. I wonder if it is the perkishness of immortality—as if his race alone were immortal. His very calmness, like that of so many of the statues he made, is an offensive contempt. It is no doubt, unreasonable, but as a living person I resent this intrusion of a preserved dead person into our warm times,—an appearance anachronistic and repellant.

But as an illustration of Egyptian customs, art, and history, the Boulak museum is almost a fascinating place. True, it is not so rich in many respects as some European collections of Egyptian antiquities, but it has some objects that are unique; for instance, the jewels of Queen Aah-hotep, a few statues, and some stelæ, which furnish the most important information.

This is not the place, had I the knowledge, to enter upon any discussion of the antiquity of these monuments or of Egyptian chronology. I believe I am not mistaken, however, in saying that the discoveries of Mariette Bey tend strongly to establish the credit of the long undervalued list of Egyptian sovereigns made by Manetho, and that many Oriental scholars agree with the directors of this museum that the date of the first Egyptian dynasty is about five thousand years before the Christian era. But the almost startling thought presented by this collection is not in the antiquity of some of these objects, but in the long civilization anterior to their production, and which must have been necessary to the growth of the art here exhibited.

It could not have been a barbarous people who produced, for instance, these life-like images found at Maydoon, statues of a prince and princess who lived under the ancient king Snéfron, the last sovereign of the third dynasty, and the predecessor of Cheops. At no epoch, says M. Mariette, did Egypt produce portraits more speaking, though they want the breadth of style of the statue in wood—of which more anon. But it is as much in an ethnographic as an art view that these statues are important. If the Egyptian race at that epoch was of the type offered by these portraits, it resembled in nothing the race which inhabited the north of Egypt not many years after Snéfron. To comprehend the problem here presented we have only to compare the features of these statues with those of others in this collection belonging to the fourth and fifth dynasties.

The best work of art in the Museum is the statue of Chephron, the builder of the second pyramid. "The epoch of Chephron," says M. Mariette, "corresponding to the third reign of the fourth dynasty of Manetho, our statue is not less than six thousand years old." It is a life-size sitting figure, executed in red granite. We admire its tranquil majesty, we marvel at the close study of nature in the moulding of the breast and limbs, we confess the skill that could produce an effect so fine in such intractable material. It seems as if Egyptian art were about to burst its trammels. But it never did; it never exceeded this cleverness; on the contrary it constantly fell away from it.

The most interesting statue to us, and perhaps the oldest image in Egypt, and, if so, in the world, is the Wooden Man, which was found at Memphis. This image, one metre and ten centimetres high, stands erect, holding a staff. The figure is full of life, the *pose* expresses vigor, action, pride, the head, round in form, indicates intellect. The eyes are crystal, in a setting of bronze, giving a startling look of life to the regard.

27

It is no doubt a portrait. "There is nothing more striking," says its discoverer, "than this image, in a manner living, of a person who has been dead six thousand years." He must have been a man of mark, and a citizen of a state well civilized; this is not the portrait of a barbarian, nor was it carved by a rude artist. Few artists, I think, have lived since, who could impart more vitality to wood.

And if the date assigned to this statue is correct, sculpture in Egypt attained its maximum of development six thousand years ago. This conclusion will be resisted by many, and on different grounds. I heard a clergyman of the Church of England say to his comrade, as they were looking at this figure :—

"It's all nonsense; six thousand years! It couldn't be. That's before the creation of man."

"Well," said the other, irreverently, "perhaps this was the model."

This museum is for the historian, the archæologist, not for the artist, except in his study of the history of art. What Egypt had to impart to the world of arts was given thousands of years ago—intimations, suggestions, outlines that, in freer circumstances, expanded into works of immortal beauty. The highest beauty, that last touch of genius, that creative inspiration which *is* genius and not mere talent, Egyptian art never attained. It achieved wonders; they are all mediocre wonders; miracles of talent. The architecture profoundly impresses, almost crushes one; it never touches the highest in the soul, it never charms, it never satisfies.

The total impression upon myself of this ancient architecture and this plastic art is a melancholy one. And I think this is not altogether due to its monotony. The Egyptian art is said to be *sui generis*; it has a character that is instantly recognized; whenever and wherever we see a specimen of it, we say without fear of mistake, "that is Egyptian." We are as sure of it as we are of a piece of Greek work of the best age, perhaps surer. Is Egyptian art, then, elevated to the dignity of a type, of itself? Is it so to be studied, as something which has flowered into a perfection of its kind? I know we are accustomed to look at it as if it were, and to set apart; in short, I have heard it judged absolutely, as if it were a rule to itself. I cannot bring myself so to look at it. All art is one. We recognize peculiarities of an age or of a people; but there is only one absolute standard; to that touchstone all must come.

It seems to me then that the melancholy impression produced by Egyptian art is not alone from its monotony, its rigidity, its stiff formality, but it is because we recognize in it an arrested development. It is archaic. The peculiarity of it is that it always remained archaic. We have seen specimens of the earliest Etruscan figure-drawing, Gen. Cesnola found in Cyprus Phœnician work, and we have statues of an earlier period of Greek sculpture, all of which more or less resemble Egyptian art. The latter are the beginnings of a consummate development. Egypt stopped at the beginnings. And we have the sad spectacle of an archaic art, not growing, but elaborated into a fixed type and adhered to as if it were perfection. In some of the figures I have spoken of in this museum, you can find that art was about to emancipate itself. In all later works you see no such effort, no such tendency, no such hope. It had been abandoned. By and by impulse died out entirely. For thousands of years the Egyptians worked at perfecting the mediocre. Many attribute this remote and total repression to religious influence. Something of the same sort may be seen in the paintings of saints in the Greek chambers of the East to-day; the type of which is that of the Byzantine period. Are we to attribute a like arrest of development in China to the same cause?

It is a theory very plausibly sustained, that the art of a people is the flower of its civilization, the final expression of the conditions of its growth and its character. In reading Mr. Taine's ingenious observations upon art in the Netherlands and art in Greece, we are ready to assent to the theory. It may be the general law of a free development in national life and in art. If it is, then it is not disturbed by the example of Egypt. Egyptian art is not the expression of the natural character, for its art was never developed. The Egyptians were a joyous race, given to mirth, to the dance, to entertainments, to the charms of society, a people rather gay than grave; they lived in the open air, in the most friendly climate in the world. The sculptures in the early tombs represent their life—an existence full of gaiety, grace, humor. This natural character is not expressed in the sombre temples, nor in their symbolic carvings, nor in these serious, rigid statues, whose calm faces look straight on as if into eternity. This art may express the religion of the priestly caste; when it had attained the power to portray the rigid expectation of immortality, the inscrutable repose of the Sphinx, it was arrested there, and never allowed in any respect to change its formality. And I cannot but believe that if it had been free, Egyptian art would have budded and bloomed into a grace of form in harmony with the character of the climate and the people.

It is true that the architecture of Egypt was freer than its sculptures, but the whole of it together is not worth one edifice like the Greek temple at Pæstum. And to end, by what may seem a sweeping statement, I have had more pleasure from a bit of Greek work—an intaglio, or a coin of the best period, or the sculptures of a broken entablature—than from anything that Egypt ever produced in art.

CHAPTER XXXV.

ON THE WAY HOME.

FOR two days after the sand-storm, it gives us pleasure to write, the weather was cold, raw, thoroughly unpleasant, resembling dear New England quite enough to make one homesick. As late as the twenty-eighth of March, this was. The fact may be a comfort to those who dwell in a region where winter takes a fresh hold in March.

We broke up our establishment on the dahabeëh and moved to the hotel, abandoning I know not how many curiosities, antiquities and specimens, the possession of which had once seemed to us of the last importance. I shall spare you the scene at parting with our crew. It would have been very touching, but for the backsheesh. Some of them were faithful fellows to whom we were attached; some of them were graceless scamps. But they all received backsheesh. That is always the way. It was clearly understood that we should reward only the deserving, and we had again and again resolved not to give a piastre to certain ones of the crew. But at the end, the obdurate howadji always softens; and the Egyptians know that he will. Egypt is full of good-for-nothings who have not only received presents but certificates of character from travellers whom they have disobliged for three months. There was, however, some discrimination in this case; backsheesh was distributed with some regard to good conduct; at the formal judgment on deck, Abd-el-Atti acted the part of Thoth in weighing out the portions, and my friend took the *rôle* of Osiris, receiving, vicariously for all of us, the kisses on his hand of the grateful crew. I shall not be misunderstood in saying that the faithful Soudan boy, Gohah, would have felt just as much grief in bidding us good-bye if he had not received a penny (the rest of the crew would have been inconsolable in like case); his service was always marked by an affectionate devotion without any thought of reward. He must have had a magnanimous soul to forgive us for the doses we gave him when he was ill during the voyage.

We are waiting in Cairo professedly for the weather to become settled and pleasant in Syria—which does not happen, one year with another, till after the first of April; but we are contented, for the novelties of the town are inexhaustible, and we are never weary of its animation and picturesque movement. I suppose I should be held in low estimation if I said nothing concerning the baths of Cairo. It is expected of every traveller that he will describe them, or one at least—one is usually sufficient. Indeed when I have read these descriptions, I have wondered how the writers lived to tell their story. When a person has been for hours roasted and stifled, and had all his bones broken, you could not reasonably expect him to write so powerfully of the bath as many travellers write who are so treated. I think these bath descriptions are among the marvels of Oriental literature; Mr. Longfellow says of the Roman Catholic system, that it is a religion of the deepest dungeons and the highest towers; the Oriental bath (in literature) is like this; the unwashed infidel is first plunged in a gulf of dark despair, and then he is elevated to a physical bliss that is ecstatic. The story is too long at each end.

I had experience of several different baths in Cairo, and I invariably found them less vigorous, that is milder in treatment, than the Turkish baths of New York or of Germany. With the Orientals the bath is a luxury, a thing to be enjoyed, and not an affair of extreme shocks and brutal surprises. In the bath itself there is never the excessive heat that I have experienced in such baths in New York, nor the sudden change of temperature in water, nor the vigorous manipulation. The Cairo bath, in my experience, is gentle, moderate, enjoyable. The heat of the rooms is never excessive, the air is very moist, and water flows abundantly over the marble floors; the attendants are apt to be too lazy to maltreat the bather, and perhaps err in gentleness. You are never roasted in a dry air and then plunged suddenly into cold water. I do not wonder that the Orientals are fond of their bath. The baths abound, for men and for women, and the natives pay a very small sum for the privilege of using them. Women make up parties, and spend a good part of the day in a bath; having an entertainment there sometimes, and a frolic. It is said that mothers sometimes choose wives for their sons from girls they see at the baths. Some of them are used by men in the forenoon and by women in the afternoon, and I have seen a great crowd of veiled women waiting at the door at noon. There must be over seventy-five of these public baths in Cairo.

As the harem had not yet gone over to the Gezeereh palace, we took the opportunity to visit it. This palace was built by the Khedive, on what was the island of Gezeereh, when a branch of the Nile was suffered to run to the west of its present area. The ground is now the seat of gardens, and of the most interesting botanical and horticultural experiments on the part of the Khedive, under charge of competent scientific men. A botanist or an arboriculturist would find material in the nurseries for long study. I was chiefly interested (since I have belief in the malevolence of some plants) in a sort of murderous East Indian cane, which grows about fifteen to twenty feet high, and so rapidly that (we were told) it attains its growth in a day or two. At any rate it thrusts up its stalks so vigorously and rapidly that the Indian tyrants have employed it to execute criminals. The victim is bound to the ground over a bed of this cane at night, and in the morning it has grown up through the body. We need such a vengeful vegetable as this in our country, to plant round the edges of our city gardens.

The grounds about the palace are prettily, but formally laid out in flower-gardens, with fountains and a kiosk in the style of the Alhambra. Near by is a hot-house, with one of the best collections of orchids in the world; and not far off is the zoological garden, containing a menagerie of African birds and beasts, very well arranged and said to be nearly complete.

The palace is a square building of iron and stucco, the light pillars and piazzas painted in Saracenic designs and Persian colors, but the whole rather dingy, and beginning to be shabby. Inside is at once a showy and a comfortable palace, and much better than we expected to see in Egypt; the carpenter and mason work are, however, badly done, as if the Khedive had been swindled by sharp Europeans; it is full of rich and costly furniture. The rooms are large and effective, and we saw a good deal of splendor in hangings and curtains, especially in the apartments fitted up for the occupation of the Empress Eugenie. It is wonderful, by the way, with what interest people look at a bed in which an Empress has slept; and we may add awe, for it is usually a broad, high and awful place of repose. Scattered about the rooms are, in defiance of the Prophet's religion, several paintings, all inferior, and a few busts (some of the Khedive) and other pieces of statuary. The place of honor is given to an American subject, although the group was executed by an Italian artist. It stands upon the first landing of the great staircase. An impish-looking young Jupiter is seated on top of a chimney, below which is the suggestion of a house-roof. Above his head is the point of a lightning-rod. The celestial electrician is discharging a bolt into the rod, which is supposed to pass harmless over the roof below. Upon the pedestal is a medallion, the head of Benjamin Franklin, and encircling it, the legend:—*Eripuit cœlo fulmen*, 1750. The group looks better than you would imagine from the description.

Beyond the garden is the harem-building, which was undergoing a thorough renovation and refurnishing, in the most gaudy French style—such being the wish of the ladies who occupy it. They are eager to discard the beautiful Moorish designs which once covered the walls and to substitute French decoration. The dormitory portions consist of passages with rooms on each side, very much like a young ladies' boarding-school; the rooms are large enough to accommodate three or four occupants. While we were leisurely strolling through the house, we noticed a great flurry and scurry in the building, and the attendants came to us in a panic, and made desperate efforts to hurry us out of the building by a side-entrance, giving signs of woe and destruction to themselves if we did not flee. The Khedive had arrived, on horseback, and unexpectedly, to inspect his domestic hearths.

We rode, one sparkling morning, after a night of heavy rain, to Heliopolis; there was no mud, however, the rain having served to beat the sand firm. Heliopolis is the On of the Bible, and in the time of Herodotus, its inhabitants were esteemed the most learned in history of all the Egyptians. The father-in-law of Joseph was a priest there, and there Moses and Plato both learned wisdom. The road is excellent and planted most of the distance with acacia trees; there are extensive gardens on either hand, plantations of trees, broad fields under cultivation, and all the way the air was full of the odor of flowers, blossoms of lemon and orange. In luxuriance and *riant* vegetation it seemed an Oriental paradise. And the whole of this beautiful land of verdure, covered now with plantations so valuable, was a sand-desert as late as 1869. The water of the Nile alone has changed the desert into a garden.

On the way we passed the race-course belonging to the Khedive, an observatory, and the old palace of Abbas Pasha, now in process of demolition, the foundations being bad, like his own. It is said that the favorite wife of this hated tyrant, who was a Bedawee girl of rank, always preferred to live on the desert, and in a tent rather than a palace. Here at any rate, on the sand, lived Abbas Pasha, in hourly fear of assassination by his enemies. It was not difficult to conjure up the cowering figure hiding in the recesses of this lonely palace, listening for the sound of horses' hoofs coming on the city road, and ready to mount a swift dromedary, which was kept saddled night and day in the stable, and flee into the desert for Bedaween protection.

At Matarééh, we turned into a garden to visit the famous sycamore tree under which the Virgin sat to rest, in the time of the flight of the Holy Family. It is a large, scrubby-looking tree, probably two hundred years old. I wonder that it does not give up the ghost, for every inch of its bark, even to the small limbs, is cut with names. The Copt, who owns it, to prevent its destruction, has put a fence about it; and that also is covered all over. I looked in vain for the name of "Joseph," but could find it neither on the fence nor on the tree.

At Heliopolis one can work up any number of reflections; but all he can see is the obelisk, which is sunken somewhat in the ground. It is more correct, however, to say that the ground about it, and the whole site of the former town and Temple of the Sun, have risen many feet since the beginning of the Christian Era. This is the oldest obelisk in Egypt, and bears the *cartouche* of Amenemhe I., the successor of Osirtasen I.— about three thousand B. C., according to Mariette; Wilkinson and Mariette are only one thousand years apart, on this date of this monument. The wasps or bees have filled up the lettering on one side, and given it the appearance of being plastered with mud. There was no place for us to sit down and meditate, and having stood, surrounded by a swarm of the latest children of the sun, and looked at the remains as long as etiquette required, without a single historical tremor, we mounted and rode joyfully city-ward between the lemon hedges.

In this spring-time, late in the afternoon, the fashionable drive out the Shoobra road, under the arches of sycamore trees, is more thronged than in winter even. Handsome carriages appear, and now and then a pair of blooded Arab horses. There are two lines of vehicles extending for a mile or so, the one going out and the other returning, and the round of the promenade continues long enough for everybody to see everybody. Conspicuous always are the neat two-horse cabriolets, lined with gay silks, and belonging to the royal harem; outriders are in advance, and eunuchs behind, and within each are two fair and painted Circassians, shining in their thin white veils, looking from the windows, eager to see the world, and not averse to be seen by it. The veil has become with them, as it is in Constantinople, a mere pretext and a heightener of beauty. We saw by chance one day some of these birds of paradise abroad in the Shoobra Garden—and live to speak of it.

The Shoobra palace and its harem, hidden by a high wall, were built by Mohammed Ali; he also laid out the celebrated garden; and the establishment was in his day no doubt the handsomest in the East. The garden is still rich in rare trees, fruit-trees, native and exotic, shrubs, and flowers, but fallen into a too common Oriental decay. Instead of keeping up this fine place the Khedive builds a new one. These Oriental despots erect costly and showy palaces, in a manner that invites decay, and their successors build new ones, as people get new suits of clothes instead of wearing the garments of their fathers.

In the midst of the garden is a singular summer-palace, built upon terraces and hidden by trees; but the great attraction is the immense Kiosk, the most characteristic Oriental building I have seen, and a very good specimen of the costly and yet cheap magnificence of the Orient. It is a large square pavillion, the centre of which is a little lake, but large enough for boats, and it has an orchestral platform in the middle; the verandah about this is supported on marble pillars and has a highly-decorated ceiling; carvings in marble abound; and in the corners are apartments decorated in the height of barbaric splendor.

The pipes are still in place which conveyed gas to every corner and outline of this bizarre edifice. I should like to have seen it illuminated on a summer night when the air was heavy with the garden perfumes. I should like to have seen it then thronged with the dark-eyed girls of the North, in their fleecy splendors of drapery, sailing like water-nymphs in these fairy boats, flashing their diamonds in the mirror of this pool, dancing down the marble floor to the music of soft drums and flutes that beat from the orchestral platform hidden by the water-lilies. Such a vision is not permitted to an infidel. But on such a night old Mohammed Ali might have been excused if he thought he was already in El Genneh, in the company of the girls of Paradise, "whose eyes will be very large and entirely black, and whose stature will be proportioned to that of the men, which will be the height of a tall palm tree, or about sixty feet;" and that he was entertained in "a tent erected for him of pearls, jacinths, and emeralds, of a very large extent."

While we were lounging in this place of melancholy gayety, which in the sunlight bears something the aspect of a tawdry watering-place when the season is over, several harem carriages drove to the entrance; but the eunuchs seeing that unbelievers were in the kiosk would not permit the ladies to descend, and the *cortège* went on and disappeared in the shrubbery. The attendants invited us to leave. While we were still near the kiosk the carriages came round again, and the ladies began to alight. The attendants in the garden were now quite beside themselves, and endeavoured to keep our eyes from beholding, and to hustle us down a side-path.

It was in vain that we said to them that we were not afraid, that we were accustomed to see ladies walk in gardens, and that it couldn't possibly harm us. They persisted in misunderstanding us, and piteously begged us to turn away and flee. The ladies were already out of the carriages, veils withdrawn, and beginning to enjoy rural life in the garden. They seemed to have no more fear than we. The horses of the out-riders were led down our path; superb animals, and we stopped to admire them. The harem ladies, rather over-dressed for a promenade, were in full attire of soft silks, blue and pink, in delicate shades, and really made a pretty appearance amid the green. It seemed impossible that it could be wrong to look at them. The attendants couldn't deny that the horses were beautiful, but they regarded our admiration of them as inopportune. They seemed to fear we might look under, or over, or around the horses, towards that forbidden sight by the kiosk. It was useless for us to enquire the age and the breed of the horses. Our efforts to gain information only added to the agony of the gardeners. They wrung their hands, they tried to face us about, they ran hither and thither, and it was not till we were out of sight of the odalisques that they recover any calmness and began to cull flowers for us, and to produce some Yusef Effendis, as a sign of amity and willingness to accept a few piastres.

The last day of March has come. It is time to depart. Even the harem will soon be going out of town. We have remained in the city long enough to imbibe its atmosphere; not long enough to wear out its strangeness, nor to become familiar with all objects of interest. And we pack our trunks with reluctance, in the belief that we are leaving the most thoroughly Oriental and interesting city in all the East.

CHAPTER XXXVI.

BY THE RED SEA.

A Gentleman started from Cairo a few days before us, with the avowed purpose of following in the track of the Children of Israel and viewing the exact point where they crossed the Red Sea. I have no doubt that he was successful. So many routes have been laid out for the Children across the Isthmus, that one can scarcely fail to fall into one of them. Our purpose was merely to see Suez and the famous Sea, and the great canal of M. Lesseps; not doubting, however, that when we looked over the ground we should decide where the Exodus must have taken place.

The old direct railway to Suez is abandoned; the present route is by Zagazeeg and Ismailia—a tedious journey, requiring a day. The ride is wearisome, for the country is flat and presents nothing new to one familiar with Egyptian landscapes. The first part of the journey is, however, enlivened by the company of the canal of Fresh Water, and by the bright verdure of the plain which the canal produces. And this luxuriant vegetation continues until you come to the still unreclaimed desert of the Land of Goshen. Now that water can be supplied it only needs people to make this Land as fat as it was in the days of the Israelites.

Some twenty miles from Cairo we pass near the so-called Mound of the Jew, believed to be the ruins of the city of Orion and the temple built by the high priest Onias in the reign of Ptolemy Philometer and Cleopatra, as described by Josephus. The temple was after the style of that at Jerusalem. This Jewish settlement was made upon old Egyptian ruins; in 1870 the remains of a splendid temple of the time of Rameses II. were laid open. The special interest to Biblical scholars of this

Jewish colony here, which multiplied itself and spread over considerable territory, is that its establishment fulfilled a prophesy of Isaiah (xix, 19, etc.); and Onias urged this prophesy, in his letter to the Ptolemy, asking permission to purge the remains of the heathen temple in the name of Heliopolis and to erect there a temple to Almighty God. Ptolemy and Cleopatra replied that they wondered Onias should desire to build a temple in a place so unclean and so full of sacred animals, but since Isaiah foretold it, he had leave to do so. We saw nothing of this ancient and once flourishing seat of Jewish enterprise, save some sharp mounds in the distance.

Nor did we see more of the more famous city of Bubastis, where was the temple to Pasht, the cat or lioness headed deity (whom Herodotus called Diana), the avenger of crimes. According to Herodotus, all the cats of Egypt were embalmed and buried in Bubastis. This city was the residence of the Pharaoh Sheshonk I. (the Shishak of the Bible) who sacked Jerusalem, and it was at that time the capital of Egypt. It was from here, on the Bubastic (or Pelusiac) branch of the Nile, that the ancient canal was dug to connect with the Heroöpolite Gulf (now the Bitter Lakes), the northernmost arm of the Red Sea at that date; and the city was then, by that fresh-water canal, on the water-way between the Red Sea and the Mediterranean. But before the Christian era the Red Sea had retired to about its present limit (the Bitter Lake being cut off from it), and the Bubastic branch of the Nile was nearly dried up. Bubastis and all this region are now fed by the canal which leaves the Nile at Cairo and runs to Ismailia, and thence to Suez. It is a startling thought that all this portion of the Delta, east, and south, and the Isthmus, depend for life upon the keeper of the gate of the canal at Cairo. If we were to leave the train here and stumble about in the mounds of Bubastis, we should find only fragments of walls, blocks of granite, and a few sculptures.

At the Zagazeeg station, where there is a junction with the Alexandria and Cairo main line, we wait some time, and find a very pleasant garden and the picturesque refreshment-house in which our minds are suddenly diverted from ancient Egypt by a large display of East Indian and Japanese curiosities on sale.

From this we follow, substantially, the route of the canal, running by villages and fertile districts, and again on the desert's edge. We come upon no traces of the Israelites until we reach Masamah, which is supposed to be the site of Rameses, one of the treasure-cities mentioned in the Bible, and the probable starting-point of the Jews in their flight. This is about the centre of the Land of Goshen, and Rameses may have been the chief city of the district.

If I knew exactly the route the Israelites took, I should not dare to disclose it; for this has become, I do not know why, a tender subject. But it seems to me that if the Jews were assembled here from the Delta for a start, a very natural way of exit would have been down the Wady to the head of the Heroöpolite Gulf, the route of the present and the ancient canal. And if it should be ascertained beyond a doubt that Sethi I. built as well as planned such a canal, the argument of probability would be greatly strengthened that Moses led his vast host along the canal. Any dragoman to-day, desiring to cross the Isthmus and be beyond pursuit as soon as possible, supposing the condition of the country now as it was at the time of the Exodus, would strike for the shortest line. And it is reasonable to suppose that Moses would lead his charge to a point where the crossing of the sea, or one of its arms, was more feasible than it is anywhere below Suez; unless we are to start with the supposition that Moses expected a miracle, and led the Jews to a spot where, apparently, escape for them was hopeless if the Egyptians pursued. It is believed that at the time of the Exodus there was a communication between the Red Sea and the Bitter Lakes—formerly called Heroöpolite Gulf—which it was the effort of many rulers to keep open by a canal. Very anciently, it is evident, the Red Sea extended to, and included, these lakes; and it is not improbable that, in the time of Moses, the water was, by certain winds, forced up to the north into these lakes; and again, that crossings could easily be made, the wind being favorable, at several points between what is now Suez and the head of the Bitter Lakes. Many scholars make Chaloof, about twelve miles above Suez, the point of passage.

We only touched the outskirts of Ismailia in going on to Suez. Below, we pass the extensive plantation and garden of the Khedive, in which he has over fifty thousand young trees in a nursery. This spot would be absolute desert but for the Nile-water let in upon it. All day our astonishment has increased at the irrigation projects of the Viceroy, and his herculean efforts to reclaim a vast land of desert; the enlarging of theSweet-Water Canal, and the gigantic experiments in arboriculture and agriculture.

We noticed that the Egyptian laborers at work with the wheel-barrow (instead of the baskets formerly used by them) on the enlargement of the canal, were under French contractors, for the most part. The men are paid from a franc to a franc and a quarter per day; but they told us that it was very difficult to get laborers, so many men being drafted for the army.

At dark we came in sight of the Bitter Lakes, through which the canal is dredged; we can see vessels of various sorts and steamers moving across them in one line; and we see nothing more until we reach Suez. The train stops " at nowhere," in the sand, outside the town. It is the only train of the day, but there are neither carriages nor donkeys in waiting. There is an air about the station of not caring whether anyone comes or not. We walk a mile to the hotel, which stands close to the sea, with nothing but a person's good sense to prevent his walking off the platform into the water. In the night the water looked like the sand, and it was only by accident that we did not step off into it. However, it turned out to be only a couple of feet deep.

The hotel, which I suppose is rather Indian than Egyptian, is built round a pleasant court; corridors and latticed doors are suggestive of hot nights; the servants and waiters are all Hindoos; we have come suddenly in contact with another type of Oriental life.

Coming down from Ismailia, a friend who was with us had no ticket. It was a case beyond the conductor's experience; he utterly refused backsheesh and he insisted on having a ticket. At last he excepted ten francs and went away. Looking in the official guide we found that the fare was nine francs and a quarter. The conductor, thinking he had opened a guileless source of supply, soon returned and demanded two francs more. My friend countermined him by asking the return of the seventy-five centimes overpaid. An amusing pantomime ensued. At length the conductor lowered his demand to one franc, and, not getting that, he begged for backsheesh.

I was sorry to have my high ideal of a railway-conductor, formed in America, lowered in this manner.

We are impatient above all things for a sight of the Red Sea. But in the brilliant starlight, all that appears is smooth water and a soft picture of vessels at anchor or aground, looming up in the night. Suez, seen by early daylight, is a scattered city of some ten thousand inhabitants, too modern and too cheap in its buildings to be interesting. There is only a little section of it, where we find native bazaars, twisting streets, overhanging balconies, and latticed windows. It lies on a sand peninsula, and the sand-drifts close all about it, ready to lick it up, if the canal of fresh water should fail.

The only elevation near is a large mound, which may be the site of the fort of ancient Clysma, or Gholzim as it was afterwards called—the city believed to be the predecessor of Suez. Upon this mound an American has built, and presented to the Khedive, a sort of *châlet* of wood—the whole transported from America ready-made, one of those white, painfully unpicturesque things with two little gables at the end, for which our country is justly distinguished. Cheap. But then it is of wood, and wood is one of the dearest things in Egypt. I only hope the fashion of it may not spread in this land of grace.

It was a delightful morning, the wind west and fresh. From this hillock we commanded one of the most interesting prospects in the world. We looked over the whole desert-flat on which lies the little town, and which is pierced by an arm of the Gulf that narrows into the Suez canal; we looked upon two miles of curved causeway which runs down to the docks and the anchoring place of the steam-vessels—there cluster the dry-docks, the dredges, the canal-offices, and just beyond the shipping lay; in the distance we saw the Red Sea, like a long lake, deep green, or deep blue, according to the light, and very sparkling; to the right was the reddish limestone range called Gebel Attàka—a continuation of the Mokattam; on the left there was a great sweep of desert, and far off—one hundred and twenty miles as the crow flies—the broken Sinai range of mountains, in which we tried to believe we could distinguish the sacred peak itself.

I asked an intelligent railway official, a Moslem, who acted as guide that morning,

"What is the local opinion as to the place where the Children of Israel crossed over?"

"The French," he replied, "are trying to make it out that it was at Chaloof, about twenty miles above here, where there is little water. But we think it was at a point twenty miles below here; we must put it there, or there wouldn't be any miracle. You see that point away to the right? That's the spot. There is a wady comes down the side."

"But where do the Christians think the crossing was?"

"Oh, here at Suez; there about, at this end of Gebel Attaka."

The Moslems' faith in the miraculous deliverance is disturbed by no speculations. Instead of trying to explain the miracle by the use of natural causes, and seeking for a crossing where the water might at one time have been heaped and at another forced away by the winds, their only care is to fix the passage where the miracle would be most striking.

After breakfast and preparations to visit Moses' Well, we rode down the causeway to the made land where the docks are. The earth dumped here by the dredging-machines (and which now forms solid building ground) is full of a great variety of small sea-shells; the walls that enclose it are of rocks conglomerate of shells. The ground all about gives evidence of salt; we found shallow pools evaporated so that a thick crust of excellent salt had formed on the bottom and at the sides. The water in them was of a decidedly rosy colour, caused by some infusorial growth. The name, Red Sea, however, has nothing to do with this appearance, I believe.

We looked at the pretty houses and gardens, the dry-dock and the shops, and the world-famous dredges, without which the Suez Canal would very likely never have been finished. These enormous machines have arms or ducts, an iron spout of semi-elliptical form, two hundred and thirty feet long, by means of which the dredger working in the centre of the channel could discharge its contents over the bank. One of them removed, on an average, eighty thousand cubic yards of soil a month. A faint idea may be had of this gigantic work by the amount of excavation here done by the dredgers in one month —two million seven hundred and sixty-three thousand cubic yards. M. de Lesseps says that if this soil were "laid out between the Arc de Triomphe and the Place de la Concorde, it would cover the entire length and breadth of the Champs Elysées, a distance equal to a mile and a quarter, and reach to the top of the trees on either side."

At the pier our felucca met us, and we embarked and sailed into the mouth of the canal. The channel leading to it is not wide, and is buoyed at short intervals. The mouth of the canal is about nine hundred feet wide and twenty-seven deep,* and it is guarded on the east by a long stone mole projected from the Asiatic shore. There is considerable ebb and flow of the tide in this part of the canal and as far the Bitter Lakes, where it is nearly all lost in the expanse, being only slightly felt at Lake Timsah, from which point there is a slight uniform current to the Mediterranean.

From the canal entrance we saw great ships and steamboats in the distance, across the desert, and apparently sailing in the desert; but we did not follow them; we turned, and crossed to the Asiatic shore. We had brought donkeys with us, and were soon mounted for a scrambling gallop of an hour and a half, down the coast, over level and hard sand, to Moses' Well. The air was delicious and the ride exhilarating. I tried to get from our pleasant Arab guide, who had a habit of closing one eye, what he thought of the place of the passage.

"Where did the Children of Israel cross?"

"Over dat mountain."

"Yes, but where did they cross the Sea?"

"You know Moses?"

"Yes, I know Moses. Where did he cross?"

"Well," closing his eye very tight, "him long time ago, not now. He cross way down there, can't see him from here."

On the way we passed the white tents of the Quarantine Station on our right by the shore, where the caravan of Mecca pilgrims had been detained. We hoped to see it; but it had just set out on its desert march further inland. It was seen from Suez all day, straggling along in detachments, and at night camped about two miles north of the town. However, we found a dozen or two of the pilgrims, dirty, ragged, burned

---

* Total length of canal, 100 miles. Width of water-line, where banks are low, 328 feet; in deep cuttings, 190; width at base, 72; depth, 26.

by the sun, and hungry, lying outside the enclosure at the wells.

The Wells of Moses (or *Ain Moosa*, "Moses' Well," in the Arabic) are distant a mile or more from the low shore, and our first warning of nearness to them was the appearance of some palms in a sandy depression. The attempt at vegetation is rather sickly, and the spot is but a desolate one. It is the beginning of the route to Mount Sinai, however, and is no doubt a very welcome sight to returning pilgrims. Contrast is everything; it is contrast with its surroundings that has given Damascus its renown.

There are half a dozen of these wells, three of which are some fifteen to twenty feet across, and are in size and appearance very respectable frog-ponds. One of them is walled with masonry, evidently ancient, and two shadoofs draw water from it for the garden, an enclosure of an acre, fenced with palm-matting. It contains some palms and shrubs and a few vegetables. Here also is a half-deserted house, that may once have been a hotel, and is now a miserable *trattoria* without beds. It is in charge of an Arab who lives in a hut at the other side of the garden, with his wife and a person who bore the unmistakable signs of being a mother-in-law. The Arab made coffee for us, and furnished us a table, on which we spread our luncheon under the verandah. He also gave us Nile water which had been brought from Suez in a cask on camel-back; and his whole charge was only one bob (a shilling) each. I mention the charge, because it is disenchanting in a spot of so much romance to pay for your entertainment in "bobs."

We had come upon what I may truly call a sentimental pilgrimage, on account of Moses and the Children of Israel. If they crossed over from Mount Attaka yonder, then this might be the very spot where Miriam sang the song of triumph. If they crossed at Chaloof, twenty miles above, as it is more probable they did, then this might be the Marah whose bitter waters Moses sweetened for the time being; the Arabs have a tradition that Moses brought up water here by striking the ground with his stick. At all events, the name of Moses is forever attached to this oasis, and it did not seem exactly right that the best well should be owned by an Arab who makes it the means of accumulating bobs. One room of the house was occupied by three Jews, traders, who establish themselves here a part of the year in order to buy, from the Bedaween, turquoise and antiquities which are found at Mount Sinai. I saw them sorting over a peck of rough and inferior turquoise, which would speedily be forwarded to Constantinople, Paris, and London. One of them sold me a small intaglio, which was no doubt of old Greek workmanship, and which he swore was picked up at Mount Sinai. There is nothing I long more to know, sometimes, than the history of wandering coins and intaglios which we see in the Orient.

It is not easy to reckon the value of a tradition, nor of a traditional spot like this in which all the world feels a certain proprietorship. It seemed to us, however, that it would be worth while to own this famous Asiatic well; and we asked the owner what he would take for it. He offered to sell the ranche for one hundred and fifty guineas; this, however, would not include the camel,—for that he wanted ten pounds in addition; but it did include a young gazelle, two goats, a brownish-yellow dog, and a cat the color of the sand. And it also comprised, in the plantation, a few palms, some junipers of the Biblical sort; the acacia or "shittah" tree of the Bible, and, best of all, the large shrub called the tamarisk, which exudes during two months in the year a sweet gummy substance that was the "manna" of the Israelites.

Mother-in-law wore a veil, a string of silver-gilt imitation coins, several large silver bracelets, and a necklace upon which was sewed a string of small Arabic gold coins. As this person more than anyone else there, represented Miriam,—not being too young,—we persuaded her to sell us some of the coins as mementoes of our visit. We could not determine, as I said, whether this spot is associated with Miriam, or whether it is the Marah of bitter waters; consequently it was difficult to say what our emotions should be. However, we decided to let them be expressed by the inscription that a Frenchman had written on a wall of the house, which reads:—*Le cœur me palpitait comme un amant qui revoit sa bien-aimée.*

There are three other wells enclosed, but unwalled, the largest of which—and it has near it a sort of *loggia*, or open shed, where some dirty pilgrims were reposing—is an unsightly pond full of a green growth of algæ. In this enclosure, which contains two or three acres, are three smaller wells, or natural springs, as they all are, and a considerable thicket of palms and tamarisks. The larger well is the stronger in taste and most bitter, containing more magnesia. The water in all is flat and unpleasant, and not enlivened by carbonic acid gas, although we saw bubbles coming to the surface constantly. If the spring we first visited could be aërated, it would not be worse to drink than many waters that are sought after. The donkeys liked it; but a donkey likes anything. About these feeble plantations the sand drifts from all directions, and it would soon cover them but for the protecting fence. The way towards Sinai winds through shifting sand-mounds, and is not inviting.

The desert over which we return is dotted frequently with tufts of a flat-leafed, pale-green plant, which seem to thrive without moisture; and in the distance this vegetation presents an appearance of large shrub growth, greatly relieving the barrenness of the sand-plain. We had some fine effects of mirage, blue lakes and hazy banks, as of streams afar off. When we reached an elevation that commanded a view of the indistinct Sinai range, we asked the guide to point out to us the "rosy peaks of Mount Sinai" which Murray sees from Suez when he is there. The guide refused to believe that you can see a rosy peak one hundred and twenty miles through the air, and confirmed the assertion of the inhabitants of Suez that Mount Sinai cannot be seen from there.

On our return we overtook a caravan of Bedaween returning from the holy mount, armed with long rifles, spears, and huge swords, swinging along on their dromedaries,—a Colt's revolver would put the whole lot of braggarts to flight. One of them was a splendid specimen of manhood, and we had a chance to study his graceful carriage, as he ran beside us all the way; he had the traditional free air, a fine face and well-developed limbs, and his picturesque dress of light-blue and buff, somewhat in rags, added to his attractions. It is some solace to the traveller to call these fellows beggars, since he is all the time conscious that their natural grand manner contrasts so strongly with the uncouthness of his more recent and western civilization.

Coming back into Suez, from this journey to another continent, we were stopped by two customs-officers, who insisted upon searching our lunch-basket, to see if we were attempting to smuggle anything from Asia. We told the guide to give the representatives of his Highness, with our compliments, a hard boiled egg.

Suez itself has not many attractions. But we are much impressed at the hotel by the grave Hindoo waiters, who serve at table in a close-fitting habit, like the present extremely narrow gown worn by ladies, and ludicrous to our eyes accustomed to the flowing robes of the Arabs. They wear also, while waiting, broad-brimmed, white, cork hats, slightly turned up at the rim. It is like being waited on by serious genii. These men also act as chambermaids. Their costume is Bengalee, and would not be at all "style" in Bombay.

Suez is reputed a healthful place, enjoying both sea and desert air, free from malaria, and even in summer the heat is tempered. This is what the natives say. The English landlady admits that it is very pleasant in winter, but the summer is intensely hot; especially when the Khamseen, or south wind, blows—always three days at a time—it is hardly endurable; the thermometer stands at 110° to 114° in the shaded halls of the hotel round the court. It is unsafe for foreigners to stay here more than two years at a time; they are certain to have a fever or some disease of the liver.

The town is very much depressed now, and has been ever since the opening of the canal. The great railway business fell off at once, all freight going by water. Hundreds of merchants, shippers and forwarders are out of employment. We hear the Khedive much blamed for his part in the canal, and people here believe that he regrets it. Egypt, they say, is ruined by this loss of trade; Suez is killed; Alexandria is ruined beyond reparation, business there is entirely stagnant. What a builder and a destroyer of cities has been the fluctuation of the course of the East India commerce!

CHAPTER XXXVII.

"WESTWARD HO!"

WE left Suez at eight in the morning by rail, and reached Ismailia in four hours, the fare—to do justice to the conductor already named—being fourteen francs. A part of the way the Bitter Lakes are visible, and we can see where the canal channel is staked out through them. Next we encountered the Fresh-Water-Canal, and came in view of Lake Timsah, through which the Suez canal also flows. This was no doubt once a fresh-water-lake, fed by water taken from the Nile at Bubastis.

Ismailia is a surprise, no matter how much you have heard of it. True, it has something the appearance of a rectangular streeted town, dropped ready-made at a railway station on a western prairie; but Ismailia was dropped by people of good taste. In 1860 there was nothing here but desert sand, not a drop of water, not a spear of vegetation. To-day you walk into a pretty village, of three or four thousand inhabitants, smiling with verdure. Trees grow along the walks; little gardens bloom by every cottage. Fronting the quay Mohammed Ali, which extends along the broad Fresh-Water-Canal, are the best residences, and many of them have better gardens than you can find elsewhere, with few exceptions, in Egypt.

The first house we were shown was that which had most interest for us—the Swiss-like *châlet* of M. de Lesseps; a summerish, cheerful box, furnished simply, but adorned with many Oriental curiosities. The garden which surrounds it is rich in native and exotic plants, flowers and fruits. On this quay are two or three barn-like, unfurnished palaces built hastily and cheaply by the Khedive for the entertainment of guests. The finest garden, however, and as interesting as any we saw in the East, is that belonging to M. Pierre, who has charge of the waterworks. In this garden can be found almost all varieties of European and Egyptian flowers; strawberries were just ripening. We made inquiry here, as we had done throughout Egypt, for the lotus, the favorite flower of the old Egyptians, the sacred symbol, the mythic plant, the feeding upon which lulls the conscience, destroys ambition, dulls the memory of all unpleasant things, enervates the will, and soothes one in a sensuous enjoyment of the day to which there is no to-morrow. It seems to have disappeared from Egypt with the papyrus.

The lotus of the poets I fear never existed, not even in Egypt. The lotus represented so frequently in the sculptures, is a water-plant, the *Nymphæa lutea*, and is I suppose the plant that was once common. The poor used its bulb for food in times of scarcity. The Indian lotus, or *Nelumbium*, is not seen in the sculptures, though Latin writers say it existed in Egypt. It may have been this that had the lethean properties; although the modern eaters and smokers of Indian hemp appear to be the legitimate descendants of the lotus-eaters of the poets. However, the lotus whose stalks and buds gave character to a distinct architectural style, we enquired for in vain on the Nile. If it still grows there it would scarcely be visible above water in the winter. But M. Pierre has what he supposes to be the ancient lotus-plant; and his wife gave us seeds of it in the seed-vessel—a large flat-topped funnel-shaped receptacle, exactly the shape of the sprinkler of a watering pot. Perhaps this is the plant that Herodotus calls a lily like a rose, the fruit of which is contained in a separate pod, that springs up from the fruit in form very like a wasp's nest; in this are many berries fit to be eaten.

The garden adjoins the water works, in which two powerful pumping-engines raise the sweet water into a stand-pipe, and send it forward in iron pipes fifty miles along the Suez Canal to Port Saïd, at which port there is a reservoir that will hold three days' supply. This stream of fresh water is the sole dependence of Port Saïd and all the intervening country.

We rode out over the desert on an excellent road, lined with sickly acacias growing in the watered ditches, to station No. 6 on the canal. The way lies along Lake Timsah. Upon a considerable elevation, called the Heights of El Guisr, is built a *château* for the Khedive; and from this you get an extensive view of the desert, of Lake Timsah and the Bitter Lakes. Below us was the deep cutting of the Canal. El Guisr is the highest point in the Isthmus, an elevated plateau six miles across and some sixty-five feet above the level of the sea. The famous gardens that flourished here during the progress of the excavation have entirely disappeared with the cessation of the water from Ismailia. While we were there an East India bound steamboat moved slowly up the canal, creating, of course, waves along the banks, but washing them very little, for the speed is limited to five miles an hour.

Although the back streets of Ismailia are crude and unpicturesque, the whole effect of the town is pleasing; and it enjoys a climate that must commend it to invalids. It is dry, free from dust, and even in summer not too warm, for there is a breeze from the lakes by day, and the nights are always cooled by the desert air. Sea-bathing can be enjoyed there the year round. It ought to be a wholesome spot, for there is nothing in sight around it but sand and salt-water. The invalid who should go there would probably die shortly of ennui, but he would escape the death expected from his disease. But Ismailia is well worth seeing. The miracle wrought here by a slender stream of water from the distant Nile is worthy the consideration of those who have the solution of the problem of making fertile our western sand-deserts.

We ate at Suez and Ismailia what we had not tasted for several months—excellent fish. The fish of the Nile are nearly as good as a New-England sucker, grown in a muddy mill-pond. I saw fishermen angling in the salt canal at Ismailia, and the fish are good the whole length of it; they are of excellent quality even in the Bitter lakes, which are much salter than the Mediterranean—in fact the bottom of these lakes is encrusted with salt.

We took passage towards evening on the daily Egyptian paquet-boat for Port Saïd—a puffing little cigar-box of a vessel, hardly fifty feet long. The only accommodation for passengers was in the forward cabin, which is about the size of an omnibus, and into it were crammed twenty passengers, Greeks, Jews, Koorlanders, English clergymen, and American travellers, and the surly Egyptian mail-agent, who occupied a great deal of room, and insisted on having the windows closed; some of us tried perching on the scrap of a deck, hanging our legs over the side, but it was bitterly cold, and a strong wind drove us below. In the cabin the air was utterly vile; and when we succeeded in opening the hatchway for a moment, the draught chilled us to the bones.

I do not mean to complain of all this; but I want it to appear that sailing on the Suez Canal, especially at night, is not a pleasure-excursion. It might be more endurable by day; but I do not know. In the hours we had of daylight I became excessively weary of looking at the steep sand-slopes between which we sailed, and of hoping that every turn would bring us to a spot where we could see over the bank.

At eight o'clock we stopped at Kataunah for supper, and I climbed the bank to see if I could obtain any information about the Children of Israel. They are said to have crossed here. This is the highest point of the low hills which separate Lake Menzaleh from the interior lakes. Along this ridge is still the caravan-route between Egypt and Syria; it has been for ages unnumbered the great highway of commerce and of conquest. This way Thothmes III., the greatest of the Pharaohs and the real Sesostris, led his legions into Asia; and this way Cambyses came to repay the visit with interest.

It was so dark that I could see little, but I had a historic sense of all this stir and movement, of the passage of armies laden with spoils, and of caravans from Nineveh and Damascus. And, although it was my first visit to the place, it seemed strange to see here a restaurant, and waiters hurrying about, and travellers snatching a hasty meal in the night on this wind-blown sand-hill. And to feel that the stream of travel is no more along this divide but across it? By the half-light I could distinguish some Bedaween loitering about; their little caravan had camped here, for they find it very convenient to draw water from the iron pipes.

It was quite dark when we presently sailed into Lake Mensaleh, and we could see little. I only know that we held a straight course through it for some thirty miles to Port Saïd. In the daytime you can see a dreary expanse of morass and lake, a few little islands clad with tamarisks, and flocks of aquatic birds floating in the water or drawn up on the sand-spits in martial array—the white spoonbill, the scarlet flamingo, the pink pelican. It was one o'clock in the morning when we saw the Pharos of Port Saïd and sailed into the basin, amid many lights.

Port Saïd was made out of nothing, and it is pretty good. A town of eight to ten thousand inhabitants, with docks, quays, squares, streets, shops, mosques, hospitals, public buildings; in front of our hotel is a garden and public square; all this fed by the iron pipe and the pump at Ismailia—without this there is no fresh water nearer than Damietta. It is a shabby city, and just now has the over-done appearance of one of our own western town inflations. But its history is a record of one of the most astonishing achievements of any age. Before there could be any town here it was necessary to build a standpoint for it with a dredging machine.

Along this coast from Damietta to the gulf of Pelusium where once emptied the Pelusiac branch of the Nile, in a narrow strip of sand, separating the Mediterranean from Lake Menzaleh; a high sea often breaks over it. It would have saved much in distance to have carried the canal to the Pelusium gulf, but the Mediterranean is shallow there many miles from shore. The spot on which Port Saïd now stands was selected for the entrance of the canal, because it was here that the land can be best approached—the Mediterranean having sufficient depth at only two miles from the shore. Here, therefore, the dredgers began to work. The lake was dredged for interior basins; the strip of sand was cut through; the outer harbor was dredged; and the dredgings made the land for the town. Artificial stone was then manufactured on the spot, and of this the long walls, running out into the sea and protecting the harbor, the quays, and the lighthouses were built. We saw some enormous blocks of this composite of sand and hydraulic lime, which weigh twenty-five tons each.

It is impossible not to respect a city built by such heroic labour as this; but we saw enough of it in half a day. The shops are many, and the signs are in many languages, Greek being most frequent. I was pleased to read an honest one in English—"Blood-Letting and Tooth-picking." I have no doubt they all would take your blood. In the streets are vagabonds, adventurers, merchants, travellers, of all nations; and yet you would not call the streets picturesque. Everything is strangely modernized and made uninteresting. There is, besides, no sense of permanence here. The traders appear to occupy their shops as if they were booths for the day. It is a place of transit; a spot of sand amid the waters. I have never been in any locality that seemed to me so nearly nowhere. A spot for an African bird to light on a moment on his way to Asia. But the world flows through here. Here lie the great vessels in the Eastern trade; all the Mediterranean steamers call here.

The Erymanthe is taking in her last freight, and it is time for us to go on board. Abd-el-Atti has arrived with the baggage from Cairo. He has the air of one with an important errand. In the hotels, on the street, in the steamer, his manner is that of one who precedes an imposing embassy. He likes state. If he had been born under the Pharaohs he would have been the bearer of the flabellum before the king; and he would have carried it majestically, with perhaps a humorous twinkle in his eye for some comrade by the way. Ahman Abdallah, the faithful, is with him. He it was who made and brought us the early morning coffee to-day,—recalling the peace of those days on the Nile which now are in the dim past. It is ages ago since we were hunting in the ruins of Abydus for the tomb of Osiris. It was in another life, that delicious winter in Nubia, those weeks following weeks, free from care and from all the restlessness of this driving age.

"I shouldn't wonder if you were right, Abd-el-Atti, in not wanting to start for Syria sooner. It was very cold on the boat last night."

"Not go in Syria before April; always find him bad. 'Member what I say when it rain at Cairo!—'This go to be snow in Jerusalem.' It been snow there last week, awful storm, nobody go on the road, travellers all stop, not get anywhere. So I hunderstand."

"What is the prospect for landing at Jaffa to-morrow morning?"

"Do' know, be sure. We hope for the better."

We get away beyond the breakwater, as the sun goes down. The wind freshens, and short waves hector the long sea swell. Egypt lies low; it is only a line; it fades from view.